The Languages of Africa and the Diaspora

NEW PERSPECTIVES ON LANGUAGE AND EDUCATION
Series Editor: Professor Viv Edwards, *University of Reading, Reading, Great Britain*
Series Advisor: Professor Allan Luke, *Queensland University of Technology, Brisbane, Australia*

Two decades of research and development in language and literacy education have yielded a broad, multidisciplinary focus. Yet education systems face constant economic and technological change, with attendant issues of identity and power, community and culture. This series will feature critical and interpretive, disciplinary and multidisciplinary perspectives on teaching and learning, language and literacy in new times.

Full details of all the books in this series and of all our other publications can be found on http://www.multilingual-matters.com, or by writing to Multilingual Matters, St Nicholas House, 31–34 High Street, BS1 2AW, UK.

NEW PERSPECTIVES ON LANGUAGE AND EDUCATION
Series Editor: Professor Viv Edwards, *University of Reading*

The Languages of Africa and the Diaspora

Educating for Language Awareness

Edited by

Jo Anne Kleifgen and George C. Bond

MULTILINGUAL MATTERS
Bristol • Buffalo • Toronto

In memory of our parents
Mildred Hovig Kleifgen and Arthur F. Kleifgen
Ruth Clement Bond and J. Max Bond

Library of Congress Cataloging in Publication Data
A catalog record for this book is available from the Library of Congress.
The Languages of Africa and the Diaspora: Educating for Language Awareness
Edited by Jo Anne Kleifgen and George C. Bond.
New Perspectives on Language and Education: 12
Includes bibliographical references and index.
1. Language and education. 2. Language policy. 3.Blacks–Languages.
4. Linguistic minorities. 5. Language awareness.
I. Kleifgen, Jo Anne. II. Bond, George C.
P40.8.L38 2009
408.9'96-dc22 2008035196

British Library Cataloguing in Publication Data
A catalogue entry for this book is available from the British Library.

ISBN-13: 978-1-84769-134-7 (hbk)
ISBN-13: 978-1-84769-133-0 (pbk)

Multilingual Matters
UK: St Nicholas House, 31–34 High Street, Bristol, BS1 2AW, UK.
USA: UTP, 2250 Military Road, Tonawanda, NY 14150, USA.
Canada: UTP, 5201 Dufferin Street, North York, Ontario M3H 5T8, Canada.

Copyright © 2009 Jo Anne Kleifgen and George C. Bond.

All rights reserved. No part of this work may be reproduced in any form or by any means without permission in writing from the publisher.

The policy of Multilingual Matters/Channel View Publications is to use papers that are natural, renewable and recyclable products, made from wood grown in sustainable forests. In the manufacturing process of our books, and to further support our policy, preference is given to printers that have FSC and PEFC Chain of Custody certification. The FSC and/or PEFC logos will appear on those books where full certification has been granted to the printer concerned.

Typeset by Wordworks Ltd, Gairloch.

Contents

Acknowledgements

The impetus for this book was a gathering of scholars in African linguistics, creolistics, African American English and education, along with teachers and educational policy makers, at Teachers College, Columbia University, where many of the themes and issues we explore in these pages were initially aired. The meeting was organized in part to honor the work of Clifford A. Hill, Arthur I. Gates Professor of Language and Education Emeritus, who began his scholarly career in West Africa with an ethnolinguistic study of oral art in Hausa culture. During his years at Teachers College, Clifford examined ways in which the resources of oral culture can be used in language and literacy development among speakers of African American English. His cross-cultural studies of language, space and time have shown connections between linguistic representations of spatial/temporal points of view in African languages and in African American English. We owe him a debt of gratitude for his leadership in language and education and for his support of this volume.

The students who helped organize this intellectual exchange infused a great deal of time, energy and new ideas into the project. Their enthusiasm greatly influenced our decision to bring together the work of the participants, along with additional invited papers, into an edited volume. They are Maureen Matarese, who chaired the group, along with Jane Bean-Folkes, Leigh L. Graham, Kiran Jayaram, Tavis Jules, Gillian Kasirye, Shilisha October, Shelley Sams and Donna Tonini. We also benefited from the support of students and colleagues from various locations around the Columbia campus: the African Studies Working Group, the Center for African Education, Center for Educational Outreach and Innovation, the Center for Multiple Languages and Literacies, the Institute for Research in African-American Studies, the School of International and Public Affairs and the TESOL/AL Roundtable.

In addition, we thank many friends and colleagues in and outside of academia and education, who have in various ways contributed to this volume: Dawn Arno, Tammy Arnstein, Darlyne Bailey, Lesley Bartlett, Linda Beck, John Borghese, Marion Boultbee, Lambros Comitas, Susan Fuhrman, Ofelia García, Edmund Gordon, Steven Gregory, Farah J. Griffin, George Irish, Yvonne Pratt Johnson, Suzanna McNamara, Michael Rebell,

Janice Robinson, Aleesha Taylor, Halima Touré, Rudolph C. Troike, Hervé Varenne and Frances Vavrus. The final copy-editing for this book was skillfully completed by Abigail Bucuvalas, whose work we gratefully acknowledge.

Contributors

John Baugh received his PhD in linguistics from the University of Pennsylvania (1979). Prior to joining Washington University as the Margaret Bush Wilson Professor in Arts and Sciences and Director of the African and African American Studies Program, he served as Professor of Education and Linguistics at Stanford University. Professor Baugh is the author of *Black Street Speech: Its History, Structure and Survival*, *Out of the Mouths of Slaves: African American Language and Educational Malpractice* and *Beyond Ebonics: Linguistic Pride and Racial Prejudice*. Professor Baugh is a sociolinguist who studies the social stratification of linguistic diversity in advanced industrialized societies, with particular attention to the linguistic plight of socially dispossessed populations. He also serves as director of the American Linguistic Heritage Survey, an ongoing study sponsored by the Ford Foundation to examine the prevalence of linguistic profiling in the United States.

George Clement Bond is the Director of the Center for African Education and William F. Russell Professor for Anthropology and Education at Teachers College, Columbia University. His interests include education and elite formation in the United States and Africa, African studies, African religions and politics, agrarian transformations and cultural dimensions of urban and minority populations. He has conducted research on political and religious change among the Tumbuka-speaking peoples of Zambia and Malawi, social dimensions of AIDS in Southern Uganda, and privatization, democratization and the plight of the poor in northern Zambia. Dr Bond has been the Director of the Institute of African Studies at Columbia University and President of the Association for Africanist Anthropology. His most recent publications include *Contested Terrains and Constructed Categories: Contemporary Africa in Focus* (2002) and *Witchcraft Dialogues: Anthropological and Philosophical Exchanges* (2001).

Susan E. Cook is a cultural and linguistic anthropologist interested in language and social change in contemporary South Africa. In addition to her work on language ideologies, language policy and urban dialects in Africa, Professor Cook has also worked extensively on issues of comparative genocide, particularly in Rwanda and Cambodia. From 1999–2001, Professor Cook was the director of the Cambodian Genocide Program at Yale University. She edited a book entitled *Genocide in Cambodia and Rwanda, New Perspectives* (2006, Transaction Publishers). She is currently completing a study of the social and political dimensions of nonstandard urban dialects in South Africa entitled *Black Voices White Noise: Language and the Limits of Ethnicity in South Africa*. Professor Cook was Associate Professor of Anthropology and Archaeology at the University of Pretoria from 2003–2008. She is currently Head of Research and Planning for the Royal Bafokeng Nation in South Africa and adjunct professor of research at the Watson Institute for International Studies at Brown University. She received her PhD from Yale University.

Michel DeGraff is Associate Professor of Linguistics at MIT. He obtained his PhD at the University of Pennsylvania in 1992. His research interests and scholarly publications mostly concern the morphology, syntax and semantics of 'Creole' languages, with focus on his native Haitian Creole. Professor DeGraff is also interested in the joint study of linguistic creolization, language change and language acquisition and how such study may help elucidate the mental bases of language development in individual speakers and across generations of speakers. This is the topic of the volume he edited, entitled *Language Creation and Language Change: Creolization, Diachrony and Development* (MIT Press, 1999). This volume and subsequent work are part of a long-term project documenting why 'Creole' languages cannot be distinguished in any fundamental way from other languages on structural or developmental grounds. From this non-exceptionalist perspective, the synchronic and diachronic properties of individual 'Creole' languages can in principle shed light on the Human Language faculty, without any *sui generis* stipulation about a 'Creole typology' or about 'Creole genesis'. Another interest of Professor DeGraff relates to the Foucauldian relationship between power and (mis)knowledge, as in the history of the Caribbean and of Creole studies. He has written about the consequences of this relationship both on current theories about Creole languages and on contemporary issues of education and language policy in Creolophone societies such as Haiti.

Christa de Kleine is Associate Professor of Education at the College of Notre Dame in Baltimore, Maryland, where she coordinates the MA TESOL program and teaches linguistics courses at the MA and PhD levels. Dr de Kleine holds degrees in linguistics from the University of Groningen in the Netherlands (MA) and the City University of New York (PhD), where she specialized in language contact issues, including creolization. She has recently published a book on Surinamese Dutch (*A Morphosyntactic Analysis of Surinamese Dutch*, Lincom Europa, 2007) and has published on other creole-influenced and creolized language varieties, including Afrikaans and Negerhollands (a Dutch-lexifier creole language once spoken in the Virgin Islands). Dr de Kleine's current research, conducted in public schools in the Baltimore-Washington metropolitan area, examines the acquisition of Standard American English by West African immigrant students in ESL programs who are native speakers of English-lexifier creole language varieties.

Jo Anne Kleifgen is Associate Professor of Linguistics and Education at Teachers College, Columbia University. She is a founding member and co-director of the Center for Multiple Languages and Literacies and is president-elect of the International Linguistic Association. She has conducted research on discourse in multilingual classrooms, the language of the Internet and the use of technologies to strengthen bilingualism and biliteracy in Haitian and Latino populations. She has also studied communicative practices in a high-tech, multilingual workplace in the Silicon Valley of California. Her articles have been published in *Anthropology and Education Quarterly, Discourse Processes, Language in Society, Research on Language and Social Interaction* and *Reading Research Quarterly*, among others. Currently, she is involved in a project that addresses the digital divide in communities with low-income, multiple-language populations, focusing on computer support for Latino middle-school students' biliteracy development in New York.

Sinfree Makoni holds a PhD in Applied Linguistics from Edinburgh University. He currently teaches at Pennsylvania State University in the departments of Applied Linguistics and African and African American Studies. His main research interests are in language in education, language planning, language and health and police communication. He has published extensively in a number of journals including; *Current Issues in Language Planning, Journal of Cross-Cultural Gerontology, International Journal of Critical Language Studies* and *Language and Society*. He has co-authored *Language and Aging in Multilingual Contexts* with Kees de Bot (Clevedon: Multilingual Matters, 2005). He has edited a number of volumes including *Disinventing and Reconstituting Language* with Alastair Pennycook (Clevedon: Multilingual Matters, 2006) and *Black Linguistics: Language, Society and Politics in Africa and the Americas* with Geneva Smitherman, Arnetha Ball and Arthur K. Spears (London: Routledge, 2003).

Peter Mtesigwa is Principal Language Research Officer at the National Kiswahili Council of Tanzania. He received his doctorate at Teachers College, Columbia University in 2001. He has taught several linguistics courses in the Kiswahili Department at the University of Dar es Salaam and was lecturer at the University of Port Harcourt, Nigeria from 1987–1991 in the Department of Linguistics and African Languages. He is a panel member of two Swahili localization computer programs: Jambo OpenOffice of the Linux Program (Kilinux, accessible at www.kilinux.udsm.ac.tz) and the Microsoft Swahili localization program that has so far translated and compiled a Kiswahili glossary of basic terms along with over 20,000 string commands and phrases applied in Microsoft Office and Windows Programs. These projects aim at meeting the growing computer literacy demand to the large non-English speaking Kiswahili population in East and Central Africa. Dr Mtesigwa is currently teaching Kiswahili at Sebha University, Libya.

Shondel Nero is Associate Professor in the Steinhardt School of Culture, Education and Human Development at New York University (NYU). She is an applied linguist who focuses on the education of second language and second dialect speakers. Her research examines the politics, challenges and strategies of educating students who speak and/or write in varieties of English that are at variance with academic discourse. She has researched the language and literacy needs of speakers of Caribbean Creole English in New York City public schools and colleges. Her work has appeared in such journals as *TESOL Quarterly, Language and Education, World Englishes* and *English Today.* A native of Guyana, she is the author of *Englishes in Contact: Anglophone Caribbean Students in an Urban College* (2001) and editor of a volume, *Dialects, Englishes, Creoles and Education* (2006). She earned her doctorate in applied linguistics from Columbia University's Teachers College in 1997 and taught in the School of Education at St John's University for nine years prior to joining the NYU faculty.

Kate Parry is a professor at Hunter College of the City University of New York, where she teaches linguistics courses in the Department of English. She spends summers and intersessions in Uganda, working on various literacy projects. Chief among these is the Kitengesa Community Library, which she administers with the help of Ugandan colleagues. She is Chair of the Uganda Community Libraries Association (www.ugcla.org) and also, in the United States, Executive Director of Friends of African Village Libraries (www.favl.org) with responsibility for its activities in East Africa. She has taught for extensive periods in Uganda, Nigeria and China and has conducted research on literacy practices in all three countries. Her publications include many articles on literacy and vocabulary acquisition as well as several collections of papers on language and literacy in China and Africa.

Casmir Rubagumya (PhD) is Associate Professor in the Department of Foreign Languages and Linguistics, University of Dar es Salaam, Tanzania. He has taught English as a foreign language at secondary school level for six years, and has been teaching English/Linguistics at the University of Dar es Salaam for the last 25 years. His research interests include language in education in Africa, bilingualism and bilingual education in multilingual settings, language and power and language and gender. His publications include two edited volumes published by Multilingual Matters: *Language in Education in Africa* (1990) and *Teaching and Researching Language in African Classrooms* (1994). He has undertaken consultancy work on language in education for various clients, including the International Development Research Centre (1996), Tanzania Ministry of Education (1998), The World Bank Institute (2000) and Zanzibar Ministry of Education (2005). He is currently working on a research project on improving the quality of education in Tanzania through language and literacy development.

Ellen M. Schnepel received her PhD in Anthropology from Columbia University in 1990. An independent scholar and practicing anthropologist, she is principal of her own consulting business in New York City. She has conducted field research in Andorra, the French West Indies and Mauritius on language politics, nationalism and ethnic identity, gender relations and changing patterns of food distribution and consumption. Her involvement in domestic and overseas projects has included applied work in public health, education, women's cooperatives, youth empowerment, international and sustainable development. She is co-editor of a special issue of *The International Journal of the Sociology of Language*, entitled *Creole Movements in the Francophone Orbit* (1993) and author of the monograph, *In Search of a National Identity: Creole and Politics in Guadeloupe* (Hamburg: Buske, 2004). Her articles have appeared in numerous academic and applied journals, including *Ethnic Groups, Recherches Féministes, Etudes Créoles, Plantation Society in the Americas* and *Gastronomica*. She currently is cultivating a lively interest in the history and culture of cacao and chocolate.

Arthur K. Spears (PhD) is affiliated with The City University of New York (CUNY). At the City College, he is Professor and Chair in the Anthropology Department and Director of the Black Studies Program. At the Graduate Center, he is professor in both the Linguistics and the Anthropology Programs. His research interests include (1) African American English, (2) creole languages, especially Haitian, (3) language and education and (4) race and ideology. Among his books are *The Structure and Status of Pidgins and Creoles* (co-editor, John Benjamins, 1997), *Race and Ideology: Language, Symbolism and Popular Culture* (editor, Wayne State University Press, 1999), *Black Linguistics: Language, Society and Politics in Africa and the Americas* (co-editor, Routledge, 2003). Believing in the importance of disseminating scholarship, he has presented information connected with his areas of specialization through frequent media appearances on the British Broadcasting Corporation ('The Story of English'), Black Entertainment Television, ABC, National Public Radio, WBAI and Inner City Broadcasting's WLIB, among other media organizations.

Barbara Trudell (PhD, Edinburgh) has been active in facilitating local-language literacy and language development since 1982, in both South America and sub-Saharan Africa. Currently she is the director of academic affairs for SIL International's Africa region. Her current research interests include the use of African languages in formal and non-formal learning contexts, language policy formulation and implementation and local community processes of language development and language choice. Her recent publications address reading methodologies for African languages, African perspectives on linguistic diversity, the impact of community values on multilingual education programs and motivations for local-language literacy programs in African communities.

Doris Warriner is Assistant Professor of Language and Literacy at Arizona State University and holds a PhD in Educational Linguistics from the Graduate School of Education at the University of Pennsylvania. Through the lenses of educational anthropology and applied linguistics, she explores questions of equal access and engaged participation for refugees living in the US. With a particular interest in the connections between language, power, education and identity, her research focuses on the role of language ideologies in the literacy and language learning experiences of adult women refugees. Her teaching and research interests include language diversity in education, language, discourse and power, transnational literacies and discourse/narrative analysis. Recent publications have appeared in *Women Studies Quarterly, Anthropology and Education Quarterly, Linguistics and Education* and the *Journal of Language, Identity and Education.*

Walt Wolfram is William C. Friday Distinguished Professor of English Linguistics at North Carolina State University, where he also directs the North Carolina Language and Life Project. He has pioneered research on social and ethnic dialects since the 1960s, authoring or co-authoring more than 20 books and more than 300 articles on regional, social and ethnic dialects of American English, including primary research (*The Development of African American English*, 2002), texts (*American English: Dialects and Variation*, 2006) and trade books for the public (*American Voices: How Dialects Differ from Coast to Coast*). Professor Wolfram is also vitally concerned with the application of sociolinguistic information to social and educational problems and the dissemination of knowledge about dialects to the public. In this connection, he has been involved in the production of numerous television documentaries on dialect diversity. He also has directed the construction of several museum exhibits on language and has developed dialect awareness curricula for the schools and the general public. Wolfram is former President of the Linguistic Society of America as well as the American Dialect Society.

Jon A. Yasin is Professor of English and Linguistics at Bergen Community College in Paramus, New Jersey. For seven years, he taught Linguistics and English at the United Arab Emirates University in Abu Dhabi. Moreover, Dr Yasin was Le Responsable D'Animation Rurale in N'Gabou, Senegal, West Africa for a two-year period. He studied the politics of language at the Kennedy School of Government at Harvard University, English and Rhetoric at the Indiana University of Pennsylvania and Applied Linguistics at Teachers College, Columbia University. His research interests include Hip Hop culture, particularly emceeing and communicating spoken messages in music, and using Hip Hop culture as an educational tool. In addition, Dr Yasin is engaged in an oral history project on the Muslim school system for African American children, which was under the leadership of the late Honorable Elijah Muhammad. Along with presenting at various conferences, Dr Yasin collaborated with his colleague, Charles Bordogna, in writing *African Legacy: A Cultural Heritage Through Art*. Other publications include 'Rap in the African American Music Tradition' in *Race and Ideology: Language, Symbolism and Popular Culture*; 'Keepin' it Real: Hip Hop in El Barrio' in *Latino/a Discourses*; 'Hip Hop Culture Meets the Writing Classroom' in *Multiple Intelligences, Howard Gardner and New Methods of College Teaching*; 'Motivating Students with Hip Hop Culture' in *Princeton University's Mid Career Fellows Publication 2005* and 'Using Hip Hop Culture to Motivate Millennial Students' in *Network: A Journal of Faculty Development*, which is the online journal of the Faculty Resource Network at New York University.

Chapter 1

Discourses of Linguistic Exceptionalism and Linguistic Diversity in Education

JO ANNE KLEIFGEN

This book was initially inspired by Michel DeGraff's (2005) article in *Language in Society,* which challenges the theoretical assumptions and dogmas in the linguistic sciences and in popular culture about the nature and origins of Creole[1] languages. DeGraff argues that, in Creole-origins discourse, these languages have been considered 'exceptional' – different from 'normal' languages. Such linguistic exceptionalism is not reserved for Creoles alone: exceptionalist discourse is pervasive, and it contributes to the marginalization of a great number of vernacular varieties. In this volume, the contributors pay attention to the social cost of these myths of linguistic exceptionalism in education. In spite of years of research that sets out to refute these myths, many languages and language varieties still are considered exceptional in today's educational institutions, and by extension, students who speak these languages still are treated as 'exceptional', 'abnormal' and 'deficient', and thus in need of 'repair'. The authors in this volume take the languages of Africa and the African diaspora as cases in point to address several related issues. They argue that all languages have value – that is, they are all 'normal' and realized out of humans' innate linguistic potential – and that they are potentially powerful resources for learning. They demonstrate that, like all languages, African and diasporic languages are subject to change with people's increased contact in a globalized world – in this case within and between the African continent, the Caribbean and the United States[2] – and these processes must be taken into account by educators and educational policy makers. Given these changing contexts, the authors highlight relationships between local and global dynamics of language and education within and between Africa and the diaspora. The problems related to exceptionalist beliefs in education and contravening movements toward various forms of diversity are common themes running through the chapters; the authors use different theoretical lenses and a range of empirical data to examine this diversity of voices in and out of the classroom.

From Africa to the Diaspora and Back Again

The African continent began to be linked to the western hemisphere through European trade routes from the 15th century, leading to language contact and change on both sides of the Atlantic.[3] In the 21st century, movements of people between Africa, the Caribbean and the Americas (and elsewhere) have intensified and, as a result, educators today work with increasingly diverse language groups. The chapters in this volume are arranged to address this linguistic complexity in two parts: 'Language and Education in Africa' and 'Language and Education in the Diaspora'. Contributors to the first part address the overarching concerns that educators on the African continent are confronting about the role of European languages – a legacy of the colonial era – and the use of Africa's own languages in education. In the second part, the authors examine the role of diasporic languages in educating students in the Caribbean and the US, focusing on Creole speakers in both the Caribbean and the US, recent immigrants to the US who speak African languages and speakers of African American English. The authors make both historical and contemporary connections between the African continent and diasporic milieux.

The vision for this volume is embodied in three thematic strands: *paradigms, practices* and *policies* of language in education. In terms of *paradigms*, contributors pose theoretical and empirical arguments for a shift from exceptionalist to inclusionary thinking, thus opening the doors for everyone to a high quality education through schools that understand the complexities of linguistic diversity. With regard to *practices*, the book aims to help educators formulate informed views about language and innovative teaching for the students they serve. Finally, in terms of *policies*, contributors suggest ways in which policy makers can reshape education so that students' linguistic resources can be considered for their learning potential.

In this introductory chapter, I discuss the three themes recurring throughout the volume. In terms of paradigms, I survey the theoretical terrain, paying particular attention to the discourses of exceptionalism and diversity. This brief examination of exceptionalist discourse and its critics covers Creoles, African American English (AAE) and African languages. I trace the discourses of diversity by addressing how selected language scholars have grappled with this question since the end of the 19th century. I also refer readers to two key theorizing chapters in the volume, one on exceptionalism and the other on diversity. This overview of paradigms prepares the ground for a discussion of the other two themes: practices and policies in education. I argue that the ideas and facts assembled in these chapters constitute a call for concerted action to provide theoretically-informed pedagogy, including teacher preparation and classroom instruction, as well as enlightened language-education policies on behalf of students from diverse language backgrounds. Together, these action-oriented goals constitute a comprehensive and dynamic form of language awareness that leads to a high quality education for students on both sides of the Atlantic.

Transforming Paradigms

The discourse of exceptionalism

Linguistic exceptionalism myths abound in linguistic and educational literature as well as in society in general. DeGraff, in a series of publications (e.g. DeGraff, 2001, 2003, 2005) focuses on the theoretical flaws existing in Creole studies. He and others (e.g. Chaudenson, 2001; Mufwene, 2001; Muysken, 1988) write about linguistic and sociohistorical aspects of Creole languages. They provide linguistic evidence to show that Creole languages are not typologically 'unusual' in terms of morphosyntactic structure; in other words, they are neither 'impoverished' nor 'built from scratch'. They argue that Creoles are instead products of language contact and change as are all other human languages. As Mufwene (2001: 1) clearly states, 'Creoles have developed by the same restructuring processes that mark the evolutions of non-creole languages.' Further, these authors offer sociohistorical evidence showing that exceptionalist fallacies, with roots in early Creole-genesis theories and developed around languages that emerged out of colonialism and slavery, ultimately are related to theories of race (cf. Hill, 2001). DeGraff puts it succinctly: 'Creoles are no more and no less the result of extraordinary external factors [language contact through African enslavement] coupled with ordinary internal factors [humans' innate capacity for language]' (DeGraff, 1999: 477).

Exceptionalist myths have also been spread with regard to African American English (AAE), considered by many educators as 'bad English' or 'slang' needing to be corrected in school (e.g. Bereiter & Englemann, 1966). Speakers of AAE were regarded as 'disadvantaged' or 'culturally deprived' because of their purported 'linguistic deficits' (e.g. Deutsch, 1964) until William Labov's (1972) groundbreaking work, 'The logic of non-standard English', demonstrated that AAE is a rule-governed variety of English. Unfortunately, despite the robust body of research on AAE, which grew out of Labov's work and continues to this day (e.g. Lanehart, 2001;

Lippi-Green, 1997; Morgan, 1994; Rickford, 1999a; Spears, 1999; Wolfram & Thomas, 2002), the stigma attached to AAE remains, as borne out by more recent phenomena such as the contentious responses to the penetration of Hip Hop verbal art into popular discourse (e.g. Alim, 2006; Richardson, 2006; Yasin, 2001) and the 'Ebonics controversy' about the role of AAE in educating its speakers (e.g. Baugh, 2000; Richardson, 1997; Rickford, 1999b).

In the African sociolinguistic context, similar myths of linguistic exceptionalism are found. What counts as an African 'language' is based largely on linguistic descriptions by 19th century European missionaries and shaped by religious, territorial and other colonialist frames (cf. Errington, 2001). This 'invention' of languages, as Makoni and Pennycook (2006) put it, has been critiqued by a number of scholars (e.g. Harries, 1988; Irvine & Gal, 2000; Makoni & Mashiri, 2006). Makoni and Mashiri (2006: 68) point out that those who classified African languages did not take the speakers' own perspectives into account, and they 'excluded "mixed language" contact, vehicular languages[4] and Creoles, which went undescribed because they were treated as ideologically marginal.' Given the neglect of these varieties, the languages of the colonizers became the default languages in government affairs and schooling in most countries.[5] More recently, African scholars have begun to demonstrate the value of mother-tongue education in certain contexts, but they continue to grapple with decisions regarding which languages should have priority as languages of instruction (e.g. Brock-Utne & Hopson, 2005). Besides the disregard for local community languages and language varieties, many of Africa's urban-hybrid languages are targeted today as 'illegitimate' speech that interferes with the education of youth (e.g. Cook, 2002 and this volume; Githiora, 2002; Spitulnik, 1998; Swigart, 2001). In sum, language practices across the continent cover a whole spectrum of languages, varieties, mixtures and registers that are part of students' lived experiences and potentially relevant to their academic achievement. One effect of the colonial legacy is that many speakers of Africa's marginalized languages have themselves espoused the discourse of exceptionalism and look upon the colonizers' languages as languages of power and African languages as having no educational, social, or economic value (Stroud, 2001). (We elaborate on this problem in more detail in our introductions to Part 1 and Part 2.)

In Chapter 7 of this volume, Michel DeGraff critically examines the concept of linguistic exceptionalism. He presents data from his native Haitian Creole to invalidate three canonical tropes in the exceptionalist discourse on Creoles:

(1) they are considered *degenerate varieties* of European languages;
(2) they are described as *hybrids* created by mapping the lexicon of a European language onto the syntax of an African language;
(3) they are said to have emerged suddenly in a *catastrophic break in transmission*, i.e. their structures were developed 'from scratch'.

He disproves these myths and discusses their social cost for the education of children in Haiti, where Haitian Creole is generally not considered a viable language of instruction, in spite of the fact that virtually all Haitians speak the language. DeGraff argues that a Cartesian-Uniformitarian theory of language puts speakers of Creole and African languages on a par with European languages because they are all based on universal properties of the human mind.

As DeGraff's chapter demonstrates, one way to delegitimize the discourse of exceptionalism and to dismantle false beliefs about languages is to expose their fallacies. As part of this exposure, work in generative linguistics shows that all humans possess the same linguistic capital, a Universal Grammar-based capital (cf. Chomsky, 1966). In this view, people everywhere possess the same linguistic capacity; thus their languages merit consideration as potentially legitimate vehicles for learning and other human endeavors.

The discourse of diversity

A second way to delegitimize the discourse of exceptionalism is by establishing an alternative discourse, that of *linguistic diversity*, which recognizes the complex intertwining of various language forms, which are put to different socially-situated uses. This approach takes into account both the equality underlying diverse linguistic forms and the diverse ways of communicating in society. Diversity entails, not just the languages people speak, but also the people speaking the languages. Of course, the discourse of linguistic diversity is not altogether new. As far back as the 19th century, research on multiple languages and language varieties was plentiful. Apart from dialectology, which emerged with the development of dictionaries and grammars in Western Europe, historical linguistics was concerned with how languages change over time. Historical linguists developed comparative methods that uncovered systematic structural correspondences across a wide range of languages. Their work led to the discovery that many of these languages were members of a 'family', the Indo-European family of languages with a common ancestor.

This insight gave rise to comparative work in 20th century linguistics to account for this language family's diversification and geographic spread. It also gave rise to the question of how one might theoretically reconcile the notion of language as a unifying system with the diversity of languages changing geographically and over time. Enter Ferdinand de Saussure, the father of 20th century linguistics. His lectures delivered at the University of Geneva addressed complex historical, structural and social questions about language. Saussure is best known for his *Cours de Linguistique Générale* (1916/1966), which calls for a shift from *diachronic* (historical) to *synchronic* linguistics (the language system at a given point in time), and for a focus on the formal system of grammar rather than its realization in actual verbal performance. Yet this treatise, taken alone, limits our understanding of Saussure's thinking. Recent scholarship shows that Saussure thought of language as a 'two-fold essence' such that, despite the interpretations of his students, whose notes became the structure-centric *Cours*, Saussure's intellectual life was devoted to coming to terms with the relationship between *langue*[6] and *parole* – between language as a unifying system and diversity in language use (cf. Gasparov, 2006a, 2006b; Sanders, 2006). According to notes written in his own hand, Saussure was also concerned with the social nature of language because:

> while there may be psychological facts, and while there may be phonological facts, neither of the two series alone would ever be capable of giving rise to any linguistic fact whatsoever. For there to be a linguistic fact, the two series must exist in union ... (Saussure, 2006: 68)

Meanwhile in early 20th century USSR, ideas on linguistic diversity began to emerge from the Bakhtin Circle. Vološinov (1929/1973) also faced the linguist's universality–diversity quandary. In *Marxism and the Philosophy of Language*, he asked, 'What, then is the true center of linguistic reality: the individual speech act – the utterance – or the system of language?' (Vološinov, 1929/1973: 63). In answering this question, Vološinov contrasted the privileging of language-as-system in the *Cours* (without the benefit of Saussure's own recently discovered notes) with his own approach, which gives primacy to linguistic performance. Importantly, he insisted that *'the utterance is a social phenomenon'* (Vološinov, 1929/1973: 82, emphasis in the original), where words are signs that take on meaning only through dialogue and in specific contexts. Thus, signs are, in his words, *multiaccentual*; diversity of meaning is worked out in social interaction.

Rooted in the work of Boas, Sapir and Whorf, thinking on diversity in languages and cultures in the US developed in the second half of the century, when Hymes (1972), in a response to Chomsky's notion of *linguistic competence*, used the term *communicative competence* to encompass not only the tacit knowledge of grammatical structure but also knowledge of how to use language appropriately, thus emphasizing the importance of the diversity of language practices in society. Gumperz (1964) introduced the concept of *verbal repertoire* to capture the full range of languages, varieties and styles that an individual or social group may deploy in social interaction. For Gumperz, the verbal repertoire bridges the gap between grammatical systems and human groups (1964: 54). His work on linguistic and cultural diversity includes studies of language varieties and bilingualism (e.g. Gumperz, 1971, 1982). This research focuses largely on a kind of multilingualism in which speakers have full control of all the languages and varieties that they use.

More recently, the notion that speakers have full control of every language and variety in their verbal repertoires has begun to shift to include the use of languages with uneven proficiency. This attention to a broader concept of verbal repertoire reflects intensified language contact around the world. Contemporary political and economic events have propelled greater flows of people within and across national borders. Concurrently, the emergence of digital technologies has induced local and global changes in the nature of communication – global changes in the multilingual reach and accelerated flow of communication and local changes in the way it is appropriated and enacted (Castells, 2007; Jacquemet, 2005; Kleifgen & Kinzer, forthcoming). Given these changes, Coste (2001) suggests that the term *verbal repertoire* may be too static to encompass contemporary language use. He and others propose the concept of *plurilingualism* to describe people's complex linguistic repertoires, which may include the use of varieties and mixtures with varying proficiency (e.g. Clyne, 2003; García *et al.*, 2007). Plurilingualism involves practices and values that are not equivalent or even homologous in different languages; instead, they are integrated, variable, flexible (Coste, 2001) and equal in value, even though they may serve different functions (Beacco & Byram, 2003). Plurilingualism, then, takes into account two overarching aspects of linguistic diversity: the complex interplay of unevenly developed competences in a variety of languages, dialects and registers and the valuing of these complexities of use.

Diversity and value

Languages are intrinsically equal, yet they are not equally valued in society; thus the notion of valuing complexities of use embodied in plurilingualism is to a great extent something one must constantly strive for. Ways of speaking, those aspects of communication that comprise the linguistic repertoires of speakers – multiple languages, varieties and mixtures, along with registers, modes and styles associated with them – are weighted differently, sometimes, as this volume demonstrates, with dire educational consequences. Hymes (1996: xii), in a book of essays on ethnography and linguistics in education, reminds us that 'however much all language may be the same from certain standpoints, it does not count the same in life.' He argues that one must distinguish between languages as potentially equal and languages as assigned unequal values in society, particularly regarding their particular roles and functions within given speech communities. He defines diversity as 'the adaptation of languages and varieties to one another, and their integration into special roles and complex speech communities' (Hymes, 1996: 30) and stresses the importance of understanding how members of speech communities themselves evaluate diversity – 'as both a human problem and a human resource' (34). Following Hymes's thinking, Blommaert (2005: 393) points out that 'every difference in language is socially valued and marked as to degree of fit in particular contexts.' Blommaert goes on to note that people may have differential access to forms (such as school-based discourse and literacy) and to contexts of interpretation (like knowing how to 'do' being a good student in the classroom); taken together, differential access to form and context can constitute a nexus of inequality. Language use is tightly bound to evaluations of what counts as meaningful, given the rules for interaction and norms of interpretation, many of which are anchored in centers of power such as the school and the state (Blommaert, 2005: 395–396).

Here let us turn again to Vološinov, who recognizes the centrality of language expressed in different genres, in particular contexts, and sometimes with conflicting goals. Vološinov, however, while recognizing the ideological aspect of language use controlled by larger centers of power, argues that power relations are expressed even in everyday social interactions. He puts it this way: 'There is no such thing as word without evaluative accent' (Vološinov, 1929/1973: 103). People as individuals and as members of complex speech communities express particular orientations towards the roles and status of their ways of speaking, and they also have the potential to surmount inequalities of access to linguistic forms and contexts in education.

In Chapter 2 of this volume, Sinfree Makoni and Barbara Trudell examine different values and beliefs with regard to linguistic diversity in the African context. They describe three types of discourses of diversity. The first portrays linguistic diversity as an enumeration of autonomous objects (languages) that exist apart from their use in society. Because languages are examined as objects, this discourse does not address realities on the ground, such as local communicative practices and people's language choice for education in Africa's multilingual environment. A second type of discourse treats linguistic diversity as a 'problematic oddity'. In this view, African languages are seen as exotic, an evaluation that can be traced back to colonialist education policies, which privileged European languages. This view is perpetuated under post-colonial governments pressured by Western donor organizations that value European languages as media of instruction in the name of globalism. The third type of discourse links linguistic diversity to identity and rights. In this discursive approach, language is inextricably tied to cultural identities and values, and it is associated with questions of power, particularly with respect to speech communities with fewer speakers. Makoni and Trudell explore the complexities and tensions around language-rights discourse among African speech communities, especially with regard to language choice in education, and note that the significant value Africans place on multilingualism holds promise for positive discourses of linguistic diversity on the continent.

The *langue–parole* connection has been an age-old conundrum in the study of language and communicative practices, and this is reflected in the various ways in which the concept of linguistic diversity is portrayed in this volume. While some authors celebrate the human capacity for language with its diverse manifestations of form, others celebrate the diversity of communicative practices. Ultimately, however, language use requires an intricate relationship between form and function. William Hanks (1996) puts it this way:

> While linguistic systems are governed in part by principles unique to language, grammar is neither self-contained nor entirely independent from the social worlds in which the language is used. How people talk has an impact on, and is influenced by, the structure of their language. ... There is no necessary contradiction between the idea of grammar and the idea of practice, since the two focus on different aspects of the total social fact. (Hanks, 1996: 235–236)

Transforming Practice and Policy: Educating for Language Awareness

In the last section, particular attention was paid to the first thematic strand, paradigms – theories about language in education. Here, I discuss the authors' thinking about two other thematic strands – practices and policies in education – with the aim of showing how these provide the ingredients for a novel approach to *language awareness*. Language awareness has been defined as 'a person's sensitivity to and conscious awareness of the nature of language and its role in human life' (Donmal, 1985: 7). The concept emerged in Britain out of concerns that language pedagogy should incorporate explicit teaching about language structures and language use in society (Hawkins, 1987). There is abundant scholarship on language awareness in Europe and the British Isles (e.g. Balboni, 1993; Cheshire & Edwards, 1998; Goethals, 1993; Hawkins, 1999; James & Garrett, 1991; McCarthy, 1994; Van Essen, 1992). Language awareness pedagogy is active in many European schools, giving students the opportunity to learn about and appreciate different languages. Elements in the language awareness curriculum include fostering understanding about language patterns, changing attitudes about languages and language varieties, and developing an ability to communicate about language (Donmal, 1985). Fairclough's (1989) work in critical discourse analysis, with its emphasis on the relationship between language, values and power relations, influenced the inclusion of these elements into language awareness pedagogy, thus giving the concept its more recent name, critical language awareness (Clark *et al.*, 1990, 1991). Language awareness policies and pedagogy have received less attention in the US, with a few notable exceptions. Alim (2005) Smitherman (2006), Smitherman and van Dijk (1988) and Smitherman and Villanueva (2003) have called for critical language awareness curricula in US schools and, under Walt Wolfram's leadership, a state-wide 'dialect awareness' curriculum has been developed for the public schools of North Carolina (Adger *et al.*, 2007; Wolfram, this volume). Language awareness has also gained traction in South African education (e.g. Janks, 1993, 2001; Ngwenya, 2006). Janks has developed and tested critical language awareness tools for South African secondary schools, and these are now being used elsewhere. Siegel (2002, 2006, 2007) has written about critical language awareness in relation to Creoles and other marginalized languages in the Caribbean and around the world.

Critical language awareness creates an opening that can be used to reconsider assumptions about whether certain languages are appropriate as resources for students' education. Contributors to this volume collectively offer a *comprehensive language awareness* approach that understands consciousness-raising in the broadest sense. That is, awareness efforts are not restricted to teachers and students, but extend also to makers of language-education policy and even to language theorists and researchers.

Providing knowledge and tools for practice

Several contributions in this volume offer ways to intensify language awareness approaches to pedagogy. There is, first, the work of authors who provide valuable linguistic data and curricular materials that can be used in the school to inculcate knowledge about linguistic diversity and, second, other work that addresses questions of language and literacy practices found outside school settings. In three chapters, linguistic data are provided that can increase teachers' knowledge about the linguistic resources that their students bring to school and help teachers instruct students about their own and others' languages. Christa de Kleine (Chapter 10) presents examples of the writing of Creole-speaking students from Anglophone West Africa enrolled in ESL classes in the US. Their writing shows grammatical transfer from their native Krio and Vernacular Liberian English (such as omission of plural marking and articles), which stem from different underlying grammatical functions or distributions. Because these languages are closely related to English, de Kleine argues that students may not notice the differences between their mother tongue and English. She suggests that ESL teachers need to understand and anticipate this challenge in order to meet the linguistic needs of these students.

Arthur Spears (Chapter 13) discusses a number of factors that contribute to what he calls 'shallow grammar' in the descriptions of African American English (AAE). When aspects of AAE are overlooked in research, teachers do not have requisite knowledge and awareness of the language for themselves and their students. Spears provides an antidote to this state of affairs by showing, first, that AAE is not a monolithic *variety*; rather, there are AAE *varieties* like African American Standard English (AASE) and African American Vernacular English (AAVE). (See also Walt Wolfram's chapter in this regard.) Second, Spears presents data obtained through participant observation showing the use of auxiliary verbs that express tense, mood and aspect in AAVE. He argues that such deeper knowledge about AAE can help to counteract exceptionalist beliefs in classrooms.

Similarly, DeGraff (Chapter 7) provides comparative lexical and morphological examples from French, English and Haitian Creole to demonstrate that Creole languages are on a par with non-Creoles. He argues that English, whose lexicon and grammar are influenced by other languages such as French, is just as 'hybrid' as Haitian Creole. He also equips educators with lexical, morphological and syntactic examples to demonstrate that Haitian Creole did not start from 'scratch' but developed differently from its French 'ancestor' just as English developed differently from its early historical stages. Finally, DeGraff suggests that, by engaging students in linguistic research on their own languages, teachers can help dispel exceptionalist beliefs.

Moving from classroom practices to system-wide curricular development, Walt Wolfram's contribution (Chapter 14) highlights the importance of a theoretically-based program to educate the public about language diversity. Like Spears, Wolfram demonstrates that AAE is significantly more diverse than often assumed in prior research, and offers examples based on a decade of research that challenges several assumptions about AAE variation and change. Wolfram then describes an ambitious dialect awareness curriculum, piloted in North Carolina's middle schools. He presents several curricular examples that illustrate a critical language awareness approach, in which teachers, using multimedia resources, show students how to critique language prejudice, compare grammatical patterns in AAE and other regional and social varieties of English, observe AAE speakers' skills in language shifting according to different speech situations and examine generational variation in AAE speech. The results of this pilot project show changes in knowledge and attitudes among students and teachers alike; Wolfram cautions, though, that entrenched language ideologies may take generations to change.

A comprehensive language awareness approach also includes transforming practices outside the school. In some cases, the educative experience can take place in the community, and in other cases 'funds of knowledge' from the community can become a resource for the school. John Baugh (Chapter 12) exposes to public view a racist practice in the form of linguistic profiling, as when people of color inquire about apartment rentals in some neighborhoods in California. Through experimentally controlled telephone calls, Baugh shows a high rejection rate of callers who speak a non-standard dialect, resulting in unequal access to housing. Baugh's contribution to public language awareness is especially important for equal educational access because, as he notes, in the US, better schools are located in higher income neighborhoods. The results of this research provide stark evidence that, however equal every language variety may be from an analytical linguistic perspective, languages are weighted differently in practice.

Whereas Baugh's work focuses on communities' *speaking* practices, Kate Parry's research (Chapter 5) is concerned with *literacy* practices in community settings. In the African context, Parry discusses ways to offer access to literacy through community libraries. Drawing on her research and experience in Uganda and Nigeria, Parry describes how these countries' multilingual situations often require multiple literacies – in the mother tongue, an African *lingua franca* and English – each serving different functions. Arguing that literacy practices in complex speech communities attend to different needs, her work resonates with Hymes's point that not all languages are equally suitable for particular purposes. Libraries provide the multiple literacy resources that schools are unable to offer. Parry's work in promoting such libraries in Uganda shows that, by affording access to materials in multiple languages, community libraries can supplement and enhance both school-based and everyday literacy practices.

In Chapter 15, Jon Yasin demonstrates how some educators, largely through ignorance of their origins and creative value, denigrate certain out-of-school language and literacy practices. Through his sociohistorical description of the development of Hip Hop culture, Yasin presents an argument for its value, not only as a counter-hegemonic discourse that strengthens group identity, but also as a potential gateway to other literacies. His description of Hip Hop practices situates this kind of discourse within the wider verbal repertoire, thus holding out insights that outsiders may not otherwise appreciate. Through his research and college-level work with students who identify with this culture, Yasin presents examples of Hip Hop elements brought into the classroom to support students' academic writing development. Yasin argues that teachers should become aware of the valuable contributions that community 'funds of knowledge' like Hip Hop can bring to the classroom.

Strengthening language awareness at the policy level

Clearly, language awareness at the level of theory and practice cannot effect change from linguistic exceptionalism to an engagement in linguistic diversity without enlightened educational policies. Because language policy issues can differ markedly from one region to another, this section outlines what authors have to say about policy in their specific contexts. Probably no other place in the world is more concerned with language-education policy than Africa, where hard questions are being asked about current policies. Several authors point to the linguistic legacy of European expansionism and the so-called *mission civilisatrice* in Africa and the Americas. Makoni and Trudell (Chapter 2) describe the colonialists' view that African languages and cultures were exotic, and their decisions to impose the 'more valuable' European languages and educational approaches; thus, colonialist language-education policies, for the most part, ignored African languages. Post-colonial language policies continued to give primacy to non-African languages in education until more recent efforts turned the gaze of the continent back toward its own linguistic diversity as a potential educational resource. Makoni and Trudell offer an example of the Tonga people of Zimbabwe, who are strong advocates for the right to use their language as a medium of instruction in the schools.

This work is complemented by Casmir Rubagumya's (Chapter 3), which looks broadly at language-education policies across the continent and argues that monolingual policies, especially the use of former colonial languages in education, do not work in Africa's multilingual societies. He shows that these policies have failed to provide a good education for students because they are not based on research evidence. Instead, policy decisions depend on what language projects get funded, popular misconceptions about languages of instruction, and poor communication between policy makers and teachers. Rubagumya offers hopeful alternatives with examples of successful mother-tongue education projects in Nigeria, South Africa, Zambia, Mali and Burkina Faso.

Peter Mtesigwa (Chapter 4) takes Tanzania's educational situation as a case in point to discuss Kiswahili language policy. Kiswahili is an example of an African *lingua franca*, since it is a language spoken in several countries of Eastern Africa. In spite of its widespread use in Tanzania, Kiswahili is used as a medium of instruction only at the primary level, whereas English is the language of instruction at the secondary and post-secondary levels. Mtesigwa describes beliefs and assumptions behind using English, and presents arguments that favor the use of Kiswahili beyond primary education; these include teacher and student higher proficiency in Kiswahili rather than English, access to high-level jobs requiring Kiswahili, and Kiswahili as a vehicle of national development and identity. Finally, while still recognizing the need to respect other mother tongues in Tanzania, Mtesigwa takes what some consider a controversial stand in favor of regional *lingua francas* in African education.

Meanwhile, Susan Cook (Chapter 6) adopts a different stance regarding language-education policy based on her research in South Africa. Rather than debating African vs. European languages, Cook states that policy makers should consider instead which varieties of African languages might be used in the classroom. She presents data from her ethnographic research on language use by teachers and students in Setswana-medium schools. Teachers rhetorically embrace 'pure' Setswana in school, which is associated with ethnic identity, while at the same time they use Street Setswana, a pan-ethnic hybrid variety signaling a more cosmopolitan allegiance. At the same time, Street Setswana, rather than standard Setswana, is the language spoken by students. Yet, because they do not speak the standard variety, teachers maintain that students need 'remedial' instruction to root out their 'bad' Setswana. The contradictory communicative practices and attitudes displayed by teachers and students are a signal of a major disconnect between policy and practice. Cook's work highlights the need for policy informed by awareness of on-the-ground linguistic practices in the former ethnic 'homelands' of South Africa.

Turning to the Caribbean context, we are treated to a rich sociohistorical description by Ellen Schnepel (Chapter 8) of the language-education policy shifts that have taken place in Guadeloupe in the French Antilles. Schnepel begins by charting the development and use of the Creole language starting with French colonization and the importation of slaves in the 17th century. With this background, she traces the changes in language policy, starting with the nationalist movement of the 1980s, to assert Guadeloupean ethnocultural identity through the local language. This activism resulted in transforming policy from the exclusive use of French to the acceptance of Creole in the schools as a legitimate language. Schnepel lays out the sociolinguistic situation in Guadeloupe and then goes on to consider in detail some of the debates relating to educational language policies, such as the orthography question, which entails creating a writing system that reflects the local language rather than French; the controversial pilot effort at a Capesterre secondary school to incorporate Creole as a bridge to French; and the design of an examination certifying secondary school teachers in the Creole language for the French Antilles and beyond.

As for the Anglophone Caribbean, Shondel Nero (Chapter 9) tells us how misguided language-education policies in Jamaica are failing students both on the island and in the US. Nero reviews the British colonial influence on educational policies: the use of English as the sole medium of instruction and the exceptionalist view that Jamaican Creole is a corrupted form of English. Within this context, she describes the policy of tracking in Jamaican schools (and elsewhere in the Caribbean), in which students are put into separate classes according to their language and socioeconomic level. Students from the upper middle class, who come to school already proficient in standard English, are put on a higher-level track, whereas the majority Jamaican Creole speakers, typically from the lower class, are assigned to low-performing schools, resulting in their academic failure. The policy also affects the education of Creole-speaking immigrants to the US, where there is a lack of awareness about Anglophone Creole languages. Nero recommends abolishing tracking practices in Jamaica and including a strong language awareness component in teacher-education programs in both Jamaica and the US.

With regard to the US, several of the authors writing about speakers of AAE at least implicitly direct readers' attention to problems in language-education policies. Here, it is useful to examine how these policies affect a different language group. Doris Warriner (Chapter 11) describes a little-researched area, which is the effect of American education policies on refugees from war-torn African regions. Her research addresses a concern expressed by Rubagumya in the African context: the persistence of monolingual language-education policies in an increasingly multilingual country. Warriner's data are drawn from research on the plight of refugee women from the Sudan who have settled in the US, a country that has

English-only policies complicated by high-stakes tests that every student must pass, regardless of language background or whether or not they have suffered an interrupted education, religious persecution or economic hardship. These women enrolled in an adult ESL program in order to assist themselves and their children in adjusting to a new culture and school system. In interviewing these women, Warriner learns how exceptionalist beliefs, expressed in widely-circulating discourses extolling the power and prestige of English, shape the women's views about the value of English as a vehicle to jobs and education. These broader discursive influences also shape the negative value they attach to their own home language, their 'accented' English and their sense of adequacy as family educators. In the face of policies that give English primacy in American education, Warriner recommends sensitizing ESL educators and learners to critical language awareness pedagogies so that refugees like these women are not marginalized still further.

Conclusion

Contributors to *The Languages of Africa and the Diaspora* address the dynamic contact and flow of African and diasporic languages, literacies and cultures across oceans, islands and continents. They show how valuing linguistic diversity can be an antidote to false exceptionalist beliefs and can even occasion access to identity, power and educational equity. By exploring the linkages among speakers of diverse languages and language varieties, the contributors illustrate both hegemonic tendencies by dominant languages and certain powerful influences exerted by non-dominant ones. They argue that these tensions and other processes of increased linguistic diversity in a globalized world must be taken into account by educational researchers, practitioners and policy makers. Taken together, the chapters in this volume make the case that a comprehensive language awareness is central to remedying the false beliefs of linguistic exceptionalism. Moreover, they suggest ways in which the affirmative dimensions of linguistic diversity might be advanced through creative improvements to pedagogy and policy so that all students gain access to an excellent education and quality of life.

Notes

1. Some of the contributors to this volume have written *creole* in lower case unless they are referring to a specific Creole language. However, in this chapter and in our introductions to Parts 1 and 2, we capitalize the term throughout to acknowledge that creoles are on a par with other languages, including 'Englishes'.

2. Although this volume's focus is on linkages between Africa and countries across the Atlantic, it is important to recognize that African connections span the globe (such as French-based Creoles in the Indian Ocean region discussed by Chaudenson, 2001). In Europe, many countries have received people from their former colonies in Africa and the New World. Examples include the Netherlands – with immigrants from Surinam, Somalia, Dutch Antilles/Aruba and others (e.g. Van der Avoird *et al.*, 2001), the United Kingdom – whose immigrants come from Ghana, Guyana, Jamaica, the Virgin Islands and elsewhere (e.g. Edwards, 2001; Nwenmely, 1996) and France – with immigrants from countries of the Maghreb (e.g. Caubet, 2001).
3. With regard to language contact in slave-trade contexts on both sides of the Atlantic, McWhorter (2000) argues that 'new world' Creoles did not have their origins on plantations, but instead originated and developed in West African trade settlements.
4. Vehicular languages – *lingua francas* such as Sango and Lingala – were used among Africans for business and commerce, yet largely ignored by European colonizers (Samarin, 1989); thus they were not considered worthy of description.
5. Bamgbose (2004) points out that colonial language-education policies in a few countries under British and Belgian influence did favor teaching in African languages during the early school years.
6. Space considerations do not permit adequate development of Saussure's notion that *langue* is both a mental and a social entity.

References

Adger, C.T., Wolfram, W. and Christian, D. (2007) *Dialects in Schools and Communities*. New York: Taylor & Francis Group.

Alim, S.H. (2005) Critical language awareness in the United States: Revisiting issues and revising pedagogies in a resegregated society. *Educational Researcher* 34 (7), 24–31.

Alim, S.H. (2006) *Roc the Mic Right: The Language of Hip Hop Culture*. London: Routledge.

Balboni, P.E. (1993) Language awareness in the national curriculum for language awareness for Italy. *Language Awareness* 2, 187–192.

Bamgbose, A. (2004) *Language of Instruction Policy and Practice in Africa*. Prepared for UNESCO. Online at www.unesco.org/education/languages_2004/language instruction_africa.pdf. Accessed 12.8.08.

Baugh, J. (2000) *Beyond Ebonics: Linguistic Pride and Racial Prejudice*. New York: Oxford University Press.

Beacco, J-C. and Byram, M. (2007) *From Linguistic Diversity to Plurilingual Education: Guide for the Development of Language Education Policies in Europe* (rev. edn). Strasbourg: Council of Europe. Online at http://www.coe.int/t/dg4/linguistic/Source/FullGuide_EN.pdf. Accessed 12.8.08

Bereiter, C. and Engelmann, S. (1966) *Teaching Disadvantaged Children in the Pre-school*. Englewood Cliffs, NJ: Prentice Hall.

Blommaert, J. (2005) Situating language rights: English and Swahili in Tanzania revisited. *Journal of Sociolinguistics* 9 (3), 390–417.

Brock-Utne, B. and Hopson, R.K. (eds) (2005) *Languages of Instruction for African Emancipation: Focus on Postcolonial Contexts and Considerations*. Cape Town: Center for Advanced Studies of African Society (CSAS).

Castells, M. (2007) Communication, power and counter-power in the networked society. *International Journal of Communication* 1, 238–266.

Caubet, D. (2001) Maghrebine Arabic in France. In G. Extra and D. Gorter (eds) *The Other Languages of Europe* (pp. 261–277). Clevedon: Multilingual Matters.

Chaudenson, R. (2001) *Creolization of Language and Culture* (revised in collaboration with S. Mufwene). London: Routledge.

Cheshire, J. and Edwards, V. (1998) Knowledge about language in British classrooms: Children as researchers. In A. Egan-Robertson and D. Bloome (eds) *Students as Researchers of Culture and Language in their Own Communities* (pp. 191–214). Creskill, NJ: Hampton Press.

Chomsky, N. (1966) *Cartesian Linguistics: A Chapter in the History of Rationalist Thought*. New York: Harper & Row.

Clark, R., Fairclough, N., Ivanič, R. and Martin-Jones, M. (1990) Critical language awareness Part I: A critical review of three current approaches to language awareness. *Language and Education* 4 (4), 249–260.

Clark, R., Fairclough, N., Ivanič, R. and Martin-Jones, M. (1991) Critical language awareness Part II: Towards critical alternatives. *Language and Education* 5 (1), 41–54.

Clyne, M. (2003) *Dynamics of Language Contact*. Cambridge: Cambridge University Press.

Cook, S. (2002) Urban language in a rural setting: The case of Phokeng, South Africa. In G. Gmelch and W. Zenner (eds) *Urban Life* (4th edn; pp. 106–114). Prospect Heights, IL: Waveland Press.

Coste, D. (2001) *La notion de compétence plurilingue.* Actes du séminaire: L'enseignement des langues vivantes, perspectives [*The Notion of Plurilingual Competence.* Seminar proceedings: The Teaching of Living Languages, Perspectives]. Paris: Ministère de la Jeunesse de l'Education et de la Recherche, DES. At http://eduscol.education.fr/D0033/langviv-acte3.htm. Accessed 12.8.08.

DeGraff, M. (1999) *Language Creation and Language Change: Creolization, Diachrony and Development*. Cambridge, MA: MIT Press.

DeGraff, M. (2001) On the origin of Creoles: A Cartesian critique of 'neo'-Darwinian linguistics. *Linguistic Typology* 2/3, 213–310.

DeGraff, M. (2003) Against Creole Exceptionalism. *Language* 79, 391–410.

DeGraff, M. (2005) Linguists' most dangerous myth: The fallacy of Creole Exceptionalism. *Language in Society* 34, 533–591.

Deutsch, M. (1964) The disadvantaged child and the learning process. In F. Riessman, J. Cohen and A. Pearl (eds) *Mental Health of the Poor* (pp. 172–187). New York: Macmillan.

Donmal, A. (ed.) (1985) *Language Awareness*. London: CILT.

Edwards, V. (2001) Community languages in the UK. In G. Extra and D. Gorter (eds) *The Other Languages of Europe* (pp. 243–260). Clevedon: Multilingual Matters.

Errington, J. (2001) Colonial linguistics. *Annual Review of Anthropology* 30, 19–39.

Fairclough, N. (1989) *Language and Power.* London: Longman.

García, O., Bartlett, L. and Kleifgen, J. (2007) From biliteracy to pluriliteracies. In P. Auer and L. Wei (eds) *Handbook of Multilingualism and Multilingual Communication* (pp. 207–228). New York: Mouton.

Gasparov, B. (2006a) The Saussurean concept of arbitrariness of linguistic signs in the light of early Romantic dialogism. Fourteenth Annual Leonard Hastings Schoff Memorial Lectures. Columbia University, New York, Nov. 13.
Gasparov, B. (2006b) Indo-European linguistics from Schlegel to Saussure: Reconstruction or mythological recollection? Fourteenth Annual Leonard Hastings Schoff Memorial Lectures. Columbia University, New York, Nov. 20.
Githiora, C. (2002) Sheng: Peer language, Swahili dialect or emerging Creole? *Journal of African Cultural Studies* 15 (2), 159–181.
Goethals, M. (1993) Language awareness in Belgium: More of an implicit fact than a clear curriculum item. *Language Awareness* 2 (1), 15–24.
Gumperz, J.J. (1964) Linguistic and social interaction in two communities. In J.J. Gumperz and D. Hymes *The Ethnography of Communication* (*American Anthropologist* special publication) 66 (6, Part 2), 137–153.
Gumperz, J.J. (1971) *Language in Social Groups*. Stanford, CA: Stanford University.
Gumperz, J.J. (1982) *Discourse Strategies*. Cambridge: Cambridge University Press.
Hanks, W.F. (1996) Language form and communicative practices. In J.J. Gumperz and S.C. Levinson (eds) *Rethinking Linguistic Relativity* (pp. 232–270). Cambridge: Cambridge University Press.
Harries, P. (1988) The roots of ethnicity: Discourse and the politics of language construction in South-East Africa. *African Affairs: Journal of the Royal African Society* 86 (346), 25–52.
Hawkins, E. (1987) *Awareness of Language: An Introduction* (rev. edn). New York: Cambridge University Press.
Hawkins, E. (1999) Foreign language study and language awareness. *Language Awareness* 8 (3–4), 124–142.
Hill, J. (2001) The racializing function of language panics. In R. Dueñas González and I. Melis (eds) *Language Ideologies: Critical Perspectives on the Official English Movement. History, Theory and Policy* (Vol. 2; pp. 245–267). Mahwah, NJ: Laurence Erlbaum.
Hymes, D. (1972) On communicative competence. In J.B. Pride and J. Holmes (eds) *Sociolinguistics* (pp. 269–293). Harmondsworth: Penguin.
Hymes, D. (1996) *Ethnography, Linguistics, Narrative Inequality*. Bristol, PA: Taylor & Francis.
Irvine, J. and Gal, S. (2000) Language ideology and linguistic differentiation. In P.V. Kroskrity (ed.) *Regimes of Language: Ideologies, Polities and Identities* (pp. 35–84). Santa Fe, NM: School of American Research Press.
Jacquemet, M. (2005) Transidiomatic practices: Language and power in the age of globalization. *Language & Communication* 25, 257–277.
James, C. and Garrett, P. (eds) (1991) *Language Awareness in the Classroom*. London: Longman.
Janks, H. (1993) *Critical Language Awareness Series*. Johannesburg: Hodder and Stoughton and Witts University Press.
Janks, H. (2001) Critical language awareness: Curriculum 2005 meets the TRC. *Southern African Linguistics and Applied Language Studies* 19 (3–4), 241–252.
Kleifgen, J. and Kinzer, C.K. (forthcoming) Alternative spaces for education with and through technology. In E. Gordon and H. Varenne (eds) *Comprehensive Education*. Lewiston, NY: Mellen Press.
Labov, W. (1972) The logic of non-standard English. In W. Labov *Language in the Inner City* (pp. 201–240). Philadelphia, PA: University of Pennsylvania Press.

Lanehart, S. (ed.) (2001) *Sociocultural and Historical Contexts of African American English*. Philadelphia, PA: John Benjamins.

Lippi-Green, R. (1997) *English with an Accent: Language, Ideology and Discrimination in the United States*. New York: Routledge.

Makoni, S. and Mashiri, P. (2006) Critical historiography: Does language planning in Africa need a construct of language as part of its theoretical apparatus? In S. Makoni and A. Pennycook (eds) *Disinventing and Reconstituting Languages* (pp. 62–89). Clevedon: Multilingual Matters.

Makoni, S. and Pennycook, A. (eds) (2006) *Disinventing and Reconstituting Languages*. Clevedon: Multilingual Matters.

McCarthy, J. (1994) The case for language awareness in the Irish primary school curriculum. *Language Awareness* 3 (1), 1–9.

McWhorter, J. (2000) *The Missing Spanish Creoles: Recovering the Birth of Plantation Contact*. Berkeley, CA: University of California Press.

Morgan, M. (1994) The African-American speech community: Reality and sociolinguists. In M. Morgan (ed.) *Language and the Social Construction of Identity in Creole Situations* (pp. 121–148). Los Angeles, CA: The Center for Afro-American Studies, UCLA.

Mufwene, S. (2001) *The Ecology of Language Evolution*. Cambridge: Cambridge University Press.

Muysken, P. (1988) Are Creoles a special type of language? In F. Newmeyer (ed.) *Linguistics. The Cambridge Survey* (Vol. 2); *Linguistic Theory: Extensions and Implications* (pp. 285–301). Cambridge: Cambridge University Press.

Ngwenya, T. (2006) Introducing critical language awareness in IsiZulu: The why and the how. *Southern African Linguistics and Applied Language Studies* 24 (2), 165–173.

Nwenmely, H. (1996) *Language Reclamation: French Creole Language Teaching in the UK and the Caribbean*. Clevedon: Multilingual Matters.

Richardson, E. (2006) *Hip Hop Literacies*. New York: Routledge.

Richardson, E. (1997) The anti-Ebonics movement: 'standard' English only. *Journal of English Linguistics* 26 (2), 156–169.

Rickford, J.R. (1999a) *African American English: Features, Evolution and Educational Implications*. Malden, MA: Blackwell.

Rickford, J.R. (1999b) The Ebonics controversy in my backyard: A sociolinguist's experiences and reflections. *Journal of Sociolinguistics* 3 (2), 267–275.

Samarin, W.J. (1989) *The Black Man's Burden: African Colonial Labor on the Congo and Ubangi Rivers, 1880–1900*. Bolder, CO: Westview Press.

Sanders, C. (2006) Introduction. In S. Bouquet and R. Engler with A. Weil (eds) *Writings in General Linguistics* (trans. from French by C. Sanders and M. Pires with P. Figueroa) (pp. xviii–xxx). New York: Oxford University Press.

Saussure, F. de (1966) *Course in General Linguistics*. C. Bally and A. Sechehaye with A. Riedlinger (eds) (trans. from French by W. Baskin). New York: McGraw-Hill Book Company (original work published 1916).

Saussure, F. de (2006) *Writings in General Linguistics*. S. Bouquet and R. Engler with A. Weil (eds) (trans. from French by C. Sanders and M. Pires with P. Figueroa). New York: Oxford University Press.

Siegel, J. (2002) Applied creolistics in the twenty-first century. In G. Gilbert (ed.) *Pidgin and Creole Linguistics in the Twenty-first Century* (pp. 7–48). New York: Peter Lang.

Siegel, J. (2006) Language ideologies and the education of speakers of marginalized language varieties: Adopting a critical awareness approach. *Linguistics and Education* 17 (2), 157–174.

Siegel, J. (2007) Creoles and minority dialects in education: An update. *Language and Education* 21 (1), 66–86.

Smitherman, G. (2006) *Word from the Mother: Language and African Americans*. New York: Routledge

Smithrman, G. and van Dijk, T. (eds) (1988) *Discourse and Discrimination*. Detroit: Wayne State University Press.

Smitherman, G. and Villanueva, V. (eds) (2003) *Language Diversity in the Classroom: From Intention to Practice*. Carbondale, IL: Southern Illinois University Press.

Spears, A.K. (1999) Race and ideology: An introduction. In A.K. Spears (ed.) *Race and Ideology: Language, Symbolism and Popular Culture* (pp. 11–58). Detroit: Wayne State University Press.

Spitulnik, D. (1998) The language of the city: Town Bemba as urban hybridity. *Journal of Linguistic Anthropology* 8 (1), 30–59.

Stroud, C. (2001) African mother tongues and the politics of language: Linguistic citizenship vs. linguistic human rights. *Journal of Multilingual and Multicultural Development* 22 (4), 339–353.

Swigart, L. (2001) The limits of legitimacy: Language ideology and shift in contemporary Senegal. *Journal of Linguistic Anthropology* 10 (1), 90–130.

Van der Avoird, T., Broeder, P. and Extra, G. (2001) Immigrant minority languages in the Netherlands. In G. Extra and D. Gorter (eds) *The Other Languages of Europe* (pp. 215–242). Clevedon: Multilingual Matters.

Van Essen, A. (1992) Language awareness in the Netherlands. *Language Awareness* 1 (1), 19–26.

Vološinov, V.N. (1973) *Marxism and the Philosophy of Language*. Cambridge, MA: Harvard University Press (original work published 1929).

Wolfram, W. and Thomas, E. (2002) *The Development of African American English*. Malden, MA: Blackwell.

Yasin, J.A. (2001) Rap in the African-American music tradition. In A.K. Spears (ed.) *Race and Ideology: Language, Symbolism and Popular Culture* (pp. 197–223). Detroit: Wayne State University.

Part 1

Language and Education in Africa

Introduction

GEORGE C. BOND

Jo Anne Kleifgen's first chapter introduction provided an overview of the volume and its central ideas. This section is specifically directed toward the sociological issues of policies, paradigms and practices in different African contexts and educational situations. The five chapters in this part of the book recognize the inherent politics of language, that stem from relationships of domination and subjugation, as they have been expressed in the policies of rulers, the responses of subjects and citizens and in the everyday lives of ordinary people. The chapters are themselves part of the historical debate over language, its use and those who use it. They focus on the interaction of 'official' and minority languages and the manner in which they represent sectional interests. The school becomes the arena in which these sectional interests intersect, providing the opportunity to see the effects of policies in the everyday lives of individuals. Within schools one may also observe the responses to educational policies as well as the history of patterns of inclusion and exclusion, reflected in the school's 'official' language of instruction. In multilingual societies, languages are often ranked, a ranking that is expressed in the educational progression from primary to tertiary schooling and one that reflects the history of its constituent social groupings. In many African countries, the progression is from the 'mother tongue' to an African lingua franca such as Swahili to the language of the former colonial rulers, English, French, or Portuguese. The colonial languages represent the metropole, the former centers of colonial power, and many African elites set them as a measure of their own individual and collective accomplishments. On the other side are African intellectuals who disclaim colonial languages and advocate the sole use of African languages. As we will see, these two positions have their own cluster of challenges.

In his discussion in Part 2, DeGraff observes that one of the fundamental characteristics of 'creolistics' is that its own genesis is 'deeply steeped in the history of White[1] hegemony in the New World and its ensuing dualism vis-à-vis the (non)humanity of those who were deemed "slaves by nature"' (Chapter 7). He makes a series of observations related to social history and the legality and legitimacy of languages; the distribution of power, wealth and privilege; and the capacity of languages to operate effectively within specific technical or environmental domains. He explores the situational use of languages related to the private and public aspirations, interests and goals of different constituencies ranging from individuals to government departments.

The story of African languages contains all of these complexities and interrelationships. Within the context of European colonial rule African languages were treated as deficient in their capacity to handle the economic and technological realities of the modern world. As these essays make clear, politicians, scholars and average people within Africa, Europe and the Americas continue to struggle over (or debate) the history, the legality, legitimacy and the capacities of African languages and African peoples. Thus, as Errington's article 'Colonial Linguistics' (2001) implies, there has been an intimate relationship between the ruler and the ruled and the dominated and the subjugated. In their conquest of African peoples, Europeans generated an 'African linguistics' related to their emphasis on literacy, syntactic analysis, modes of inscription, representation of sound, assignment of meaning and understanding of structure. The struggle is related to the distribution of power, wealth and privilege, and the social history of the users and the capacity of languages to operate effectively within specific technical or environmental domains. These essays explore the situational use of languages related to the private and public aspirations, interests and goals of different constituencies ranging from individuals to government departments.

In this section, much of the discussion of African languages begins with a critical exploration of the European colonial premise that African languages are exceptional linguistic forms, 'vernaculars' that do not embody the full properties and capacities of 'standard' languages. To refute this position, scholars have taken on the challenge of analyzing African languages and demonstrating that they should not be treated as exceptions. The primary question centers on the relations between different languages, their use within and between different private and public domains and their proficiency in incorporating new social and technical forms. These domains may include the family (or domestic unit), the street, the neighborhood and the school. Each domain has its own situational and structural logic as to the appropriateness of different linguistic forms.

In Chapter 2, Sinfree Makoni and Barbara Trudell confront the implicit politics of language. They examine the nature of linguistic diversity and the types and sources of beliefs about it. They identify three main positions related to linguistic diversity. The first views language as an autonomous phenomenon with its own linguistic properties, and thus, as a form of human expression or activity that can be studied unto itself, independent of its human agents. Following Saussure's distinction, though expressed in a particular setting as speech, the structure of language can be abstracted from the instances of speech and undergo comparative analysis. This mode of analysis is fundamental to a particular school of sociological thought that looks for structure in repetitive human action and relationships derived from the abstraction of regularities. In turn, it postulates that the expression of human action conforms to these regularities and yet, it is aware that rules may not always be followed, giving rise to contradictions that lead to structural transformations. It includes two intellectual traditions designated as structural/functionalism and structuralism (see Durkheim, 1938/1958; Levi-Strauss, 1966; Barth, 1967; Radcliffe-Brown, 1952; and also Murphy, 1971). The analysis incorporates both structural stasis and dynamics; however, the two approaches differ as to the location of structure. One postulates that it is in the social reality itself and the other, in the abstraction generated by the analyst.

The other two positions identified by Makoni and Trudell are cut from the same cloth and intimately interrelated. They are mainly anchored in individualized social perspectives and public policy. One position sees linguistic diversity 'in a negative light, either as exotic or politically unwelcome,' and the other sees it 'in terms of the political and cultural rights of local speech communities'. Here there is the question of rights, entitlements and identities expressed in the conflicting interests of those persons with power and wealth along with the central government on the one hand, and the common folk or average people and their local communities, on the other. During the colonial period, the language of the European rulers was declared the official language of the state and imposed on colonial citizens and subjects (see Mamdani, 1996). (For example, within the British Empire, English was the language of government and the major institutions affiliated with it.) In their turn, local peoples sought to preserve their indigenous languages as best they could. It is not by accident that the system of schooling became and has remained one of the central arenas of language contestation. Schools penetrate the integument of domestic units. It is through them that the central government's educational policies confront the range of local peoples and their individual languages. Schools also provided potential opportunities for individuals to enter into the newly emergent political and economic world that transcended local, parochial situations.

In their chapters, Makoni and Trudell and Rubagumya and Mtesigwa explore these themes, focusing on educational policy and formal systems of schooling. During the period of colonial rule, local languages were the primary medium of instruction in primary schools, after which point the instruction shifted to the language of the colonial rulers. The problem of language diversity did not go away with independence, but became one of the central issues for African nationalist movements, independent African governments and African scholars. The challenge was how to maintain language diversity and yet impose an official language without creating linguistic exceptionalism and its accompanying attribution of stigmatizing local indigenous languages as deficient. Interestingly enough, the reality is a political one and not one concerning the capacity of African languages, though it is framed in this way. English itself has been described as a Creole language and yet, its ability to handle the complexities of the modern world is very rarely questioned.

The chapters by Rubagumya and Mtesigwa test the waters of language diversity and exceptionalism from the perspective of monolingual language policies in multilingual societies. They focus on Tanzania and Kiswahili as their primary examples. Once again, one may argue that fundamentally the challenge is not in fact the incapacity of African languages to deal with the complexities of the modern world, but the political and cultural issues tied into designating one as the national, official language of the state.

Casmir Rubagumya (Chapter 3) adds a further twist in that he explores the relation of language to establishing a quality education. He brings us directly into the school and the classroom where he explores the material conditions, mode of teaching, the proficiency of the teacher in the language of instruction and the student's ability to understand the lesson being taught. He identifies a series of disconnects related to the languages that affect the process of learning.

Three main languages may be used in schools: the local mother tongue, the African language of primary instruction, and the language of the former colonial rulers. Though the issues of language use are complex, the pattern is understandable in multilingual situations. The language spoken at home may not be the 'official' language of the school. There is an important disconnect between the domestic unit and the school and between the student and the teacher. In this situation, teachers neither exploit nor build upon the local human and cultural capital that students bring with them into the school. Since the home and primary school languages are often of the same linguistic family, the greatest disconnect does not occur at this juncture. It is most pronounced when English becomes the main language of instruction. Rubagumya argues strongly and convincingly in favor of teaching children to read and write in their own language. Though he does not mention it, this may well be a contributing factor to the success of mission education or having a religious affiliation that requires competence in knowledge of written religious texts such as the 'Book' (see McCracken, 1964; Ipenburg, 1992). The child is not only taught in his (or her) own language, but is also exposed to a worldview that transcends the local situation. At home children may speak one language, in the neighborhood another, and at school and church they may speak and read still another language.

In his essay (Chapter 4), Peter Mtesigwa further examines issues raised by Rubagumya. He explores the potential of using African lingua francas such as Kiswahili, as languages of instruction. The exposition reviews arguments in favor of keeping English, the language of the former colonizers, and those opposed to using Kiswahili, Tanzania's official language. He starts from the premise that all languages are equal and have the same potential and capacities. He recognizes the challenge of selecting one African language over others to be the 'national' or 'official' language of a country with many different languages. Few of Africa's over 2000 languages possess the same attributes as Kiswahili. As a lingua franca, it transcends locality and region and is spoken widely in East, Central and Southern Africa. It is used in many social and economic transactions, and as a Bantu language it possesses many of the linguistic and cultural features of the Bantu languages spoken by local peoples. It provides an ideal language for schools, an African language that serves to meet the challenges confronting Tanzania. For example, within Tanzania it provides for an easy transition from domestic unit into school and serves to overcome ethnicity and language as a basis for action. Externally, it is an international language that transcends national and state boundaries. Moreover, it does not carry the stigma of being the language of the former colonial rulers. It has acquired the reputation of being a universal, unifying language.

Kate Parry's chapter (Chapter 5) explores the role of community libraries for advancing the development of literacy within linguistically diverse states. The chapter is a reflective essay that outlines many of the problems confronting multilingual societies. It emphasizes their linguistic and social diversity. Having undertaken research in Nigeria and Uganda, Parry is concerned with providing practical solutions to seemingly complex, intractable problems In her analysis, she explores social differences and their implication for learning in a cost-effective way. She identifies three main languages: English, the language used in schools and by the social elites, an African lingua franca, and the mother tongue used by students at home and in their everyday interactions. Each language is associated with a different social group and is used under different conditions for different purposes. Libraries provide an opportunity that enables culturally diverse peoples to enter into the world of literacy and participate in a broader world of learning. Information is not mediated through teachers whose knowledge of the official school language and reading skills may be limited. In community libraries both children and adults gain knowledge directly through confronting the text itself, and adults may share in a common experience of reading and learning. Community libraries collapse linguistic and social boundaries and the values attached to them. They are centers of public learning beyond the school.

Susan Cook's essay (Chapter 6) brings us into the social complexities of multilingual African societies and the effect of government language policies on schools and the behaviors of teachers and students. She explores the use of urban-hybrid languages, especially among youth, and the consequences for classroom and domestic interactions. Her study of South African classrooms transcends the debate as to the value that should be attached to the use of European colonial languages in schools. Instead she looks at the situational use of African languages and their relationship to identity, culture and class. Cook examines the logic that frames a particular context and the type of linguistic forms, styles and expressions that it elicits. She looks at the interrelation and interaction of structure (*langue*) and actual behavior (*parole*) within the context of public and private situations and the manner in which individuals draw upon elements of different normative orders to provide their actions with meaning. The teacher as a teacher demands that students learn and use the 'pure' form of Setswana, one of the nine official South African languages. Though students may comply within the classroom, in their personal interactions they use 'street Setswana'. The two forms of Setswana, the pure and the hybrid, are a source of tension in that one expresses and seeks to maintain an ethnic identity and the other, a national synthesis. The hybrid form represents Africa in the making and the pure one represents Africa in the past. Thus, in this instance, the language of exceptionalism is emerging as the language of the dominant expression of the future. Cook's essay provides us with a new perspective. Creolisation is an ongoing and expected process and English may be taken as a prime example.

Note

1. Some of the contributors to this volume have written black/white in lower case, whereas others have chosen to capitalize the terms as a way of identifying with their own disciplinary traditions and communities. We have left this decision to the discretion of each author.

References

Barth, R. (1967) *Elements of Semiology.* London: Jonathan Cape.

Durkheim, E. (1938/1958) *The Rules of Sociological Method.* Glencoe: Free Press.

Errington, J. (2001) Colonial linguistics. *Annual Review of Anthropology* 30, 19–39.

Ipenburg, A. (1992) *'All Good Men': The Development of Lubwa Mission, Chinsali, Zambia, 1905–1967.* New York: Peter Lang.

Levi-Strauss, C. (1966) *The Savage Mind.* London: The Garden City Press.

Mamdani, M. (1996) *Citizen and Subject: Contemporary Africa and the Legacy of Late Colonialism.* Princeton, NJ: Princeton University Press.

McCracken, K.J. (1977) *Politics and Christianity in Malawi, 1875–1940.* Cambridge: Cambridge University Press.

Murphy, R. (1971) *The Dialectics of Social Life.* New York: Basic Books.

Radcliffe-Brown, A.R. (1952) *Structure and Function in Primitive Society.* London: Cohen and West.

Chapter 2

African Perspectives on Linguistic Diversity: Implications for Language Policy and Education

SINFREE MAKONI AND BARBARA TRUDELL

Beliefs about the nature of linguistic diversity are shaped by the discourses within which it is defined. Such beliefs are largely unexamined in popular use, and yet they are highly influential in a broad range of contexts, from national-level language planning to local decisions regarding education and language choice. It is thus important to understand the discursive sources of these beliefs, the perspectives to which each discourse is hospitable and how the different discourses play out in policy-setting contexts. These issues are the focus of this chapter. Discourses regarding linguistic diversity in Africa can be grouped into three broad categories: those that view language as an autonomous phenomenon; those that see linguistic diversity in a negative light, either as exotic or politically unwelcome; and those that see linguistic diversity in terms of the political and cultural rights of the local communities which speak those languages.

Linguistic Diversity and the Autonomy of Language

The propensity to regard language as autonomous has a long history in linguistics. With roots in positivistic paradigms of scientific inquiry, linguistics developed as the science of language (Yngve, 1996; Yngve & Wasik, 2004). The focus of linguistic enquiry and description has tended to be on the nature of language itself; language data are seen as largely unrelated to humans except as they are the necessary source of that data. The fundamental belief underpinning such linguistic description is the belief that languages are natural and not historically contingent, and that they are countable, discrete and bounded. This belief in the autonomy of language is best captured by Johnstone (1996: 188) when she draws a distinction between the 'linguistics of language and the linguistics of the individual speaker'.

Mühlhaüsler (1996) describes this discourse as concerned with the enumerability of language. When languages are seen as discrete phenomena, they can be distinguished from each other and counted. Thus, Adegbija (2004) lists over 450 languages in Nigeria. The *Ethnologue* (Gordon, 2005), arguably the most exhaustive catalogue of languages of the world, is also located in this discourse. Related to the notion of enumerability is that of 'language as object'. This is the argument that language has existence and value apart from its actual use in a society. Languages can thus be objectified, studied and counted with at most only a passing reference to their location within particular human cultures (Wurm, 1996). Terms such as *language shift* and *language loss* (Fasold, 1990) have characteristically been used to describe sociolinguistic processes linguistically, with minimal reference to the societal or political causes or impact of such processes.[1]

The notion of language as an autonomous object has recently come under sustained criticism from a number of different theoretical positions including Harris (1980, 1998), Yngve (1996, 2004a, 2004b), Reagan (2004) and Makoni and Pennycook (2005, 2006). Canagarajah (2002) argues that one way out of this conceptual impasse is to include locally grounded views of language; still, not all locally grounded views of language can necessarily form the basis on which a viable applied linguistics project can be founded (Makoni & Meinhof, 2006).

The ecology of language

An important development within the discourse of linguistic autonomy has been the ecological approach to linguistic diversity (Nettle & Romaine, 2000). In this paradigm, languages are seen not as isolates, but as existing in a larger psychological and sociolinguistic environment. UNESCO (n.d.) describes this paradigm as treating language as an analogue to biodiversity, maintaining that 'just as there are hotspots of biodiversity, there are also hotspots of linguistic diversity.' Thus, language ecology is the study of the interactions between a language and this larger environment (Haugen, 1972). Hornberger (2003) more specifically describes language ecology as encompassing processes of language evolution, language environment and language endangerment.

The biodiversity analogy has engendered the use of metaphors such as *survival* and *death* (Crystal, 2000) and, even more emotively, *killer languages* and *linguistic genocide* (Skutnabb-Kangas, 2000). This terminology highlights an ethical judgement that language loss is morally wrong, regardless of the particular conditions of its social uses, and that linguistic diversity is inherently good. This is a radical departure from the positivist approach to language change that has for so long been a hallmark of linguistic theory

The notion of language endangerment in particular has caught the popular imagination in the West and has fuelled the arguments of language rights advocates. Keebe (2003: 47) describes this as a claim 'that the loss of a language is the permanent, irrevocable loss of a certain vision of the world, comparable to the loss of an animal or a plant.' Losing a language, irrespective of the number of speakers of that language, deprives humanity of a part of our universal human heritage insofar as the language embodies a unique worldview and knowledge of local ecosystems (Nettle & Romaine, 2000: 166).

Clearly, the ecological approach to linguistic diversity takes into account the sociolinguistic and political milieu of language development and language change, in a way which earlier linguistic paradigms have not. However, it is important to note that in this discourse, language is still described as an autonomous phenomenon, and at times is itself accorded agency. This perspective may be seen in UNESCO's argument for language preservation:

> The world's languages represent an extraordinary wealth of human creativity. They contain and express the total 'pool of ideas' nurtured over time through heritage, local traditions and customs communicated through local languages. (UNESCO, n.d.)

The view of language as autonomous is the basis of most criticism of such approaches. Ecological paradigms, it is argued, fundamentally misrepresent the nature of language (and by implication linguistic diversity) because they treat language as if it were a natural, independently-occurring phenomenon that is only a vehicle of culture, rather than as a cultural artefact in itself. This inhibits opportunities for understanding the role of human and political agency in language change and shifts in language ecology. Certainly, human existence is enriched through biological diversity, and the strongest ecosystems are characterized by diversity; but if languages are cultural artefacts rather than natural phenomena, then the ecological argument regarding the social good served by linguistic diversity is considerably weakened. It thus cannot be assumed that because biological diversity enriches human heritage, linguistic diversity necessarily has the same effect (Keebe, 2003; Pennycook, 2007).

Another risk of the ecological discourse regarding linguistic diversity is its potential for allowing 'language' to take the place of 'people', minimizing the essentially communicative and symbolic role of language within human society; Romaine (2004), an advocate of the ecolinguistics discourse, acknowledges this risk.

Describing minority languages in terms of endangered biodiversity carries a further risk: it tends to exoticize the people who speak those languages or treat the speakers 'as if they were plants' (England, 2002: 141).

Clearly, protection of vulnerable languages must not encourage the marginalization of the speakers of those languages; the rhetoric of endangerment must not do disservice to the very people it is seeking to protect. As an indigenous person of South America once told one of the authors, 'we are not interested in being in a human zoo'. The voices of the communities whose languages are being threatened have to be given substantial attention.

Other, less-contested assumptions about linguistic diversity that are made in the ecological approach include the individuality and equal value of all languages, including the weakened and endangered ones. This particular assumption derives from a belief in the value of all human cultures and individuals, no matter how vulnerable or disempowered. Elson articulates this view in his 'linguistic creed':

> [A]ny language is capable of being a vehicle for complicated human interaction and complex thought, and can be the basis for a complex culture and civilization. Therefore, all languages deserve respect and careful study... . Interest in and appreciation of a person's language is tantamount to interest in and appreciation of the person himself. All languages are worthy of preservation in written form by means of grammars, dictionaries and written texts. This should be done as part of the heritage of the human race. (Elson, 1987)

The values expressed in this statement underlie much of the work currently carried out in the documentation and development of endangered languages. The value set on language in this context is directly related to its use by a unique people. The reference to language as a heritage of the human race also expresses the notion of the universal value of language; this notion informs the universalist approach to language rights that is discussed below.

Linguistic diversity and language preservation

In the arguments recounted above, language preservation is assumed to be a key strategy for maintaining linguistic diversity. However, the notion of language preservation is not in itself unproblematic. It tends to ignore the diversity within languages in favor of one form. The fact that standardization and corpus planning are generally carried out under the aegis of non-native speakers of the languages adds further to the possibility that the written form of a language may not be perceived by its speakers as belonging to them in the way the oral forms of the language do.

This prompts another observation. Notions of linguistic autonomy and ecolinguistics have their roots in Western philosophical traditions and current Western values. Although that fact does not negate their utility, it does raise the question of whether African correlates to these discourses exist and, given a concern with diversity, what their implications might be. The following African examples suggest some of the issues.

One interesting case in which ecological concerns and cultural concerns have been combined is the celebrated environmental work of Dr Wangari Maathai, a Kenyan activist and Nobel Peace Prize winner. Dr Maathai has clearly linked preservation of the natural environment with the vitality of Kenyan cultures (Green Belt Movement website). It is notable, however, that her articulation of this link does not extend specifically to the preservation of local languages, some of which are significantly under threat. The same attitude may be seen in a variety of disciplines in which environmental discourses are used,[5] but rarely in connection with language preservation.

In other cases, however, the need for language development and cultural preservation is clear to threatened ethnic communities. Abundant anecdotal evidence from the ethnic communities of southern Sudan indicates that, as these communities have been faced with what they perceive as ethnocide at the hands of the northern Sudanese government, their interest in committing the details of their culture and languages to writing has soared (Gilley, 1999). This vivid perception of language endangerment on the part of the speakers themselves has led to active participation in local language planning and development activities. It appears that people's perception of the importance of their linguistic (and cultural) distinctives is enhanced when they find themselves in such a climate of extreme hostility to their ethnic and cultural identity.

Still, it appears that the notions of linguistic autonomy and ecolinguistics strike few familiar chords among African language communities. For African scholars, the concern with linguistic diversity tends to centre far more on issues of multilingualism and political inclusion (Adejunmobi, 2004; Muthwii & Kioko, 2004; Roy-Campbell & Qorro, 1997). An exception to this is the recent work by Batibo (2005: vii), in which the author makes an impassioned case for the need to 'deal with the problem of language shift and death among the minority languages.'

The implications of the ecolinguistics discourse for education in Africa are not especially strong. Use of African languages in learning contexts is certainly seen as a way to ensure their sustainability and dynamic nature; however, few clues are available from this discourse regarding language choice in multilingual environments, or how to navigate the political and social realities of education in Africa today. This failure to address the complexities of social and educational realities may account for the lack of resonance with this discourse among African scholars in language and education.

Language Diversity as a Problematic Oddity

The discourse set that sees linguistic diversity as both exotic and problematic arguably has its genesis in the colonial domination of Africa. The supposedly 'exotic' nature of African languages, along with their associated cultures, was a theme of colonial European sociopolitical discourse. Linguistic features such as tone, length and phonemes (e.g. clicks) not found in European languages contributed to the perception, as did the rich range of language varieties found in many parts of the continent (see, for example, Migeod, 1925). To the Europeans, this made African languages of curious academic interest.

The evidence of abundant linguistic diversity also led merchants, colonial officers and mission authorities in the British colonies to conclude that English was a preferable alternative to local languages for the administrative, communicative and educational tasks they had set themselves in Africa (Migeod, 1925: 21). An English-based Pidgin developed in the British colonial holdings in West Africa (Vernon-Jackson, 1967), affirming the belief that any variety of English was preferable to attempting to communicate in the plethora of African languages in use by the colonized populations. Similar developments and beliefs in the French-held African colonies led to the dominance of French in those countries.

The swift takeover of European-style education – in European languages – in African communities over the first decades of the colonial era confirmed the marginalized place of African languages and cultures in the new world order. Further marginalization of African languages in 'modern' Africa came with local responses to so-called *adapted education* in the British colonies (King, 1971). This attempt at education reform, originating in the United States and Britain, advocated a curriculum embedded in local knowledge and local languages (Wolf, 2001). The vigorous rejection of adapted education by African parents, who suspected it was an attempt to keep them from acquiring European knowledge and power (Ball, 1983), included rejection of both the local knowledge curriculum and the local language in which it was to be taught. This sense of the inappropriateness of African language as a medium of conveying knowledge in the formal classroom continues to be a widespread perception among African parents.

As independence swept across the African continent in the second half of the 20th century, the influence of the discourse of linguistic diversity as both exotic and anachronistic continued. The economic and political agenda of African states' new Western partners continued to favour the primacy of non-African languages and cultures in the continent's sociocultural development. At the Conference of African States on the

Development of Education in Africa (1961), ministers of the newly-independent African nations presented their hopes for a uniquely African education that would include serious attention to cultural and linguistic diversity. In response, their Western partners at the conference emphasized the need to refashion African education to match their own vision for economic development – a vision that revolved around global realities, not African ones. In the end, recognition of cultural and linguistic diversity failed to appear on the international agenda for the development of African education.

So it has been that post-colonial governments have maintained and even extended the position of European languages in national education and political systems. Adegbija analyzes the post-colonial place of European languages in this way:

> Post-colonial policy makers in Africa have largely rubber-stamped or toed the line of language and educational policies bequeathed to them by the colonial masters... . Educational systems, which have widened and extended beyond what they were in colonial days, have been further used to entrench and perpetuate the feeling of the inviolable worth of colonial languages. (Adegbija, 1994: 33–4)

In this environment, linguistic diversity becomes a characteristic to ignore as far as possible.

However, in recent decades challenges have emerged to the entrenched notion that linguistic diversity is troublesome and anachronistic. Spear-headed by international institutions such as UNESCO, there have been powerful moves to popularize the idea that linguistic diversity deserves to be addressed in political and educational spheres. As a result, African government language policies tend to be increasingly positive towards acknowledgement of the languages within their borders, and in their educational systems.

Is the discourse of linguistic diversity as exotic and problematic any less foreign to Africa than the discourse of linguistic autonomy and ecology of language, discussed above? Certainly, both originated with Western views of African languages and cultures. Their embedding in post-colonial national policies can be traced to the nature of the political structures brought about by colonial domination of the continent. However, after so many decades of neglectful or negative policy regarding linguistic diversity by African governments, it is difficult to maintain that the discourse in which linguistic diversity is conceived as problematic is essentially foreign to Africa any more.

The educational implications of this view of language diversity can be seen across the continent, where international languages are given by far the greatest priority as languages of instruction. Despite the negative educational outcomes associated with this approach, it is still highly popular with African parents, school authorities and government decision makers.

Linguistic Diversity, Identity and Rights

A third discourse set regarding linguistic diversity focuses on the maintenance of language as an aspect of cultural identity, political enfranchisement and human rights. The implications of this discourse for education are significant, as educational access is seen as one of the fundamental rights that are claimed.

The discourse of language and identity is grounded in the belief that language and culture are profoundly entwined. Whether language actually predisposes its speakers to see the world in a certain way (Sapir, 1929: 207), or whether language is itself a reflection of culture, the role of language in mediating and defining social relations is considered within this discourse to be crucial (Kramsch, 1998: 77). This is not to say that the nature of the language–culture connection is static; but as May (2001: 129) argues, language is nevertheless a significant feature of ethnic identity.

In sub-Saharan Africa, certainly, language functions as one of the most obvious markers of culture. Webb and Kembo-Sure (2000: 122) note that, in Africa, people are often identified culturally primarily (and even solely) on the basis of the language they speak. Describing the role of language in traditional Zambian societies particularly, Serpell (1993: 97) notes that Zambian languages are intimately tied with indigenous values and practices. In this discourse, linguistic diversity becomes symbolic of cultural diversity, and the maintenance or revitalization of language signals ongoing or renewed validity of the culture associated with that language. For speakers of those African languages that are unwritten and largely unacknowledged, this is a powerful argument for language development and the preservation of linguistic diversity.

A related discourse links language use and language choice to issues of power imbalance. It is undeniably true that language communities with fewer speakers tend also to be the less politically-empowered communities. Indeed, May (2000) contends that language loss is not fundamentally a linguistic issue; rather, it is clearly related to issues of power, with language loss rarely occurring in privileged language communities. Romaine (2004) also describes the power imbalances underlying the material, political and economic domination of 'most of the world's small language communities'.

And, in his study of the motivations underlying language planning and policy, Ager notes that:

> because of their majority or minority status, many communities within the state are vociferous in support of their own identity and desire to ensure that their language, customs and traditions are not lost .... Language is an almost inevitable point of contention between communities. (Ager, 2001: 158)

This discourse of language-related power imbalances could be seen as contradicting Bamgbose's (1991) contention that linguistic diversity is not in itself an inherent threat to national unity. However, both of these arguments are linked by the crucial point that linguistic diversity per se is not a political problem: rather, *ignoring* linguistic diversity is the problem. Distinct language practices are often a feature of communities that are marginalized from access to resources and power, but national unity need not imply cultural or linguistic uniformity. Indeed, as national authorities recognize the right of individual communities to distinct language and cultural practices, and do not withhold resources or power from such communities, the resulting unity is likely to be stronger and more representative.

Linguistic human rights

In a further move along the continuum of language and politics, the discourse that relates language issues to the political and cultural rights of communities gives rise to a more militant approach to linguistic diversity that focuses on the dominance and perceived imperialism of large, prestigious world languages – primarily English (Phillipson, 1992) – over the smaller languages of the world. The notion of linguistic human rights arises within this discourse. Freedom to use one's own language is seen as a human right, and language diversity becomes symbolic of the defence of this universal human right. This discourse may at times use the terminology of language ecology to describe endangered and disempowered language communities (Skutnabb-Kangas, 2000), but its basis is not actually that of biodiversity nor of language as a natural phenomenon needing protection from endangerment. Rather, a legal and political framework underlies the discourse of language rights (*Universal Declaration of Linguistic Rights*, 1998).

Rights discussions became increasingly prominent in the 1990s, a period characterized by the appearance of democratic movements and multiparty elections in Africa. The interest and commitment to human rights regimes by African states can also be seen at a pan-African level. A number of important pan-African structures have been set up to implement and protect human rights regimes, including (1) the Pan-African Parliament, (2) the African Court of Justice, (3) the Economic, Social and Cultural Council, (4) the Peace and Security Council and (5) the African Commission on Human Rights and People's Rights.

However, the African state's abiding concern for political security has complicated state support for human rights. The situation is further complicated by the controversy in African scholarship on the nature of rights as a construct (Bhebhe & Ranger, 2001; Zeleza, 2004). Those who make a universalist argument insist that every individual has inalienable rights, and that these rights are not contingent upon a specific historical context. Those who maintain a relativist position, on the other hand, argue that a unique set of rights and discourses has developed in Africa as a product of its unique historical context. These rights are expressed and articulated in a paradigm that places a premium on human dignity rather than rights. Language diversity is not a defining characteristic of this type of rights discourse.

Nevertheless, the discourse of linguistic human rights does draw from this larger rights discourse. Ogechi (2003: 280) identifies the United Nations Universal Declaration of Human Rights, promulgated in 1948, as a primary pillar of language rights:

> Everyone is entitled to all the rights and freedoms set forth in this Declaration (of human rights) without distinction of any kind, such as race, colour, sex, language, religion, political or other opinion, national or social origin, property, birth or other status. [2]

Ogechi further notes that language rights are integral to numerous subsequent UN documents. Musau (2004: 59) describes a broad range of linguistic human rights, 'aimed at the promotion of linguistic justice and the removal or prevention of linguistic inequalities or injustices that may occur because of language'. Musau and Ogechi do not entirely agree in their analyses of the status of linguistic rights in their country of focus – Kenya – but both are clearly situated in the rights discourse regarding linguistic diversity.

On the other hand, the notion of linguistic human rights has been subjected to considerable criticism (Makoni & Pennycook, 2005, 2006; Stroud, 2000). This criticism coalesces around a deep-seated scepticism regarding the definition of language that underpins this discourse, itself related to scepticism regarding Western notions of language in non-Western contexts. This perspective can be understood as part of a broader critique of linguistics and some of its notions of language (see Harris, 1981; Makoni & Pennycook, 2006; Yngve, 1996; Yngve & Wasik, 2004).

For other scholars, such as Ngugi wa Thiong'o and Mazisi Kunene, however, it is only through a renewed focus on the use of indigenous languages in language rights discourse that rights may be protected and enhanced. These scholars see contemporary discourses of rights as deeply entrenched in, and shaped by, European linguistic constructs. Rights discourses that are entrenched in European idiom will not have the desired effect when the people who are meant to be affected have limited knowledge of European languages (Mazrui, 2004).

In the light of this complex situation, it is important to ask to what extent the discourse of identity, culture and rights resonates among African citizens and decision makers. The identification of specific languages with specific cultures varies across the continent, depending in part on the role that the various languages play in these cultures. Certainly for the 66% of African citizens who live in rural areas[3] (and so are unlikely to be fluent in international languages), the mother language is closely identified with their way of life. The desire to preserve and develop their languages is not uncommon among language communities with fewer speakers in countries as diverse as Kenya, the Democratic Republic of the Congo, Ghana, Senegal, Cameroon, Benin, Uganda and Sudan.

One particular example of such local interest in promoting local language is the case of the Tonga people of Zimbabwe, examined by one of the authors. The Tonga are an impoverished minority group who were forcibly removed from their land to make way for the construction of the Kariba Dam (which forms the biggest man-made lake in Africa). The Tonga were moved into a dry area of the country; this deprived them of their primary livelihood, fishing.

One striking feature of the Tonga's attitude towards their language can be seen in their energetic advocacy over the years for recognition of their language and its use as a medium of instruction in formal education. This campaign to promote Tonga has not been as benign as one might assume language promotion to be. In fact, the Tonga were known to have used threats to convince community teachers and principals to use the Tonga language in schools.

Another striking feature of this situation is that the Tonga seemed much more committed to the process than were other minority groups in Zimbabwe. In a sense, the Tonga were at the forefront of a process that led to the formation of an Association composed of other minority language communities such as the Venda, Sotho, Nambya and others. These other communities might have been committed to seeing their languages used as a medium of instruction and to improving the status of those languages, but these groups were not willing to take similar risks on behalf of those goals. It appears that their stance was affected by the political climate at the time: lobbying for the promotion of minority languages was taking place in a sensitive political context in which the Zimbabwean government was under immense pressure from its opposition party. As a result, most minority groups felt their campaign for the promotion of their languages would be construed as a thinly veiled act of opposition to the ruling Zimbabwean government. The Tonga, however, did not let such concerns hinder their advocacy efforts on behalf of their language rights.

A third unique feature of this situation lies in those who led the campaign. The literature from the Tonga records that the campaign for the promotion of Tonga was led by lobbyists and chiefs. The project was also partially funded by the Catholic Church for the Justice of Peace. Very little participation by the schoolchildren of the area is recorded, even though the children were seen to be in favour of the promotion of Tonga. This exclusion was a result of the belief that the students themselves were contributing towards the dilution of Tonga culture and language – exactly the situation which the campaigners sought to rectify. It seems that this campaign to promote the Tonga language was based partly on a view of the cultural and linguistic purity of Tonga, an idea that was not reflected in the realities of the Tonga youth.

Tonga women were also found to be excluded from the language promotion campaign. This exclusion of women from the language promotion exercise might be construed as reflecting gender imbalances within the Tonga community. It could also suggest the patriarchal nature of the Tonga, as well as their perception that language promotion was in fact a serious matter: important issues of political rights such as this needed men to deal with them, not women.

Further evidence that this language promotion initiative was truly locally shaped lay in the fact that it took local sensitivities into account, including at the level of discourse. The Tonga felt that the term 'minority' was negative and preferred the term 'indigenous' instead; thus the Association which they formed was called an Indigenous Association, rather than a Minority Language Association. They argued that, in the geographical areas in which they lived, they were not a minority.

The Tonga example also demonstrates ways in which the promotion of minority languages tends to be based on the equation of language with ethnicity. It was assumed that 'the Tonga speak Tonga', even though an analysis of data from secondary school students reveals a more complex relationship between language and ethnicity (in which some students who claimed to be ethnically Tonga also said they spoke the Dombe language). These data indicate the need to understand more fully the potential effects of minority language promotion on the relationship between ethnicity and language.

So it is clear that the rights discourse has a strong recent history on the African continent. Whether language is widely considered to be a human right is debatable, however; scholarly attention to compliance with linguistic human rights by African nations does not seem to be matched by a more general sense of the place of language in human rights discourse.

Where language *is* associated with a human rights discourse, education is a key context in which these rights are played out. Adoption of the Education for All and Millenium Development goals, both of which highlight the need for access to quality education, is leading African government policy-makers to consider a more central role for African languages in both formal and non-formal learning contexts. Thus this discourse provides the framework for broadening language use options in education, including multi-language initiatives. However, local beliefs about the superiority of international languages, as well as the desire for forms of education that lead to positive economic outcomes, give rise to a certain degree of opposition to such pro-African language initiatives.

Conclusion

In examining the array of discourses of linguistic diversity that influence beliefs and policy in sub-Saharan Africa, a few conclusions seem clear. One is that Africans tend to value multilingualism highly (Roy-Campbell & Qorro, 1997; Simire, 2004). This deep-seated and generalized value is highly pragmatic, with few obvious theoretical roots in discourses of ecology or rights. However, the fact that it is so widespread lends support to positive discourses of linguistic diversity on the continent.

Another conclusion is that the pressure of a largely monolingual movement towards global culture, added to the already-existing prestige of colonial languages, is maintaining English and French in a place of dominance in the minds of many Africans. Formal schooling, higher education, the Internet and modern telecommunications all increase the value of fluency in international languages. This fact, although not inherently inimical to multilingualism or the maintenance of African languages, does provide fuel to those discourses that denigrate African languages.

These colliding values account for the tension that exists between the various discourses of linguistic diversity as they are found in sub-Saharan African societies. Constructive resolution of this tension is only possible as the value of multilingualism, including fluency in European languages, is broadened to allow space for the continued development of minority languages for education and communication.

A related tension also characterizes discussion of linguistic diversity in Africa: the tension between regarding language as simply a means of communication and regarding language as a profound marker of cultural identity. Discourse choices that downplay the self-identity role of language by denying its bounded nature entirely are not adequate models of linguistic diversity for Africa. Equally, those discourses that ignore the contingency of language on social and communicative choices are incomplete models. The discourse of 'language as communicative tool' must be balanced where needed by the discourse of 'language as cultural marker' if the benefits of both are to be attained by the millions of Africans who live the reality of linguistic diversity.

Notes

1. One notable exception to this rule is the linguistics text *African Voices* (Webb & Kembo-Sure, 1999). Intended primarily as an introductory linguistics text, this treatment of linguistics is heavily seeded with sociopolitical commentary on linguistic processes as played out in African societies.
2. United Nations Universal Declaration of Human Rights, as quoted in Ogechi (2003).
3. Population Reference Bureau (http://www.prb.org). The definition of 'rural' used in this database of population statistics is a community environment of less than 2000 persons.

References

Adegbija, E. (1994) *Language Attitudes in Sub-Saharan Africa: A Sociolinguistic Overview*. Clevedon: Multilingual Matters.

Adegbija, E. (2004) *Multilingualism: A Nigerian Case Study*. Lawrenceville, NJ: Africa World/Red Sea.

Adejunmobi, M. (2004) *Vernacular Palaver*. Clevedon: Multilingual Matters.

Ager, D. (2001) *Motivation in Language Planning and Language Policy*. Clevedon: Multilingual Matters.

Ball, S.J. (1983) Imperialism, social control and the colonial curriculum in Africa. *Journal of Curriculum Studies* 15 (3), 237–263.

Bamgbose, A. (1991) *Language and the Nation: The Language Question in Sub Saharan Africa*. Edinburgh: Edinburgh University Press.

Batibo, H. (2005) *Language Decline and Death in Africa: Causes, Consequences and Challenges*. Clevedon: Multilingual Matters.

Bhebhe, N. and Ranger, T. (2001) *The Historical Dimensions of Democracy and Human Rights in Zimbabwe: Precolonial and Colonial Legacies*. Harare: University of Zimbabwe Press.

Canagarajah, A.S. (2002) Celebrating local knowledge on language education. *Journal of Language, Identity and Education* 1 (4), 243–261.

Conference of African States on the Development of Education in Africa, Addis Ababa (1961) *Final Report*. UNESCO.
Crystal, D. (2000) *Language Death*. Cambridge: Cambridge University Press.
Elson, B.F. (1987) *Linguistic Creed*. Available online at http://www.sil.org/sil/linguistic_creed.htm. Accessed 10.01.06.
England, N. (2002) Commentary: Further rhetorical concerns. *Journal of Linguistic Anthropology* 12 (2), 141–143.
Fasold, R. (1990) *The Sociolinguistics of Language*. Oxford: Blackwell.
Gilley, L. (1999) Facilitating orthography development with mother-tongue speakers. *Notes on Linguistics* 2 (4), 185–192.
Gordon Jr, R.G. (ed.) (2005) *Ethnologue* (15th edn). Dallas: SIL International.
Green Belt Website (n.d.) At http://greenbeltmovement.org/c.php?id=5. Accessed 20.1.06
Harris, R. (1980) *The Language-makers*. Ithaca, NY: Cornell University Press.
Harris, R. (1981) *The Language Myth*. London: Duckworth.
Harris, R. (1998) *Introduction to Integrational Linguistics*. London: Pergamon.
Haugen, E. (1972) *Linguistic Ecology*. Stanford, CT: Stanford University Press.
Hornberger, N. (2003) Multilingual language policies and the continua of biliteracy: An ecological approach. In N. Hornberger (ed.) *Continua of Biliteracy: An Ecological Framework for Educational Policy, Research and Practice in Multilingual Settings*. Clevedon: Multilingual Matters.
Johnstone, B. (1996) *The Linguistic Individual: Self Expression in Language and Linguistics*. Oxford: Oxford University Press.
Keebe, D. (2003) Language policy and linguistic theory. In J. Marais and M. Morris (eds) *Languages in a Globalising World* (pp. 47–58). Cambridge: Cambridge University Press.
King, K. (1971) *Pan-Africanism and Education: A Study of Race, Philanthropy and Education in the Southern States of America and East Africa*. Oxford: Clarendon Press.
Kramsch, C. (1998) *Language and Culture*. Oxford: Oxford University Press.
Makoni, S. and Meinhof, R. (2006) Lingüística aplicada na África: Desconstruindo a noção de lingua. In P. Moita-Lopes (ed.) *Por uma Lingüística Aplicada Indisciplinar* (pp. 191–211). Sao Paulo: Parábola Editorial.
Makoni, S. and Pennycook, A. (2005) Disinventing and reconstituting language. *International Journal of Critical Language Studies* 2 (3), 137–156.
Makoni, S. and Pennycook, A. (eds) (2006) *Disinventing and Reconstituting Languages*. Clevedon: Multilingual Matters.
May, S. (2001) *Language and Minority Rights: Ethnicity, Nationalism and the Politics of Language*. Essex: Pearson Education Ltd.
May, S. (2000) Uncommon languages: The challenges and possibilities of minority language rights. *Journal of Multilingual and Multicultural Development* 21 (5), 366–385.
Mazrui, A.M. (2004) *English in Africa after the Cold War*. Clevedon: Multilingual Matters.
Migeod, F. (1925) *Through British Cameroons*. London: Heath Cranton.
Mühlhaüsler, P. (1996) *Linguistic Ecology: Language Change and Linguistic Imperialism in the Pacific Region*. London: Routledge.

Musau, P. (2004) Linguistic human rights in Africa: Challenges and prospects for indigenous languages in Kenya. In M.J. Muthwii and A.N. Kioko (eds) *New Language Bearings in Africa: A Fresh Quest* (pp. 155–165). Clevedon: Multilingual Matters.
Nettle, D. and Romaine, S. (2000) *Vanishing Voices.* Oxford: Oxford University Press.
Ogechi, N.O. (2003) On language rights in Kenya. *Nordic Journal of African Studies* 12 (3), 277–295.
Pennycook, A. (2007) *Global Englishes and Transcultural Flows.* London: Routledge.
Phillipson, R. (1992) *Linguistic Imperialism.* Oxford: Oxford University Press.
Reagan, T. (2004) Objectification, positivism and language studies: A reconsideration. *Critical Inquiry in Language Studies: An International Journal* 1, 47–60.
Romaine, S. (2004) Linguistic diversity, sustainable development and the future of the past. Paper given at the Linguapax 2004 Conference on Linguistic Diversity, Sustainability and Peace, Barcelona.
Roy-Campbell, Z. and Qorro, M. (1997) *Language Crisis in Tanziania: The Myth of English vs. Education.* Dar es Salaam: Mkuki Na Nyota Publishers.
Sapir, E. (1929) The status of linguistics as a science. *Language* 5, 207–214.
Serpell, R. (1993) *The Significance of Schooling.* Cambridge: Cambridge University Press.
Simire, G.O. (2004) Developing and promoting multilingualism in public life and society in Nigeria. In M.J. Muthwii and A.N. Kioko (eds) *New Language Bearings in Africa: A Fresh Quest* (pp. 231–244). Clevedon: Multilingual Matters.
Skutnabb-Kangas, T. (2000) *Linguistic Genocide in Education: Or Worldwide Diversity and Human Rights?* Mahwah, NJ: Erlbaum.
Stroud, C. (2000) Language and democracy: The notion of linguistic citizenship and mother tongue. In K. Legère and S. Fitchat (eds) *Talking Freedom: Language and Democratization in the SADC Region* (pp. 67–74). Windhoek: Gamsberg Macmillan.
UNESCO (n.d.) *The Earth's Linguistic, Cultural and Biological Diversity.* Online at http://portal.unesco.org/education/en/ev.php-URL_ID=18391&URL_DO=DO _TOPIC&URL_SECTION=201.html. Accessed 20.1.06.
Universal Declaration of Linguistic Rights (1998) Barcelona: Universal Declaration of Linguistic Rights Follow-up Committee.
Vernon-Jackson, H.O.H. (1967) *Language, Schools and Government in Cameroon.* New York: Teachers College Press.
Webb, V. and Kembo-Sure (eds) (2000) *African Voices.* Oxford: Oxford University Press.
Wolf, H.G. (2001) *English in Cameroon.* Berlin: Mouton de Gruyter.
Wurm, S.A. (1996) *Atlas of the World's Languages in Danger of Disappearing.* Paris: UNESCO.
Yngve, V. (1996) *From Grammar to Science: New Foundations for General Linguistics.* Philadelphia: John Benjamins.
Yngve, V. (2004a) Issues in hard science linguistics. In V. Yngve and Z. Wasik (eds) *Hard-Science Linguistics* (pp. 14–27). New York: Continuum.
Yngve, V. (2004b) An introduction to hard-science linguistics. In V. Yngve and Z. Wasik (eds) *Hard-Science Linguistics* (pp. 27–35). New York: Continuum.
Yngve, V. and Wasik, Z. (2004) *Hard-Science Linguistics.* New York: Continuum.
Zeleza, P. (2004) Human rights and development in Africa: New contexts, challenges and opportunities. Paper presented at the International Conference on the African Commission on Human and People's Rights, Uppsala, Sweden.

Chapter 3

Language in Education in Africa: Can Monolingual Policies Work in Multilingual Societies?

CASMIR M. RUBAGUMYA

Language is without doubt the most important factor in the learning process, for the transfer of knowledge and skills is mediated through the spoken or written word.
Ayo Bamgbose (1992)

The main thesis of this chapter is that the problems of language in education in Africa stem from pursuing monolingual policies in predominantly multilingual societies. The chapter starts by looking at the relationship between quality of education and language. It is argued that proficiency in the medium of instruction is a necessary, though not sufficient condition to ensure quality in the learning/teaching process. The chapter then goes on to survey research that has been done in Africa, and elsewhere where relevant, concerning the effect of a foreign medium of instruction on educational quality. Some good practices, even though they are an exception in Africa, are pointed out. The chapter also briefly discusses why public policy regarding the medium of instruction is usually based on political expediency, not on research results. It is argued that language attitudes based on 'common sense' assumptions, dependency syndrome, pegging educational innovations on 'project' funding and lack of meaningful dialogue between policy-makers and practitioners are all part of this problem.

The Relationship between Quality Education and Language

The words of Professor Ayo Bamgbose (quoted above), an eminent Nigerian linguist and educationalist, may seem too commonplace to merit any serious consideration. Yet, it is precisely the taking of language in education for granted that has to a large extent caused a number of pedagogical problems in educational systems in Africa, thus undermining the quality of our education.

Why is language a crucial factor in ensuring quality education? Clegg (2005) has made two important points in this regard. First, you cannot learn if you do not understand the lessons. It goes without saying that you cannot understand the lessons if you do not understand the language in which those lessons are taught. Secondly, you cannot teach effectively and efficiently if you are not confident enough in the language of learning and teaching. Thus, both learners and teachers need to have a certain level of proficiency in the language of instruction if meaningful learning and teaching are to take place. Qorro (2003) had made an interesting analogy between education and electricity. It is not possible to have an electricity supply without copper wires, which act as a conduit of electricity. In the same manner, it is not possible to have education without a language through which that education is transmitted. So, saying you want quality education without paying attention to language is like saying you want electricity but you do not care about the wiring system.

In the same vein, talking about education in Africa, Obanya has clearly shown the importance of language in education:

> It has always been felt by African educationalists that the African child's major learning problem is linguistic. Instruction is given in a language that is not normally used in his immediate environment, a language which neither the learner nor the teacher understands and uses well enough. (Obanya, quoted in Brock-Utne, 2000: 141)

What we see here then is that language is a necessary, though not sufficient, condition for quality education. For this reason, any attempt to raise the quality of education has to address the language issue.

Let us begin with the instructional side of language use in the classroom. In educational contexts where 'frontal teaching' of 'talk and chalk' predominate, as in many African countries, up to 80% of class time can be taken up by teacher talk (Griffin, 1991). In such an environment, the role of language can hardly be overemphasized. This kind of teaching/learning environment does not only rely heavily on teacher talk, it also places great importance on text materials used in the classroom.

All this means that the language of the teacher as well as the language used in classroom text materials (which language and at what level of complexity) play a big role in determining the quality of instructional delivery.

Cleghorn *et al.* succinctly sum up the importance of language in education:

> When teachers (and learners) cannot use language to make logical connections, to integrate and explain the relations between isolated

pieces of information, what is taught cannot be understood ... and important concepts cannot be mastered. (Cleghorn *et al.*, 1989: 36)

I would like to suggest that, in many African countries, it is precisely this lack of logical connections that threatens the quality of education. Although the quotation above is referring to lack of logical connections in content, the language factor has a lot to do with this problem. My first proposition then is that, unless the different languages used at the various levels of the educational system are seen as connected, the quality of education will continue to suffer. In Tanzania, for example, education is disconnected at two points in the system. When children, especially in rural areas, start going to school, they go into the classroom with hardly any knowledge of Kiswahili. They will, however, be competent in their ethnic community language. Once in the classroom, the teacher takes it as his/her duty to stamp out the vernacular and teach these children Kiswahili. This is the first disconnection that the children experience. What they bring from home is not built upon; it is eliminated, and they have to start afresh to get 'knowledge' in Kiswahili as if they came as empty vessels.

At secondary level, the same disconnection happens again. Here children jump from Kiswahili to English medium of instruction. Kiswahili here is seen as a 'problem', which interferes with pupils' mastery of English and the subject content through the medium of English, just as ethnic community languages are seen as a 'problem' at primary level. The net effect of this is that what is learnt at primary level is not built upon. The language resources accumulated at primary school level are abandoned, and pupils have to start afresh building up new resources in a different language. The argument here is that the change in the language of instruction at various levels in a disjointed manner has a negative impact on logical connections in content. Admittedly, the transition from the ethnic community language to Kiswahili is less stressful than that from Kiswahili to English. This is because learners find it much easier to learn Kiswahili, which in many ways has similarities to ethnic community languages, most of which are, like Kiswahili, Bantu languages.

Language in education in Africa: What do we know so far?

There is ample research evidence to demonstrate that using a foreign language as a medium of instruction has a negative effect on the teaching and learning process. For example, Mlama and Matteru (1978) have clearly shown that English medium of instruction at secondary school level in Tanzania leads to ineffective and inefficient teaching and learning. Subsequent research in Tanzania has corroborated this finding (Brock-Utne *et al.*, 2003; Rubagumya, 1993).

Similar findings have been documented elsewhere. For example, Heller and Martin-Jones talking about research in South Africa and Peru, refer to what has been called 'safe talk'. This is:

> Classroom talk that allows participation without any risk of loss of face for the teacher and for the learners and maintains an appearance of 'doing the lesson' while in fact little learning is actually taking place ... [T]his particular style of interaction arises from teachers' attempts to cope with the problem of using a former colonial language, which is remote from the learners' experiences outside school, as the main medium of instruction. (Heller & Martin-Jones, 2001: 13)

A litany of similar findings can be recited, such as in Burundi (Ndayipfukamiye, 1994), Botswana (Arthur, 1994) and Kenya (Bunyi, 2001). Bunyi (2001: 90) for instance, cites a reading lesson in a Kenyan classroom in which the learners could not make sense of a reading text in English. Although the children seemed enthusiastic at the beginning, this enthusiasm seemed 'to derive more from the opportunity afforded to them to shout out loud the unfamiliar English sounds. Many of the children were not even looking at the reading text as they chanted.'

There are several reasons why instruction in the former colonial languages (i.e. English, French and Portuguese) has failed in Africa. First, learners are required to use a foreign language as the language of instruction before they have acquired the requisite competence in that language. Cummins (1979) has made a distinction between Basic Interpersonal Communication Skills (BICS) and Cognitive Academic Language Proficiency (CALP). Whereas BICS refers to the ability to use language in day-to-day communication, CALP refers to the level of language proficiency that allows the learner to use that language to make sense of the content s/he is learning. CALP is therefore required before one can use a language as the language of instruction. In most African countries, BICS is assumed to be enough for a foreign language to be used as the language of instruction. In Tanzania, for example, English-medium primary schools submerge children in English-medium education from day one at school. This is 'sink or swim' pedagogy. In this case, children start English-medium education before even BICS has been acquired in English (Rubagumya, 2003). These practices negatively affect the learning process. Even if a learner is able to handle a foreign language in 'small talk' fairly fluently, this does not mean the learner is ready to use the language as a medium of instruction. As Cummins (2000: 35) correctly points out, 'while a student may be able to speak and understand English at fairly high levels of proficiency within the first three years of school, academic skills in English reading and writing take longer for students to develop.'

Secondly, education in most African countries does not exploit the advantages of bilingualism in education. Even where there are bilingual programs, these tend to be subtractive rather than additive in nature. De Mejia describes additive bilingualism thus:

> Additive bilingualism refers, on the one hand to the positive outcomes which result from being bilingual at an individual level, and on the other, to the enrichment of language, culture and ethno-linguistic identity at a societal level. In these cases an individual acquires or learns a second or foreign language without detracting from the maintenance and development of his or her first language. The second or foreign language is seen as 'adding to' and enriching language experience, rather than replacing the first language. (de Mejia, 2002: 40)

The problem in Africa is that learning English (or French, or Portuguese) is conceived in terms of subtractive bilingualism. The aim is often to replace African languages by English, with disastrous educational outcomes (Rubagumya, 2004). In Tanzania for example, in English-medium primary schools as well as all secondary schools (where the medium of instruction is supposed to be English), students are not allowed to use any language besides English, with the assumption that, if other languages are prohibited, students will learn English faster. However, this has never been a successful policy, for two reasons. For one, policing students to ensure that they speak only English is an impossible task, especially as teachers themselves do not speak English all the time. In addition, as pointed out earlier in this chapter, forcing learners to use a language they are not proficient in is counter-productive because they cannot efficiently use it to learn subject content.

A third reason why instruction in the former colonial languages has failed is that teaching is usually teacher dominated. Learners have very little opportunity to use the language of instruction in a meaningful way. At the same time teachers have not been oriented towards being conscious of the importance of language in education. The concept of Language Across the Curriculum (LAC) is still not mainstreamed in the education systems of most African countries (see Rea-Dickins *et al.*, 2005, for the case of Zanzibar).

On a more positive note, there is also research evidence to show that good practice can produce desired results. In a review prepared for the ADEA 2006 Biennial Meeting, the authors found that mother-tongue and bilingual instruction in a large selection of African countries has positive social and economic consequences for those countries if the students receive this instruction for at least six years (Alidou *et al.*, 2006). In Nigeria, the Yoruba Six Year Primary Project (SYPP) shows that primary school children educated using Yoruba, their mother tongue, were better in mathematics and English than those educated through the medium of English. The outcomes of the SYPP provide strong support for the use of the child's first language as a medium of instruction. Learning how to read and write in the mother tongue becomes much easier, and the formation and understanding of concepts in a language that the child is already familiar with facilitates the learning process (Akinaso, 1993; Bamgbose, 2005). At the same time, the SYPP demonstrates that learning a second language does not suffer when other subjects are taught in the mother tongue. On the contrary, a good mastery of the mother tongue can in fact facilitate the learning of the second language.

In South Africa, the Molteno Project has been very successful for several decades now in preparing reading materials and teaching initial literacy in African languages. The project, started in 1974, was based at Rhodes University and funded by a grant from the Molteno Brothers Trust from which it derives its name. From research conducted in schools where African languages are spoken, it was found that learners were failing to learn English mainly because they were failing to learn to read in their mother tongue. By 1985, the project had already prepared reading materials in Setswana, isiZulu, Sepedi, Tchivenda and Tsonga (Molteno website, n.d.).

In Zambia, the New Breakthrough to Literacy (NBTL) program, based on the Molteno Project described above, has been very successful in ensuring that children become literate in their mother tongue before they start learning English. Several factors have contributed to the success of this program:

(1) using the mother tongue for initial literacy enables children to learn from the known to the unknown;
(2) the methodology is child-centered and allows the teacher to meet the children in small groups;
(3) the teaching/learning materials are appropriate to the age and culture of the learners;
(4) there is adequate teacher training, both in-service and pre-service;
(5) key stakeholders are sensitized about the language policy and its benefits. (Sampa, 2003: 176)

In-service teacher training has been at the center of this program. It started with 30 teachers, 10 Teacher Training College lecturers and 10 curriculum language specialists from the Curriculum Development Center, making a total of 50 Trainers of Trainers.

In Mali, Convergent Teaching methodology (*Pedagogie Convergente*) has been used in a number of schools since 1987. These schools use interactive methodology, with a syllabus that integrates school learning with everyday life skills. One of the main aims of this methodology is the maintenance of Malian languages, introducing French gradually as an additional language. Comparative test results carried out in 1998 and 1999 show that students in Convergent Teaching schools did better in mathematics and French than students in Traditional Schools where French is the only medium of instruction (Canvin, 2007).

In Burkina-Faso, *Ecoles Bilingues* (Bilingual Schools) are another success story. In these schools, the national language is used as a medium of instruction in all five grades of primary education, being reduced gradually from 90% in Grade 1 to 10% in Grade 5. Alidou and associates have argued that the success of *Ecoles Bilingues* in Burkina-Faso can be attributed to:

> Teaching methods (that) help children develop not only academic and functional literacy but also help them make connections between the act of studying and the act of producing. They also promote positive cultural values; they seek parents' active participation in their children's education by using a common language and connecting, whenever possible, school activities to socio-economic and cultural activities run by the village. (Alidou *et al.*, 2006: 112)

Outside Africa, success stories that we can learn from include schemes in Bolivia in Latin America and Papua New Guinea in the Pacific. In Bolivia, the Bolivian National Education Reform of July 1994 has to some extent succeeded in making Bolivian education intercultural and participatory. It has introduced all Bolivian languages into the educational system as subjects and as media of instruction. The three main tenets of this reform are as follows:

(1) Education has to be intercultural: all cultures of the Bolivian people have to be valued, and the teaching of, and in, the indigenous language is one way of giving value to these languages and the cultures they embody.
(2) Education has to be bilingual: learners will use two (or more) languages as media of instruction and learn two (or more) languages as subjects in the school curriculum.
(3) Education has to be participatory: the participation of all the stakeholders at the grassroots level in decision making is given priority.

In terms of implementation, a lot of headway has been made in the three major indigenous languages (Quechua, Guarani and Aymara). Many resources have been put into preparing teaching and learning materials, training of teachers and researching these languages (Hornberger & Lopez, 1998).

Another success story we can learn from is the Tok Ples Pri Skul (TPPS) program in Papua New Guinea in the 1980s and early 1990s. In this program, over 200 indigenous languages were used as media of instruction in vernacular pre-schools. The success of the TPPS initiative was in the main due to high level of community control and support in teacher selection, finances, curriculum development, planning and monitoring. Some of the achievements of the program include:

(1) higher academic performance in the early years of the formal system of education in all subjects, including English;
(2) children could learn the basic skills necessary for reading faster when initial instruction was in the mother tongue;
(3) children participating in the program were integrated more successfully within village life;
(4) there was language maintenance and increased production of reading materials in the local languages and increased knowledge of the local culture. (Siegel, 1997)

Finally, in a stock-taking review of mother-tongue and bilingual instruction in a large selection of African countries, the authors found that using African languages to teach students for at least six years has positive social and economic consequences for those countries (Alidou *et al.*, 2006).

There are several lessons that we can learn from these good practices. First, policies that are initiated at the grassroots level and that are wholly owned and controlled by the local community have more chances of success than those imposed from above. In other words, if local communities are not involved in the decision-making process, and if they feel that their interests have not been taken into consideration, resistance at the level of implementation is likely.

Secondly, it follows from the point made above that, if major stakeholders (parents, students, etc.) are not convinced of the usefulness of the language of instruction in question, they will not cooperate in its implementation. Tanzanian parents' quest for their children to learn English by sending them to English-medium schools is a case in point. However, as Vavrus (2003) argues, education in itself should not be seen as a panacea. She demonstrates that, despite efforts by parents in Kilimanjaro Region (northern Tanzania) to send their children to school, most of them end up getting disillusioned because education has not been able to solve their socio-economic problems. For Tanzania, this disillusionment is generally more pronounced for female students because they find it more difficult to access quality education, especially science education, than male students.

Thirdly, changing the medium of instruction by itself is not enough. In order for the change to make a significant impact, the teaching and learning environment must be improved. Teachers must be well trained to use the mother tongue as a medium of instruction. Likewise, teaching and learning materials must be adequate both in quality and quantity (Rubagumya, 2000). At this point it might be useful to say something in some detail on the implications for teacher education of the language issue in African education.

According to Nunan and Lam (1998), a teacher in a multilingual/multicultural classroom setting needs to have a number of skills, including knowledge of the discipline s/he is assigned to teach, linguistic competence (i.e. proficiency in the target language and the learners' languages), communicative effectiveness in the classroom, ability to teach in the language of instruction, and an appreciation of the learners' culture(s) and the ability to respond positively to a multilingual/multicultural setting.

Language policies in many African countries usually assume that, once a teacher has grasped the subject matter (e.g. biology, history), s/he can teach that subject matter in the prescribed language of instruction. This assumption is not well grounded. Academic discourse needs a mastery of decontextualized language skills (Cummins, 2000). It goes without saying that a teacher must acquire these skills himself/herself before helping the learners to acquire them. Institutions involved in teacher education therefore have the responsibility of ensuring that the teacher trainees acquire both contextualized and decontextualized language skills, as well as the methodologies of imparting the same to their students once they become qualified teachers.

What is said above points to the importance of Language Across the Curriculum (LAC). 'LAC can be defined as teachers' and learners' practical concern and responsibility for the way language is used as a means of access to, and communication about, the curriculum' (Young, 1995: 110). Because language is a key to knowledge, the philosophy behind LAC is that every teacher should be concerned with the language issue in his/her classroom. Whether one teaches mathematics, geography or chemistry, one has to pay attention to the language used to teach these subjects. I am therefore suggesting that any teacher education program that does not give LAC its due emphasis is not likely to be successful in preparing effective teachers.

To What Extent is Public Policy Regarding Medium of Instruction Based on Informed Debate?

If there is overwhelming evidence that using a second/foreign language as a medium of instruction does not work, why is it that public policy is usually not informed by this research evidence? In many African countries, language policy is based on political expediency rather than informed debate or research results. For example, one issue that is politically explosive has always been which language(s) to choose among several contending candidates. Would choosing one language not be construed as favoring one ethnic group at the expense of others? In such cases, a European language is always chosen by default because of its supposed neutrality. However, this kind of 'logic' is problematic. To start with, the idea of choosing one language in a multilingual society does not make sense. The issue should not be which language to choose, but how different languages in a given society can be drawn upon as resources. Equally problematic is the idea that European languages are neutral. They cannot be neutral because they are the languages of the elite in Africa. By choosing a European language in order to avoid ethnic conflict, one is in fact creating a small but very powerful 'ethnic group' of English (or French, or Portuguese) speakers. Those who are not part of this group are marginalized because they cannot have access to services and resources that need one to be fluent in the official language.

However, behind this justification of a so-called 'neutral' language lies a more fundamental issue: the struggle for resources and power. As Heller and Martin-Jones correctly argue:

> Linguistic practices are central to struggles over controlling production and distribution of resources and over the legitimation of relations of power, which are, in the end, what such control amounts to. All our debates about who should speak what and how are really, we argue, debates over who gets to decide what counts as legitimate language ... Debates over linguistic norms and practices are, in the end, debates over controlling resources. (Heller & Martin-Jones, 2001: 2)

So-called 'common sense' assumptions (Fairclough, 1989) about language in education usually influence African policy-makers in making language policy decisions. Such assumptions, however, have been proved to be misguided. For example, Qorro (2004) has analyzed arguments put forward in favour of English-medium instruction in Tanzania and has clearly shown that they are all based on 'common sense' assumptions, but not supported by any research evidence. In Africa, these assumptions are grounded in a more general discourse of language-related power imbalances. In this discourse, linguistic diversity is seen as problematic, and national cohesion is believed to be possible only if one language (usually the language of the former colonial power) is promoted. However, as Makoni and Trudell (Chapter 2, this volume) argue:

> (L)inguistic diversity per se is not a political problem: rather, *ignoring* linguistic diversity is the problem. Distinct language practices are often a feature of communities that are marginalized from access to resources and power, but national unity need not imply cultural and linguistic uniformity. Indeed, as national authorities recognize the right of individual communities to distinct language and cultural practices, and do not withhold resources or power from such communities, the resulting unity is likely to be stronger and more representative.

Dependency syndrome has also been one of the reasons that militate against making decisions based on research evidence. Because most African countries depend on Western donor countries and institutions to balance their budgets, sometimes donor interests, even if in good faith, do not necessarily coincide with local priorities. In such a case, as the saying goes, 'he who pays the piper calls the tune'. Mazrui (2004) has succinctly demonstrated this in the case of the World Bank. While the World Bank accepts that instruction in a child's first language enhances learning and the development of basic cognitive skills, the Bank at the same time asserts that:

> There are many instances when early immersion – that is, instruction in the European languages, in an all European language environment, from day one of schooling – is more appropriate than instruction in local languages, and that such immersion may be the only pragmatic option available to a nation. (cited in Mazrui, 2004: 45)

Mazrui (2004) goes on to argue that this stance of the World Bank shows that any interest that it might have in mother-tongue instruction is merely using the mother tongue as a means of making a transition to a European language as a medium of instruction.

Furthermore, educational innovations related to language in education are usually not sustainable beyond the 'project' timeframe. Since the 'project' money is almost always in the form of donor funds to be expended within a specific period of time, at the end of this period the recipient country is either unable or unwilling to find the resources to sustain the innovation started by the project. (See Rea-Dickins *et al.*, 2005, for the case of Zanzibar.)

Another problem militating against language policy being informed by research evidence has to do with lack of meaningful dialogue between researchers, practitioners and policy-makers. This point was recently underscored during the 7th International Conference on Language and Development held in Addis Ababa, Ethiopia in October 2005. Whereas researchers are seen by politicians and policy-makers as being engaged in 'ivory tower' theorizing, these latter are mistrusted by researchers and academicians as pursuing a different agenda that serves the interests of the ruling class.

Some Unanswered Questions

Although evidence for the many advantages of using the child's mother tongue as the medium of instruction seems to be generally accepted, there are still questions that need answers. In discussing these, I will take Tanzania as a case in point. Despite the fact that Kiswahili has been the medium of instruction at primary school level (Grades 1 to 7) since 1967, there is a lot of talk about the falling standards of primary school education in Tanzania. Conversely, recently established private English-medium primary schools are said to be providing better quality education (see Rubagumya, 2003, for a more detailed discussion). Several questions would be in order here:

(1) Is the quality of education deteriorating in Kiswahili-medium primary schools?
(2) If it is deteriorating, is it because of Kiswahili-medium instruction?
(3) Do English-medium primary schools give access to better quality education?
(4) If they do, is it because of English-medium instruction?

Even assuming that there is some truth in the assertion that the quality of education is deteriorating in Kiswahili-medium primary schools, there are factors other than language that might be involved. These include large classes, unqualified teachers, insufficient teaching/learning materials, a non-inclusive environment (e.g. absence of desks, hungry children, distance covered from home to school and back, etc.), the assumption that any teacher who speaks Kiswahili can teach in Kiswahili without any training and, finally, inappropriate teaching methods.

Given these factors, it would seem to me that comparing the performance of English-medium and Kiswahili-medium primary schools in Tanzania and concluding that instruction in English leads to better performance is a futile exercise. This kind of comparison would make sense if the medium of instruction were the only variable that is controlled. However, even a cursory look at private English-medium primary schools reveals that they tend to be better resourced than public Kiswahili-medium primary schools. Any difference in the quality of education offered by the two groups of schools would, in my view, be accounted for in terms of resources available to each, rather than the 'superiority' of English as a medium of instruction.

Some of the problems associated with mother-tongue literacy have been discussed by Wedin (2004) in her study of literacy practices in Karagwe District, northwestern Tanzania. In her interviews with primary school teachers on their classroom practices, one of the teachers said:

> Learning to read and write they do in standard 1 and 2. After that it's mainly to answer questions. That's what they write, answers to questions. We do it together in class. If everyone is to do it individually some will only write single letters. (Wedin, 2004: 86)

Another teacher had this to say:

> They (i.e. pupils) read to exercise. They sit together many pupils with one book. Some only watch, they don't read. Every pupil maybe reads three times a week. (Wedin, 2004: 87)

If this is what happens in many Tanzanian primary schools with respect to Kiswahili literacy, one would not be surprised that some pupils will complete their primary education not fully literate in Kiswahili. There is no reason to think that what is described by Wedin (2004) is peculiar to Karagwe District or for that matter to Tanzania. All public schools in Tanzania and probably in other African countries face more or less the same problems. In my view, the problems of large classes, inadequate resources, and inappropriate methodology, made apparent in the two quotations above, can be generalizable across the whole of Africa. See, for example, Bunyi (2005) for Kenya and Ndayipfukamiye (2001) for Burundi. It is only the extent of the problems that differs from country to country. If this is the case, the consequences are very serious indeed. For instance, one wonders how pupils can learn how to read and write by 'doing it together in class'. How can the teacher know that each individual pupil has learnt these skills? How can pupils learn how to read and write by only watching others?

Which Way Forward?

The language question in African educational systems is complex and, as such, it probably calls for complex, multi-pronged approaches in addressing it. All too often the debates on language in education have generated more heat than light, accusations and counter-accusations. As Ouane (2005: 1) points out, 'we must stop pointing the finger at policy-makers and take another look at the role of education specialists and other advisors.' In other words, we should be asking ourselves: have we done enough? What is it that we are capable of doing but have not yet done? At a Conference on Bilingual Education and Use of Local Languages, which was held in Windhoek, Namibia in August 2005, participants generally agreed on the following points:

(1) language policies should not be seen separately from the challenges of addressing poverty and the development of democratic societies through education;
(2) colonial monolingualism should be gradually replaced by African bi/multilingualism;
(3) bi/multilingual education and the use of local languages should be implemented through the additive language model as the objective for all African countries facing multilingualism within their societies;
(4) institutional frameworks that allow and promote positive reforms of language-in-education policies in African must be established;
(5) open and clear communication between experts, policy-makers, the public and other stakeholders is crucial since the question of language still raises fear and suspicion, leading to resistance to change.

I suggest that we adopt these five points as our guiding principles; and each one of us should ask him/herself: what can I do to change these principles into practices that will contribute to solving the language problem in education in Africa? It has very often been said that what is lacking is not research-based knowledge to guide policy-makers on what policies to pursue, but rather lack of political will to make and implement the right policies. I think the biggest challenge we face as professionals is to convince policy-makers of the pedagogical usefulness of using African languages in education, not *instead* of European languages, but *in addition* to them.

References

Akinaso, F.N. (1993) Policy and experiment in mother-tongue literacy in Nigeria. *International Review of Education* 39 (4), 255–285.

Alidou, H., Boly, A., Brock-Utne, B., Diallo, Y.S., Heugh, K. and Wolff, H.E. (2006) *Optimizing Learning and Education in Africa: The Language Factor.* Paris: ADEA. Online at www.adeanet.org/biennial-2006/doc/document/B3_1_MTBLE_en.pdf. Accessed 11.6.08.

Arthur, J. (1994) English in Botswana primary classrooms: Functions and constraints. In C.M. Rubagumya (ed.) *Teaching and Researching Language in African Classrooms* (pp. 63–78). Clevedon: Multilingual Matters.

Bamgbose, A. (1992) Language policy options in basic education: Implications for policy formulation. Language Policy, Literacy and Culture Round-Table: International Conference on Education. Geneva, 18 September.

Bamgbose, A. (2005) Mother-tongue education: Lessons from the Yoruba experience. In B. Brock-Utne and R.K. Hopson (eds) *Language of Instruction for African Emancipation: Focus on Post Colonial Contexts and Considerations* (pp. 231–257). Cape Town: CASAS.

Brock-Utne, B. (2000) Whose education for all? *The Recolonization of the African Mind.* London: Falmer Press.

Brock-Utne, B., Desai, Z. and Qorro, M. (2003) (eds) *Language of Instruction in Tanzania and South Africa* (LOITASA). Dar es Salaam: E&D Limited.

Bunyi, G. (2001) Language and educational inequality in primary classrooms in Kenya. In M. Heller and M. Martin-Jones (eds) *Voices of Authority: Education and Linguistic Difference* (pp. 77–100). London: Ablex.

Bunyi, G. (2005) Language classroom practices in Kenya. In A. Lin and P.W. Martin (eds) *Decolonization, Globalization: Language-in-Education Policy and Practice* (pp. 131–152). Clevedon: Multilingual Matters.

Canvin, M. (2007) Language and education issues in policy and practice in Mali, West Africa. In N. Rassool (ed.) *Global Issues in Language, Education and Development* (pp. 157–186). Clevedon: Multilingual Matters.

Clegg, J. (2005) Towards bilingual education in Africa. A paper presented at the 7th International Conference on Language and Development. Addis Ababa, Ethiopia, 26–28 October.

Cleghorn, A., Merritt, M. and Abagi, J. (1989) Language policy and science instruction in Kenyan primary schools. *Comparative Education Review* 33 (1), 21–39.

Cummins, J. (1979) Linguistic interdependence and the educational development of bilingual children. *Review of Educational Research* 49, 222–251.

Cummins, J. (2000) *Language, Power and Pedagogy.* Clevedon: Multilingual Matters.

de Mejia, A.M. (2002) *Power, Prestige and Bilingualism.* Clevedon: Multilingual Matters.

Fairclough, N. (1989) *Language and Power.* London: Longman.

Griffin, R.K. (1991) The burden of comprehension: Classroom discourse in Tanzania secondary schools. Unpublished MEd dissertation, University of Leeds.

Heller, M. and Martin-Jones, M. (eds) (2001) *Voices of Authority: Education and Linguistic Difference.* London: Ablex.

Hornberger, N.H. and Lopez, L.E. (1998) Policy, possibility and paradox: Indigenous multilingualism and education in Peru and Bolivia. In J. Cenoz and F. Genesee (eds) *Beyond Bilingualism: Multilingualism and Multilingual Education* (pp. 206–242). Clevedon: Multilingual Matters.

Mazrui, A.M. (2004) *English in Africa after the Cold War.* Clevedon: Multilingual Matters.

Mlama, P. and Matteru, M. (1978) *Haja ya Kutumia Kiswahili kama Lugha ya Kufundishia katika Elimu ya Juu.* Dar es Salaam: BAKITA.

Molteno Project (n.d.) *A History of the Molteno Project.* Online at http//: www.molteno.co.za. Accessed 2.5.08.

Ndayipfukamiye, L. (1994) Code-switching in Burundi primary classrooms. In C.M. Rubagumya (ed.) *Teaching and Researching Language in African Classrooms* (pp. 79–95). Clevedon: Multilingual Matters.

Ndayipfukamiye, L. (2001) The contradictions of teaching bilingually in Burundi: From nyakatsi to maisons en etages. In M. Heller and M. Martin-Jones (eds) *Voices of Authority: Education and Linguistic Difference* (pp. 101–116). London: Ablex.

Nunan, D. and Lam, A. (1998) Teacher education for multilingual contexts: Models and issues. In J. Cenoz and F. Genesee (eds) *Beyond Bilingualism: Multilingualism and Multilingual Education* (pp. 117–140). Clevedon: Multilingual Matters.

Ouane, A. (2005) Learning, but in which language? *ADEA Newsletter* 17 (2), 1–2.

Qorro, M. (2003) Unlocking language forts: The language of instruction in post-primary education in Africa with special reference to Tanzania. In B. Brock-Utne, Z. Desai and M. Qorro (eds) *Language of Instruction in Tanzania and South Africa (LOITASA)* (pp. 187–196). Dar es Salaam: E&D Limited.

Qorro, M. (2004) Popularizing Kiswahili as the language of instruction through the media in Tanzania. In B. Brock-Utne, Z. Desai and M. Qorro (eds) *Researching the Language of Instruction in Tanzania and South Africa* (pp. 93–116). Cape Town: African Minds.

Rea-Dickins, P., Clegg, P.J. and Rubagumya, C.M. (2005) *Evaluation of the Orientation Secondary Class in Zanzibar.* Zanzibar: Ministry of Education, Culture and Sports.

Rubagumya, C.M. (1993) The language values of Tanzanian secondary school pupils: A case study in Dar es Salaam Region. Unpublished PhD thesis, Lancaster University.

Rubagumya, C.M. (2000) *Social and Political Dimensions of Language of Instruction.* Consultancy Report submitted to the World Bank Institute, Human Development Group, Washington, D.C.

Rubagumya, C.M. (2003) English medium primary schools in Tanzania: A new linguistic market in education? In B. Brock-Utne, Z. Desai and M. Qorro (eds) *Language of Instruction in Tanzania and South Africa* (pp. 149–169). Dar es Salaam: E & D Limited.

Rubagumya, C.M. (2004) English in Africa and the emergence of Afro-Saxons: Globalization or marginalization? In M. Baynham, A. Deignan and G. White (eds) *Applied Linguistics at the Interface* (pp. 133–144). London: BAAL/Equinox.

Sampa, F. (2003) Mother-tongue Literacy in the Zambian New Breakthrough to Literacy Programme. In E.A. Arua (ed.) *Reading for All in Africa: Building Communities where Literacy Thrives* (pp. 173–178). Newark: International Reading Association.

Siegel, J. (1997) Formal vs non-formal vernacular education: The education reform in Papua New Guinea. *Journal of Multilingual and Multicultural Development* 18 (3), 206 –222.

Vavrus, F. (2003) *Desire and Decline: Schooling amid Crisis in Tanzania.* New York: Peter Lang.

Wedin, A. (2004) *Literacy Practices In and Out of School in Karagwe.* Stockholm: Centre for Research on Bilingualism.

Yates, R. (1995) Functional literacy and the language question. *International Review of Education* 15 (4), 437–447.

Young, D. (1995) Preparing teacher trainees to teach in multilingual classes. In K. Heugh, A. Siegruhn and P. Puddemann (eds) *Multilingual Education in South Africa* (pp. 107–112). Johannesburg: Heinemann.

Chapter 4

Perspectives, Challenges and Prospects of African Languages in Education: A Case Study of Kiswahili in Tanzania

PETER C.K. MTESIGWA

As long as African countries continue to educate the continent's future leaders primarily through foreign languages, they will remain dependent. Education for liberation and self-reliance must begin with the use of languages that do not impede the acquisition of knowledge. This is the challenge for the 21st century.
Roy-Campbell (2001: 197)

The Executive Council Meeting of the African Union (AU) held in Sudan in January 2006, declared year 2006 the Year of African Languages. This declaration served as a reminder to most African countries of the vision set at independence in the 1960s of empowering indigenous African languages in order to establish national identity and facilitate social, economic, political and cultural development. In the globalization era we live in today, Africa needs to constantly keep herself committed not only to this vision, but also to exploiting opportunities to demonstrate what she can contribute to the global village. Africa's colonial language policies, imposed on her by colonial governments on the one hand and the struggle to establish adequate language policies in education after independence on the other, are still among key issues that need to be addressed toward obtaining meaningful education.

This chapter presents first a broad picture of the language situation in Africa today and the complicated linguistic implications commonly experienced in a multilingual setting. It also gives an overview of how Kiswahili, one of the continent's most flourishing indigenous languages, has grown over time in terms of geographical expansion in use in both official and non-official domains. Kiswahili is presented here to demonstrate the potential that African languages have for education if adequate language planning is provided. It thus challenges the notion that African languages are doomed, underdeveloped, unable to express concepts in science and technology and, therefore, incapable of being used as languages of education. The chapter also presents what challenges must be faced and gives suggestions on what might be done to develop African languages as languages of instruction in an era dominated by globalization.

The Language Situation in Africa

The figures regarding the number of languages that exist in Africa vary from researcher to researcher. According to Gordon (2005), there are over 2000 languages in Africa. Given the complex sociolinguistic situation that dominates in many African countries, even this number cannot be taken to be unchanging. Some languages with a growing number of speakers are being 'discovered', while others with few speakers are being 'eliminated'. This mass of African languages is classified into four language phyla:

(1) Niger-Congo phyla: 1514 languages (within which there are 500 cluster members);
(2) Afro-Asiatic phyla: 375 languages;
(3) Nilo-Saharan phyla: 204 languages;
(4) Khoisan phyla: 27 languages.

We need to note that this figure of over 2000 languages represents nearly one third of the world's languages. Thus, according to Gregersen (1977), Africa, with an area of less than a quarter of the world's geographical size and with about 10% of the world's population, accommodates a very substantial share of languages.

The reliability of the criteria applied in identifying or counting languages is subject to a number of questions. Foremost is the lack of a clear sociolinguistic boundary between what may be defined as a language and what as a dialect. The difference between given speech varieties may not be reliable enough to determine the language–dialect boundary. Although intelligibility between languages declines with increase in distance among languages on a continuum, dialects are considered to be related to the same language even though they might exist on the far ends of that continuum. Secondly, a language is often recognized based on having national status, having a written form, being the standard form of a range of speech varieties, being unintelligible to speakers of other 'languages' and having a relatively large number of speakers. There are countless numbers of widely-used African languages that do not have a written form. Furthermore, it is difficult to determine what number qualifies as a 'large number' of speakers.

But more importantly, besides determining the figure for the number of African languages, Africa has sterner and more practical sociolinguistic problems. Many people, even within the same nation, fail to communicate owing to language barriers. In Nigeria, for example, there are 510 living languages, many of which are mutually unintelligible. Cameroon has 279 living languages, and in many other African countries, there are at least 100 languages spoken within each country (for most recent numbers, see Gordon, 2005). Failure among people within the same nation to communicate has, in many countries, led to failure to agree on the choice of an indigenous national or official language. In some cases, such failure has been experienced even in the choice of the standard variety of the same language. This multilingual situation in many African countries has led many to adopt the former colonial masters' languages as official languages.[1]

Heine and Nurse (2000) observe that multilingualism is the norm rather than the exception, especially among most African adults. Heine and Nurse further note that, in Africa, multilingualism is manifested at three levels:

(1) at the level of a nation whence the state profile is considered;
(2) the degree of multilingualism within a given state;
(3) the status rank of indigenous languages within that same state, which divides them into 'majority' and 'minority' languages.

At the nation-state level profile, if having 90% of the population speaking the same language is taken to be an indicator of whether or not a nation is monolingual, then only a handful of countries qualify as monolingual in Africa. These are Botswana (Setswana), Burundi (Kirundi), Lesotho (Sotho), Madagascar (Malagasy), Mauritius (Mauritian Creole), Rwanda (Kinyarwanda), Seychelles (Creole), Somalia (Somali) and Swaziland (Seswati). The remaining African countries are multilingual. The degree of multilingualism within a given state, however, varies from country to country regardless of the extent of its population or geographical area. In Nigeria, with approximately 105 million people, 410 languages are spoken; in The Democratic Republic of Congo (DRC), with a population of 30 million people, 206 languages are spoken; and in Cameroon, with 8 million people, 185 languages are spoken, to mention but a few examples.

Apart from being a sociolinguistic feature, multilingualism in Africa is further complicated by institutional multilingualism based on language status. According to Obanya (1999), language status is based on two dimensions, namely, the demographic status and the social status. Demographically, very few people (10–15%) in African countries speak former colonial masters' languages (i.e. English, French and Portuguese). In terms of social status, however, these are the languages that carry very high status as official languages or languages of education. This criterion is applied in identifying African countries according to the language of their former colonial master. We thus have 'Anglophone', 'Francophone' and 'Lusophone' Africa in spite of the fact that, in these countries, at least 90% of the population do not speak those languages. The indigenous African languages spoken by most people in any given country – including prominent lingua francas such as Kiswahili, Hausa, Wolof and Bambara – are given low social status. Very few among these languages enjoy the status of national languages, not to speak of being official languages or languages of education in their nations. As far as language in education is concerned, it ought to be noted that language status is vividly reflected since local languages as languages of instruction are limited to primary education. In many African countries, children are taught in their mother tongue for the first two years in elementary math, reading and writing. In the third year, children are introduced to the 'majority' language spoken in the locality. It is at this level, too, where a former colonial language (English, French, or Portuguese) is introduced and gradually takes over as a medium of instruction by the fourth or fifth year. Thereafter, the foreign language becomes the medium of instruction for all subjects except for the local language(s), if they are lucky to survive as subjects to be studied – along with geography, science and so on – as part of the official curriculum. In most cases, it is the majority language or the lingua franca that survives. At the secondary and tertiary levels of education, local languages (as opposed to foreign languages), especially tribal languages (belonging to specific ethnic groups), are rarely heard of except in cases where they are the subject of linguistic or literature research in colleges or universities. Educational language policies deliberately prohibit or seriously discourage the use of local languages as languages of instruction. The bilingual education system with which the child starts schooling comes to an abrupt end.

It may be argued that, given the complexity of multilingualism in Africa, using colonial languages in education is a rational choice to maintain national unity. Convincing as the argument may sound, we dare not forget that the choice of a language for education demands several considerations including, in particular, for whom education is to be delivered and for what purpose. These two factors are among the major pillars that must determine what language of instruction is to be used. Before choosing to use foreign languages in education, African countries need to compare and contrast their educational policies with the colonial government policies that came before.

Kiswahili: An Overview

Tanzania is a multilingual nation and, according to Rubagumya (1990), Kiswahili is spoken by about 90% of Tanzania's people, who also speak other indigenous languages. Because of its long history and geographical spread in Tanzania, Kiswahili constitutes about 80% of everyday language use in public places, especially in urban areas (Polomé, 1980). Kiswahili is not a monolithic language, however; there are standard and non-standard varieties and even an emergence of mixed forms such as the urban speech of Dar es Salaam youth, who are members of the Hip Hop generation (cf. Blommaert, 2005; see also Yasin, Chapter 15 this volume). As an official language, standard Kiswahili is used in parliament, the judiciary and education. In parliament, it is the language in which discussions are predominantly conducted, although members can contribute to discussion in English. Bills are, however, drafted in English and tabled in Kiswahili, but the Hansard (the discussion record) is written in both English and Kiswahili. In the judiciary, Kiswahili dominates in primary and district courts. All hearings are carried out in Kiswahili, although judges take notes in English and judgments are recorded in English. In formal education, Kiswahili is both a subject and the medium of instruction at the primary level and in primary level teacher-training colleges. It is also the medium of instruction for Adult Education. At secondary level, however, Kiswahili is taught as a subject, but the medium of instruction for other subjects is English. A similar procedure generally obtains at the tertiary level, although Kiswahili is the medium of instruction for courses offered in colleges that train teachers for primary schools. Kiswahili is also used as a medium of instruction in degree courses offered by the Kiswahili Department at the University of Dar es Salaam. The Open University of Tanzania offers an option for students to take their degree courses in Kiswahili.

Kiswahili is extensively used in many non-official domains like politics, religion, in homes, public cultural activities, local business and trade. Kiswahili is also widely used by nearly all publicly- and privately-owned radio and television stations. Today in Tanzania there are more than 50 registered newspapers and magazines published in Kiswahili. Concerning the facilitation of modern information and communication technology, two Kiswahili localization projects have been launched for translating a number of computer programs at the University of Dar es Salaam. These are the Kilinux OpenOffice operated by the Computer Science Department and two other Microsoft programs, namely, Microsoft Office and Microsoft Windows programs operated by Kiswahili Department. Through these projects, glossaries totaling over 3000 terms and over 20,000 string commands and phrases have been translated.

English is used in fewer domains in Tanzania, probably because only about 10% of the population seriously need it for communication, as already mentioned. Being a world language, however, English serves international functions that link Tanzania to the international community, such as international diplomatic functions, conferences, trade, business and information exchange. In the judiciary, it is used in resident magistrate courts, the high court and the court of appeals where Kiswahili interpretation or translation services are made available on request. The original language of the Constitution of the United Republic of Tanzania is Kiswahili, although laws are still written in English. Recently, however, the demand for translating laws into Kiswahili has grown. Two sensitive Parliament Acts that touch the everyday life of most people and which are instrumental in mobilizing the masses for successful implementation have been translated into Kiswahili. These are The Village Land Act No. 5 of 1999 (*Sheria ya Ardhi ya Vijiji* Na. 5 ya Mwaka, 1999) and The Environmental Management Act No. 20 of 2004 (*Sheria ya Kusimamia Mazingira Na.20 ya Mwaka*, 2004). Various individual lawyers, law organizations, NGOs and the public sector are working on translating several others. Members of the geneal public recognize the need to understand the law, and will best be able to do so if the law is accessible in the language they speak, even if legal technicalities and interpretation may be a work exclusively for law professionals. Many policies and government guidelines have also been translated into Kiswahili. In fact, some policies such as the Policy on Culture of 1997 (Ministry of Education and Culture, no date) were first formulated in Kiswahili, and then translated into English.

Within Eastern Africa, Kiswahili is accorded various statuses depending on the level of use. It is both a national and an official language of Kenya (debate for a similar status continues in Uganda), one of the national languages in the DRC and Comoro Islands, a lingua franca in Rwanda and Burundi and a language of wider communication in Eastern Malawi, Northern Mozambique, Southern Sudan, Southern Somalia, North East Madagascar and parts of the Seychelles. It is also one of the working languages of the East African Community.

Outside Eastern Africa, Kiswahili is one of the official and working languages of the African Unity (AU). According to Tanzania's Ministry of Information, Culture and Sports (2006), there are plans to include it as one of the official languages of the Southern African Development Community (SADC). Kiswahili is currently sixth amongst the mostly widely used languages of the world, the second most widespread (after Arabic) among

African indigenous languages and the first to be widely spread and spoken among Bantu languages in Africa. The desire to learn Kiswahili in African countries outside East and Central Africa has increased following two events in particular. The first was its introduction in use by various heads of states during the AU meeting in Addis Ababa in July, 2004. The second is the use of Kiswahili in Africa's Parliament as one of its official languages since the inception of that institution in October 2004 in Cape Town. The use of Kiswahili at these two levels has sparked interest in and increased the demand for learning Kiswahili at various levels in several African countries, particularly Nigeria, Libya, Ghana and Namibia.

Outside Africa, Kiswahili enjoys an atmosphere that is amenable for growth and further spread. This is evidenced by the fact that Kiswahili has now spread to every continent in the world, either through broadcasting over Kiswahili radio or by being taught as a foreign language in schools, colleges and universities. The National Kiswahili Council of Tanzania estimates that not less than 30 radio stations in various countries outside Africa have Kiswahili broadcasting programs and not less than 200 institutions outside Africa either teach in Kiswahili or conduct research on the language.

Kiswahili as a Medium of Instruction in Tanzania

As already noted, Tanzania is among the very few countries in Africa that uses an African language, Kiswahili, as a language of instruction throughout the primary school education system. At one point after independence, there were plans that Kiswahili would be used as a medium of instruction in secondary schools and even the university. Unfortunately, the government changed that view in the early 1980s for social and economic rather than linguistic reasons. It is important to add, as already pointed out, that in Tanzania, which is a multilingual country with no less than 120 indigenous languages, Kiswahili is spoken by 90% of the population. Strictly speaking, Kiswahili is the mother tongue of the population living along the east coast and in Zanzibar, but it is learned at an early age in most of Tanzania. It is increasingly becoming the first language of the young generation in urban areas and among the working class population.

It is also worth noting that, while many African countries opted for the language of their former colonial rulers as their official language as the best alternative for maintaining national unity, historical circumstances had shaped Kiswahili so strongly in Tanzania that, by independence in 1961, the language had become acceptable as a non-antagonistic unifying local language. The use of other local languages was, therefore, discouraged in official domains, including education. This measure has helped Tanzania not only in maintaining and strengthening her national unity but also in concentrating her meager resources for education in Kiswahili. What remains debatable and astonishing as far as the language of instruction is concerned in Tanzania, is why Kiswahili, despite having all these qualities, is not accepted as a language of instruction in secondary schools and higher education, where English remains the only language that plays that role.

Several studies on the use of English as a language of instruction in Tanzanian secondary schools have shown that little content learning takes place in class, mainly because students are not competent enough in English (Criper & Dodd, 1988; Mlama & Matteru, 1977; Mtesigwa, 2001; Roy-Campbell & Qorro, 1997). A common characteristic noted in classes where these studies were conducted is that the students' level of English is far too low and insufficient to enable them to learn as expected. Their participation in class is minimal because of the language barrier. It was further observed that effective learning takes place in classes where Kiswahili is used or where teachers venture to switch to Kiswahili in order to clarify important points in their classes. One wonders whether using English as a medium of instruction serves the purpose of learning and whether the society is able to benefit from such learning. Roy-Campbell and Qorro comment on this saying:

> If the objective of our education system is to prepare young people for their future role in society, which is 90% Kiswahili speaking, then it is only logical that that preparation should be undertaken through Kiswahili ... . (Roy-Campbell & Qorro, 1997: 104)

Despite the weak record of success in using English as a language of instruction in secondary schools, various arguments have been advanced in favor of maintaining it. As cited in Mulokozi (1991), Roy-Campbell and Qorro (1997) and Rubagumya (1990), the most common reasons for using English are as follows:

(1) English is the international language that Tanzania needs in order to communicate with the outside world in studies, trade, politics, and so on. Using Kiswahili will isolate Tanzania from the international community.
(2) English is the language of science and technology. Kiswahili needs more time to develop before it can be used in teaching science and expressing technology.
(3) There is no funding available to meet the cost of such a changeover, especially for training teachers and for translating teaching materials now available in English.

(4) English will die out if it is eliminated as a medium of instruction in Tanzania. There would be no incentive to learn it.

The reasons given against Kiswahili may be applied to other African languages, especially where a foreign language dominates. Ansre (1977, 1979) distills and critiques four major rationalizations put forward by highly-placed West Africans for maintaining former colonial languages as media of instruction, and these apply to most African countries. They include the fear of the *anticipated cost of producing educational material in indigenous languages*, the fear of being *isolated* in an era when the world is 'shrinking' (globalizing), the need for *detribalization* of African nations through use of foreign languages since they are deemed neutral, and the *inadequacy of African languages* to express science and technology.

Let us summarize a critique of these rationalizations, which will help us consider what the reality is today in practical context. Foremost, the fact that a language is international does not dictate that it has to be a medium of instruction in the educational system of a given country. At most, owing to its important role in communication, a foreign language needs to be taught and mastered well as a subject in schools. There are countries that use English or French for international communication but do not use them as the medium of instruction. Secondly, the argument that English is the language of science and technology is a weak one because, given the opportunity for careful language planning, every language is able to become a language of science and technology for its users. German, Greek, Italian, French, Russian, Japanese, Chinese, Finish, Arabic and many other languages express science and technology adequately and are being used as media of instruction by their users. Science, like knowledge, is neutral to any language. What is more important here is that if science or knowledge is to benefit the society at large, it must be expressed in the language the community understands. On whether a language (Kiswahili or any other African language for that matter) needs to wait until enough terms are created before being allowed as the medium of instruction, one should not ignore the fact that language is not merely an object to be planned but is used by its people, so its lexicon should develop in use and not wait until that time when it is thought to be fully 'developed'.

On the fear of insufficient funding for the changeover to a country's own language, this is a question of financial planning rather than a linguistic problem. In a society where language is considered a resource, proper language planning should guide the government to allocate adequate funds for language development. Once a government commits itself to treating language as one of its priorities, it cannot fail to allocate the resources to meet the costs of that decision. With regard to the fear that a foreign language may die if not used as a medium of instruction (the argument used for maintaining English as a medium of instruction in Tanzania), this only demonstrates the inadequacy of foreign language teaching methodology in Tanzania. Contrary to this claim, research on bilingual education (e.g. Baker, 1996; Hakuta, 1986; Krashen *et al.*, 1998) has confirmed that learning in the first language, apart from making learning more effective and meaningful to the learner, also facilitates better learning and mastery of the second (foreign) language. Among the prominent studies with regard to using African languages in education is the Six-Year Primary Education Project that was conducted in Nigeria on the use of Yoruba as a language of instruction compared with English. Bamgbose (1991) points out that evaluation studies repeatedly showed that pupils educated through the medium of Yoruba were more proficient in school subjects, including English, than pupils educated through the medium of English alone.

Finally, the argument on the use of a foreign language for maintaining unity in Africa's multilingual societies (because of its neutrality) in order to solve tribal rivalry in Africa leaves much to be desired. Tribal rivalry in Africa is rooted more deeply in social, economic and political inequalities in the ethnic groups concerned rather than in languages. If linguistic difference were synonymous with tribal rivalry, we would not see civil wars, unrest and genocide in Rwanda, Burundi or Somalia, which are virtually monolingual societies as earlier noted. Thus, these arguments of 'fear' often given for not using Kiswahili, or any other African languages for that matter, do not hold up.

Brock-Utne (2000) notes that the choice of language of instruction in Africa is a political choice rather than a rational one that embraces the redistribution of power in a global context within and outside the country concerned. Within the African country, it often safeguards the interests of the elite or the ruling class, by assuring that education remains the possession of the few and that the medium of instruction acts as a strong gatekeeper for social mobility. Outside the country, as Fafunwa (cited in Brock-Utne, 2000) argues, there is a correlation between underdevelopment and the use of a foreign language as the official language of instruction. While knowledge is imparted in foreign languages, the masses perform their daily tasks in their local languages. Fafunwa contends, therefore, that unless the hidden agenda is perpetuation of dependency, why should the masses not be helped to improve their social, economic and political activities in the languages they best understand, namely, their mother tongues? It is to a wider theoretical globalization framework we now turn for discussion of educational language policy in Africa.

Globalization in Educational Language Policy in Africa

Sweeting (1996) expresses globalization as a process of becoming 'global', that is, visualizing the whole world as 'our home planet'. In other words, globalization is regarding the world through a 'one world system' approach in which the world is a global village and modern humans belong to one tribe. Sweeting argues that today's world is a standardized, undifferentiated one, in which there is an assumption of similarity of social, economic and geographical circumstances and problems. It is a notion for people both in the developing and in the developed countries to believe that they are part of the same world, and that world forces are instrumental in determining the nature of problems and their solutions.

Little (1996) shares the 'one village' concept in defining globalization as the system in which economic, political and cultural arrangements transcend national boundaries and achieve integration on a world scale. Economically, globalization advocates for the free movement of labor markets between nation states. Politically, it advocates for the weakening of the nation state and strengthening of common global political values. Culturally, globalization anticipates deterritorialized cosmopolitanism and diversity. Locating the role of education in globalization, Stewart (1996) holds the view that education affects labor productivity and a country's ability to compete in international markets. Thus, the availability of human resources is critically important in the new context of a global economy. Based on this, Stewart emphasizes that globalization rewards countries that have the human resources to exploit while penalizing those who do not. In terms of access to high-quality learning, there is therefore the potential of competition between unequal partners in which a deliberate effort of the more powerful group globalizes the less powerful. Here is where the language of education matters and whose interest the language serves matters.

How does this theoretical framework apply to educational language policy in Africa? It is obvious that education is crucial to mass participation, a means of upward social mobility, and a source of manpower training and development. Above all, it is a tool towards the full realization of human potential and the utilization of this potential as a nation's resource for the benefit of all. Prah notes:

> Therefore, in free societies, knowledge transfer takes place in the language or languages of the masses; the languages in which the masses are most creative and innovative; languages which speak to them in their hearts and minds most primordially. Cultural freedom and African emancipation, therefore, cannot be cultivated, expanded or

> developed where the LOI [Language of Instruction] is different from the languages or language the people normally speak in their everyday lives. (Prah, 2003: 17)

In short, knowledge is power, and the language of education is the language of power. The choice regarding which language is used in education can result in either a powerful or powerless polity.

According to Mazrui (1997), through the policies and implementations of the more powerful developed world, the present trend in Africa is focused on maximum convergence between Euro-languages and secular education, and maximum divergence between Afro-ethnic languages and school. Elaborating this view, Brock-Utne (2000) points out that the World Bank, for instance, is the most powerful institution that formulates educational policies in Africa. Bilateral aid agencies operate with a determined World Bank hand behind them. The World Bank favors the use of African languages in the early grades of primary school only as a strategy for smoother transition to the European languages as languages of instruction. Furthermore, it plays a substantial role in determining the publication of schoolbooks and even the educational language policy in African countries. Individual European countries also play a part in assuring that their languages dominate. For instance, about 90% of schoolbooks for secondary schools in 'Francophone Africa' are produced in France and Belgium (International Bank for Reconstruction and Development / The World Bank, 2008). There have also been cases in which donors will not give aid to the publication of schoolbooks or to an education program unless a certain national language policy or educational language policy of their preference is pursued. In Tanzania, for example, aid from Britain to raise the standard of English in Tanzania's secondary schools through the English Language Teaching Support Project (ELTSP) was subject to the condition that Tanzania uses English as a medium of instruction in secondary and higher education, even though research conducted by the British Council had demonstrated that English was no longer an effective medium of instruction at that level (Roy-Campbell, 1992). This condition has remained the basis for maintaining English as a medium of instruction in secondary and higher education in Tanzania.

Against this background, there are solid reasons why Kiswahili must be the rational choice as a medium of instruction. Here are four basic reasons:

(1) Kiswahili is the language that teachers and students understand well and therefore the language in which they can best communicate and enable effective learning to take place. Using Kiswahili, students do

not have to resort to rote learning, but can to synthesize what they learn and cultivate an inquiring mind for further learning.

(2) Kiswahili is the language through which forms of knowledge, including science and technology, can be passed on to all sectors of society. It is the language in which the elite and experts render their services to society; thus, graduates skilled in the spoken and written standard can gain access to science and technology positions.

(3) Since national development requires the efforts of every Tanzanian, Kiswahili enables active participation of the masses in various social and economic campaigns such as illiteracy, poverty eradication, the war against AIDS, good governance and democracy, and so on.

(4) Kiswahili is increasingly becoming a symbol of African identity in the international community. Using it as a medium of instruction gives it a chance to express diverse ways of knowing and contributing knowledge to the international community that is unique to the African environment and culture.

What is said of Kiswahili might also be applied to the use of African languages in other regions of the continent.

A Way Forward

African countries need to seriously reassess their language planning and policies such that they will focus on making their languages the media of instruction. In this view, Africans should consider their multilingual situation an asset, and not a liability. The following suggestions might help toward that goal:

(1) If African countries recognize that language and knowledge are separate issues, then their language policies will extend preference for the use of indigenous languages. This is the preferred policy position because foreign languages do not impart deeply enough what learners need to grasp the material. Since learning takes place best in the language that both the teacher and the learner communicate, efforts should be made to develop indigenous languages as languages of instruction. In addition, programs must be developed to improve methods of teaching and learning foreign languages.

(2) In language planning, priority should be given to forming language boards that comprise members from various disciplines including linguists or language planning experts, educationists and policy makers. These experts should have a thorough knowledge through ethnographic research about actual language use in the African

context (see Cook, Chapter 6 this volume). Such a strategy may help such boards in facilitating decision-making and implementation. Where conferences, seminars or workshops are held, a similar composition of attendants needs to be ensured.

(3) Well aware that such boards are responsible for implementing language policy, governments must also ensure that their budgets allocate sufficient funding for the boards to enable them to move through all necessary stages in order that African languages might qualify as media of instruction at various levels of education.

(4) Regional languages used across nations should be given priority in being developed and used as media of instruction. At the same time, the treasures of other languages and varieties should be supported as far as possible and always respected, as they represent diverse African voices.

Conclusion

This chapter has presented two overviews pertaining to languages in Africa – the general sociolinguistic situation on the African continent, and the situation of Kiswahili in Tanzania (as well as across Africa and the rest of the world). Both overviews served to identify some problems that underlie official and educational language policies with regard to African languages. To this end, recommendations have been given towards achieving preferable and feasible policies for effective and meaningful education in Africa. It remains with Africans themselves to keep in mind that the language of education is also the language of power. As African nations become increasingly important players in a globalized world, they must give careful consideration to whether their language policies in education empower all their people to contribute to the global village and to attain a good quality of life through a high-quality education.

Notes

1. Others have looked for different solutions. In the case of Nigeria, there have been calls to make Nigerian Pidgin a national language (e.g. Ndolo, 1989).

References

Ansre, G. (1977) Four rationalizations for maintaining the European languages in Africa. *Kiswahili: Journal of The Institute of Kiswahili Research, University of Dar es Salaam* 47 (2), 55–61.

Ansre, G. (1979) Four rationalizations for maintaining the European languages in Africa: A critique. *African Languages/Langues Africaines* 5 (2), 10–17.

Baker, C. (1996) *Foundations of Bilingual Education and Bilingualism* (2nd edn). Clevedon: Multilingual Matters.

Bamgbose, A. (1991) *Language and the Nation: The Language Question in Sub-Saharan Africa*. Edinburgh: Edinburgh University Press for The International African Institute.

Blommaert, J. (2005) Situating language rights: English and Swahili in Tanzania revisited. *Journal of Sociolinguistics* 9 (3), 390–417.

Brock-Utne, B. (2000) *Whose Education for All? The Recolonization of the African Mind*. New York: Falmer Press.

Criper, C. and Dodd, W. (1988) Report on the English Language Support Programme Extensive Reading Scheme. Edinburgh, mimeo.

Gordon Jr, R.G. (ed.) (2005) *Ethnologue: Languages of the World* (15th edn). Dallas, TX: SIL International. Online version: http://www.ethnologue.com/. Accessed 21.8.08.

Gregersen, E.A. (1977) *Language in Africa: An Introductory Survey*. New York: Gordon and Breach Science Publishers.

Hakuta, K. (1986) *Mirror of Language: The Debate on Bilingualism*. USA: Basic Books.

Heine, B. and Nurse, D. (eds) (2000) *African Languages: An Introduction*. Cambridge: Cambridge University Press.

International Bank for Reconstruction and Development/The World Bank (2008) *Textbooks and School Library Provision in Secondary Education in Sub-Saharan Africa*. World Bank Working Paper No. 126. Washington, DC: The World Bank.

Krashen, S.D., Tse, L. and McQuillan, J. (eds) (1998) *Heritage Language Development*. Culver City, CA: Language Education Associates.

Little, A.W. (1996) Globalization and educational research: Whose context counts? *International Journal of Educational Development* 16 (4), 427–438.

Mazrui, A. (1997) The World Bank, the language question and the future of African education. *Race and Class. Journal for Black and Third World Liberation* 38 (3), 35–49.

Mlama, P. and Matteru, M. (1977) *Haja ya Kutumia Kiswahili Kufundushia Katika Elimu ya Juu*. Dar es Salaam: BAKITA.

Ministry of Education and Culture (n.d.) *Sera ya Utamaduni* [*Policy on Culture*]. At http://www.tzonline.org/pdf/serayautamaduni.pdf.

Ministry of Information, Culture and Sports (2006) The case for using Kiswahili as SADC's working language. Position paper by the United Republic of Tanzania presented to the meeting of SADC's PS/DGs of education. Kasane, Botswana, 7–9 March.

Mulokozi, M.M. (1991) English versus Kiswahili in Tanzania's secondary education. In J. Blommaert (ed.) *Swahili Studies: Essays in Honour of Marcel Van Spaandonck* (pp. 7–14). Ghent: Academia Press.

Mtesigwa, P.C.K. (2001) Tanzania's educational language policy: The medium of instruction at the secondary level. Unpublished doctoral dissertation, Teachers College, Columbia University.

Ndolo, I.S. (1989) The case for promoting the Nigerian Pidgin language. *The Journal of Modern African Studies* 27 (4), 679–684.

Obanya, P. (1999) Education, equity and transformation from the perspectives of language education. In L. Limage (ed.) *Comparative Perspectives on Language and Literacy: Selected Papers from the Work of the Language and Literacy Commission* (pp. 17–30). Dakar, Senegal: UNESCO – BREDA.

Polomé, E.C. (1980) Tanzania: A sociolinguistic perspective. In E.C. Polomé and C.P. Hill (eds) *Language in Tanzania*. Oxford: International African Institute.

Prah, K.K. (2003) Going native: Language of instruction for education, development and African emancipation. In B. Brock-Utne, Z. Desai and M. Qorro (eds) *Language of Instruction in Tanzania and South Africa (LOITASA)* (pp. 14–34). Dar es Salaam: E&D Ltd.

Roy-Campbell, Z.M. (1992) Power or pedagogy: Choosing the medium of instruction in Tanzania. PhD thesis, University of Wisconsin.

Roy-Campbell, Z.M. (2001) *Empowerment through Language: The African Experience: Tanzania and Beyond.* Trenton, NJ: Africa World Press.

Roy-Campbell, Z.M. and Qorro, M. (1997) *Language Crisis in Tanzania: The Myth of English versus Education.* Dar es Salaam: Mkuki na Nyota Publishers Ltd.

Rubagumya, C.M. (1990) Language in Tanzania. In C.M. Rubagumya (ed.) *Language in Education in Africa* (pp. 5–14). Clevedon: Multilingual Matters.

Sheria ya Ardhi ya Vijiji Na. 5 ya Mwaka (1999) [*The Village Land Act No. 5 of 1999*]. At http://www.parliament.go.tz/Polis/PAMS/Docs/4-1999.pdf.

Sheria ya Kusimamia Mazingira Na.20 ya Mwaka (2004) [*The Environmental Management Act No. 20 of 2004*]. At http://parliament.go.tz/bunge/docs/mazingira.pdf. Accessed 16.4.08.

Stewart, F. (1996) Globalization and education. *International Journal of Educational Development* 16 (4), 327–333.

Sweeting, A. (1996) The globalization of learning: Paradigm or paradox? *International Journal of Educational Development* 16 (4), 379–391.

Chapter 5

Languages, Literacies and Libraries: A View from Africa

KATE PARRY

One of the most notorious consequences of 19th century imperial ventures in Africa was the grouping together into colonial states of peoples who differed widely in language and culture. Now these states have become independent, and their greatest political problem is how to weld their peoples into coherent national units. The formal education system is one of the most important instruments for doing so, but the effectiveness of the system is frequently undermined by linguistic diversity. In most African countries, the various peoples speak a wide variety of languages, creating not only communication difficulties but also serious dilemmas with regard to which languages to use for the teaching of literacy skills and for the promotion of literacy practices. The different languages are, in effect, producing different literacies, none of which, as taught in the schools, is adequate. Yet individuals can find ways to develop the literacies they need if, but only if, they have access to appropriate materials and an environment in which they can read them freely. Such access can be provided by libraries, and I will cite my own experience in Nigeria and Uganda to make the case.

Languages

Everyone knows that the world is a multilingual place – though native speakers of English tend to forget that fact – and Africa is one of its most linguistically diverse regions (see Mtesigwa, previous chapter). According to *Ethnologue*, there are nearly 7000 languages in the world, of which 2000 or so are spoken in Africa (Gordon, 2005; Heine & Nurse, 2000). These 2000 languages are grouped in four large phyla:

- the Afro-Asiatic, spoken across North Africa, into the Horn and across the savannah belt of the Western Sudan;
- the Nilo-Saharan, spoken in the eastern part of the Sahara and southwards into Uganda and Kenya;

- the Khoisan, spoken among the hunter-gatherer peoples of Southern Africa;
- and the Niger-Congo, which includes most of the languages spoken in the forest belt of West Africa and the large family of Bantu languages that dominates the Central, Southern and much of the Eastern parts of the continent.

In many individual countries, more than one of these phyla are represented, both Uganda and Nigeria being cases in point. In Uganda, the people of the south all speak more or less closely related Bantu languages, but those of the north speak languages that belong to two quite different families within the Nilo-Saharan phylum. Altogether, there are over 40 different languages in the country, in a population of under 30 million. As for Nigeria, all the major phyla except Khoisan are represented, and among the country's more than 100 million people, there are some 500 languages in all (Hansford *et al.*, 1976). What this means at the level of individual experience is illustrated by the 20 boys whom I taught at my last teaching post in Nigeria (Parry, 1986). They had among them no fewer than 12 mother tongues and including all the languages that they claimed they could speak, they had a total of 23 – besides the English that I was teaching them. And, closely related though some of those languages may have been, many were completely unrelated to one another, some belonging, for instance, to the Afro-Asiatic phylum and others to the Niger-Congo phylum – as different from one another in morphology and syntax as either is from English.

Such is the linguistic diversity we are facing when we try to promote literacy in Africa, and it creates tremendous practical problems. In the early 1990s, the newly installed National Resistance Movement (NRM) government of Uganda proudly declared a policy of teaching every child in his or her mother tongue, at least in the rural areas (Uganda Government, 1992). But the proviso points immediately to one difficulty: in the urban areas populations are too mixed for it to be practicable to provide mother-tongue teaching; even in some rural areas, the populations are equally diverse (Sanyu, 2000). It also proved, and continues to prove, very difficult in the case of many of the mother tongues to find teachers able and willing to teach them or to write materials for the purpose (Keshubi, 2000; Parry, 1999). The same problems are found all over Africa and, indeed, in much of the rest of the world too. Everyone wants mother-tongue education – to oppose it would be like opposing motherhood itself – but for speakers of most of Africa's languages, nobody has figured out how it can be done.

Part of the problem is that not all languages are equal. That assertion may cause some indignation, for linguists have long accepted that all languages are equally sophisticated and equally capable of expressing human thought and feeling – there is no such thing as a primitive language (Pinker, 1995). But the fact is that some languages are used by more people than others are, and the languages that are spoken by the largest numbers tend also to be associated with the greatest political and economic power. The equation is not exact: it takes time for linguistic practice to catch up with political and economic developments and other factors, such as artistic achievement and religious belief, also have strong effects on a language's prestige. Nevertheless, there is no doubt that individual people make language choices according, not to the intrinsic qualities of particular languages, but to the perceived power and influence of the people who speak them.

The way these facts play out in Africa is that people like the boys I taught in Nigeria typically speak at least three languages (Parry, 1999). The first of these is their mother tongue, and that emotive term is entirely appropriate, for it is the language of home and intimate relations, the language spoken with the elders of the village, including and especially the speakers' mothers. The second language is an African *lingua franca,* which is usually encountered while children are still young and is widely used outside the confines of the home and the home village. In the case of my Northern Nigerian students this language is Hausa, but in Southern Nigeria it is often Yoruba or Igbo, while in East Africa it is generally Kiswahili – except in Southern Uganda, where the African lingua franca is usually Luganda. All of these languages, it should be noted, are the mother tongues of particular ethnic groups, but they are widely spoken as second languages by other groups as a result of political and economic relationships; and because the dominance of certain languages reflects past, if not present, patterns of political and economic dominance, there are sometimes tensions associated with their use and promotion. It is these lingua francas, moreover, that are, in many cases, the most immediate threat to the mother tongues (Mekacha, 1994; Roy-Campbell & Qorro, 1997; Rubagumya, forthcoming). Finally, my Nigerian students, like all Africans who have had formal schooling beyond the elementary level, speak a European language. In the Nigerian case, that language is English, but in many African countries the language of schooling is French or Portuguese. This third language reflects even more powerfully than the lingua francas do the experience of political and economic domination, and its use and promotion is even more bedevilled by tensions and, in some cases, hostility. The Kenyan writer Ngugi Wa Thiong'o (1986) is a famous exponent of such feelings, but they are often expressed by others too (see, for instance, the quotation with which Peter Mtesigwa begins Chapter 4 in this volume). Further examples appear in 'dreams' that were invoked at a retreat on the subject of African university education organized by the Ford Foundation in 2001 (Mama & Hamilton, 2003; the emphases are mine):

> I dreamt of a university that one could call a Swahili university, where instructions and communication and everything was done in the Swahili language. All forms of knowledge were transmitted *in the language of the people*. (p. 33)
>
> I imagine a place where all the teaching is done, first and foremost, *in African languages*, whether it be Swahili or Yoruba, or Wolof. And where, secondly, many major African languages are taught, so as to favor intra-African comprehension ... (p. 35)
>
> In my dream ... language is no object. Technology has been very useful here. It's come up with a device that enables us *to speak whichever language we choose*, but be heard. (p. 36)

The unease at the dominance of the colonial languages is evident, but the fact that that unease is here expressed in English suggests that the dominance, for the present at least, is escapable only in dreams.

In fact the dominance of English, in particular, is only increasing. Much has been said about the role of globalization in this development – how the English-speaking juggernauts of international business are crushing other languages beneath them, and how the insidious tentacles of English-dominated media are reaching into people's homes and planting the alien language there (Crystal, 2003; Mazrui, 2004; Pennycook, 1994). All this is true, but we have to recognize that there are also local forces at work. While some educated successful Africans, like the people quoted above, lament the fact that their education and success are predicated on English, those who are not yet educated or successful do everything that they can to learn it. Even the humblest peasants in adult literacy programs in Uganda express a desire to learn the language (Carr-Hill *et al.*, 2001; Uganda Government, 1997), and many of the users of the rural library with which I am particularly concerned value the library precisely because it provides access to English books (Dent & Yannotta, 2005). This popular desire to learn English is well founded: people know very well that they cannot access professional status or political power without it and that it greatly increases their chances of economic prosperity. Any attempt to withhold English, then, however justified in terms of cultural identity, will be interpreted by those who are least influenced by European and American culture as an attempt to prevent them from getting ahead in the world. In a similar situation in India, when the Marxist government of Bengal State announced in the 1980s that the teaching of English would be discontinued in government primary schools, a graffito in Calcutta made a trenchant statement of the problem:

> My son won't learn English. Your son won't learn English. But Jyoti Basu [the Chief Minister] will send his son abroad to learn English.

As Salman Rushdie comments, with reference to this graffito, 'One man's ghetto of privilege is another's road to freedom' (Rushdie & West, 1997: xii).

Literacies

These problematic relationships among languages are closely tied in with questions of literacy, or rather of literacies, as denoted in my title. This use of *literacy* in a plural form goes back to Brian Street's book *Literacy in Theory and in Practice*, in which he asserts that the ways in which written text is used in different social and cultural contexts are so diverse that, 'we would probably more appropriately refer to "literacies" than to any single "literacy"' (Street, 1984: 8). I am thus invoking the line of thinking initiated by Street and subsequently developed by many scholars, which considers literacy not as a single discrete skill but as a complex of practices surrounding the use of written text. Some scholars, in fact, define the term still more broadly as the practices associated with the use of any coding system (Cope & Kalantzis, 2000: 5). I prefer, however, to stick to the traditional association between literacy and writing, because present technological developments are making writing – that is, the visual representation of language – more important than ever in human communication. We need, then, to retain a term for the use of written language, and *literacy*, for me, is that term.

Literacy practices, so defined, are embedded in social situations, just as oral practices are, and they reflect the relationships and ideology of those who participate in them. Thus they vary from one culture to another and, indeed, in different circumstances within the same culture. Street, for example, identifies three different literacies in the Iranian mountain village where he did his fieldwork in the late 1970s:

(1) *makhtab* literacy, or the religious use of written text in Arabic;
(2) commercial literacy, or the use of the script learned in the *makhtab* for keeping track of transactions in the fruit trade;
(3) school literacy, including reading and writing in English, which was acquired in the towns by people who attended Western-type schools.

All these literacies are associated with different patterns of behavior and have different ideological implications. I have tried in earlier papers to come up with a comparable inventory of the literacies that I have observed in Africa (Parry, 2000, 2006). It is extremely difficult, because the different literacies overlap, and practices are often transferred from one to another – in fact, that is the way in which new literacies develop. It is a little easier, however, to identify the different literacies associated with particular languages. Here I shall use the linguistic framework outlined above in order to do so.

To begin, then, with *mother-tongue literacy*. The phrase, like *mother tongue* itself, raises warm associations for many people, inspired by memories of sitting comfortably in bed as their mother reads a story. That sort of literacy practice is the norm in many, perhaps most, middle-class communities in which the mother tongue is English or some other European language, and it is also common in middle-class families in Asia, for example in Japan and China (Hatano, 1986; Parry & Su, 1998). Several studies have shown that children whose first literacy develops in this way have a head start as compared to others when they learn new kinds of literacy practice in school (Cook-Gumperz, 1986; Heath, 1994; Scollon & Scollon, 1981). So shouldn't we encourage the development of that kind of mother-tongue literacy in Africa? Maybe we should, but we must recognize the difficulties, especially for the vast majority of African families that live in rural areas. In the first place, mother often can't read or, if she can, she doesn't have time. In the second place, there are probably no books at home or, if there are, there is no light at night by which to read them. In the third place, and this is probably the greatest impediment, there are few books published in most of Africa's mother tongues, and in some of them there are none at all. Those books that are published are often not suitable for reading to children. The *Index of Nigerian Languages*, for example, records Saint Mark's Gospel as the sole publication in a number of languages (Hansford *et al.*, 1976), and though more recently in Uganda I have come across non-devotional vernacular texts, they are often titles such as *Abakyala mumanye eddembe lyammwe* [*Women Know your Land Rights*] (Uganda Women's Network, 2000) and *Abakyala mu mirimu gyeby'obusubuzi* [*Women in Business*] (Lockhead, 1990). Adults may find these books relevant and absorbing, but it is unlikely that children will (cf. Carr-Hill *et al.*, 2001).

This is not to say that mother tongue literacy is insignificant. The religious texts, for instance, are of central importance to Christians, especially Protestants, so that mother tongue literacy is for many a religious literacy – to read is to pray. 'The Bible is very important for my life,' said one informant in western Uganda, 'so I read it whenever I find time' (Openjuru, forthcoming), while in a study that covered all regions of Uganda, in all but one district over 50% of the adult literates surveyed claimed to read religious books (Carr-Hill *et al.*, 2001). Speakers of four of Uganda's languages (Luganda, Ateso, Lwo and Runyankore) can also read newspapers in their mother tongue, which constitutes perhaps a more practical kind of literacy, and there are also the texts, exemplified above, that are meant to promote social and economic development (though none of Openjuru's Runyankore-speaking informants mentioned reading them). In all these cases, though, mother-tongue literacy is an adult literacy, and it is associated with people who live in the village, as opposed to the city, and especially with those who are devout.

In southern Uganda, it is hard to distinguish *lingua franca literacy* from literacy in the mother tongue, because the most widely-spoken African language, Luganda, is also the mother tongue of the Baganda people, who comprise the largest cultural group. Members of other, smaller, groups, though, use Luganda as a second language, especially in the south and east. Kiswahili is spoken in the armed forces and as a second language by people in the north but, despite government policy that it should be taught in secondary schools (Uganda Government, 1992), Kiswahili literacy is neither widespread nor widely valued in Uganda. The situation in Kenya and Tanzania, however, is quite different, with Kiswahili having much higher status and Kiswahili texts of all sorts being much more widely available (Mtesigwa, Chapter 4 of volume; Pawlitzky, forthcoming). Tanzania, indeed, achieved high levels of literacy in Kiswahili in the 1970s and early 1980s, though there was a drastic falling off after Julius Nyerere retired from public life and Tanzania submitted to World Bank demands for cuts in government spending (Mazrui, 2004; Rubagumya, forthcoming). Nonetheless, both Tanzania's experience and Pawlitzky's study of adult readers in Kenya suggest that there is tremendous potential in lingua franca literacy, especially when, as in Kiswahili and in Hausa, there is a long precolonial tradition of writing. For those who speak them as second languages, these lingua francas may not express personal identity in the way that their mother tongues do, but they are undeniably African, they have a rich literary tradition and a wide range of texts, and learning to read in them is infinitely easier than learning to read in a foreign language such as English or French. No wonder the 'dreamers' quoted above mentioned Kiswahili as a language for the African university that they envisioned (see also Mazrui, 2004: 102).

In literacy, though, as in education, Kiswahili is overshadowed by English, even in Tanzania (Roy-Campbell & Qorro, 1997). Mtesigwa (this volume) attributes that fact to the World Bank's hostility to African languages, but *English literacy* is even beginning to overshadow literacy in the former colonial languages of Lusophone and Francophone Africa. A friend from Burundi, for example, told me recently that Burundians regard the Anglophone countries of East Africa as lands of riches and opportunity and are attributing Rwanda's relative success to the fact that the country is adopting English for use in government (see Crystal, 2003). As for Anglophone countries like Uganda, people often seem to consider English literacy to be the only literacy that counts. Another anecdote will illustrate the point. In 1998, when I was interviewing the headteacher of one of the schools where I was doing research, he told me that most of the students' parents were 'illiterate'; yet he also told me that they often sent him notes, written in Luganda. The main reason for such attitudes is undoubtedly the association of English with wealth and prestige, but another important reason is that there is much more written material in English than in any other language (Crystal, 2003). This phenomenon is self-increasing as, at one end of the scale, more and more European and Asian scholars decide that competence in written English is essential to academic success, while, at the other, increasing numbers of businesses, whether through signboards or the Internet, take to advertising their wares in English.

The problem, for rural Africans, is that they encounter English only in school, where they are taught by teachers who are often not confident of their own command of the language. The situation is exacerbated by the fact that rural schools hardly ever have enough books (Liang, 2002; Muwanga *et al.*, 2007), even though books in English are much more readily available than in African languages. So the teaching of reading, in English as well as in other languages, often takes the form of choral recitation in response to text written on a blackboard or wall chart. After the first few sessions, this is not much fun for anybody, and students have little hope of learning enough to become independent readers. The results are manifest at the end of secondary school, when students focus narrowly on exams and, in their desperation to pass and their fear that they will not do so, resort to learning by rote what their teachers have told them (cf. Serpell, 1981). As a senior staff member in an especially forward-looking Ugandan university told me of the undergraduates he was teaching,

> The weakness basically is general literacy ... I suspect it has to do with the fact that [the students] have not really been given an opportunity to be themselves. ... [They] haven't been equipped with the ability to go out and find information on their own. Because of the way that the system has been, they have been told that the teacher is correct and if you give

back what the teacher has given you, you are a good student. (Field notes, Uganda Martyrs University, 30 January, 2007)

This kind of *schooled literacy*, as I like to call it, provides little access to information; still less does it nourish the imagination or foster critical thinking.

Libraries

But this is where libraries come in, for they can provide a means of developing literacy practices *beyond the school*. The kind of library considered here is not the traditional school library. These have long existed in Uganda (though certainly not in all schools), and some of them are very good, but they have little impact outside the schools in which they are located, and those schools are largely the preserve of the professional elite. Nor are the libraries in question centrally-administered public ones such as those operated by Uganda's Public Libraries Board from the 1960s to the 1990s. Those libraries were set up in district capitals and catered for an educated urban population; then they were starved of funds from the 1970s, and even now they are a low priority for the local government authorities that are responsible for them. These libraries have few books, such as they have are usually old and shabby, and as institutions they are often seen as irrelevant. Yet Ugandans are responding eagerly to the efforts of local and foreign benefactors to provide community libraries – institutions located usually in rural areas that cater to all the people resident there by providing reading material and organizing activities associated with literacy (cf. Mostert, 1998, on community libraries in South Africa).

My own work in Uganda is increasingly focused on promoting libraries of this sort. Since 1999, I have, with the help of the director of a local secondary school, been running one near a village called Kitengesa in Masaka District in the Luganda-speaking Central Region (Kitengesa Community Library, 2008). From 2006 to 2007 I worked to set up a Uganda Community Libraries Association (UgCLA), with the aim of encouraging the growth of such libraries across the country. The Association has, at the time of writing, only just been launched, but its work will be to put these libraries in touch with one another and, we hope, with donor communities elsewhere; to provide training workshops for their managers; and to raise funds that can be funneled into specific library projects in the form of small grants. These libraries can be regarded as constituting 'innovative multicultural library services for all,' as was stated in the theme of the conference at which this paper was first presented. They are *innovative* because they have emerged in Uganda only in the past decade. They are *multicultural* because they serve, potentially at least, all the different cultures of the country and also introduce readers to cultures of other parts of the world; and they are *for all* because their membership is unrestricted and because they can have a dramatic impact on the lives of the whole community.

The easiest service for such libraries to provide is to complement the education system by giving access to secondary school textbooks and reference books, which are almost all in English, as well as to supplementary reading materials, also in English. This is what students in the schools want, and it is such students who provide the core membership of the Kitengesa library and of the other libraries with which I have been working. To begin with, I was reluctant to respond to the demand for textbooks and especially for what the students call 'pamphlets' – potted notes that are geared to exam subjects – but my recent research has convinced me that even these materials, provided in the context of a community library, help to take literacy beyond the school, or at least beyond the narrow teaching and learning strategies described above. In the first half of 2007, I interviewed upper level secondary school students in a couple of different libraries, and they came up with remarks like this:

> When teachers don't cover the whole syllabus you can find a book and read it (Field notes, Kitengesa Community Library, 16 May 2007)

> You can use the library for reference and check whether what the teachers have told you is true or false. (Field notes, Kitengesa Community Library, 16 May 2007)

> You should read a textbook with a friend. For example, when it is difficult to understand the teacher, you should get a textbook and explain it to others. It helps you so much because something you teach others you cannot forget it. (Field notes, Caezaria Public Library, 24 May 2007)

Such remarks suggest that by using the library these students are developing some independence from their teachers and are learning how to seek and find, information for themselves.

I have also found that, despite their focus on exams, students both enjoy and appreciate the value of reading for 'relaxation'. A common strategy in both libraries, it seems, is to spend an hour or two studying and then to break off to read some other material. One boy showed me his 'relaxation' book, which he had already taken down from the shelf although he was still occupied in his studies; the book was *An Animal Encyclopedia,* and to explain why he enjoyed it he showed me a picture of a cobra and pointed out its qualities as an artistic design. A later conversation with some of this boy's friends went like this:

J: If I feel like I'm bored I go to Traditional Stories or Modern Stories [two of the categories used in the library].
C: We also use the newspapers.
G: Biography [is] good for relax[ation]. E.g. Isaac Newton.
M: [You can use] dictionaries for relaxation.
P: [Or for] getting vocabulary – to challenge young people.
J: [For] Swahili and English. Idioms. Proverbs. (Field notes, Kitengesa Community Library, 30 May 2007)

In the other library, the students gave different examples: *Romeo and Juliet* in 'story form', which must be a simplified reader; 'vernacular' novels such as *Guluma Gusa*; a title called *Jude the Nun*; and *The Da Vinci Code* – this last from a particularly sophisticated student who is now at university (Field notes, Caezaria Public Library, 24 May 2007). In short, the availability of a range of books is enabling these young people, if only in occasional spare moments, to go beyond the reading dictated by their exam syllabuses and to explore their own interests.

All this is good, but if we stop at secondary school students, we are not doing our job. What about the adults in the community? The most educated ones are teachers, whether at secondary or primary level, and they are easy enough to attract with much the same range of books. Those that I talked to at Kitengesa told me that they use the library mainly for preparing lessons, but also for reading novels and newspapers. Indeed, one of them claimed that he never spends a day without coming to the library in order to keep up with the news – and I know it is true, for I always find him there when I go. These people are a minority, though. Most of the people in the village are peasant farmers, with hard lives and little leisure to spare; if they have spent years without reading a book, why should they start now? Moreover, many of them are not comfortable reading in English, and some of them cannot read at all.

We have adopted two strategies for reaching such people. One is to help them get access to written material, partly by teaching them directly and partly by explaining to them, in Luganda, the information found in English texts. Thus, one of our librarians runs a women's group, to which he invites local experts in subjects such as horticulture and stock-raising; the experts explain, for example, how to look after cows when you do not allow them out to graze, and the librarian shows them any books we have on the subject. The other librarian recently gave them a striking example of how empowering the knowledge found in books can be. She herself has two cows which she 'zero-grazes', to use the Ugandan expression. In early 2007, one of her cows was in calf, and the vet wanted 60,000 shillings (about

$US40) to help her deliver. Our librarian was not willing to pay that money, so she borrowed *Where There is No Vet* (Forse, 1999) from the library, read all the sections about pregnancy and birth in cows, and when the time came followed the instructions. When I visited her in May 2007, she had a fine calf, and a cow that was producing eight liters of milk a day. With such a model before them and with the support they can give to one another, the women have a strong incentive to build up their literacy skills and the little English that they have; and of course we try to help them by purchasing material that is both likely to be interesting and is written at a level that is accessible to them.

The second strategy is to try to provide material in Luganda, which is the mother tongue of most people in the area. So we have a policy of buying every Luganda book that we can find, but, alas, by June 2007 that meant only 159 titles. This number of titles is better than none, but it is not enough to establish reading habits, so we are increasingly trying to produce Luganda texts ourselves. During the school holidays in May 2007, a group of students, including two of those quoted above, undertook to collect and write out Luganda stories for me – with English translations so that I could understand them and also send them to the United States, where, for a fundraising ploy, a friend has promised to print them out for sale to her colleagues. There is also a Writers' Club at the school where the library is located, and that, too, is working to produce Luganda texts. Meanwhile, we subscribe to the Luganda newspaper, *Bukedde*, and to a Luganda magazine, *Entanda ya Buganda*, and these materials are proving particularly attractive, not only to adults but to students too.

A final group that we are working to reach is children. In 2005, I did a survey of the library's membership and borrowing patterns and was dismayed to find that children hardly featured at all. So in 2006, we began a campaign to bring children in by inviting a friend from Kampala (formerly the children's librarian for the national Public Libraries Board) to facilitate a Children's Reading Tent for us. We hired a tent, put all our children's books on display, and invited children and teachers from ten primary schools, as well as various local dignitaries, to participate. There were tables set up for painting, drawing, writing, reading aloud and silent reading; there were speeches, of course, and there were songs; and everyone was given a good meal. Since then, we have been holding Children's Days two or three times a term, when we invite children from one school at a time and offer much the same range of activities, though on a smaller scale. More recently, moreover, younger children have begun to come to the library without being invited at all. They simply showed up one Saturday when a Children's Day was scheduled, so they were welcomed and given paper to draw on and books to look at. Since then they have been coming every Saturday expecting to be entertained, and the librarian has arranged for student helpers to be on hand to look after them.

On June 2, 2007, I attended one of the Children's Days and was particularly impressed by how the young woman whom we had recently hired as a library assistant was handling the bilingual situation that the library represents. She was reading a book aloud to a group of five children, a traditional story from Northern Uganda called *When Hare Stole Ghost's Drum* (Ocwinyo, 2005). The book was in English (although its author heard it originally in Lwo), but for a time I thought it must be a bilingual text because from one sentence to another the young woman was translating into Luganda, easily and fluently, with lively intonation, and turned the book towards the children from time to time so that they could see the pictures. The children listened eagerly, laughing when Hare got beaten by Odobo, and nodding with understanding when the reader showed how his back escaped because it was protected by a drum. These children were having an experience of reading that will prepare them well for the multilingual and multicultural world in which they will live their lives, for they were hearing how the tales of one culture can be expressed in the language of another, and how that language can itself be translated orally into one that is easier for the people present to understand. They were also, of course, being exposed to English, the language that they are already aware of as the one of power and prestige; but at the same time, their mother tongue was being affirmed as a language equally appropriate for literacy.

Conclusion

In promoting literacies, then, in multiple languages, I nail my colors firmly to the cause of community libraries. In their aim of serving entire communities, they can provide for the natural desire to learn the languages of power, but they can also address the need for material in the languages that local communities speak; and because, unlike schools, they are not governed by centrally-imposed curricula, they can adopt creative means of doing so, drawing on the linguistic skills of community members. I hope therefore that within a few years, there will be libraries like the Kitengesa one scattered all over Uganda, and my present work is focused on encouraging that to happen. There are some community libraries besides Kitengesa already, and their managers, like our own librarians, are working hard to bring people in who have not hitherto thought of reading and to help them overcome the linguistic barriers that make written text inaccessible to so many. It is an exciting movement, one that will, I trust, prove that people can learn the languages that will give them access to information at the national and global levels, while at the same time developing, enriching and preserving the ones that express their own local identities and represent the rich multiplicity of African cultures.

Acknowledgement

This chapter is a revised version of a keynote address presented on 17 August 2007 at a satellite conference of the International Federation of Library Associations and Institutions (IFLA), organized in Pretoria, South Africa, by IFLA's Section on Library Services to Multicultural Populations in cooperation with the Libraries for Children and Young Adults Section and the Reading Section. I am grateful to the conference organizers for inviting me to speak and to the participants for their warm and encouraging feedback. My home institution, Hunter College of the City University of New York, generously released me from teaching in the spring semester of 2007 to do the research reported here. The research was funded by grant number 68074-00 37 from the PSC-CUNY Research Foundation and from a fellowship in the Fulbright New Century Scholars Program for 2007–2008. My main colleagues in the work of administering the Kitengesa library are Mawanda Emmanuel, director of Kitengesa Comprehensive Secondary School, in Masaka District, Uganda and our two librarians, Daniel Ahimbisibwe and Lucy Namwanje. Francis Kigobe, director and manager of the Caezaria Public Library in Buikwe County, Mukono District has been very helpful in providing information and putting me in touch with library users. I have also received much support from my fellow trustees on the Board of the Uganda Community Libraries Association. Finally, I would like to thank the many people in the libraries mentioned above and in Uganda Martyrs University who kindly agreed to be interviewed.

References

Carr-Hill, R.A., Okech, A., Katahoire, A.R., Kakooza, T., Ndidde, A.N. and Oxenham, J. (2001) *Adult Literacy Programmes in Uganda*. Washington, DC: World Bank.

Cook-Gumperz, J. (ed.) (1986) *The Social Construction of Literacy.* Cambridge: Cambridge University Press.

Cope, B. and Kalantzis, M. (eds) (2000) *Multiliteracies: Literacy Learning and the Design of Social Futures*. London: Routledge.

Crystal, D. (2003) *English as a Global Language* (2nd edn). Cambridge: Cambridge University Press.

Dent, V.F. and Yannotta, L. (2005) A rural community library in Africa: A study of its use and users. *Libri* 55, 39–55.

Forse, B. (1999) *Where There is No Vet*. London: Macmillan.

Gordon Jr, R.G. (ed.) (2005) *Ethnologue: Languages of the World* (15th edn). Online at http://www.ethnologue.com/. Accessed 26.11.07.

Hansford, K., Bendor-Samuel, J. and Stanford, R. (1976) *An Index of Nigerian Languages*. Accra, Ghana: Summer Institute of Linguistics.

Hatano, G. (1986) How do Japanese children learn to read? Orthographic and ecocultural variables. In B.R. Foorman (author) and A.W. Siegel (ed.) *Acquisition of Reading Skills: Cultural Constraints and Cognitive Universals* (pp. 81–114). Hillsdale, NJ: Lawrence Erlbaum Associates.

Heath, S.B. (1994) What no bedtime story means: Narrative skills at home and school. In J. Maybin (ed.) *Language and Literacy in Social Practice: A Reader* (pp. 73–95). Clevedon: Multingual Matters Ltd in association with the Open University.

Heine, B. and Nurse, D. (eds) (2000) *African Languages: An Introduction*. Cambridge: Cambridge University Press.

Keshubi, H. (2000) Teaching local languages in Primary Teachers' Colleges. In K. Parry (ed.) *Language and Literacy in Uganda: Towards a Sustainable Reading Culture* (pp. 46–50). Kampala, Uganda: Fountain Publishers.

Kitengesa Community Library (2008) Website at www.kitengesalibrary.org. Accessed 14.8.08.

Liang, X. (2002) *Uganda Post-primary Education Sector Report* (No. 26706). Washington, DC: World Bank

Lockhead, A. (1990) *Abakyala mu mirimu byeby'obusubuzi [Women in Business]*. Kampala: Quaker Service Norway and DENIVA

Mama, A. and Hamilton, G. (2003) *Envisioning the African University of the Future: A Report of a Retreat on Higher Education*. Nairobi: The Ford Foundation.

Mazrui, A.M. (2004) *English in Africa after the Cold War.* Clevedon: Multilingual Matters.

Mekacha, R.D. (1994) Language death: Conceptions and misconceptions. *Journal of Pragmatics* 21, 101–116.

Mostert, B.J. (1998) Community libraries: The concept and its application, with particular reference to a South African Library System. *International Information and Library Review* 30 (1), 71–85.

Muwanga, N.K., Aguti, J.N., Mugisha, J.F., Ndidde, A.N. and Siminyu, S.N. (2007) *Literacy Practices in Primary Schools in Uganda: Lessons for Future Interventions*. Kampala: Fountain Publishers.

Ngugi wa Thiong'o. (1986) *Decolonising the Mind: The Politics of Language in African Literature*. London: Heinemann/J. Currey.

Ocwinyo, J. (2005) *When Hare Stole Ghost's Drum*. Kampala: Fountain Publishers.

Openjuru, G. (forthcoming) Literacy practices in a rural Ugandan community. In K. Parry (ed.) *Reading in Africa: Beyond the School*. Kampala: Fountain Publishers.

Parry, K. (1986) Readers in context: A study of Northern Nigerian students and school certificate texts. Unpublished doctoral dissertation, Teachers College, Columbia University.

Parry, K. (1999) Language and literacy in African contexts. *Language Matters: Studies in the Languages of Southern Africa* 30, 113–130.

Parry, K. (2000) Literacy policy and literacy practice. In K. Parry (ed.) *Language and Literacy in Uganda: Towards a Sustainable Reading Culture* (pp. 59–65). Kampala: Fountain Publishers.

Parry, K. (2006) Which literacy matters? And why? Paper presented at the Reading Association of South Africa 2nd Annual Literacy Conference.

Parry, K. and Su, X. (eds) (1998) *Culture, Literacy and Learning English: Voices from the Chinese Classroom*. Portsmouth, NH: Heinemann.

Pawlitzky, C. (forthcoming) Understanding the reader: Reading preferences of Kikuyu and Luo speakers in Kenya. In K. Parry, S. Andema and L. Tumusiime (eds) *Reading in Africa: Beyond the School*. Kampala: Fountain Publishers.

Pennycook, A. (1994) *The Cultural Politics of English as an International Language*. London: Longman.

Pinker, S. (1995) *The Language Instinct: The New Science of Language and Mind*. London: Penguin Books.

Roy-Campbell, Z. and Qorro, M (1997) *Language Crisis in Tanzania: The Myth of English versus Education*. Dar es Salaam: Mkuki-na-Nyota.

Rubagumya, C.M. (forthcoming) The policy of language and literacy in Africa: The experience of Tanzania. In K. Parry, S. Andema and L. Tumusiime (eds) *Reading in Africa: Beyond the School*. Kampala: Fountain Publishers.

Rushdie, S. and West, E. (eds) (1997) *Mirrorwork: 50 Years of Indian Writing 1947–1997*. New York: Henry Holt.

Sanyu, F. (2000) Difficulties of teaching in the mother tongue. In K. Parry (ed.) *Language and Literacy in Uganda: Towards a Sustainable Reading Culture* (pp. 43-45). Kampala: Fountain Publishers.

Scollon, R. and Scollon. S.B. (1981) *Narrative, Literacy and Face in Interethnic Communication*. Norwood, NJ: Ablex.

Serpell, R. (1981) The cultural context of language learning: Problems confronting English teachers in Zambia. *English Teachers Journal* 5 (1), 18–33.

Street, B.V. (1984) *Literacy in Theory and Practice*. Cambridge: Cambridge University Press.

Uganda Government (1992) *Education for National Integration and Development*. Government White Paper on implementation of the recommendation of the report of the Education Policy Review Commission. Kampala: Uganda Government.

Uganda Government (1997) *Functional Adult Literacy Programme*. Report on the review of post-literacy programme in Uganda. Kampala: Ministry of Gender and Community Development.

Uganda Women's Network (2000) *Abakyala mumanye eddembe [Women Know your Land Rights]*. Kampala: Uganda Women's Network

Chapter 6

Street Setswana vs. School Setswana: Language Policies and the Forging of Identities in South African Classrooms

SUSAN E. COOK

The ongoing debate around the status of European versus African languages in South Africa (specifically English and Afrikaans versus the nine major Bantu languages)[1] recalls similar debates from other African countries, as well as other parts of the post-colonial world. Michael Meeuwis described a situation in the former Zaire where language planners and policy makers, as well as the general public, argued whether French, the colonial language, should remain official in post-colonial Zaire, or whether African languages should ascend to that status (Meeuwis, 1999). Meeuwis argues that this 'language ideological debate' served to erase a prior debate about varieties of African languages, including different dialects of Kiswahili and the urban hybrid Lingala. Similarly, arguments about the appropriate role for 'European' versus 'African' languages in contemporary South Africa (see for example Thwala, 2007) have eclipsed the question of which varieties of African languages are the 'proper' ones, worthy of policy attention and budget expenditure. With a focus on this less visible debate, this chapter starts from the premise that language, and in particular the distinction between standard and non-standard varieties of African languages, provides a critical lens into the process of identity formation, ideological tensions and social change in post-apartheid South Africa.

The South African constitution of 1996 articulates a policy of multilingual inclusion, and specifically seeks to promote the status of previously disadvantaged languages, in particular African and Khoi-San languages. There are government bodies tasked with operationalizing these goals, and legislation that attempts to steer behavior, at least in official domains, towards a more multilingual practice (Perry, 2004). But one cannot read change out of official rhetoric and policy. Everyday language practices and dominant language ideologies are at least as important a gauge of processes of change, and the points of tension and contestation with regard to these changes. Non-standard speech varieties such as Tsotsitaal, Is'camtho, Pretoria Sotho and Street Setswana,[2] the variety examined in detail here, are the languages of everyday life for most black South Africans. They incorporate lexical material from a wide range of languages (as well as a high number of neologisms) into a grammatical structure most commonly based on one of the African languages (Myers-Scotton, 1993; Slabbert & Finlayson, 2000). These highly expressive and rapidly-changing speech forms are not only uncodified, for the most part, but they also are actively sanctioned in the language classroom. Their hybrid nature is ideologically construed as 'mixed up' and 'confused' at best, and socially and morally degenerate at worst. Language purists (often black elite intellectuals) decry the effects of these speech forms, and argue for a return to more 'authentic' linguistic practices, which usually means the promotion of the standard versions of the nine major Bantu languages spoken in South Africa. There is irony in this position of course. These nine 'languages' are themselves a legacy of European missionary activity in southern Africa in the early-to-mid-19th century as well as white rule later (Harries, 1988; Herbert, 1992). Confronted with a broad spectrum of closely-related speech forms, missionary linguists drew boundaries where there were none, and identified distinct 'languages' (hence also distinct 'cultures' and 'nations'). So, for example, Sesotho, Sepedi and Setswana were identified as three languages, despite the fact that they were probably nearly indistinguishable 200 years ago, and remain mutually intelligible today (Cook, 2006).

Nevertheless, the language purists of today, many of them respected educationalists, seek to enforce the boundaries between these codes, imaginary linguistic walls that are directly threatened by the hybrid varieties that effectively overlook the entire history of boundary enforcement between black people. Put more simply, where the language purists seek to maintain ethnic boundaries and 'authentic' ethnic identities, the use of hybrid codes marginalizes ethnic identity in favor of a more general black, urban South African identity. Despite the fact that this conflict is enacted everyday in thousands of South African classrooms, where teachers dutifully correct language 'mistakes' that violate the standard language policy, the debate itself is almost completely overshadowed by the debate surrounding African languages versus European languages as the medium of communication in universities, government, business and the media. This 'erasure' (Cook, 2006; Gal & Irvine, 1995) of one 'language ideological debate' by another diverts attention from the contestation around the very notion of what it means to be a [black] South African today. Are you a Zulu first, a black second and a South African third? What community do you feel most a part of, and where do your social, economic and political allegiances lie? These questions have been asked and answered many times since South Africa's formal liberation from apartheid in 1994, most often through the lenses of political science, sociology and even marketing (Burgess, 2002; Chipkin, 2007). Examining the tension between language policies and language behaviors in black communities shifts the focus away from the broader contours of racial inequality (between blacks and whites), and from the assumed/purported/constructed existence of 'ethnic conflict' (as between Xhosas and Basotho). It allows us to examine a more subtle and, I would argue, more far-reaching shift from the privileging of ethnic identities in everyday life to the practice of an urban black identity and perspective that transcends the boundaries so entrenched in policy.

This chapter therefore examines the role played by Setswana-medium government schools in inculcating language habits and attitudes, and their corresponding social values and identities. The data presented here suggest that the language classrooms where ethnic Tswana children 'learn' their mother tongue are an important site of social reproduction, not only of Tswana ethnic identity, but also of black urban aspirations. These different forces are evident in seemingly contradictory behaviors and attitudes on the part of both teachers and students. Observation of Setswana classrooms reveals that young people learn to divide their feelings about Afrikaans between the official position, in which it is a foreign language of oppression, and everyday practice, where it is a popular way to swear, joke and interact with friends. And, although schools attempt to confine English to the role of 'language-of-wider-communication' (i.e. an out-group language), teachers themselves are unwitting examples of English's currency *within* the Tswana community as the language of upward mobility, urban sophistication and (inter)national pop culture. So while the school curriculum itself may not accurately reflect students' social and economic concerns, the teachers' unofficial behavior often does. Motivating this dual emphasis on standard Setswana and 'foreign' language learning is an idea of Tswana ethnic identity that teachers still cleave to, but that is difficult to impart to children (or adults) for whom it promises few tangible rewards. Schools are thus a useful place to examine the split between South Africans' understanding of where they belong on the one hand, and of what they want on the other.

Street Setswana

Street Setswana is a non-standard form of Setswana that incorporates lexical material from English, Afrikaans, Zulu and Tsotsitaal, among others. Better described as a range of speech styles than a single 'language', these styles are all linked by the fact that they index urbanity.

The transcript in Figure 6.1 is a 35-second excerpt from a conversation between a group of young men. Caleb and Bisto,[3] both 23 years old, are sitting inside a friend's house, talking about the price of portable stereos. Words of Setswana origin are in plain typeface, English-derived words are in **bold type**, Afrikaans-derived words are underlined and words borrowed from other African languages are in *italics*. While lexical features

TRANSCRIPT	*ENGLISH GLOSS*
C: Nno, o tsoo reka **redio** e eturang, man. Nkampan' kao reka... soo se se botlhale bogolo ge e le **theipi** ya bo **handred e samthing** bo **thu handred en samthing**, le gone e ya **handred samthing** e botoka m'na, kana tsotsotlhe ke bo **thu handred en samthing**...	C: Hey, you bought an expensive **radio**, man. I'd rather buy something bigger instead of a **tape player** for around **a hundred and change, two hundred and change**, and the one for **a hundred and change** is better, man, since they all cost around **two hundred and change**.
B: **Noo** mar... C: Eh! ... 'OMEGA' mothakoole onthaare nkaereka ka... B: Nee mar waitse...yonee botlhalenyana...	B: **No**, but... C: Hey, that guy told me I can buy an OMEGA for... B: Uh, but you know...that one is better...
C: OMEGA onthare nkaereka ka trii **handred en**... B: [whistles] C: Ka re 'waatsenwa.' B: OMEGA?!	C: He told me I can buy an OMEGA for three **hundred and**... B: [whistles in disbelief] C: I said 'you're crazy.' B: OMEGA?!
C: A re trii **handred en** mang nare? ee. B: Kana mo **dishopong** tse dingwe ke *triikllipa* **khapol** waitse?	C: He said three **hundred and** what, right? Yeah. B: But in the **shops** others are *three hundred* **and something** you know?
C: Ka re nka se reke OMEGA monna ka sose, nka mpene ka o patella... B: Ga ke e khompera le mokgatla o koo kreileng maabane ole, yerr... o bona fela gore nno, goo sa tsamae, o o nyala kgaitsadio	C: I'm saying I cannot buy an OMEGA for that, but I'd rather pay ... B: If I **compare** it with the one I got yesterday, hey... you realize that if you don't shop around, you end up marrying your sister.

Figure 6.1 Transcript, Street Setswana

Key: **English,** Afrikaans, *other African language*

are not the only way that Street Setswana differs from the standard form, choice of vocabulary carries a great deal of symbolic weight in the non-referential (socially indexical) functions of this speech form, thus meriting special attention.

Structurally, this speech form differs very little from standard Setswana, especially in terms of syntax. In the area of morphophonemics (sound combinations), many otherwise distinct sounds are combined in Street Setswana (as they are in the spoken forms of many languages). Good examples of this can be seen in line 1, where 'o tsoo' would be rendered 'o ntse o' in standard written Setswana, and line 3, where 'soo se' would be 'selo se' in the standard form. In addition, many sound combinations are found in Street Setswana that are 'disallowed' in the sound system of standard Setswana. Like other Bantu languages, Setswana does not contain consonant clusters, making such combinations as 'ndr' in 'ha**ndr**ed' (line 5) impossible. (Bantu lexemes follow a CVCV structure: consonant-vowel-consonant-vowel). Likewise, Setswana does not have an inter-dental fricative sound (IPA symbol è), making 'samthing' (line 5) impossible in the standard Setswana. Finally, a brief note about semantics. Street Setswana typically includes standard Setswana words to convey non-standard meanings. An example from this transcript is the word 'botlhale', which appears in lines 3 and 15 (in the latter in a diminutive form), and means 'clever' or 'intelligent' in standard Setswana. Here, it conveys a sense of 'good' or 'desirable'.

The prevalence of Street Setswana as a mode of communication is at odds with many people's ideas of what it means to be ethnically Tswana. Investigating people's communicative practices in light of their ideological conceptions of language reveals the co-presence of two identity formations in contemporary South Africa. Tswana ethnic nationalism, promoted by the apartheid and Bantustan regimes and also present in certain policies of the ANC-led government, is reflected in people's allegiance to standard Setswana as a symbol of ethnic authenticity. People's day-to-day use of Street Setswana – a dynamic variety that is mutually intelligible with other South African hybrid varieties – reflects a desire to identify with a broader black South African identity. These two sets of ideas appear to co-exist in many individuals I interviewed, but they exist in tension. Ethnic identity relies on a notion of purity and exclusivity, allegiance to agrarian practices and traditions and a linguistic practice that is emblematic of these values. Urban black identity, on the other hand, eschews ethnic difference in favor of a more cosmopolitan South African (and global consumer) culture, rejects anachronistic agrarian values in favor of market-oriented and individualistic economic orientation, and dismisses language purity in favor of rapidly-changing pan-ethnic hybrid codes.

The tension between these two ideologies seems unsustainable, and likely to resolve itself in favor of one or the other. The language teaching practices in Setswana-medium government schools in the North West Province offer clues as to the direction of change. Bourdieu and other influential reproduction theorists identify schools as one of the main institutions where values, identities and class structures are produced and reproduced (Bernstein, 1971; Bourdieu & Passeron, 1977). In her work on Catalan in Spain, however, Woolard (1985) cautions against focusing too much attention on formal institutions such as schools as the primary sites of social reproduction. Rather, she notes, it is on the 'primary economic relations on arrangements for everyday living, and on the informal structures of experience in daily life' that we should focus our attention (Woolard: 1985: 742). If, however, government schools are viewed *both* as formal institutions charged with the task of inculcating official attitudes towards Setswana language and culture, *and* as places of informal behavior where young people see, hear and learn to emulate the everyday behaviors of their teachers, then schools' role as a site of social reproduction is not overdetermined based on its status as a government institution, nor is it ignored as an important site of 'the informal structures of experience in everyday life' (Woolard, 1985: 742).

Educators and policy makers in post-apartheid South Africa are working hard to ensure that languages such as Setswana, marginalized by the apartheid regime, are given new status and legitimacy. Many South Africans understand that children have the right to acquire literacy and basic concepts in their home language, and that they also have the right to learn the language(s) used in higher learning and the economic marketplace. These principles manifest themselves in schools where knowledge of standard Setswana is strongly encouraged in theory, English proficiency is strongly encouraged in practice, and Afrikaans has lost some of the status it acquired under the apartheid regime.

Neither at the local nor the national level, however, do school authorities acknowledge, much less accept, that the wider social and economic environment is not easily reconciled with these policies. Students' home language in the communities I studied is not Standard Setswana, but rather Street Setswana. Because Street Setswana is not treated as a legitimate speech variety by schools, students learn to read and write in what amounts to a non-native dialect.

Standard Setswana in the Classroom

Setswana instruction in government schools is viewed as perhaps the most important bulwark against the 'deterioration' or 'corruption' of the language. Administrators, teachers, parents and even students agree that if language standards are not maintained in the schools, then the fight for linguistic purity is lost. The Setswana curriculum reflects this objective, even to the point of testing students' vigilance against non-standard items on the national matriculation exam (see below). While school policy is clear-cut in its support for standard Setswana, it is the people who implement those policies who are charged with promoting the standard language. This is no easy task. Nevertheless, teachers and principals embrace it as their mission, confident that their efforts are a vital contribution to the preservation of Tswana culture and identity.

In Tlhabane and Phokeng, the two communities where I conducted fieldwork, children attend six years of primary school, three years of middle school and three years of high school. When children enter the first grade, they are taught exclusively in standard Setswana, presumed to be the 'home language' for most. English is introduced informally in the first grade, and then more formally in the second year. Afrikaans is introduced as a subject in the third grade, and by the fourth grade most subjects are taught in English. Setswana remains a mandatory subject through Grade 12, when students write their national exams. The following discussion is based on my observations of fifth and sixth grade Setswana teachers and their students, in and outside the classroom, at two primary schools: Sunnyside Primary in Tlhabane, and Hillside Primary in Phokeng. I chose to focus on this age group because it is around the ages of 11 or 12 that children become aware of the social status of Street Setswana and start emulating older speakers of it more consciously.

As the purveyors and promoters of standard Setswana language and culture, school administrators and language teachers see themselves as an important line of defense against the negative influences of urban life and modern values. Mr Tau, the principal and fifth grade Setswana teacher at Hillside Primary, feels he is responsible first and foremost for equipping his students to pass the national matriculation exam at the end of high school. The Setswana portion of the exam is mandatory for all first-language Setswana speakers, and tests not only the student's knowledge of Setswana grammar, composition and literature, but also their knowledge of Setswana culture. Mr Tau acknowledges that many students don't acquire a good foundation in standard Setswana at home, and many lack the cultural information they need in order to pass their exams and graduate:

... in grade 12, then they are going to encounter problems. There they test the quality of the language. We must try to give them at least the acceptable language that will help them when they reach the high school.[4]

Although Hillside Primary is located in the village of Phokeng, where children are presumed to know something about herding cattle, weaving baskets, making clay pots and preparing traditional foods, Mr Tau finds that students are often unfamiliar with these things. It is therefore an explicit part of the Setswana curriculum to coach students in the official version of 'Setswana traditional culture.'

In addition, given that most adults don't use standard Setswana in their everyday interactions, children from Tswana-speaking homes usually require remedial instruction in the 'correct' form of the language as well. Students enter school not only with simplified grammar and limited vocabulary – a normal stage of language acquisition – but with a lot of non-standard words that teachers must find a way to excise from their vocabulary. These range from words that are standard in 'another' South African language to words that are borrowed into Setswana from English and Afrikaans and 'Setswanalized' (the local term for mophosyntactic incorporation of non-Tswana words into Setswana). Some examples of the words I heard being banned from Setswana classrooms are shown in Table 6.1

Most of these words are conventional in everyday speech, having been used by Setswana speakers for generations, and are considered 'foreign' only by language purists. Setswana teachers not only label these words 'incorrect,' but feel they symbolize a dangerous trend towards abandoning or contaminating Setswana culture and identity. As teachers of 'pure'

Table 6.1 Some words banned from Setswana classrooms

Word	*Derivation*	*English gloss*	*Standard Setswana*
etsa	Sotho: *etsa*	do	*dira*
mama/papa	Afrikaans: ma/pa	mother/father	*mme/rre*
konomaka	Afrikaans: *skoonmaak*	clean	*phepafatsa*
kamore	Afrikaans: *kamer*	room	*phaposi*
distories	English: stories	stories	*dikgang*
Krismas	English: Christmas	Christmas	*Botsalo jwa Morena*
dikwatlele	Afrikaans: *kwatel*	dishes	*dijana*

Setswana, these professionals thus see themselves as ethnic nationalists fighting for the survival of their culture. This perceived threat of linguistic and moral degeneration is revealed in the way teachers characterize lexical borrowing in Setswana. Mr Tau refers to lexical borrowing as 'stealing.' At Sunnyside Primary in the township, Mrs Mmutle, a fifth grade Setswana teacher, regards borrowing as laziness at best, cultural treason at worst. She carefully corrects her students as they give oral presentations, cautioning them to use *sejanaga* instead of *bese* (bus), *peretshitswana* instead of *baesekele* (bicycle) and *terena* instead of *sitimela* (train).[5] After class, I told her that I couldn't find *peretshitswana* in my Setswana/English dictionary. 'What did they say for bicycle?' she asked. '*Baesekele.*' 'No, they are being lazy!' she said. 'We are trying to phase out that language; we want to speak OUR language.' It should be noted that most Setswana speakers consider terms like *sejanaga* and *peretshitswana* arcane, and say that it would be very unusual to hear them in conversation.

While Setswana teachers don't like to admit that standard Setswana is not the only form of spoken Setswana, they do so implicitly by calling this variety 'pure Setswana' or 'clean Setswana' (*Setswana se se phepa, Setswana se se tlhapileng*). Thus, the state-sponsored version of Setswana is not only linguistically correct, but also morally superior to other varieties. The importance of distinguishing between 'pure Setswana' and some other (unnamed) variety has even found its way into the Setswana portion of the national matriculation exam. The following section appeared in the 1996 test:[6]

(g) *Kwala mafoko a a latelang ka Setswana se se phepa*
(Write the following words in pure Setswana)

(i) *Silabase* ('syllabus' from English)
(ii) *Sepitikopo* ('speed cop' from English)
(iii) *Tshampione* ('champion' from English)
(iv) *Ripoto* ('report' from English)
(v) *Sepatshe* ('wallet' from Afrikaans)

Although lexical borrowing is considered a normal social process elsewhere, Setswana teachers associate change in the language with destruction of the culture. The connection between standard Setswana and Setswana culture is often explicit in Mrs Mmutle's classroom.

Zulu people speak their language, Sotho people speak their language, and we, we speak OUR language!
(*Mazulu a bua puo ya ga bona, Basotho ba bua puo ya ga bona; rona, re bua puo ya RONA!*)

Mrs Mmutle links standard Setswana to authentic Tswana identity when she tells her class 'we speak pure, traditional Setswana' (*re bua Setswana se se phepa, sa bogologolo*). In fact, she regularly evaluates her students' Tswana-ness based on their command of the standard language. For example, when she introduced a seldom-used Setswana term, and found that the children didn't know it, she exclaimed, 'Hey, you people are not Tswana!' (*Batho we, ga le Batswana!*). This kind of remark usually refers to the students' *lack* of Tswana-ness, but the inverse situation also occurs. When a boy in her class correctly identified '*go ja nala*' as a Setswana idiom meaning 'to visit,' she congratulated him by saying '*O Motswana*!' ('You're a Tswana!').

This consistent interweaving of standard Setswana with Tswana ethnicity is not the only way that schools seek to reproduce language behaviors and ethnic identity. Setswana teachers also consciously or unconsciously weave identity issues together with language instruction via their own attitudes about rural versus urban lifestyles. 'Pure Setswana culture' (*Setswana se se phepa*) is closely identified with the rural way of life that Tswana speakers led before they were colonized by Europeans in the early 19th century. Traditions that originate in the typical Tswana cattle-herding, grain-growing economy are the emblems of traditional Tswana prosperity and well-being. The move to cities, townships and white-owned farms in the last 150 years has contributed to the gradual obsolescence of much of that agrarian knowledge and practice. Although Hillside Primary is located in a village, few people in Phokeng are farmers. Although Mr Tau is not a Mofokeng[7] and lives in Tlhabane, he characterizes his approach to Setswana teaching as 'rural,' meaning he encourages his students to appreciate the link between the language and the agrarian mode of production it emblemizes. When discussing the occurrence of borrowing, Mr Tau says different teachers have different standards for accepting borrowed terms in the Setswana classroom, and the standard also varies from area to area. According to Mr Tau, teachers from rural areas are more vigilant about preserving the purity of Setswana. In a roundabout way, Mr Tau implies that urban dwellers have less of a stake in retaining or promoting their ethnic identity.

> Those ones in Tlhabane, for example, don't mind it [borrowing]. Even the teacher there doesn't mind. Let me say they don't care. So the one in the village must take due care when coming to the Tswana terminologies. In fact, we are to be rather too strict to reduce stealing words from other languages, especially when we come to their [the students] mother tongue, you see.

In his Setswana classes, Mr Tau takes every opportunity to remind the students that they are not only Tswana, but Bafokeng (the sub-ethnic identity linked to the particular chieftaincy that Phokeng falls under). He tells them that their schools were built by the tribal authority (unlike those in the townships that were built by the 'homeland' regime), and his classroom is decorated with pictures of crocodiles, the totemic symbol of the Bafokeng people. He encourages his students to talk about the history of their school, its location in relation to certain hills and rivers, and the hereditary structure of the local governance system. The students at Hillside Primary are taught to be proud of their school, their village, their ethnicity and the language that symbolizes it.

At Sunnyside Primary in Tlhabane, teachers also emphasize the urban/rural opposition, and again, urban dwellers are constructed as culturally and morally deficient. Miss Metshe, a young ethnic Mofokeng who lives in the township, teaches Setswana to sixth graders at Sunnyside Primary. Her students are mostly from Setswana-speaking homes, although they represent a wide range of sub-ethnic identities. Some trace their roots to the Batlokwa to the north, others to the Bahurutshe to the west. A few students come from non-Tswana speaking homes, and are often the children of migrant laborers working in the mines. Miss Metshe frequently tells her class that the reason they don't know certain words or concepts in Setswana is because they live in a township: 'You are town-dwellers; you don't know what *kgaogana* [split up] means' (*Lona ke batho ba toropong; ga lo itse gore 'kgaogana' ke go dira eng*.) When she asked the class the meaning of another word concerning cattle-rearing, and got no response, she asked who in the class comes from Phokeng. One girl raised her hand, and Miss Metshe called on her, assuming she would know the answer. (She didn't.) Another time, Miss Metshe digressed from a reading comprehension lesson in order to teach the class a short civics lesson on how villages are governed differently from townships. She asked for names of villages, and when one child gave the name of a township, she firmly corrected him. 'Boitekong is a village? It's not a village! It's a township! A township, like Tlhabane. I want villages ... home villages!' ('*Boitekong ke motse? Ga se motse! Ke motse se toropo, jaka Tlhabane. Ke batle metse ... magaeng*!') When I asked Miss Metshe how many of her students come from outside Tlhabane, she replied that although some students commute from nearby villages, none of them actually 'comes from' Tlhabane, implying that a real home is, by definition, a lineage based in a rural area. Resonant with Mr Tau's subtle comments that rural teachers care more about standard Setswana, Miss Metshe's claim that no one is native to Tlhabane reflects the common perception that ethnic identity in South Africa is indivisible from rural origins.

Mrs Mmutle (at Sunnyside in Tlhabane) also seems to privilege discussions about rural themes in her classroom. She encourages her class to talk about their visits to relatives in villages, and listens enthusiastically to stories of boys herding cattle or riding on donkey carts and of girls collecting water or firewood and helping their grannies cook porridge in iron pots. When she focuses any attention on the children's experiences in the township (where they spend the vast majority of their time), it is to admonish them about the dangers of handguns and to tell them to go to church on Sunday rather than playing in the street. While it can be argued that teachers in the townships are obliged to expose urban children to rural themes so that they are not handicapped on the national Setswana exam, it is clear that teachers' negative attitudes about urban living influence how they inculcate ideas of good and bad in their students. The pedagogical imperative to teach Setswana rural traditions falls into an ideological matrix wherein 'pure' Setswana language and culture reside in the rural areas, while in the townships, linguistic laxness and ethnic diversity lead to a kind of un-ethnic anomie.

If standard Setswana is threatened by unscrupulous borrowing and Tswana cultural knowledge is in decline, then who or what is responsible for this moral and social decay? No one suggests that it has anything to do with the apartheid regime's insidious Bantu Education policies designed to systematically under-educate blacks while providing white students with world-class educations. If anything, teachers credit the homeland regime with doing more to promote 'pure Setswana' than the current administration. Mrs Mmutle says that teachers are now allowed to present more borrowed words in the Setswana curriculum than they were under President Mangope's regime, a policy shift she does not condone.

Teachers as Black Urban South Africans

On the list of what and who is socially prestigious in South Africa, Tswana-ness ranks near the bottom. Where Zulus celebrate the history of their feared warrior, Shaka and Sothos can explain how Chief Moshoeshoe founded the Sotho nation, there is no heroic figure or epic event that Tswanas regularly refer to with pride. Despite the fact that Tswanas were at the vanguard of many of the first encounters between indigenous people and 'modern' ways in South Africa (see Comaroff & Comaroff, 1991, 1996), Tswana people themselves are more likely to regurgitate circular logic about how they are proud of their language simply because other South Africans are proud of theirs. Ironically, this kind of statement purports to be 'about'

Tswana ethnic identity, but it is implicitly more 'about' national identity, i.e. the desire to embrace an ethnic identity like other South Africans.

But unlike Zulu ethnicity, urbanity or the ability to speak English, there is little social capital to be gained from foregrounding one's Tswana-ness. Individuals seeking prestige in mainstream middle-class South Africa must identify with prestigious social spaces through their (socially symbolic) behavior. How then, do members of the professional class such as teachers become such strong proponents of standard Setswana, going against their socioeconomic interests in the process? How can they carry the banner for the traditional, rurally-based emblem of Tswana identity when their position in society would suggest they are interested in the trappings of modern, urban life?

In fact, teachers behave very much within the confines of their class interests, and their professional status as Setswana teachers is full of contradictions. By observing Setswana teachers both inside and outside the classroom, I quickly learned that they only identify themselves *rhetorically* with the standard language, and thus, by association, with 'pure Setswana culture'. In practice, they are avidly seeking the trademarks and privileges of middle-class culture, and must therefore distance themselves from anything that would mark them as ethnic Tswanas.

Teachers' speech behavior outside the classroom instantly reveals this split between ideology and practice. In the staffroom at Sunnyside Primary, teachers speak to one another in Street Setswana, often codeswitching into English. Examples abound. One day, I was sitting in the staffroom when Miss Metshe went to her classroom to quiet her class before I visited them for the first time. When she came back to get me, another teacher inquired, '*Ba shap*?' ('Are they ok?' from the English *sharp*). On another occasion in the staffroom, Mrs Mmutle used *vroeg* ('early morning' in Afrikaans), and *klina* ('to clean,' from English). Given her insistence that her students use the standard Setswana term *phepafatsa* rather than the Afrikaans-derived *konomaka* ('to clean'), I was surprised to hear her using other non-standard terms in her own speech. When I gave some of my boiled maize to Miss Metshe during lunch one day, she exclaimed, '*susan ke chomi ya ka!*' ('Susan is my friend!'), using the Tsotsitaal term for friend (*chomi*), derived from the English 'chum' and the possessive pronoun from Sepedi. I went to cheer on the Sunnyside kids at a local sports competition. A teacher I don't know well greeted me saying, '*Ba a siana alright*?' (Are they running well?).

It is tempting to assume that Setswana teachers feel obliged to impart formal language skills in the classroom, but shift to a more informal speech register when they are offstage. This turns out to be only partly true. In fact, their speech behavior in the classroom also includes Street Setswana. Here is a small sample of teachers' utterances in the classroom, with English glosses (non-standard items are in **bold**):

Mr Tau:

(1) *'**moattende**...'* (from Eng.) 'please attend to him/her'

(2) *'yo o **etsang** ...'* (from Sotho) 'the one who does ...'
(shortly after telling the class not to use *etsa*)

(3) *'**kom**!'* (Afrikaans) 'come!'

Mrs Kobo (a first grade teacher at Hillside Primary):

(4) *'go **shotang**?'* (from Eng. 'short') 'what's missing?'

Mrs Mmutle:

(5) uses ***papa*** (from Afrikaans) to address boys.

(6) *'**ok, dankie**, ke a leboga'* 'ok, thanks, thank you.'

Example 6 is a good example of codeswitching to reiterate a point. It may also suggest an effort on the teacher's part to censor herself, i.e. she follows her initial utterance in English and Afrikaans with the school Setswana for 'thank you'. But if teachers are conscious of the extent to which they use Street Setswana in the classroom, they rarely admit it. I asked Mr Tau whether he explained to his students that they need to know standard Setswana for certain purposes, but can also use the mixed version in their daily interactions. He said no, he would prefer that his students use the standard version at all times, but added 'where possible' in tacit acknowledgment of the fact that any child who did so would be considered socially inept. The above examples of teachers' use of non-standard Setswana in the classroom are all from moments of informal discourse, not the formal presentation of the lesson. In other words, these offstage shifts into Street Setswana illustrate (to the students as well as to the researcher) that standard Setswana is inappropriate for informal interactions.

In addition to frequent slips into Street Setswana, teachers codeswitch into English frequently. Rather than a case of using language to identify with urban culture, the use of English in the classroom reveals the extent to which many students simply do not understand standard Setswana terms. In the case of Mr Tau, who teaches science and math (in English) in addition to Setswana, it is unsurprising that he switches to English to refer to topics or concepts he has already discussed in his science/math lessons. For example, when reading a Setswana poem about the sun, Mr Tau digresses slightly, reminding the students that, 'Food will only be manufactured in the presence of sunlight.' More revealing are the instances where Mr Tau resorts to English when a student doesn't get the point in Setswana. When trying to teach one student the terms for 'right' and 'left' in Setswana (*moja, molema*), Mr Tau repeats '*seatla sa* ***molemeng***' (the left hand) several times, to no avail, until he gives up and says '*seatla sa mo* ***left***'. Similarly, when discussing the geographic location of Hillside, Mr Tau lists the cardinal directions in Setswana. Students have difficulty distinguishing them, so he explains it using '*bo-north*', '*bo-south*', etc. to make it clearer. Outside the classroom, numbers are hardly ever expressed in Setswana, almost always in English. In the effort to speak 'correctly,' though, the teachers often insist that students give the date or other numbers in Setswana. For example, Mr Tau corrected a boy who said that people entered a room '*ka one one*' (one by one). On another occasion, though, Mr Tau struggled to say the year that Hillside Primary was built, 1968, in Setswana ('*sekete kgolo a robong' 'some a marataro, le robedi*'). Not only are many students more familiar with certain English terms than with their standard Setswana equivalents, but they are more comfortable with English in general than standard Setswana. Mr Tau reluctantly gives evidence of this when he resorts to English to make instructions clear to the class. For example, when explaining to his class that he wanted them to write a four-paragraph description of their school, he said, '*O na le* ***dikarolo tse nne***' (You have four paragraphs), then reinforced the instruction by repeating (twice), '*O na le* ***four paragraphs***'.

Although codeswitching in Afrikaans also occurs in the Setswana classroom, it is often a symbolic assertion that Afrikaans has no place there, as when Mrs Mmutle says to her class, '*Ons praat nie Afrikaans!*' (We don't speak Afrikaans!). The students' ability to make sense of this statement presupposes that they *do* understand Afrikaans, but they also know that it is considered out of place in Setswana class. Interestingly, Mrs Mmutle's statement wouldn't make as much sense if it were about English, i.e. if she said 'We don't speak English!' In fact, codeswitching in Afrikaans is highly marked behavior, whereas the use of English in the Setswana classroom often goes unnoticed.

In her study of language use among high school pupils, Malimabe (1990: 18) observes that 'some teachers mix English and Setswana words when speaking'. She identifies this as one of the reasons students make mistakes in their written Setswana assignments. Although Malimabe is reluctant to identify social reasons for students' so-called 'mistakes' (i.e. use of a non-standard variety of the language), she does relate the teachers' codeswitching to the issue of social prestige. Regardless of its social value, though, codeswitching is a 'major problem for teachers', according to Malimabe, especially because 'they are not conscious of its presence in their language' (Malimabe 1990: 19). What Malimabe constructs as an educational problem can otherwise be seen as a social fact: teachers are middle-class professionals who wish to identify with urban, black South African culture. Their desire for the status symbols associated with urban, educated status includes speaking English on the level of symbolic behavior.

The final evidence of teachers' unwillingness to practice what they preach when it comes to being 'pure' Tswanas lies in the decisions they make on behalf of their own children. All of the teachers mentioned here (those teaching in Phokeng as well as those teaching in Tlhabane) live in the more up-scale neighborhoods of Tlhabane (i.e. Fox Lake, Bester). When I asked Miss Metshe, a proud Mofokeng who so frequently extols the qualities of Phokeng to her students, why she doesn't live in the village, she was slightly embarrassed. She prefers the lifestyle of the township, she admitted. And despite their insistence that Tswana children must learn 'good' Setswana at school in order to preserve their identity as Tswana people, *all* of these teachers send their children to English-medium schools in Rustenburg. When I ask why, the answer is simple. They want their children to have the socioeconomic advantages that proficiency in English brings in contemporary South Africa. Mrs Mmutle beautifully demonstrated the conflict inherent in striving to be upwardly-mobile South Africans and Tswanas at the same time upon our first meeting at Sunnyside Primary. 'We encourage the students to speak pure English [sic] at home,' she declared, before recovering herself. This slip-of-the-tongue is hardly coincidental. When I visited Mrs Mmutle at her home in Bester, I noted that she and her husband (a high school principal) speak to their children almost exclusively in English.

Students' Language Attitudes

What do students make of the mixed messages about Setswana language and culture they receive at school? On the one hand, they are told over and over again that they should be proud of their cultural heritage and ethnic identity, embodied in 'school Setswana,' (as the students sometimes refer to the standard variety). The version of Setswana they speak at home, after school and on the playground is constantly corrected, insulted and demeaned in the classroom. On the other hand, their teachers (often their only models for the white collar jobs they aspire to), behave in a way that downplays standard Setswana's status and practicability. As authority figures and government employees, teachers seek to impress upon students the social, cultural and even moral superiority of standard Setswana and the traditional, rural lifestyle it symbolizes. The Street Setswana they occasionally use in the classroom and almost always among themselves, however, bears little relation to the symbols of Tswana-ness they extol in their classrooms. Miss Metshe is a good example of this. She wears trendy clothing, sports gold tooth caps and carries herself in a manner that is markedly urban. But far from being linguistically paralyzed or culturally confused by all of this, the students happily mirror (or at least mimic) their teachers' contradictory attitudes towards Setswana, and model themselves much more closely after the teachers as middle-class urban professionals than as 'pure' Tswanas.

Although the students speak Street Setswana at home, they soon learn how to censor themselves in the classroom, based on what the teachers tell them is 'good' and 'bad' Setswana. For example, when I was talking informally with a sixth grade class at Sunnyside Primary (and Miss Metshe was absent), one student used the word *chomi* (friend). The other students immediately corrected him, telling him to use the school Setswana equivalent *tsala*. (See previous example where Miss Metshe refers to me as her *chomi*.) The students appeared a little uncomfortable when I told them that I myself use the word *chomi*.

In a more formal interview that my research assistant conducted with five fifth graders at Hillside Primary, the same split emerged between how people speak, and how they talk about their speech. As the students were speaking very enthusiastically about 'school Setswana,' they were using Street Setswana (for example, *khota pas thu* for 2:15). Reflecting the official school policy, the students asserted that they speak standard Setswana during their Setswana lesson, English during English class and Afrikaans during Afrikaans class. When I interjected that I have heard them using English in their Setswana lessons, they agreed. They admitted that their teacher (Mr Tau) likes to speak English, but they can't give a reason why. My assistant, Holiness, suggested to the students that perhaps there are English words they encounter in their lessons that they understand better than the Setswana equivalents. The students denied this at first, but soon agreed that they can often understand English better than school Setswana.

The students also revealed their school to be less ethnically homogenous than one would infer from listening to Mr Tau address them all as 'Batswana' and 'Bafokeng'. In fact, there are Zulus and Sothos who attend Hillside. Although these students speak Setswana at school, they do so imperfectly. The children joke about a Sotho student who uses *aowa* instead of *nyayaa* for 'no'.

Aware of the rural/urban opposition that correlates with good and bad Setswana in their teachers' rhetoric, the students claim that when playing in the street they speak only [standard] Setswana. Some of the children then volunteer that kids from other schools speak English in the street, but that they themselves do not. Holiness then explored their attitudes about English and Afrikaans, and again the reflex answers differ somewhat from the responses that emerge after some prodding and reflection. As for Afrikaans, they say they don't like it, it's a difficult subject, and many are failing it (*'Nna ke* ***feila*** *Afrikaanse'* – 'Me I'm **failing** Afrikaans'). When asked why they fail it, they say it's difficult (*e thata*), and it's not their own language (*ga se puo ya rona.*) They say they like English a lot, though, and when reminded that English is also a foreign language to them, they say it's easy because they are used to it. They learn it on the street (*mo strateng*) and in the newspapers (*mo dipampiring.*) After a little more back and forth about Afrikaans, one boy who commutes to Hillside from his home in a township ventures that he actually likes Afrikaans. It emerges that Afrikaans conveys a certain amount of covert prestige, especially among male speakers. In a village primary school, though, this boy's declaration provokes an uncertain response. At first the rest of the children in the group laugh at his statement, but then another student, a girl, says she also likes speaking Afrikaans. Another girl joins in by joking about their classmates who confuse the Afrikaans '*suiker*' (sugar) with '*skêr*' (scissors). This diffuses the tension a bit, and the consensus emerges that Afrikaans isn't that bad.

The children are not at all hesitant to say that they like to speak English. As the interview progresses, in fact, the students become more and more explicit about the social superiority of English to Setswana, despite Holiness's mock protests. The students unanimously agree that they would prefer to go to English-medium schools in town, rather than their Setswana/English medium village school. Why? 'So we can speak English with them [kids in town]' (*Gore re re bue S'kgowa le bona*). When Holiness asks 'Why do you want to speak English; didn't you just say that you like Setswana?' (*Why le batl'o bua S'kgowa? S'tswana, akere l'a re S'tswana l'a se rata?*), they answer that they will need English in the future in order to work. A long debate ensues in which Holiness tries to make the students say that it's not necessary to speak English in order to work a white-collar job, that if your boss is white, s/he should learn Setswana, or if your boss is black, you can use your mother tongue. The students remain unswayed, though, and assert over and over that no matter what the racial or ethnic make-up of the workplace, managers and bosses will always require their subordinates to speak English. Three of the children say they want to be doctors, one wants to be a manager, and the other a policeman. Holiness then asks, 'So, do you mean that [standard] Setswana has no purpose, in the end?' (*So, o ra'a gore S'tswana ga se na mmereko ko pele?*). The boy from the township doesn't hesitate, 'Yes' (*Ee*).

This interview was deliberately arranged such that the students were not encouraged to perform their 'correct' Setswana speech and attitudes. Although they were at school, the interview took place away from their classroom, and Holiness consistently spoke Street Setswana in order to distance himself from the role of teacher. To the best of my understanding, my presence did not exert any pressure on the students to speak 'better' Setswana. In fact, their speech seemed very natural, that is, full of non-standard lexical and grammatical features common in Street Setswana. Significantly, it took the students some time to move away from the official attitudes towards Setswana, English and Afrikaans that clearly contradict their own feelings and experiences of these languages. These children, then, are a testament to their teachers' success in imparting the idea that Tswana identity is indivisible from speaking standard Setswana and maintaining allegiance to some kind of ideal rural culture. At the same time, the students emulate their teachers' offstage speech and urban orientation when it comes to thinking about their futures in practical terms.

This kind of divided consciousness about language and culture is what Malimabe (1990) seems to be proposing in her study. While she recognizes that codeswitching in English is prestigious, and that being urban is cool, she remains prescriptive about Setswana instruction. 'Until codeswitching is accepted as a universal bilingual strategy, it should be discouraged in class especially where it interferes with the purity of standard language' (Malimabe, 1990: 19). But as she herself admits, students and teachers do not think and act one way in school, and another way in real life. As the observations from Tlhabane and Phokeng attest, Tswana-speakers are constantly faced with the challenge of identifying with two very different sets of values about who they are.

Conclusion

Black South Africans living in the North West Province are caught in a double bind of identity construction. Tswana ethnic nationalism – with its roots in European intellectual traditions and with its South African heyday in the homeland period – remains a powerful ideology in the minds of residents of Tlhabane and Phokeng. The school curriculum reinforces the idea that standard Setswana language symbolizes ethnic purity, while social and linguistic deviations from that ideal, in the form of urban lifestyles or mixed speech forms, are discouraged. But Tswana-ness does not carry the social prestige, economic potential and cultural cachet that black South Africans aspire to today. In the new South Africa, where racial discrimination is no longer part of national policy, blacks desire better education, middle-class lifestyles and access to the national, urban culture. In acquiring, or even aspiring to, this class status, Tswana-ness is a liability, associated with rural-ness, a lack of urban style and street-smarts and a tendency to political accommodation of the previous status quo. It is in this atmosphere that a new generation of Tswana speakers is being educated in schools that purport to be bastions of linguistic purity and ethnic integrity. Ironically, though, the practitioners charged with inculcating a knowledge of, and appreciation for, 'pure' Setswana in their students are those with the least incentive to identify themselves with the symbols of Tswana ethnicity. As educated professionals oriented towards black urban culture, teachers are among those most likely to mark themselves as upwardly mobile South Africans by means of their clothes, cars, homes and language. In fact, this uneasy mix of rural ethnic identity and urban national identity may be better exemplified by Setswana teachers than by anyone else. Although they may intend to compartmentalize their identities into onstage and offstage linguistic personae, close observation reveals that they are almost always in the throes of this double bind. Schools, then, effectively reproduce not only these two ideologies – ethnic identity and black urban identity, but also the tension between them. As students' own behavior and attitudes demonstrate, they readily incorporate both lessons as they forge their own identities. Loyal to the standard form of the language that symbolizes their ethnic heritage, but simultaneously aware of the incentives and practicalities of speaking English, being popular and having an urban outlook, students emulate the ideological tensions embodied in their role models. This is as true today as it was when the data for this study were collected a decade ago. While there may be more conscious acknowledgement on the part of language professionals of the problems involved in promoting standard Setswana today, there are still very few voices advocating for an honest and critical assessment of the status quo. Meanwhile, as educators and policymakers start to grapple with the obvious contradictions between their classroom ideologies and their real-life aspirations, millions of average people have already voted with their mouths, as it were, embracing styles, trends, role-models and speech forms that mark them as modern black South Africans. As a result, classroom time that might be spent exploring the possibilities of a vibrant, contemporary speech form like Street Setswana is used instead to promote a linguistic symbol of ethnic authenticity that offers 21st century Batswana little in the way of symbolic or practical rewards.

Notes

1. South Africa's 11 official languages are isiZulu, isiXhosa, siSwati, isiNdebele, Setswana, Sesotho, Sepedi, Tshivenda, Xitsonga, English and Afrikaans.
2. Street Setswana is my translation of '*setswana sa mo strateng*' (literally, Setswana of the street), which is how many of my informants referred to their everyday variety of Setswana.
3. All names of persons and schools are pseudonyms.

4. This and subsequent quotations are excerpted from interviews I conducted in 1996–1997.
5. Ironically, both *terena* and *sitimela* are derived from English ('train' and 'steam').
6. The 2006 exam did not include such a section.
7. Mo-fokeng – person from Bafokeng community (singular).
   Ba-fokeng – people from Bafokeng community (plural).

References

Bernstein, B. (1971) *Class, Codes and Control*. London: Routledge.

Bourdieu, P. and Passeron, J.C. (1977) *Reproduction in Education, Society and Culture*. London: Sage.

Burgess, S.M. (2002) *SA Tribes: Who We Are, How We Live and What We Want From Life in the New South Africa*. Cape Town: David Phillip.

Chipkin, I. (2007) *Do South Africans Exist? Nationalism, Democracy and the Identity of 'the People'*. Johannesburg: Witwatersrand University Press.

Comaroff, J. and Comaroff, J.L. (1991) *Of Revelation and Revolution: Christianity, Colonialism and Consciousness in South Africa*. Chicago, IL: University of Chicago Press.

Comaroff, J.L. and Comaroff, J. (1996) *Of Revelation and Revolution: The Dialectics of Modernity on a South African Frontier*. Chicago, IL: University of Chicago Press.

Cook, S.E. (2006) Language policies and the erasure of multilingualism in South Africa. In M.L. Achino-Loeb (ed.) *Silence: The Currency of Power* (pp. 52–69). New York: Berghahn Books.

Gal, S. and Irvine, J. (1995) The boundaries of languages and disciplines: How ideologies construct difference. *Social Research* 62 (4), 967–1001.

Harries, P. (1988) The roots of ethnicity: Discourse and the politics of language construction in South-East Africa. *African Affairs: Journal of the Royal African Society* 86 (346), 25–52.

Herbert, R.K. (1992) *Language and Society in Africa: The Theory and Practice of Sociolinguistics*. Johannesburg: Wits University Press.

Malimabe, R. (1990) The influence of non-standard varieties on the standard Setswana of high school pupils. Unpublished MS thesis, Rand Afrikaans University.

Meeuwis, M. (1999) Flemish nationalism in the Belgian Congo vs. Zairean anti-imperialsim: Continuity and discontinuity in language ideological debates. In J. Blommaert (ed.) *Language Ideological Debates: Language, Power, and Social Process*. Berlin: Mouton de Gruyter.

Myers-Scotton, C. (1993) *Duelling Languages: Grammatical Stucture in Codeswitching*. Oxford: Clarendon.

Perry, T. (2004) *Language Rights, Ethnic Politics: A Critique of the Pan South African Language Board. PRAESA Occasional Papers No. 12*. Cape Town: UCT Press.

Slabbert, S. and Finlayson, R. (2000) 'I'm a cleva!': The linguistic makeup of identity in a South Africa urban environment. *International Journal of the Sociology of Language* 144, 119–135.

Thwala, N. (2007) Reflections on the mother language. *Mail & Guardian*, 17 March 2007. Online at mg.co.za. Accessed 16.9.07.

Woolard, K. (1985) Language variation and cultural hegemony: Toward an integration of sociolinguistic theory. *American Ethnologist* 12 (4), 738–748.

Part 2

Language and Education in the Diaspora

Introduction

JO ANNE KLEIFGEN

'Truth' is linked in a circular fashion with systems of power which produce and sustain it, and to effects of power which it induces and which extend it.
Foucault, 1980: 133

In his Introduction to Part 1, George Bond presents a sociological perspective on languages and education in the African context. Parallels are drawn here for the nine chapters comprising Part 2, where the authors explore the role of diasporic languages in Caribbean and US educational systems. Issues comparable to the politics of language in Africa are addressed in these essays. We see, for example, in the three chapters on Caribbean Creole languages and education, striking similarities between the metropole's imposition of language policies on African peoples and the policies imposed on Africans enslaved on plantations in the Caribbean beginning in the 17th century. Michel DeGraff's essay (Chapter 7) leads the way by exposing the underlying racism that led to describing the African slaves in Haiti as 'nonhumans' and characterizing their Creole as the 'inferior dialect' of the masters' language – a 'corrupted French.' Recognizing the role of the school in enacting policies that reflect power relations in the larger society, DeGraff outlines the failed language-education policy in Haiti, which, despite the government's recognition of Haitian Creole as an official language, still reflects for all practical purposes a French-only policy. He demonstrates the legitimacy of Haitian Creole as a 'normal' rather than an 'exceptional' language and therefore a valid and powerful medium of instruction for students in Haiti as well as for Haitian Creole speakers throughout the diaspora.

Likewise, in her essay (Chapter 8), Ellen Schnepel lays out the complex political and sociolinguistic situation in Guadeloupe from 17th century French colonization and enslavement of Africans on plantations to 19th century emancipation. During this period, language contact in plantation society resulted in the emergence of Creole as the primary language of the slaves. The colonial education system, established in the second half of the 19th century, became the site of social class divisions, where French was given primacy as the language of education for the elite, and where freed slaves were not considered worthy to be educated or even to speak French. By the time Guadeloupe became a French overseas department in the mid-20th century and compulsory education was established for all children, the French and Creole languages had become markers of race, class, culture and education. Schnepel describes the struggle for Guadeloupean cultural autonomy since that period and the eventual recognition of Creole as a regional language in the French Antilles; she also details efforts to introduce the language into the education system, and outlines for us some efforts to validate the teaching and study of Creole as a legitimate discipline in secondary schools.

Along with French rule, British colonial expansionism and the slave trade in the mid-17th century resulted in the establishment of sugar plantations and the transport of Africans to work these plantations throughout the Anglophone Caribbean. Shondel Nero's Chapter 9 presents the current situation of language and education in Jamaica, where English is the language left by its former colonial masters, and Jamaican Creole is the language that emerged through language contact among masters, slaves from Africa and indentured laborers from elsewhere. Slavery was eventually abolished in 1838, and, in time, the former slave population was 'permitted' to receive a British-style education. Like the situation faced by Creole speakers in the French Antilles, the education of Jamaican Creole speakers was (and continues to be) imbued with relations of power. The distribution of power is manifested through a kind of socio-economic apartheid in Jamaica's schools called 'streaming' (tracking), a practice by which school authorities assign students to separate classrooms based on some measurement of their academic 'ability' (see Oakes, 1985, for a study of tracking in US schools). Nero describes the effect of an educational policy in which sociolinguistic stratification and attendant school tracking of Jamaican Creole speakers in effect fashions two vastly different kinds of education, depending on students' language variety (Standard Jamaican English or Jamaican Creole) and socioeconomic status. As a result, education for speakers of the Jamaican 'standard' becomes a 'success story' while the inequities in educating Jamaican Creole speakers becomes a story of failure. This parallel narrative, as Nero calls it, also occurs with Jamaican immigrants to the US because of educators' differential perceptions of their Jamaican students.

The question posed in Part 1 by Rubagumya, Mtesigwa and Makoni and Trudell regarding whether education policy in Africa adequately accounts for the linguistic diversity of students, is similarly addressed in Part 2 with regard to US immigrant learners of English. Two contributions explore what happens when an English-only education policy collides with the diversity of languages spoken by African newcomers to American shores. Having been labeled 'English language learners' – signaling an exceptionalist ideology in the halls of government – students learning English more appropriately should be recognized as 'emergent bilinguals' (Garcia *et al.*, 2008), given their potential path to bilingualism and even to multilingualism. But, as Christa de Kleine (Chapter 10) and Doris Warriner (Chapter 11) each demonstrate in their detailed studies on the plight of immigrants trying to adjust to an educational system in the US, these efforts by the students and their families are thwarted in a system that adheres to a monolingual education policy within a growing multilingual society. Both authors' contributions to this volume fill an enormous gap in research on the particular language-in-education needs of the African immigrant communities they study. The research by de Kleine is concerned with students from Anglophone West Africa, who speak different varieties of Creole English. These students – speakers of Krio from Sierra Leone and speakers of Vernacular Liberian English from Liberia – face unique educational challenges. Because students and their teachers are unaware of subtle underlying grammatical differences between school-based English and Creole English, students do not often fare well in English writing. The students' home languages are stigmatized, even by the immigrants themselves, and considered 'broken English'. Through her analysis, de Kleine shows that this exceptionalist discourse can only be replaced with teachers' increased awareness of these subtle differences. Similarly, Warriner describes 'exceptionalist' ideologies and beliefs embedded in American language policies, and she shows the effect of these policies on the attitudes of Sudanese refugee women regarding their educative role as parents and their own developing English. Warriner's focus on these women's experiences highlights the fact that schools stigmatize parents of refugee students and consider them incapable partners in their children's education owing to their limited formal schooling and 'imperfect' English. In these two examples of the immigrant situation in the schools, their apparent internalization of the school's discourse, which devalues their home languages and their emergent English, resonates with Foucault's (1980) notion of power/knowledge relations where institutions and their members are 'complicit' in 'naturalizing' or shaping social practice.

This anti-diversity discourse in the US educational system is not reserved for immigrants alone. Four contributors provide sociohistorical information and contemporary research on questions of schooling and opportunity in the US for speakers of African American English (AAE), a vernacular variety that has long been subjected to exceptionalist beliefs.

John Baugh's essay (Chapter 12) returns us to matters of language, race and class relationships by scrutinizing unfair housing practices directed at African Americans. Baugh observes that discrimination and segregation, which existed from the inception of slavery, still exist today for Americans who are descendents of African slaves. This is borne out in his research on linguistic profiling, in which AAE speakers, who make telephone calls to inquire about the availability of rental properties, are denied equal access to housing simply for 'sounding Black' on the telephone.

In Chapter 13, Arthur Spears discusses further the question of the relationship between racial and linguistic prejudice. For Spears, the dearth of detailed description of many AAE features, a phenomenon he calls 'shallow grammar,' reinforces the exceptionalist belief that AAE is an impoverished language. In short, as DeGraff argues in the case of Creoles, Spears contends that a great deal of theory about AAE is based on limited data. Despite the fact that this variety has been studied extensively, Spears' recent work has documented a number of grammatical features, such as a fuller development of the AAE auxiliary system (described in this chapter), and associated communicative practices, which until now have not been given attention in the literature. Spears' contribution demonstrates that, in order for educators and those they educate to become more sociopolitically engaged language users, they first must have the opportunity to explore such intricacies of linguistic diversity and variation.

This brings us to Walt Wolfram's and Jon Yasin's chapters. Their writings take us into schools and classrooms, the arena where, as George Bond describes in his introduction to Part 1, one can 'see the effects of policies in the everyday lives of individuals'. As with the English-only policies, which negatively affect the education of emergent bilinguals, 'standard English' is a state-sanctioned variety that favors some groups over others. Wolfram (Chapter 14), like Baugh and Spears, is concerned about the linguistic effects of racism and the clashes in language ideologies in the US. Yet, rather than confronting these issues through ideological debate, Wolfram's approach is to change public perceptions about AAE and other vernacular varieties through judicious use of the media and with informed pedagogy. His chapter describes outreach programs in the state of North Carolina such as documentaries on dialect diversity for public television and linguistic material for units on language variation in the school curriculum. Through these programs, both the viewing public and students can examine diversity inductively and within a positive frame. Wolfram argues that misinformed language ideologies circulating in the wider society can be transformed through such language-awareness programs.

In Chapter 15, Jon Yasin also places emphasis on sociopolitical values accorded to language and communicative practices in his description of the development and spread of Hip Hop verbal art from New York City to elsewhere in the US and around the world. Hip Hop's emergence in New York coincided with the energy of the Civil Rights and Black Power movements, and the socially-conscious artist pioneers steered many young people away from gang violence and toward creative performance 'battles', skill-building and a new discourse of resistance and identity. With roots in African verbal art, the discourse of Hip Hop has circulated throughout the US, the Caribbean and the African continent. It is a discourse used by many, especially the youth in these regions, to contest social injustices. Yasin describes how Hip Hop, with its rich historical and cultural basis and global spread, can be brought into the classroom as a motivating resource for its followers. He shows how Hip Hop is a vehicle students can use for the development of their academic language and literacy, which they can add to their already imaginative verbal repertoire.

Foucault (1980) argues that knowledge expressed discursively in institutional settings serves to regulate conduct. Yet subalterns have voices and agency, as Valentin Vološinov (1973) has argued, to develop alternative discourses at the level of social interaction. Projects that open up reflexive understanding of linguistic diversity (be it to contest a government's monolingual language-education policies, to expose practices of linguistic profiling, to challenge the monolithic standardized discourses regimented by institutions or to raise awareness of language and dialect variation in the schools and the public arena) can contribute to a new kind of discourse, 'a new politics of truth' (Foucault, 1980: 133).

References

Foucault, M. (1980) *Power/Knowledge: Selected Interviews and Other Writings 1972–1977* (C. Gordon, ed.). New York: Pantheon.

García, O., Kleifgen, J. and Falchi, L. (2008) *From English Language Learners to Emergent Bilinguals: Research Review Series Monograph, Campaign for Educational Equity.* New York, NY: Teachers College, Columbia University.

Oakes, J. (1985) *Keeping Track: How Schools Structure Inequality.* New Haven, CT: Yale University Press.

Vološinov, V.N. (1973) *Marxism and the Philosophy of Language.* Cambridge, MA: Harvard University Press (original work published 1929).

Chapter 7

Creole Exceptionalism and the (Mis)Education of the Creole Speaker

MICHEL DEGRAFF

A recent article in the *Miami Herald* (Bailey, 2006) described the efforts of a local elementary school to incorporate Haitian Creole as a language of instruction alongside English for Creole-speaking Haitian students. The article argued that the early use of Creole in the classroom is critical to the education of Creole-speaking children. This article caused a stir among readers, and subsequent letters to the article's author, Peter Bailey, contained comments such as:

- '[T]hat lousy, disgusting Creole ... is not even a legitimate language. It's just badly bastardized French.'
- 'Creole is not even a language. It is slave lingo.'
- 'Why on earth are we spending public funds to teach kids in school the language of peasants?'
- 'The absence in Creole of complex concepts and fine shadings of meaning should suggest that it is fine if Haitian parents want to speak it at home, but it should not be "taught" in schools any more than "Spanglish" or "Ebonics" should be.'

These comments convey more than negative attitudes about a language; the comments are riddled with demeaning remarks related to race and class. Faced with such virulent anti-Creole attitudes, how should linguists and educators respond? Although one might assume that linguists are in a good position to help change these false beliefs about Creole languages and their speakers, a change in attitude towards Creoles must start in linguistics itself, which, historically, has played a major role in producing and maintaining these beliefs.

In this chapter, I examine ways in which what I call 'Creole Exceptionalism' beliefs, going back to the 19th century, have been manufactured and transmitted over time by linguists. In this context, I show how Creole Exceptionalism has historically been a means of maintaining power. Then I survey theoretical and empirical arguments that show that these beliefs are, indeed, false, and that Creoles are on a par with other languages. Finally, I argue that the lack of understanding about the legitimacy of Creole languages as valued resources in the classroom and elsewhere comes at a great social cost for the education of Creole speakers. In the conclusion, I propose a few directions for change.

Some Definitions and Facts

The term *Creole languages* typically, though not exclusively, refers to the speech varieties that were created in many of the emerging communities in and around the colonial forts and plantations of Africa and the 'New World' from the 15th to 19th centuries. In the New World, these Creole communities emerged relatively abruptly as the result of Europe's colonization of the Caribbean, subsequent to Columbus's expeditions. Caribbean Creole languages thus developed among Europeans and Africans. They are linguistic side effects of a peculiar type of 'globalization', so to speak – the slave trade and other mercantilist practices by the Europeans (British, French, Portuguese, Dutch and Spanish) in Africa and the Americas. In modern linguistics, the term is often extended to include any new language variety that is considered to have emerged relatively abruptly from contact between groups of speakers of distinct languages. Under this extended definition, there are some 20 million speakers of Creole languages worldwide, including the Greater Caribbean, the USA. (e.g. Louisiana Creole, Gullah in the Sea Islands of Georgia and South Carolina, Hawaiian Creole), Africa, the Indian Ocean and the Pacific. Strikingly, most of these languages are located around the Equator. This geographical significance is not accidental; the term arose as a result of Europe's imperialist expansion into tropical lands. But, can a linguistic-structural concept be validly assigned a geographical correlate, when language contact occurs everywhere? Could there be typological features that are exclusively reserved for languages that grew out of colonization?

In this chapter, I draw on data from Haitian Creole, my native language. It is one of the most extensively studied Creole languages, and it is the Creole language with the largest community of speakers. Haitian Creole emerged during the second half of the 17th century out of contact between the regional and colloquial varieties of French, as spoken by the European colonists, and the various African languages of the Niger-Congo spoken by the Africans that were enslaved and then brought across the Atlantic to work on Caribbean colonial plantations and the related colonial infrastructure. Haitian Creole is Haiti's national language and, since 1987, a constitutionally-recognized official language, alongside French. However, most official documents in Haiti are still written exclusively in French to the detriment of monolingual Creolophones, even though French is spoken today by only about one-fifth of the population. These French-only policies effectively create a situation of 'linguistic apartheid', which mirrors Haiti's long-standing social apartheid (P. Dejean, 1989, 1993; see also Trouillot, 1990). In Haiti, the use of French by a small but powerful élite is still used to keep monolingual Creole speakers – the vast numerical but disenfranchised majority – away from the halls of power.

For many linguists, Creole languages are an exceptional window on the difficult-to-observe processes of language creation and evolution. Linguists' goals with regard to Creoles might seem lofty – to use these allegedly rapidly-emergent languages to understand how the human mind works. Yet, these exceptionalist beliefs (about Creoles' unique scientific potential) have implications that converge with the attitudes expressed in the aforementioned letters to the *Miami Herald*.

A variety of linguistic dogmas, going back to the 19th century, have maintained that Creoles constitute a special class of languages because of their grammatical structures (or lack thereof) or the ways in which these structures have emerged in the course of history. In one of the earlier studies of Creole languages, it was claimed that:

> [Creole grammar] is, therefore, a spontaneous product of the human mind, freed from any kind of intellectual culture. ... But when one studies its structure, one is so very surprised, very charmed by its rigor and simplicity that one wonders if the creative genius of the most knowledgeable linguists would have been able to give birth to anything that so completely reaches its goal, that imposes so little strain on memory and that calls for so little effort from those with limited intelligence. (Saint-Quentin, 1872/1989: 40f; my translation)

In a related vein, the current orthodoxy considers Creoles as quintessentially exotic linguistic neonates, as opposed to 'normal' languages: only the latter are 'old' languages (i.e. languages with ancient pedigrees), whereas Creoles are often considered the world's youngest languages that fall outside the family tree of 'normal' languages. They do not appear in any of the family trees of languages in the classic linguistics texts (e.g. Bendor-Samuel & Hartell, 1989; Crystal, 1987; Fromkin & Rodman, 1993). In somewhat 'Neo'-Darwinian fashion, these exceptionalist claims often correlate Creoles' alleged youth with extraordinarily reduced ('primitive') structures that limit their expressiveness and render them unusable for 'serious' purposes in the modern world. This brand of Creole Exceptionalism is an instance of linguistic 'utopia'... or 'anti-utopia' perhaps, depending on, for example, whether or not the observer is a (monolingual) Creole speaker or an individual who stands to benefit from a world order where Creole languages are considered and treated as deficient.

A Sampling of Creole-genesis Theories: Contesting Three Canonical Tropes

Here I lay out three different kinds of theory that claim Creole languages to be special, and I show why they are flawed. The first and most widespread view about Creole languages, especially among the general public (such as the readers who sent complaints to the *Miami Herald* about the use of Creole to teach school children), is that they are degenerate – 'broken' – varieties of European languages. For example, Haitian Creole and Jamaican Creole (aka Patwa) are often considered 'broken French' and 'broken English' respectively. This degeneracy view was the received wisdom in the comparative-historical linguistics of the 17th through 19th centuries, as summarized in scientific encyclopedia entries such as Larousse (1869: 490), where Creole is defined as 'corrupted French'. Similar views are rehearsed in scholarly works throughout the 19th and 20th centuries. Meillet, for example, claims that

> 'Creole' modes of speaking – Spanish Creole or French Creole – ... constitute varieties of Spanish or French that are deprived of almost all their grammar, weakened in their pronunciation, reduced to a small lexicon. (Meillet, 1924/1951: 68)

This degenerate descendant view was made most (in)famous and most explicit by Bloomfield, who stated:

> Speakers of a lower language may make so little progress in learning the dominant speech, that the masters, in communicating with them resort to 'baby-talk'. This 'baby talk' is the masters' imitation of the subjects' incorrect speech. ... When the jargon [among Negro slaves in many parts of America] has become the only language of the subject group, it is a creolized language. The creolized language has the status of an inferior dialect of the masters' speech. It is subject to constant leveling-out and improvement in the direction of the latter. (Bloomfield, 1933: 472–474)

Even in the latter half of the 20th century, certain linguists still claim that structural and linguistic factors such as incapacitating 'morphological simplicity' and a 'vocabulary [that] is extremely poor' are among the 'greatest obstacles to the blossoming of Creoles' (Valdman, 1978: 345; see also Seuren, 1998; Seuren & Wekker, 1986).[1]

A second exceptionalist view states that Creoles are hybrid languages: African grammars clothed in European-sounding words. The earliest proponent of such a view is perhaps Lucien Adam in 1883 for whom Cayenne Creole grammar, for example, 'is nothing but the general grammar of the languages of Guinée [in West Africa].' For Adam (1883: 4–5), 'African grammatical habits prevented them from adopting French grammar': such 'African grammatical habits' were viewed as too 'primitive' and 'children-like' in comparison with those of speakers of languages such as Sanskrit, Latin and French. In a related vein, the Haitian linguist Suzanne Sylvain states that Haitian Creole is 'French vocabulary in the mold of African syntax or ... an Ewe dialect with French lexicon' (Sylvain, 1936: 178). Sylvain, like Adam in 1883, readily assumes 'early crystallization of the mental powers of the Black race' as key factor in the formation of Haitian Creole (Sylvain 1936: 36f). A contemporary descendent of Adam's hybridization theory, and one that is fortunately removed from both Adam's and Sylvain's problematic race-theoretical stipulations, is Lefebvre's (1998) Relexification Hypothesis. According to the latter, Creole creators as adult language learners adopt, and adapt, words – or just phonetic strings – from the target European language (called the *lexifier* or *superstrate* language) and overlay these European-derived phonetic strings on the syntax and semantics of their native African languages (called the *substrate* languages), with the grammar of the latter transferred virtually intact into the newly-created Creole languages. This view appears in the popular press, as well. It was recently claimed in the *Times Literary Supplement* that:

> [A] creole [is] an African language, or languages, upon whose syntax the vocabulary of another language is laid. The clearest example from the New World is [Haitian Creole], a creole which appears to be composed of French vocabulary overlaid on the grammar of the African language Ewe. (Greppin, 2002)

Let us examine some basic comparative data from both lexicon and morphology (DeGraff, 2001a; Fattier, 1998) to judge whether there is really a bottleneck for lexical and morphological development in the history of Creoles – a bottleneck that would make Creoles, as the above tropes suggest, degenerate varieties or special hybrids. With respect to hybridity, the data that follow demonstrate that English, in its lexicon and morphology, has 'out-creoled' Haitian Creole. We begin with Modern English – a non-Creole language and one that is usually taken to descend from its Germanic ancestor by 'normal' processes of language change, which make English a so-called 'genetic' language in the terminology of historical linguists. We show here that English, at the very least in its lexicon and morphology, is substantially much more 'mixed' than Haitian Creole – a so-called 'non-genetic' language (i.e. one that allegedly was not created by 'normal' processes of language change). In some estimates, the lexicon of English is 65% non-Germanic, much of it due to the Norman French invasion in 1066 and its socio-historical correlates. The etymology of a sampling from the English lexicon and morphology follows:

French-based Lexicon:

(1) battle (*bataille*), ally (*allié*), alliance (*alliance*), admiral (*amiral*), march (*marche*), enemy (*ennemi*), peace (*paix*) ... ;

(2) judge (*juge*), jury (*jury*), justice (*justice*), court (*court*), defendant (*défendant*), crime (*crime*), petty (*petit*), marriage (*mariage*) ... ;

(3) clergy (*clergé*), altar (*autel*), miracle (*miracle*), pray (*prier*), sermon (*sermon*), virgin (*vierge*), saint (*saint*), friar (*frère*) ... ;

(4) cuisine (*cuisine*), sauce (*sauce*), boil (*bouillir*), filet (*filet*), soup (soup), pastry (*patisserie*), fry (*frire*), roast (*rôtir*) ... ;

French-based morphology:

(5) -or (*-eur* as in *dictateur*), -tion (as in *célebration*), -ment (as in *déguisement*);

(6) -ee (as in *payée*), -able (as in *agréable*), -age (as in *espionnage*) ... ;

English also contains borrowings from Latin, among many additional languages:

Latin-based Lexicon:

(7) kitchen (*coquina*), pan (*panna*), cup (*cuppa*), dish (*discas*), parsley (*petrosileum*) ... ;

(8) priest (*presbyter*), bishop (*episcopus*), nun (*nonna*), angel (*angelus*) ... ;

Latin-based morphology:

(9) ex- (*ex* as in *expatriare*), pre- (*prœ* as in *prœ cursor*), pro- (*pro* as in *proclamare*), dis- (*dis* as in *disjunctio*), re-, (*re* as in *recreare*), inter- (*inter* as in *intermuralis*}....

(For other and easily accessible examples of this sort, see Vajda, n.d.)

In contrast with English, the etymology of most of the Haitian Creole lexicon (over 90%) is unmistakably French (Fattier, 1998). The same observation applies to morphology: virtually all Haitian Creole affixes have cognates in French affixes, whereas English has many affixes and many words, of non-Germanic origins. So is English more of a 'Creole' than Haitian Creole?

A third view is that Creoles are the results of a catastrophic and abnormal break in transmission. This third view, like the first two, has antecedents in 19th-century Creole studies – recall Saint-Quentin's (1872/1989: 40f) above-quoted statement that Creole grammar is a 'spontaneous product of the human mind, freed from any kind of intellectual culture.' This third view, which is perhaps the most spectacular instance of Creole Exceptionalism, has received the most press, not only among linguists, but also among anthropologists, psychologists and evolution theorists. According to this hypothesis, the 'normal' transmission of language is broken in the Pidgin-to-Creole life cycle. Basic introductory linguistics texts such as O'Grady *et al.* promote this view:

> Contact situations where speakers have restricted access to each other's language can sometimes lead to the formation of a pidgin – a rudimentary language with minimal grammatical rules and a small lexicon. By definition, a pidgin has no native speakers and many pidgins are predominantly used as a lingua franca. (O'Grady *et al.*, 2001: 578)

The textbook goes on to assert 'If their children [i.e. children of pidgin speakers] then learn the pidgin as a first language and it is adopted as the native language of the new community, it becomes a Creole and is no longer considered a pidgin. When a Pidgin becomes a creole, its inventory of lexical items and grammatical rules expands dramatically, usually in only one or two generations' (2001: 579f).

It is thus that Creoles are set apart from non-Creoles. Creoles are considered to have emerged 'non-genetically' (i.e. with a Pidgin ancestor) through some abnormal and catastrophic 'break in transmission' whereas non-Creoles are considered to have evolved gradually and 'genetically' via the 'normal transmission' of a full-fledged (i.e. non-Pidgin) language. Creolists often postulate that one prominent exceptional/abnormal process in the history of a Creole is the elimination of (virtually) all morphology from the output of pidginization (see Bickerton, 1984; Hjelmslev, 1938; Jespersen, 1922; McWhorter, 1998; Seuren, 1998; Seuren & Wekker, 1986). Pidgins, in other words, are structurally impoverished languages without any morphology, so the subsequent Creoles had to create their morphological apparatus *ab ovo*.

In its most extreme form, this spontaneous-and-catastrophic-creation view turns Creoles into observable replicas of the earliest human languages in the evolutionary history of *Homo sapiens*. Bickerton has now argued that the catastrophic birth of Creoles from Pidgins recapitulates the first (i.e. most primitive) evolutionary stages of language evolution. The Pidgin-to-Creole cycle would thus approximate the transition, at the prehistoric dawn of our humanity, from *Homo erectus*' pre-human protolanguage to *Homo sapiens*' first human language. Creole speakers now become linguistic 'Adams and

Eves' and the colonial Caribbean an edenic utopia. Bickerton's hypothesis is popularized in the print media such as in *Newsweek*: 'Creole languages are the missing linguistic fossils ... the equivalent of the Galapagos to Darwin' (Begley, 1982) and in the *New York Times* quoting McWhorter: 'I suspect that [Creoles] most approximate some of the early languages. Creoles begin as Pidgin languages .... Creoles ... are the only languages which have started again' (Dreifus, 2001). In effect, Creole languages now become living linguistic fossils, one generation removed from the structureless Pidgin speech that allegedly resembles the protolanguage of our evolutionary ancestors. This is the most spectacular exceptionist scenario whereby Creoles are assigned a *sui generis* typological class.

This third view of Creole genesis can be proven flawed with a variety of linguistic data, including lexical, morphological and syntactic evidence. First, let us contrast the empirical claims about 'break in transmission' with the following samples of Haitian Creole word-formation through affixation, compounding, reduplication and apocope (from DeGraff, 2001a):

Prefixation:

(1) *de-* (cf. Fr *de-*), as in *derespekte* 'to disrespect, to insult' (cf. *respekte* 'to respect'), *dekreta* 'to cut off the crest' (cf. *krèt* n. 'crest') and *debaba* 'to mow down' (cf. *baba* adj. 'mute'; variant of *bèbè*);

(2) *en-* (cf. Fr *in-*), as in *enkoutab* adj. 'foolhardy' (cf. *koute* 'to listen');

(3) *ti-* (cf. Fr *petit*), as in *Ti-Yèyèt*, *Ti-Sonson* and *ti-chouchou*.

Suffixation:

(4) *-te* (cf. Fr *-té*), as in *bèlte* 'beauty' (cf. *bèl* 'beautiful'), *frekanste* 'insolence' (cf. *frekan* 'insolent'), *lèdte* 'ugliness' (cf. *lèd* 'ugly'), *safte* 'greed' (cf. *saf* 'greedy');

(5) *-ay* (variant: *-aj*) (cf. Fr *-age*), as in *plasay* (variant: *plasaj*) n. 'concubinage' (cf. *plase* 'to live in concubinage');

(6) *-è* (cf. Fr. *eur*), as in *djolé* n. 'boaster' (cf. *djòl* n. 'mouth');

(7) *-èt* (cf. Fr *-ette*), as in *Boukinèt* (cf. *Bouki*) and *bòlèt* n. 'lottery' and *boul* (*-bòlèt*) 'lottery number, ball';

(8) *-syon* (cf. Fr *-tion*), as in *admirasyon* (cf. *admire* 'to admire') and *tribilasyon* 'tribulation';

(9) verbal marker *-e(n)* (cf. Fr *-er*), as in *gade* 'to look', *admire* 'to admire', *mennen* 'to bring', *mache* 'to walk' (cf. *mach* n. 'march, step/stairs'), *grennen* 'to shell out' (cf. *grenn* n. 'grain');

(10) nominalizer *-man* (cf. Fr *-ment*), as in *kozman* n. 'talk, gossip' (cf. *koze* 'to talk');

(11) adverbalizer *-man* (cf. Fr *-merit*), as in *kòrèkteman* adv. (cf. *kòrèk* adj. 'correct');

(12) suffixation plus gender inflection with *-en/-èn* (cf. Fr *-en/-enne*), as in the pair *Dominiken/Dominikèn* n. (cf. *Dominikani* n. 'Dominican Republic').

Other:

(13) compounding, as in *kòk-batay* 'fighting cock';

(14) reduplication, as in *Ti-Yèyèt, Ti-Sonson, ti-chouchou* 'little darling' (affectionate) and *mache-mache* 'to walk a lot' (intensifying);

(15) apocope, as in *gen*, which is the short form of *genyen*.

It is instructive to note that, in (1), *-te* as in *bèlte* 'beauty' from *bèl* 'beautiful' is an abstraction marker par excellence: it derives nouns of quality from adjectives that describe qualities. This contradicts the oft-repeated claims by linguists such as Whinnom (1971: 109), who states that 'what cannot be generated very successfully by the combination of concrete words is abstract terms, in which it is notorious that pidgins and creoles are deficient', thus 'there may be some reason to suspect that the creole-speaker is handicapped by his language'.

The data presented here show that there was no etymological 'break in transmission' in the history of Haitian Creole. The overwhelming majority of Haitian Creole morphemes (whether free or bound) have French cognates. If we consider the inventory of Haitian Creole affixes, alongside the fact that most of these affixes have origins in French, then it is most unlikely that these affixes would have been created from the linguistic scratch of an affixless pidgin. Nor is there evidence for relexification in the history of the Haitian Creole lexicon and morphology – at least, not for *massive* relexification of the sort that is claimed in Lefebvre (1998).

Further, the basic comparative morphosyntactic data (from DeGraff, 2000, 2005a) disconfirm the orthodox dichotomy between Creole languages and non-Creole languages. In comparing the formation of Haitian Creole structures from French with the formation of Modern English structures from earlier varieties of English, it is clear that Haitian Creole cannot be taken to have evolved via some exceptional processes that would make creolization radically different from 'normal' processes of language change.

Let's start our comparison by focusing on the distribution of the nominal complements of verbs in Haitian Creole. These objects of the verb uniformly *follow* the verb that take them as complements, giving rise to the uniform word-order pattern *subject...verb...object* (SVO) as in examples (16) and (17):

(16) *Bouki* *konnen* *Boukinèt.*
Bouki know Boukinèt
'Bouki knows Boukinet.'

(17) *Bouki* *konnen* *li.*
Bouki know 3rd sg
'Bouki knows him/her/it.'

Note that pre-verbal pronouns are ungrammatical in Haitian Creole:

(18) **Bouki*[2] *li* *konnen.*

In contrast, standard French has post-verbal noun-phrase objects as in (19) but it also exhibits pre-verbal pronominal objects as in (20):

(19) *Bouqui* *connaît* *Bouquinette.*
Bouqui know Bouquinette
'Bouqui knows Bouquinette.'

(20) *Bouqui* *la* *connaît.*
Bouqui *3rd sg-f* *know*
'Bouqui knows her.'

Post-verbal pronouns are ungrammatical in standard French declarative clauses:

(21) **Bouqui connait* *la.*

The next set of data compares the placement of verb vis-à-vis certain adverbs and the negation marker *pa(s)* in the two languages. Here we can see that in Haitian Creole these adverbs and the negation marker *pa* consistently precede the verb:

(22) *Bouki* *deja* *konnen* *Boukinèt.*
Bouki already know Boukinèt
'Bouki already knows Boukinet.'

(23) *Bouki* *pa* *konnen* *Boukinèt.*
Bouki NEG know Boukinèt
'Bouki doesn't know Boukinèt.'

Note that these adverbs and the negation marker cannot intervene between the verb and its object:

(24) **Bouki* *konnen* *deja Boukinèt.*

(25) **Bouki* *konnen* *pa* *Boukinèt.*

In contrast, verb placement in French follows a different pattern: it is actually the mirror image of the Haitian pattern. In French, the finite verb *precedes* the corresponding adverbs and the negation marker *pas*:

(26) *Bouqui* *connaît* *déja* *Bouquinette.*
Bouqui know already Bouquinette
'Bouqui already knows Bouquinette.'

(27) Bouqui (ne) connaît *pas* *Bouquinette.*
Bouqui NEG know NEG Bouquinette
'Bouqui doesn't know Bouquinette.'

In French, unlike in Haitian Creole, these adverbs and the negation marker *pas* cannot precede the finite verb:

(28) **Bouqui* *déjà* *connaît* *Bouquznette.*

(29) **Bouqui (ne) pas* *connaît* *Bouquznette.*

Finally, unlike French, there are no suffixes on Haitian Creole verbs for marking features such as concord and tense. In Haitian Creole, the tense-mood-aspect markers (e.g. *te* which marks anterior, *ap* which marks future or progressive depending on the verb, and *a(va)* which marks irrealis[3] mood) are independent words that precede the verb they modify. (Also compare with English tense-mood-aspect free morphemes such as *will* and *would*, as in *she will walk* and *she would walk*, and contrast with English agreement and tense suffixes such as *-s* and *-ed*, as in *she walks* and *she walked*):

(30) { *Mwen* I *Ou* I *Li* I *Nou* I *Yo*} *konnen Boukinèt.*
lsg I 2sg I 3sg I lpl/2pl I 3pl know Boukinèt
'{I I You I He/She I We I They } know(s) Boukinèt..'

(31) *Boukinèt te* *renmen* *Bouki.*
Boukinèt ANT renmen Bouki
'Boukinèt loved Bouki.

(32) *Boukinèt ap* *renmen* *Bouki.*
Boukinèt FUT love Bouki
'Boukinèt will love Bouki.'

(33) *Boukinèt a* *renmen* *Bouki* *si ...*
Boukinèt IRR love Bouki if ...
'Boukinèt would love Bouki if ...'

Compare these structures with concord and tense suffixes in (Standard) French, which shows the following patterns:

(34) *J'aime* '1sg love + 1sg' *Nous aimons* '1pl love + lp'
Tu aimes '2sg love + 2sg' *Vous aimez* '2pl love + 2p'
Il/Elle aime '3sg + m/f love + 3sg' *Ils/Elles aiment* '3pl+m/f love +3p'

(35) *Bouquinette aim-ait Bouqui*
Bouquinette loved Bouqui

(36) *Bouquinette aim-era Bouqui*
Bouquinette will love Bouqui

(37) *Bouquinette aim-erait Bouqui si ...*
Bouquinette would love Bouqui if

The Haitian Creole and French structural contrasts illustrated above are summarized in Table 7.1.

Now compare the above French/Creole differences with similar differences in the history of English – a 'genetic' language.

Modern English is like Haitian Creole in having its negation marker and certain adverbs occur regularly in the position that *precedes* the verb and in not allowing these adverbs and the negation marker to occur between the verb and its object. Yet, Modern English, like Haitian Creole, has an ancestor where these adverbs and the negation marker regularly occurred to the *right* of the finite verb, thus intervening between the verb and its object, if any. This is exemplified in line 1744 from Chaucer's *Merchant's Tale*, 'Quene Ester looked never with switch an eye' (Kroch, 1989). Similar examples abound where, in its earlier historical stages, English allowed certain adverbs and the negation marker to *follow* the finite verb – a verb-placement pattern that is *not* allowed in Modern English (nor in Haitian Creole). Thus there isn't anything particularly 'Creole' about the fact that Haitian Creole has the adverb-verb and *pa*-verb word-order patterns while its French ancestor has the verb-adverb and verb-*pas* word-order patterns, as illustrated above. Like Haitian Creole, Modern English, a non-Creole language, has the adverb-verb and negation-verb word-order patterns

Table 7.1 Haitian Creole and French structural contrasts

	Haitian Creole	***French***
verb object pronoun	OK	NOT OK
object pronoun verb	NOT OK	OK
negation marker /adverb finite verb object	OK	NOT OK
finite verb negation marker/adverb object	NOT OK	OK
tense-mood-aspect marker verbal suffixes	NOT OK	OK

with its Middle English ancestor exhibiting the verb-adverb and verb-negation word-order patterns.

Besides, Middle English exhibited multiple inflectional affixes on its verbs with forms such as *showedest* with two consecutive suffixes (*-ed* for tense and *-est* for 2nd-singular concord) somewhat like Modern French *nous aimions* 'we loved' with *-i* a tense suffix and *-ons* a 1st plural concord suffix. Thus, in the history of English, as in the history of Haitian Creole, there has been a reduction in the inventory of suffixes that can attach to the verb to indicate tense-mood-aspect or subject-verb concord.

Similar parallels obtain between the history of Haitian Creole and the history of English in the domain of object placement. Old English, for example had pre-verbal object pronouns like Modern French has today, yet in Modern English, objects are now uniformly post-verbal as in Haitian Creole (see DeGraff, 2005a for additional details).

Given the above comparative data, the patterns of verb placement, object placement and verbal inflectional affixes in the formation of Haitian Creole fall within developmental scenarios that are instantiated in the history of non-Creole languages. In other words, these patterns in Haitian Creole history do not instantiate any sort of 'discontinuity' that would set 'creolization' apart from other instances of language development/change over time. There is no rigorous algorithm that can reliably measure the structural discontinuity that is to serve as a litmus test for distinguishing the history of Creoles from the history of non-Creoles. The above data thus dismantle the exceptionalist claim that the kind of discontinuity manifested in Creole genesis is of a significantly distinct nature in comparison to the kind of discontinuities manifested in the history of so-called 'normal' or 'genetic' languages. The above-mentioned discontinuities in the history of English seem as spectacular as, or perhaps even more spectacular than, those in the history of Haitian Creole.

Toward Post-Colonial Creolistics: Taking a Cartesian-Uniformitarian Approach

One fundamental characteristic of the study of Creole languages (aka creolistics) is that its own genesis, along with the genesis of its objects of study, is deeply steeped in the history of White hegemony in the New World (e.g. colonization and enslavement) and its ensuing dualisms vis-à-vis the (non)humanity of those who were deemed 'slaves by nature'. The genesis of creolistics may thus offer a clear case study of the linguistics-ideology interface – namely, how sociohistorically-rooted ideological and geopolitical concerns promote, and are reinforced by, certain types of linguistic (mis)analyses. In the history of creolistics as in the history of other human sciences, power did produce the sort of 'reality' – the 'régime of truth' – that benefited those in power. Creolistics, like the sociology reflexively studied by Bourdieu and Wacquant (1992: 51), has the 'scientific authority ... [and] the power to produce, to impose and to inculcate the legitimate representation of the social world', including the past, present and future (socio)linguistic world of Creole speakers. In turn, analyzing the power-knowledge cycles that make up the creolistics-ideology interface will, I hope, contribute to eliminating the recurrent myths that conspire against both a deeper understanding of Creole languages and the welfare of Creole speakers. Such an analysis is unavoidably both political and linguistic. To quote Bourdieu again:

> By uncovering the social mechanisms which ensure the maintenance of the established order and whose properly symbolic efficacy rests on the misrecognition of their logic and effects, social science necessarily takes sides in political struggles. (Bourdieu & Wacquant, 1992: 51)

The three tropes in the discourse of Creole Exceptionalism that I have laid out in this chapter can be related historically to the ideological climate of the colonial and neocolonial eras as determined by the economic, geopolitical and socio-psychological interests of the ruling and slave-holding classes and of their post-colonial and post-emancipation ideological descendants. Simultaneously, the intellectual roots of Creole Exceptionalism can be traced back textually to versions of pre- and neo-Humboldtian essentialism (e.g. Rousseau and followers; cf. Corcoran, 2001) and to pre- and post-Schleicherian-Darwinian views on both human evolution and language evolution (DeGraff, 2001a, 2001b, 2003, 2004).

Yet, our best available evidence, alongside robust results from linguistic theory and psycholinguistics, supports an approach in which Creole grammars do not form a typological class that is aprioristically and fundamentally distinguishable from that of non-Creole grammars. Thus Creole Exceptionalism is a set of socio-historically rooted dogmas with foundations in (neo-)colonial power relations, and not a scientific conclusion based on robust evidence. It could be argued that the myths of Creole Exceptionalism are still active because they implicitly serve symbolisms of power and mechanisms of inclusion and exclusion, all of which relate to identity formation, to socioeconomic hierarchies, and to modern *missions civilisatrices*.

In recent work, the joint investigation of language contact, language change and language acquisition suggests that there is not, and could not be, any deep theoretical divide between the outcome of language change and that of Creole formation (see, e.g. DeGraff, 2005a, 2005b; Mufwene,

2001; Muysken, 1988; Posner, 1985): 'The very notion of a "Creole" language from the linguistic point of view tends to disappear if one looks closely; what we have is just a language' (Muysken, 1988: 300). One basic insight in these and related works is that language contact, in some form or another, and language creation, whether seemingly gradual or seemingly abrupt, happens always and everywhere.

> [C]reoles are no more and no less than the result of extraordinary external factors coupled with ordinary internal factors...[Within mentalistic approaches to language creation and language change,] the notion of 'creolization' as a unitary and distinct linguistic phenomenon evaporates. (DeGraff, 1999: 477)

The theoretical antidote to Creole Exceptionalism beliefs can be found in what I have dubbed 'Cartesian-Uniformitarian' approaches to Creole languages. By 'Cartesian-Uniformitarian', I mean linguistic approaches that can be, in principle, extrapolated from Descartes's assumption about the species-specificity and the basic uniformity of the human mind: 'Reason ... is by nature equal in all men' (Descartes, 1637/1962: 1; cf. Chomsky, 1966). In Creole studies, such rationalist approaches were already adumbrated by Greenfield's (1830: 51f.) dictum, 'The human mind is the same in every clime; and accordingly we find nearly the same process adopted in the formation of language in every country'. In a similar vein, Sapir (1933: 155) considers all speakers to be endowed with the full-fledged knowledge of their native language; this knowledge is 'an essentially perfect means of expression and communication among every known people'. In other words, every language is 'normal,' and so are the processes whereby it is created in the minds of its native speakers. Similar prospects are found, most explicitly, in the methodology of generativists whose objects of study are Cartesian properties of mind. Cartesian-Uniformitarian linguistics from, for example, Greenfield to Chomsky is thus intrinsically egalitarian and provides a solid rational basis for undermining the traditional dualist dogmas in Creole studies (for case studies with Haitian Creole as 'prototypical' test case, see DeGraff, 2000, 2001a, 2001b, 2002, 2005a, 2005b).

Contesting Creole Exceptionalism in the (Mis)Education of Creole Speakers

Neo-colonial and exceptionalist creolistics eventually infringes on the human rights of Creole speakers. The beliefs of Creole Exceptionalism that are critiqued in this chapter and elsewhere have long served to justify the widespread exclusion of Creole speakers from a number of spheres where socioeconomic power is created, reproduced and exercised.

The most powerful tool of domination, both actual and symbolic, is the school system, which in much of the Caribbean still devalues Creole languages – even in Haiti, where all Haitians speak Haitian Creole and the vast majority speak only Haitian Creole, and where Haitian Creole is an official language on a par with French. The non-use or limited use of Haitian Creole in Haitian schools violates the pedagogically sound principle that 'education is best carried on through the mother tongue of the pupil' (UNESCO, 1953: 6, 47). Such de facto stigmatization and/or exclusion of Haitian Creole in the schools and in other formal spheres effectively make monolingual Haitian Creole speakers second-class citizens. As other contributors to this volume demonstrate, there are revealing socio-historical and sociological parallels between Creole-related orthodoxies and studies of linguistic minorities in the US such as the case of speakers of African American English (e.g. Baugh, 2000, Chapter 12 this volume; Rickford, 1999; Wolfram, 2007, Chapter 14 this volume).

How can postcolonial linguistics as a discipline help fight such stigmatization in education? In Cartesian-Uniformitarian linguistics, the mental bases of language acquisition (i.e. 'Universal Grammar') are similar across the entire human species and across recent time (say, the past 50,000 years). If we accept this view, then Creole languages cannot be singled out structurally. Cartesian-Uniformitarian linguistics is anti-exceptionalist: it aims at understanding the speaking mind, and thus our very humanity, which includes the humanity of Creole speakers, notwithstanding accidents of (post)colonial history. Cartesian-Uniformitarian linguistic research on the origins and structures of Creoles questions and ultimately invalidates the epistemological and conceptual bases of the neo-colonial and non-egalitarian paradigms of much work in contemporary creolistics whereby Creole languages are effectively devalued as 'beginning' languages, 'less advanced' languages, 'simplest' languages, 'abnormal' languages, 'broken' languages, 'corrupted' languages and so on.

In terms of pedagogy, Universal Grammar leaves no room for the still-widely-believed orthodoxy according to which Creole languages constitute a 'handicap' for Creole speakers and cannot be used as viable media for, and objects of, instruction. So, in principle, a creolistics that is informed by Cartesian-Uniformitarian linguistics may help provide Creole languages and their speakers with, among other things, 'capital' that is both symbolic, in Bourdieu's (1982) sense, and real, in the socio-cultural and economic sense. Such capital is critical in order to reverse the past and present stigmatization and dehumanization of Creole speakers and help move Creole-speaking communities toward progressive social change, especially through education.

Post-colonial creolistics must invest in this Universal Grammar-based capital, both epistemologically – to improve Creole-related linguistic research – and sociologically, to improve Creole-based education and language policy. One prerequisite of this investment is a thorough re-evaluation of the use of Creole languages in research and education. Education is the strongest bastion of socioeconomic hegemony. In Haiti, for example, the French-based (mis-)education system has, for much of Haiti's history, quite successfully kept the monolingual Haitian Creole-speaking at bay as incompetent or as failures, notwithstanding the fact that these monolingual Creole speakers are the vast numerical majority of the population.

The return on investment in our Creole capital may, in the future, be found in the widespread and constructive use and study of Creole languages as an integral part of research, education, language policy and sociocultural practices in Creole communities. From the perspective of Cartesian-Uniformitarian linguistics and contrary to the myths surveyed in this chapter and elsewhere, there is no reason to believe that Creole structures constitute an intrinsic intellectual handicap that irremediably blocks intellectual and socioeconomic progress for Creole speakers. In fact, there do exist educational virtues in using Creole languages in the education of Creole speakers (for the case of Haiti, see Y. Dejean, 1975, 1993, 1997, 1999; I. Dejan, 2006). In addition, the cognitive, intellectual and scientific benefits of engaging school children in linguistic research with their native languages as data sources have long been documented (see, for example, Hale, 1972; Honda & O'Neil, 1993).

More generally, we can apply our improved knowledge to new and truly progressive educational practice and pedagogy. Worldwide, linguists and educators devoted to Creole speakers and their cause have already started linking theory and practice via the elaboration of autonomous orthographies, literacy programs, pedagogical tools, instructional resources, guidelines for reforms, post-colonial critiques and so on. Modern Creole-related technology even includes automated orthographic conversion software (Mason, 2000). Thanks to the continuing expansion and development of these types of tools and materials, Creole speakers, like speakers of other languages, can be, and have been, taught to read and write their native languages, and to acquire and produce knowledge in and about those languages. See, for example, Y. Dejean, 1985, 1997, 1999; I. Dejan, 1995, 2006; P. Dejan, 1988; P. Dejean, 1989, and most recently Féquière Vilsaint's prolific library of pedagogical texts in Haitian Creole (as listed on http://www.educavision.com/).

Given Caribbean history and the history of Creole studies, these efforts seem to require nothing less than embracing a Foulcauldian antidote:

> 'Truth' is linked in a circular fashion with systems of power which produce and sustain it, and to effects of power which it induces and which extend it. ... The essential political problem for the intellectual [e.g. linguists and educators] is ... ascertaining the possibility of constituting a new politics of truth [toward] changing ... the political, economic, institutional régime of the production of truth. (Foucault, 1980: 133)

We can educate parents, teachers, Creole-speaking children and ourselves about the intrinsic value of Haitian Creole and other Creoles as powerful linguistic resources. This is, of course, a tall order, but the arguments set forth here can, I hope, be a small step toward achieving this goal.

Acknowledgements

Most heartfelt thanks go to my friend and colleague Jo Anne Kleifgen for the conception of this important project, for inviting me into it, for being a most delightful and stimulating host and for going beyond the call of editorial duty to bring my contribution into its published form. Jo Anne, *Mèsi anpil!*

This chapter is partly an abbreviated and adapted version of arguments presented in DeGraff, 2005b.

Note

1. For a detailed review of a number of degeneracy claims spanning four centuries of Creole studies, see DeGraff, 2001a, 2001b, 2005b.
2. The asterisk indicates that the phrase or sentence structure is unacceptable/ungrammatical to the native speaker's ear.
3. Irrealis mood is the way in which the grammar of a language indicates that the situation described by the corresponding clause has not (yet) happened at the time of speech.

References

Adam, L. (1883) *Les idiomes négro-aryen et maléo-aryen: Essai d'hybridologie linguistique*. Paris: Maisonneuve et cie.

Bailey, P. (2006) School's Creole classes causing a stir. *Miami Herald* (Miami, FL), September 18, Education.

Baugh, J. (2000) *Beyond Ebonics: Linguistic Pride and Racial Prejudice*. New York: Oxford University Press.

Begley, S. (1982) The fossils of language. *Newsweek*, 15 March, p. 80.

Bendor-Samuel, J. and Hartell, R.L. (eds) (1989) *The Niger-Congo Languages: A Classification and Description of Africa's Largest Language Family*. Lanham, MD: University Press of America.

Bickerton, D. (1984) The language bioprogram hypothesis. *Behavioral and Brain Sciences* 7, 178–203.

Bloomfield, L. (1933) *Language*. New York: Holt.

Bourdieu, P. (1982/1991) *Ce que parler veut dire: L'économie des échanges linguistiques*. Paris: Fayard. [English edition (1991) *Language and Symbolic Power* (G. Raymond and M. Adamson, ed. and trans.). Cambridge, MA: Harvard University Press.]

Bourdieu, P. and Wacquant, L. (1992) *An Invitation to Reflexive Sociology*. Chicago, IL: University of Chicago Press.

Chomsky, N. (1966) *Cartesian Linguistics: A Chapter in the History of Rationalist Thought*. New York: Harper & Row.

Corcoran, C. (2001) Creoles and the creation myth: A report on some problems with the linguistic use of 'Creole'. In J. Boyle and A. Okrent (eds) *Papers from the 36th Meeting of the Chicago Linguistic Society*. Chicago, IL: Chicago Linguistic Society.

Crystal, D. (1987) *The Cambridge Encyclopedia of Language*. Cambridge: Cambridge University Press.

DeGraff, M. (1999) Creolization, language change and language acquisition: An epilogue. In M. DeGraff *Language Creation and Language Change: Creolization, Diachrony and Development* (pp. 473–543). Cambridge, MA: MIT Press.

DeGraff, M. (2000) A propos des pronoms object dans le créole d'Haïti: Regards croisés de la morphologie et de la diachronie. *Langages* 138, 89–113.

DeGraff, M. (2001a) Morphology in Creole genesis: Linguistics and ideology. In M. Kenstowicz (ed.) *Ken Hale: A Life in Language* (pp. 52–121). Cambridge, MA: MIT Press.

DeGraff, M. (2001b) On the origin of Creoles: A Cartesian critique of 'neo'-Darwinian linguistics. *Linguistic Typology* 2/3, 213–310.

DeGraff, M. (2002) Relexification: A reevaluation. *Anthropological Linguistics* 44, 321–414.

DeGraff, M. (2003) Against Creole Exceptionalism. *Language* 79, 391–410.

DeGraff, M. (2004) Against Creole Exceptionalism (redux). *Language* 80, 834–839.

DeGraff, M. (2005a) Morphology and word order in 'creolization' and beyond. In R. Kayne and G. Cinque (eds) *Handbook of Comparative Syntax* (pp. 249–312). New York: Oxford University Press.

DeGraff, M. (2005b) Linguists' most dangerous myth: The fallacy of Creole Exceptionalism. *Language in Society* 34, 533–591.

Dejan, P. (1988) *Ki sa gouvènman peyi a janm fè ant 1943 ak 1988 pou l regle koze pa konn li ak pa Konn ekri ann Ayiti* [*What Has the Haitian Government Ever Done between 1943 and 1988 to Solve Haiti's Literacy Problem*]. Port-au-Prince: Sekreteri d Eta pou Alfabetizasyon.

Dejan, I. (1995) *Ann etidye lang nou an* [*Let's Study Our Language*]. Port-au-Prince, Haiti: Demen Miyò.

Dejan, I. (2006) *Yon lekòl tèt anba nan yon peyi tèt anba* [*An Upside-Down School in an Upside-Down Country*]. Port-au-Prince, Haiti: FOKAL (Fondason Kilti Ak Libète).

Dejean, P. (1989) *Survol des Tentatives d'Alphabétisation en Haïti par les Services Gouvermentaux, 1943–1988* [*An Overview of Literacy Projects in Haiti by State Agencies, 1943–1988*]. Port-au-Prince: Groupe d'action et de recherche pour l'éducation.

Dejean, P. (1993) *Haïti: Alerte, on tue!* [*Haiti: Help, They're Killing Us!*]. Montréal: CIDIHCA.

Dejean, Y. (1975) *Dilemme en Haïti: Français en Péril ou Péril Français?* [*Dilemma in Haiti: French in Peril or French Peril?*]. New York: Connaissance d'Haïti.
Dejean, Y. (1985) *Ann aprann òtograf kreyòl la* [*Let's Study Creole Orthography*]. Port-au-Prince: State Secretariat for Literacy.
Dejean, Y. (1993) Notre Créole à nous [Our own Creole]. *Chemins critiques* 3 (1–2), 263–283.
Dejean, Y. (1997) *Alphabétisation: Mythes et réalités* [*Literacy: Myths and Facts*]. Port-au-Prince: Lemète Zéphyr.
Dejean, Y. (1999) The native language as a medium of instruction: An issue revisited. In A. Spears (ed.) *Race and Ideology* (pp. 93–103). Detroit, MI: Wayne State University Press.
Descartes, R. (1637/1962) *Discours de la méthode*. Leyden: I. Maire. [English edition (1962) *Discourse on Method* (J. Veitch, trans.). La Salle, IL: Open Court.]
Dreifus, C. (2001) How language came to be, and change. *New York Times*, October 30, 'Science Times', p. D3.
Fattier, D. (1998) Contribution à l'étude de la genèse d'un créole: L'Atlas linguistique d'Haïti, cartes et commentaries. PhD thesis, Université de Provence (distributed by Presses Universitaires du Septentrion, Villeneuve d'Ascq, France).
Foucault, M. (1980) *Power/Knowledge: Selected Interviews and Other Writings 1972–1977* (C. Gordon, L. Marshall, J. Mepham and K. Soper, ed. and trans.). New York: Pantheon.
Fromkin, V. and Rodman, R. (1998) *An Introduction to Language* (6th edn). New York: Harcourt, Brace, Jovanovitch.
Greenfield, W. (1830) *A Defence of the Surinam Negro-English Version of the New Testament*. London: Samuel Bagster.
Greppin, J. (2002) The triumph of slang: Social, regional and racial origins of American English. Review of *The Cambridge History of the English Language* (J. Algeo, ed.). *Times Literary Supplement*, 1 February, 3–4.
Hale, K. (1972) Some questions about anthropological linguistics: The role of native knowledge. In D. Hymes (ed.) *Reinventing Anthropology* (pp. 382–397). New York: Pantheon.
Hjelmslev, L. (1938) Relation de parenté des langues créoles. *Revue des Études Indo-européenes* 2, 271–286.
Honda, M. and O'Neil, W. (1993) Triggering science-forming capacity through linguistic inquiry. In K. Hale and S.J. Keyser (eds) *The View from Building 20: Essays in Linguistics in Honor of Sylvain Bromberger* (pp. 229–255). Cambridge, MA: MIT Press.
Jespersen, O. (1922) *Language: Its Nature, Development and Origin*. London: Allen & Unwin.
Kroch, A.S. (1989) Reflexes of grammar in patterns of language change. *Language Variation and Change* 1, 199–244.
Larousse, P. (1869) *Grand dictionnaire universel du XIX siècle*. Paris: Larousse.
Lefebvre, C. (1998) *Creole Genesis and the Acquisition of Grammar: The Case of Haitian Creole*. Cambridge: Cambridge University Press.
Mason, M. (2000) Automated Creole orthography conversion. *Journal of Pidgin and Creole Languages* 15, 179–184.
McWhorter, J. (1998) Identifying the Creole prototype: Vindicating a typological class. *Language* 74, 788–818.

Meillet, A. (1924/1951) Introduction à la classification des langues [Introductory chapter of *Les langues du monde*]. In A. Meillet *Linguistique Historique et Linguistique Générale* (Vol. 1; pp. 53–69). Paris: Klincksieck.

Mufwene, S. (2001) *The Ecology of Language Evolution*. Cambridge: Cambridge University Press.

Muysken, P. (1988) Are Creoles a special type of language? In F. Newmeyer (ed.) *Linguistics: The Cambridge Survey* (Vol. 2): *Linguistic Theory: Extensions and Implications*. Cambridge: Cambridge University Press.

O'Grady, W., Archibald, W., Aronoff, M. and Rees-Miller, J. (eds) (2001) *Contemporary Linguistics: An Introduction* (4th edn). New York: Bedford/St Martin's Press.

Posner, R. (1985) Creolization as typological change: Some examples from romance syntax. *Diachronica* 2, 167–188.

Rickford, J. (1999) *African American Vernacular English: Features, Evolution, Educational Implications*. Malden, MA: Blackwell.

Saint-Quentin, A. de (1872/1989) *Introduction à l'histoire de Cayenne ... with Étude sur la grammaire créole* by Auguste de Saint-Quentin, Antibes: J. Marchand. [1989 edn: Cayenne: Comité de la culture, de l'education et de l'environnement, Région Guyane.)

Sapir, E. (1933) Language. *Encyclopaedia of the Social Sciences* 9, 155–169.

Seuren, P. (1998) *Western Linguistics: An Historical Introduction.* Oxford: Blackwell.

Seuren, P. and Wekker, H. (1986) semantic transparency as a factor in Creole genesis. In P. Muysken and N. Smith (eds) *Substrata Versus Universals in Creole Genesis* (pp. 57–70). Amsterdam: John Benjamins.

Sylvain, S. (1936) *Le créole haïtien: Morphologie et syntaxe*. Wetteren: de Meester.

Trouillot, M. (1990) *Haiti: State against Nation. The Origins and Legacy of Duvalierism*. New York: Monthly Review Press.

UNESCO (1953) *The Use of Vernacular Languages in Education. Monographs on Fundamental Education, VIII.* Paris: UNESCO.

Vajda, E. (n.d.) *History of the English Language.* Online at http://pandora.cii.wwu.edu/vajda/ling201/test3materials/History_of_English.htm. Accessed 18.5.08.

Valdman, A. (1978) *Le Créole: Structure, statut et origine* [*Creole: Structure, Status and Origins*]. Paris: Klincksieck.

Whinnom, K. (1971) Linguistic hybridization and the 'special case' of Pidgins and Creoles. In D. Hymes (ed.) *Pidginization and Creolization of Languages* (pp. 91–115). Cambridge: Cambridge University Press.

Wolfram, W. (2007) Sociolinguistic folklore in the study of AAE. *Linguistic and Language Compass* 2, 292–313.

Chapter 8

Political and Cultural Dimensions of Creole as a Regional Language in the French Antilles

ELLEN M. SCHNEPEL

Introduction: The 'Culture Wars' in the French Antilles

Since the 1970s, language militants in Guadeloupe and Martinique in the French Antilles have pressed for the recognition of Creole as a language in its own right, separate and distinct from the French language, while Antillean educators and linguists have advocated for its introduction in the school system, either as a legitimate subject of study or as a pedagogical tool to aid school children in the transition to and mastery of French. By challenging the official policy of the French educational system, which historically has given the French language the sole privileged place in schools in the Metropole and its overseas territories, efforts have now culminated in the recognition of Creole as a regional language of France, alongside Breton, Basque, Occitan and Corsican; and Creole is now taught as a course option in junior high schools (or *collèges*) in Guadeloupe and Martinique.

While the debate on language and culture is frequently sited in Martinique – where the key proponents of *négritude*, *antillanité* and *créolité* were born and reside (Edouard Glissant being the exception until the passing of Aimé Césaire on April 17, 2008) – few people who follow the controversy are aware that a parallel movement to *créolité* occurred on the 'sister island' of Guadeloupe. In the two decades prior to the 1989 publication of *Éloge de la Créolité* by three Martinicans – Jean Bernabé, Patrick Chamoiseau and Raphaël Confiant – Guadeloupean intellectuals defended their linguistic, cultural and ethnic specificity by linking Creole to the nationalist movement on their island. Brandishing Creole as symbol *par excellence* of the nationalist cause, conduit and container of an anti-assimilationist ideology, militants framed a discourse that elevated Creole while they disparaged the earlier generation of ACRA (Académie Créole des Antilles) who had founded a cultural association in the 1950s to study and re-evaluate their 'quaint *patois*.'

This chapter revisits the language question in Guadeloupe by tracing the key stages in Creole's recent evolution: the volatile period in the 1980s, when the language was intrinsically identified with the local nationalist movement (see Schnepel, 1998, 2004); the acceptance of Creole in the 1990s by all political parties and social strata, not just the nationalists, independentists, or upper-middle class and elites, as a regional language and source of cultural identity; and in 2001–2002, when the French Ministry of National Education gave official sanction to Creole by implementing an examination in the language, known as the CAPES (*Certificat d'Aptitude au Professorat de l'Enseignement du Second Degré*), for secondary school teachers in the French Antilles, French Guiana in South America and Réunion in the Indian Ocean.

The journey of Creole's change in status from *patois* to regional language, culminating in the CAPES-*créole*, has not been without trial and error or political acrimony on both sides of the Atlantic. As a case study in vernacular language promotion, it provides a fascinating story of the difficulties, technical problems and political stakes that are central to language planning in postcolonial sites.

An Overview of the Sociohistoric and Sociolinguistic Context of Guadeloupe, 1630–1946

The Creole language in Guadeloupe dates from the early years of French colonial expansion in the Caribbean, beginning with the mass importation in the 17th century of enslaved Africans as the labor force for sugar plantations. Lambert-Félix Prudent (1980), a Martinican sociolinguist, singles out four main stages in Creole's evolution in the French Antilles: the early years of French colonization, the aftermath of the enactment of the *Code Noir* in 1685, the post-abolition period from 1848–1946 and the modern era of departmentalization commencing with the law of political assimilation in March 1946.

In the early period of French colonization (1625–1685), the speech we now refer to as Creole had its genesis, and it soon became the lingua franca of the plantation for the diverse groups who shared no common language. French settlers ranged in social class from landowners, militia, overseers, indentured laborers and sailors to disgraced members or non-inheriting offspring of noble families, and they came from various provinces of France (Normandy, Brittany, the Parisian region) where regional dialects were spoken. Enslaved Africans were even more heterogeneous, drawn from different regions, ethnic and linguistic groups, and occupational niches in their homelands, and once on the plantation they were stratified according to task and status (e.g. field, skilled and domestic labor).

Plantation society was characterized by linguistic variation and instability with a degree of multilingualism, particularly among the plantation whites and successive cohorts of newly-arrived Africans who spoke different languages. Plantation owners controlled at least two language codes: non-standard French, in their social relations with their family and the European settler community, and Creole, in their work and domestic relations with the slaves. In light of the instability of African languages on the plantation and limited accessibility of the subordinate group to the speech habits of the dominant class, Creole became the primary language of the enslaved population. It was the language of socialization used by native-born (or creole) slaves to season the newly-arrived slaves from Africa, and succeeding generations of slaves born in the Antilles spoke Creole as their mother tongue. While African languages co-existed with Creole in the slaves' repertoire for longer periods than originally thought, once the slave trade from Africa was curtailed in the early 1800s, language shift to Creole was more rapid and complete.

By 1671, blacks outnumbered whites in Guadeloupe (Abénon, 1987; Lasserre, 1961). The passage of the *Code Noir* ('Black Code') in 1685 established a hierarchical social and economic structure based on an ideology of race that had existed de facto. The code solidified social boundaries and legislated social relations between enslaved Africans and the dominant class of whites. Owing to the relative absence of female colonists and a legal code that prohibited marriage between whites and blacks, sexual liaisons or concubinage between plantation owners and female slaves occurred with great frequency. As a result of these unions, an intermediary group of *sang-mêlés* (mulattoes) emerged, many of whom later formed the class of free colored. This stratum, along with domestic slaves, had greater access to the French language and in all probability spoke a variety of Creole closer to French than the 'deep' Creole of the field slaves. Imitation of French standards may even have contributed to increased social rewards or even manumission for certain slaves.

The abolition of slavery in 1848, which theoretically granted civil and political rights to the newly-freed slaves, opened the way for a degree of social mobility that hitherto had been denied the colored population in Antillean society. In the period prior to emancipation, decrees were passed prohibiting the education of the slaves and specifying the need to keep them in total ignorance in order to discourage revolts. While religious indoctrination was allowed, mutual schools for free mulattoes did not appear until the 1830s in Guadeloupe. In the second half of the 19th century, school instruction was extended in theory to the newly-freed blacks, but this right was largely limited to the mulatto class or to blacks from the professional classes.

With the establishment of a colonial education system, the school became the primary means for social advancement for an elite minority that would later form the local colored bourgeoisie. French became the language of this new social class, and its acquisition was an index of social prestige. To speak French signaled a strong association and identification with French standards and values – in culture, art, music and dress. A passage in 1944 from a Guadeloupean newspaper, *La Tribune Syndicale et Laïque*, captures particularly well the developing social-class allegiance to French as a marker of social status and prestige during the colonial epoch.

> Towards the end of the last century, French was the language of the bourgeoisie, of people distinguished by their wealth or high social position. French was the pendant of the piano, of the coach, of the pince-nez with a gold chain, and other attributes of an ostentatious and affluent bourgeoisie. It was the language of a class. Poor folk were to take pleasure in humility and dared not to practice a language which they did not have the possibility of learning adequately. Today, owing to the spread of education which ensures the vernacularization of the language, French has become quite simply the language of polite company, of men and women who show proper correctness in conduct and speech. (Narfez, 1944: 2; author's translation)

Creole continued to be the vernacular of the popular strata, used for daily communication, and the main vehicle for local creole culture. A passage in the same newspaper article reveals the low esteem in which Creole was held at the time:

> ... Creole is, above all, marked by sterility. Due to its insufficient vocabulary, the meagerness of its words, its usage is limited to the expression of common knowledge. It is incapable of translating the varied learning of modern science. It suffices only for the ignorant. Its syntax, unstable and imprecise, varies with each colony where it is used, even in parts of the same colony. ... Certainly it will continue to exist for a long time, but it will disappear nevertheless, overrun by the invading French language. It will disappear like the local dress, not by evolution but by progressive elimination. (Narfez, 1944: 2; author's translation)

In the 100-year interim between the abolition of slavery in 1848 and the passage of the departmentalist law in 1946, language usage had developed into a marker of race, class, culture and educational attainment in Guadeloupean society.

Departmentalization and its Consequences

The law of March 16, 1946, establishing Guadeloupe as a French overseas department (or DOM), heralded a post-war era of rapid social change marked by the whole-scale transplantation of French institutions to the Antilles – from the school, courts, social services and political structure to transportation and communication networks. The extension of a highly centralized French administrative structure to the Antilles naturally resulted in the creation of a substantial local bureaucracy with a need for trained personnel. Over the course of the next decades, an influx of metropolitan French filled top and middle-level positions in the administration, school system, health and social services, communications, technology, finance, agricultural management, the police and army as the French government became the primary employer in the islands.

Guadeloupeans won social security benefits, including health-care coverage and medical insurance, family allowances, welfare for single mothers, workers' insurance, pensions and guarantees for minimum wage. In addition, the 40% cost-of-living subsidy (*prime de vie chère*), which had originally applied only to metropolitan French civil servants working in the islands, was extended to cover Antillean bureaucrats as a result of union pressure and strikes in the early 1950s. This subsidy contributed to a higher standard of living for functionaries while exacerbating differentials in income and purchasing power between the various social strata.

Most significant among the institutional changes of political assimilation was the expansion of the national education system to the French Antilles. Compulsory schooling was legislated for all children until the age of 16. Secondary and technical education was added to an essentially primary school structure, and new schools were built in rural areas that had not previously been served by the system. The expansion of education led to further penetration of the French language and culture, setting up a dual system with French the acceptable language of discourse in formal or public institutional settings while Creole was relegated to the informal or private sector. Although the two languages were often complementary in their functions, they overlapped in certain domains of usage, which often carried ambivalent or dual meanings (Reisman, 1970).

In the postwar era, many local notables and upper-level functionaries questioned whether the widespread use of the local *patois* would harm the quality of spoken French, infusing it with Creole forms of pronunciation, intonation and nasalization. Educators viewed the role of the teacher to eradicate the impending L1 influence from Creole into French (known as *créolismes*), to purify the classroom of Creole and its nefarious influences, and to teach proper forms of French diction (Nainsouta, 1944). Thus the Antillean school became the site of linguistic conflict and the stage where the drama between metropolitan and local cultures played out.

Departmentalization soon gave rise to a growing crisis within the society as it became increasingly dependent upon the Metropole – politically, economically and culturally (Blérald, 1983). Agriculture was still based on production for the exterior rather than for local consumption, but declining production was further threatened by a loss of export markets as a result of increased competition from Third World countries where costs were lower. With the relative lack of an industrial sector and hyperactivity in the tertiary sector, social problems emerged and intensified: growing school failure in an educational system that had expanded rapidly; the rise of unemployment, particularly among youth between the ages of 16 and 24; large-scale migration of Antilleans to France in search of jobs, skills and education where they soon encountered racism and discrimination; and increased labor disputes and strikes by dockers, agricultural laborers, hospital workers and civil servants (Giraud, 1989).

These social and economic ills played into Antilleans' growing frustration with the islands' political status and accompanying loss of cultural autonomy. Realization of the failure of assimilation soon became part of a developing discourse in the 1950s among leftist intellectuals, who were becoming more conscious of the existence of a distinct Antillean 'personality' and a history separate from the French. A new generation of Antillean intellectuals began to question French cultural dominance and recognize the need to preserve and promote a culture that was specifically Antillean, framing the cultural question within a growing sentiment for political autonomy within the French state.

> One sees today individuals in the extreme end of the Antillean intelligentsia registering an interest in local popular life – as it exists among the folk in the towns and countryside, with the needs they endure and the values to which they adhere – and not from the false perspective of a pleasant exoticism or a noble archaism. If it's true that Aimé Césaire considered that among the youth there would be a shift toward taking stock of the cultural riches of Martinique (the collection of folktales and songs in the Creole language, the study of folk arts and traditions), the establishment of such an inventory had no real significance other than to aid the masses as bearers of these riches in coming to consciousness. If it is equally true in Guadeloupe that personalities like Rémy Nainsouta and Roger Fortuné are attached to local folklore, their interest in regional life goes together with their desire to see the material resources of the

country used more advantageously than they are and that their fellow countrymen, prone to flee the islands, return to their islands to offer their services. (Leiris, 1955: 15–16; author's translation)

A New Discourse on Creole Language and Culture

During the 1970s, interest in the promotion of Creole as a language in its own right was appropriated almost exclusively by the anti-colonialist left and far-left in Guadeloupe. Two types of 'proto-elites' formed the organizational basis of the movement: language strategists, who in their defense of Creole had created a symbol of ethnocultural identity and new group frontiers and political militants, who defined and defended group interests through the instrumental use of Creole (Schnepel, 1998, 2004).

With the development of nationalist unions in Guadeloupe, a revolutionary break with language traditions occurred. Creole, not French, began to be utilized in general assembly meetings of the non-French-aligned unions. The change was intended to liberate agricultural workers and peasants so they could understand the debate and speak freely in their mother tongue, thereby allowing them to participate fully in a context that had previously been conducted exclusively in French.

Creole also began to be used by union leaders of the two main independentist parties, the UPLG (*Union Populaire Pour la Libération de la Guadeloupe*) and the MPGI (*Mouvement Pour la Guadeloupe Indépendante*), as the language of protest at public demonstrations and during strikes to organize and mobilize workers. National liberation would be achieved by mobilizing economic resistance among the masses of agricultural workers and small farmers in the countryside, not the urban workers who with higher wages and year-round employment formed the base of the Communist unions.

Language teachers, educational specialists, linguists and university researchers formed the new generation of Creole promoters, and they were organized into pressure groups and associations with varying degrees of linkage to, or distance from, the independentist political parties. Several interest groups were formed in the decades of the 1970s and 1980s, with differing postures on Creole and their vision for its future role in Guadeloupe. These included:

- Gérard Lauriette with his innovative pedagogy using Creole in his private school;
- Dany Bebel-Gisler and her center *Bwadoubout* for at-risk youth who had dropped out of public schools;

- the activist priest Père Céleste and Christians for an Independent Guadeloupe (KPLG);
- the UPLG with its two radio stations, Radyo Tanbou (in Pointe-à-Pitre) and Radyo Banbou (in Basse-Terre), newspapers and political propaganda;
- Jean Bernabé and the research group GEREC (Groupe d'Etudes et de Recherches en Espace Créolophone), at the Campus Fouillole in Guadeloupe and later relocated to the Campus Schoelcher of the Université des Antilles et de la Guyane (UAG), in Martinique;
- the nationalist teachers' union in Guadeloupe, the SGEG;
- Hector Poullet, Sylviane Telchid and the Association KREY, with their goal of literary production and diffusion in Creole; and
- Guy and Marie-Christine Hazaël-Massieux, professors at the Université de Provence in France, which housed a center for the study of creole languages and cultures.

Coming from different socioprofessional backgrounds, these groups all competed for the Creole limelight as they channeled their ideas and popularized their linguistic choices while seeking a local following.

The Orthography Issue: The GEREC Script

The primary agenda of the language strategists was the formulation of a writing system that would integrate the two dialects of Creole, Martinican and Guadeloupean and provide an orthography that was easily accessible to other speakers of Creole in the Lesser Antilles, notably St Lucia and Dominica. Presumably the script would be for non-literate as well as educated members of these societies and the orthography would be popularized and serve as the basis for further linguistic and educational research, for the development of a written literature (e.g. grammars, dictionaries, collections of oral traditions and translations), and for the production of plays, poetry and political pamphlets.

Largely through the work of Jean Bernabé, a written system for Creole was developed and presented in a series of articles in the GEREC's publications, *Espace Créole* (Bernabé, 1976) and *Mofwaz* (Bernabé, 1977a, 1977b, 1980). Similar to the proposals of Dany Bebel-Gisler (1975, 1976), a Guadeloupean activist and sociologist, the script was heavily influenced by the Haitian experience using the newer IPN (Institut Pédagogique National) model. The very nature of the project to design a graphic system was intended to alter the status of Creole: to establish its own internal autonomy as a language in its own right with the full capacity to function like other languages. This could be accomplished *only* by breaking with the limitations of an etymological system, based on French graphic practices, and by designing a phonologically-based writing system.

The GEREC system symbolized a rupture with assimilationist tendencies and incorporated a nationalist ideology. As the writing system was based on a scientific alignment of phoneme and grapheme, with reference to the International Phonetic Alphabet, the orthography simultaneously reflected and maintained the integrity and autonomy of Creole. In turn, the autonomist system was reinforced by the principle of *déviance maximale* ('greatest difference'), which was incorporated in the notational system: that is, the phonological system of Creole would be represented by selecting graphemes that were the farthest or most distinct from French.

Originally, there was some societal opposition to the GEREC script. Guadeloupean partisans found it too closely identified with Bernabé, a Martinican, and they felt the script did not take into account certain important phonological differences between Guadeloupean and Martinican varieties of Creole. Many faulted the writing system for being too 'intellectual,' well beyond the grasp of the semi-literate or illiterate folk, while others felt that certain graphic choices, such as 'w' and 'k,' were aesthetically unpleasing or inappropriate for speakers accustomed to reading French. Several language promoters even tried to improve upon the system by introducing their own innovations (see Hazaël-Massieux, 1987, 1993; Ludwig [ed.], 1989; Poullet *et al.*, 1984). However, by the mid-1980s, the script with some changes and improvements had been widely adopted by writers, poets, journalists, the cultural avant-garde and high school and university students, as well as by those who yearned to write in their mother tongue. Even so, others continued to write Creole spontaneously in their own fashion.

Creole in the School: The Capesterre Experiment in the Early 1980s

With so many children coming from Creolophone households and experiencing difficulty with French in secondary school, teachers at union meetings and informal gatherings in the rural community of Capesterre Belle-Eau began to debate the value of incorporating Guadeloupe's language and culture into school as a means to counteract school failure and promote cultural identity.

In 1981, three teachers at the junior high school in Capesterre – Hector Poullet, Sylviane Telchid and Moïse Sorèze – launched an experimental, unauthorized program to teach Creole. The program was supplemental to

French classes and intended to improve students' mastery of French through remedial work that highlighted influences from one language in the other. Modest objectives were set for the experiment: to encourage students' spontaneity by permitting them to use Creole in class, to awaken their linguistic curiosity while eliminating many of their complexes associated with speaking French, and to provide a foundation for the transition from Creole to French by emphasizing the different structures of each language.

Although the goals were by no means revolutionary, no official French government text at that time authorized the use of Creole as a regional language in the Antillean school system. New ministerial directives in the early 1980s had alluded to the integration of Creole in schools in 'regions marked by a high incidence of school failure and education difficulty.' However, these directives singled out only Marie-Galante, an island dependency of Guadeloupe, and the French-administered side of Saint-Martin, where curiously English and English-lexicon Creole function as home languages in addition to French Creole.

Without the necessary French legislative power or official acknowledgement by the local Chancellor of Education for the Antilles and French Guiana, the Capesterre experiment continued for a second year with only the support of an enlightened principal and the pioneering work of the instructors who referred to themselves as *nèg mawon* ('maroons'), symbolizing their renegade status in the educational system while conjuring up images of rebel slaves' resistance to European domination.

In June 1982, a new ministerial directive from Paris addressed the issue of teaching regional cultures and languages in the national education system, and it mapped out a comprehensive plan to introduce regional languages into schools at the nursery, primary and secondary levels. After a period of three years' experimentation, there would be a review of the results. However, the circular was ambiguous in not even specifying which languages were considered regional languages. It prompted suspense and bewilderment among competing interest groups in the Antilles who were divided over its provisions and the interpretation of Creole's status: Was it a national language, a regional language, or just a *patois*?

A year later, in May 1983, on the occasion of the Fourth International Conference of French Creole Studies in Lafayette, Louisiana, the cultural attaché of the Chancellory of Education for the Antilles and French Guiana, Xavier Orville, made a surprise announcement of Creole's inclusion as a regional language of France and its introduction in the educational system in the Antilles. The text of the Louisiana declaration, satirically referred to in the local press as the 'Creole bomb,' is worth examining. While on the surface the document acknowledged the cultural identity and linguistic environment of the Antilles and provided a structure for the gradual inclusion of Creole in the school, no specific directives were outlined to implement such a program. The classes were to be supplementary and optional, left to the discretion of individual school directors and teachers, and subject to students' volition to participate.

Barriers to the implementation of the program existed at diverse levels within the educational system in the Antilles. No formal program had been initiated in the teachers' colleges to provide the pedagogical foundation for these changes. No process was outlined to codify Creole or to commission texts in the language, and no one was empowered to teach Creole. The document thus illuminated the ambivalence of the Ministry of National Education towards taking a firmer stand on the language issue while it highlighted the intransigence of local authorities to set policy.

The Louisiana declaration, however, did grant a certain degree of legitimacy to the teaching of Creole and, therefore, had immediate implications for the Capesterre group. It provided the necessary pressure to make the school program official, but it also had other unexpected repercussions. The Creole classes continued to be optional and supplemental to the regular school program, but now Creole became a separate study, no longer attached to French classes, with the main purpose to teach students to read and write in Creole, thus sensitizing youth to their mother tongue as an expression and instrument of their native culture.

Even with these changes, the Creole classes polarized the community in Capesterre, pitting the Creole instructors and school principal against hostile parents and vocal members of the town. The Capesterre controversy received an inordinate amount of attention in the local as well as overseas media. Arguments voiced by opponents of Creole's introduction in the school revealed that there was much more at stake than just one or two supplementary hours of instruction in the Creole language. The anti-Creole discourse of the parents raised a number of compelling issues: popular attitudes toward the vernacular, linguistic variation and its role in the process of language standardization, the qualifications of the Creole partisans, and ultimately the relationship between Creole, education and Guadeloupe's future political status.

Language Politics in the New Millennium: The CAPES-*Créole*

Since the 1980s the discourse on language has softened. Rather than being primarily associated with the nationalist current, by the 1990s, all political parties from the left to the right in Guadeloupe acknowledged

Creole as a regional language, and there was popular acceptance of the language as the source of local cultural identity.

> Today there is widespread recognition of Guadeloupe and Martinique as cultural communities in their own right, despite the fact that it is the French government that partially finances the valorization of local cultural promotion. (Daniel, 2001: 73)

Within the last few years, the polemic regarding Creole has been rekindled in the Antilles over discussion of a CAPES in Creole – a competitive examination to certify secondary school teachers in the Creole language. As a result of this examination Creole would become part of the secondary school program and newly-certified teachers would be placed in positions to teach the regional language. Many educators and language teachers were resistant to the idea of the CAPES-*créole* for they felt the examination raised more issues than it answered:

- What would be the pedagogical content of courses in Creole, since there had been several experiments with teaching Creole in secondary schools but no serious evaluation of these pioneering attempts in the 1980s and 1990s?
- Who would teach Creole? How and by whom would teachers of Creole be trained – for example, by the IUFM (Institut Universitaire de Formation des Maîtres, formerly the Ecole Normale) or the research association GEREC-F (which had since changed its acronym to incorporate the study of French and its varieties)?
- What students would take Creole as a subject? Would there be enough demand by students to warrant Creole as a bona fide discipline? Or would Creole be only a passing phase?
- How would the hours for Creole instruction affect the scheduling and content of other school subjects so tightly controlled by the Ministry of Education?

For the past two decades, numerous educational seminars, conferences and workshops in Martinique and Guadeloupe had been dedicated to the question of the introduction of Creole in school while also considering the development of a pedagogy specific to the language. A number of secondary schools in Guadeloupe and Martinique began to offer classes in Creole for junior high school students. However, the teaching of Creole still remained optional and without accreditation. There was, as yet, no mechanism in place to train and certify teachers in Creole, nor any legitimate teaching positions in the new discipline of Langues et Cultures Régionales (LCR), even though the IUFM handled teacher training in which the curriculum frequently included coursework in sociolinguistics and Creole pedagogy (Prudent, 2001: 84–89, 99–103). Degrees in LCR had been offered for two decades at the Faculty of Languages on the Schoelcher campus in Martinique in which the GEREC-F was in charge of instruction.

On October 18, 2000, in Paris, at a press conference of the education and overseas ministries, the Socialist Minister of National Education Jack Lang surprised the educational establishment by declaring that in 2001, a CAPES in Creole would be created. In his presentation, he laid out a plan for educational reform and change in the DOM that would link students with their environment and pave the way for school success through the teaching of Creole. Now a program would be put into place that would define the content of instruction, train teachers and evaluate both the teachers and their instruction. Educational administrators were finally recognizing the bilingualism of the Antilles and creating a policy to include Creole as a regional language. 'In developing local languages and our national language, we favor bilingualism, rather than focusing on the former as the cause of the high toll in school failure,' declared Lang (Prudent, 2001).

Three weeks after Lang's pronouncement, the French leftist daily newspaper *Libération* published an article, 'Les créoles à l'épreuve du CAPES,' by the French linguist Robert Chaudenson of the Université de Provence. In an arrogant style, Chaudenson (2000) asserted that the enormous educational problems in the DOM would not be resolved by the creation of a CAPES in Creole, but instead the new policy would serve only to silence the burning claims of the nationalists who hoped to sever, if not an empire, at least a principality. First, he pointed out that there was not one Creole but four different ones (i.e. Guadeloupean, Martinican, Guyanese and Réunionnais) so there would need to be four, not one, CAPES. Second, he underlined that no official orthography existed for Creole and that the GEREC graphic system was far from being accepted by everyone. Chaudenson alluded to the fact that other systems in use were technically better, though he did not elaborate. Furthermore, he stated that implementation of the educational circulars of 1982 and 1995 concerning regional languages was predicated on the willingness of teachers, students and parents, not to mention the chancellors of the academies in each department, all of whom had shown reservations regarding the teaching of Creole in school.

There soon followed invectives written by Raphaël Confiant of Martinique, Hector Poullet of Guadeloupe, and Axel Gauvin of Réunion – all Creole activists in their respective islands – denouncing the paternalist and colonialist remarks of Chaudenson. A website 'KAPES *KREOL*' was soon launched for publishing information and texts, all prepared by the

GEREC-F. But, perhaps more importantly, the electronic site served as Confiant's personal platform for refuting Chaudenson's statements, claiming that the GEREC-F was the only true research group entrusted with establishing linkages between the French and Creole languages, a position the GEREC would surely have shunned in the 1970s and 1980s. The website emphatically announced their refusal to collaborate with Chaudenson or any of his associates in designing the examination process for the CAPES-*créole*.

Curiously, since its inception in 1976, the GEREC had waffled continuously regarding the introduction of Creole in the school, but the French government authorities had been equally as ambivalent with respect to educational and linguistic reform.

> Here in effect was a government that over the years had ignored, even marginalized, movements for cultural and linguistic promotion; then, even as it pronounced the words 'historical reparations' (Giordan 1982) and was preoccupied with making up for the backwardness of these regions, it utterly ignored the materiality and vitality of the vernacular languages of the Caribbean and Indian Ocean. Why does the government throw itself suddenly into a reckless school intervention with such a zeal that borders on convulsion while choosing to lean on the most fundamentalist wing of the Martinican creolist movement? How does it pretend to proceed in a pedagogical reform whose fall-out and foreseeable results are serious for the whole cultural and political life of four distinct communities with close to two million French citizens? Is it reasonable to create a new discipline, with new programs and new evaluations without reflecting on its impact on the elementary school above all and on the adjustments with related subjects? [...] What can one reasonably hope to achieve in short and long terms in each of these territories? (Prudent, 2001: 83–84; author's translation)

The implementation of the CAPES-*créole* in the 2001-2002 academic cycle, its first year, was fraught with problems. Local committees sought to comply with the Ministry of National Education and all its circulars – which often were slow in arriving – on the development of instruction in regional languages and cultures: e.g. creation of an academic advisory council on regional languages, jury selection for the CAPES-*créole*, and developing standards, a program and a venue for the oral and written sections of the exam. Critics felt that the CAPES-*créole* was initiated precipitously and prematurely before Creole teachers had been properly trained, relevant instructional materials in Creole developed and appropriate measures put in place in the secondary school system in order for Creole instruction to be integrated with other disciplines.

In turn, certain Creole partisans objected to the selection of the secondary school as the point of entry for Creole. They favored the language's introduction at the primary school level, where the real conflict exists between home and school languages, and then proposed adding Creole progressively from junior to senior high school. (Thus, over the course of seven years of secondary school, the Creole classes would be added to scale, beginning with the first year of junior high and ending with the last year of senior high, adding a new class each year.) Others debated the relevance of a single CAPES that did not fully acknowledge the distinctions between the Creoles, variation within each Creole and the phenomenon of the *interlecte*, an intermediary linguistic zone identified and analyzed by Prudent (1980, 1981, 1993, 2005) and later discussed in terms of Guadeloupean Creole (see Managan, 2004; Meyjes, 1995). As in other metropolitan-local debates, the question surfaced why the CAPES-*créole* was patterned after the CAPES examination for other regional languages of France when the context of each DOM was drastically different. Underlying these issues was the subtext: how to resolve the equality-and-difference oxymoron.

The results of the first year of the CAPES-*créole* were particularly poor. Of the 192 original candidates, only 10 (or less than 5%) were admitted: two Guadeloupeans, two Martinicans and six Réunionnais. Given so few successful candidates and the few openings created to teach Creole, it was quite possible that a Réunionnais who successfully passed the CAPES-*créole* could be selected to teach the language (but which dialect?) in a secondary school in the Antilles, further inflaming nationalist or local sentiment. The results pointed to the haste and lack of reflection in setting up a process and structure to examine secondary school teachers in Creole, and raised the more fundamental issue of the purpose and viability of a CAPES-*créole*.

The Balance Sheet

In the years since 2002, one cannot say the CAPES program has progressed with stellar results. There have been issues of jury manipulation and polemics over every decision from the appointment of the first director of the CAPES-*créole*, Didier de Robillard (a Franco-Mauritian linguist), to selection of qualified jury members and examiners, as well as the disciplines they represent, since all of these choices are fraught with political and ideological symbolism. The fact that the Réunionnais branch of the

CAPES-*créole* has been more successful, in large part due to the vigor and quality of instruction at the Université de la Réunion, irrespective of the island's high toll of school failure, did not sit well with the Antillean contingent. In Martinique, the ensuing controversy is certainly more vocal than in Guadeloupe as the UAG's Faculty of Languages and Literature, the GEREC-F and the *créolité* triumvirate are all headquartered there.

Certainly the affair over the CAPES-*créole* points to the fact that, even as Creole has been accepted as a regional language in Guadeloupe, the language and education issue is still a bone of political, cultural and ideological contention (CAPES *Créole(s)*, 2001). While the controversy pits Antilleans in their homelands against encroachment by the French Ministry of Education, it also creates friction and fissions among the local Creole activists, sympathizers, grassroots organizations and sponsoring agencies in the various DOM in which the stakes are high. Most importantly, the conflict does not focus on the real issue of how best to serve Antillean school children in a bilingual or multilingual, post-colonial context.

References

Abénon, L-R. (1987) *La Guadeloupe de 1671 à 1759, Etude Politique, Economique et Sociale* (2 vols). Paris: L'Harmattan.

Bebel-Gisler, D. (1975) *Kèk Prinsip Pou Ekri Kréyòl*. Paris: L'Harmattan.

Bebel-Gisler, D. (1976) *La Langue Créole, Force Jugulée: Etude Sociolinguistique des Rapports de Force entre le Créole et le Français aux Antilles*. Paris: L'Harmattan.

Bernabé, J. (1976) Propositions pour un code orthographique intégré des créoles à base lexicale française. *Espace Créole* 1, 25–56.

Bernabé, J. (1977a) Ecrire le créole (Part 1): Ecriture et phonétique. *Mofwaz* 1, 11–29.

Bernabé, J. (1977b) Ecrire le créole (Part 2): Ecriture et syntaxe. *Mofwaz* 2, 11–20.

Bernabé, J. (1980) Ecrire le créole (Part 3): Présentation de la base syntaxique de l'écriture du créole; suivie d'une brève tentative d'évaluation de la socialisation de ce système orthographique après 4 années d'existence. *Mofwaz* 3, 9–15.

Bernabé, J., Chamoiseau, P. and Confiant, R. (1989) *Éloge de la Créolité*. Paris: Gallimard.

Blérald, P.A. (1983) Guadeloupe-Martinique: A system of colonial domination in crisis. In F. Ambursley and R. Cohen (eds) *Crisis in the Caribbean* (pp. 148–165). New York: Monthly Review Press.

CAPES Créole(s) (2001) Le Débat. *Études Créoles* 24 (1).

Chaudenson, R. (2000) Les creoles à l'épreuve du CAPES. *Libération* (9 novembre), 8.

Daniel, J. (2001) The construction of dependency: Economy and politics in the Antilles. In A.G. Ramos and A.I. Rivera (eds) *Islands at the Crossroads: Politics in the Non-Independent Caribbean* (pp. 61–79). Kingston: Ian Randle Publishers.

Giraud, M. (1989) Racism and immigration: French West Indians in the mainland. *New Political Science* 16–17 (Fall/Winter), 71–78.

Hazaël-Massieux, M-C. (1987) *Chanson des Antilles, Comptines, Formulettes*. Paris: CNRS.

Hazaël-Massieux, M-C. (1993) *Écrire en Créole: Oralité et Ecriture aux Antilles*. Paris: L'Harmattan.

Lasserre, G. (1961) *La Guadeloupe: Étude Géographique* (2 vols). Bordeaux: Union Française d'Impression.

Leiris, M. (1955) *Contacts de Civilisations en Martinique et en Guadeloupe*. Paris: UNESCO.

Ludwig, R. (ed.) (1989) *Les Créoles Français entre l'Oral et l'Ecrit*. Tübingen: Gunter Narr Verlag.

Managan, J.K. (2004) Language choice, linguistic ideologies and social identity in Guadeloupe. PhD dissertation, New York: New York University.

Meyjes, P. (1995) On the status of Creole in Guadeloupe: A study of present-day language attitudes. PhD dissertation, Chapel Hill, University of North Carolina.

Nainsouta, R. (1944) Créole et français ou le conflit des langues. *Liberté: Organe Guadeloupéen de Progrès Économique et Social* 2ème année (29), 1–3.

Narfez, A. (1944) La vulgarisation du français par l'école. *La Tribune Syndicale et Laïque* 7ème année (23), 2.

Poullet, H., Telchid, S. and Montbrand, D. (1984) *Dictionnaire Créole-Français*. Fort-de-France, Martinique: Hatier-Antilles.

Prudent, L-F. (1980) *Des Baragouins à la Langue Antillaise: Analyse Historique et Sociolinguistique du Discours sur le Créole*. Paris: Editions Caribéennes.

Prudent, L-F. (1981) Diglossie et interlecte. *Langages* 61, 13–38.

Prudent, L-F. (1993) Pratiques langagières martiniquaises: Genèse et fonctionnement d'un système créole. Thèse de doctorat d'Etat en linguistique, Université de Rouen.

Prudent, L-F. (2001) La reconnaissance officielle des créoles et l'aménagement d'un CAPES dans le système éducatif de l'Outre-mer français. *Etudes Créoles* 24 (1), 80–109.

Prudent, L-F. (2005) Interlecte et pédagogie de la variation en pays créoles. In L-F. Prudent, F. Tupin and S. Wharton (eds) *Du Plurilinguisme à l'Ecole: Vers une Gestion Coordonnée des Langues en Contextes Educatifs Sensibles* (pp. 359–378). Berne: Peter Lang.

Reisman, K. (1970) Cultural and linguistic ambiguity in a West Indian village. In N.E. Whitten, Jr and J.F. Szwed (eds) *Afro-American Anthropology: Contemporary Perspectives* (pp. 129–144). New York: The Free Press.

Schnepel, E.M. (1998) The language question in Guadeloupe: From the early chroniclers to the post-war generation of ACRA. *Plantation Society in the Americas* V (1), 60–94.

Schnepel, E.M. (2004) *In Search of a National Identity: Creole and Politics in Guadeloupe*. Hamburg: Helmut Buske Verlag.

Chapter 9

Success or Failure? Language, Tracking and Social Stratification of Anglophone Caribbean Students

SHONDEL NERO

The literature on, and general perception of, the academic performance of Anglophone Caribbean[1] students in the United States in the last 30 years have reflected what I call 'parallel narratives'; that is to say, the Caribbean student is, depending on which narrative is being constructed, either the immigrant success story (Kalmijn, 1996; Kao & Tienda, 1995; Model, 1991; Rong & Brown, 2001) or the failing student (Kirkwood, 2002; Sontag, 1992; West-White, 2003). These seemingly contradictory narratives are, arguably, both true to some degree, although the failing student narrative has been gaining ground as more recent waves of Caribbean students, mostly from the lower socioeconomic class, have entered North American schools and colleges.

The narratives reflect the significant disparity in academic achievement among Anglophone Caribbean students both in the Caribbean and abroad. In order to gain a deeper understanding of the academic performance of Caribbean students in the US, it is first necessary to go to the source – to examine critically the history, structure and quality of education in the Caribbean itself. While there are obviously differences among the various Anglophone Caribbean islands and countries in the extent and manifestation of the issue, the historical context of education and the core institutional structures are sufficiently similar that studying the case of one country can be illustrative. Thus, in this chapter, I will use Jamaica as a microcosm of the region because it is the most populous island, and also because the situation there, linguistically and socioeconomically speaking, is representative of the underlying factors that I believe lead to the development of the parallel narratives alluded to above.

I argue that the practice of streaming (aka tracking) in Jamaican and other Caribbean schools, largely indexed by socioeconomic class and language use (on a continuum from Creole to Standard English) is a major contributory factor in Caribbean students' success or failure in school both in the Caribbean and abroad (Evans, 2001). Furthermore, to the extent that proficiency in Standard English is used as an index of academic ability, Jamaican and other Caribbean students who come to school already proficient in standard English (a minority, usually from the upper middle class) are put on track for academic success. while other students (the Creole-speaking majority, typically of lower socioeconomic class) are assigned to low-performing classes and schools, putting them on track for a cycle of underachievement and/or failure. This paper calls for a critical re-examination of the practice of tracking in Caribbean schools, and the implementation of a more equitable and inclusive language policy for Caribbean students at home and abroad, which does not perpetuate the socially stratified system of academic success for a minority, and underachievement for the majority.

A Brief History of Social Stratification, Language Development and Education in the Anglophone Caribbean

With the exception of the indigenous peoples, the Caribbean area is mostly populated by transplanted groups of peoples from Africa, Asia and Europe brought to the region as cheap labor during the era of the British slave trade. The large number of Black Africans brought to the Caribbean to work on the sugar plantations vastly outnumbered their White British slave masters, reflected in the Black majority populations of most Anglophone Caribbean nations. After the abolition of slavery, a shortage of labor on the plantations was remedied by the importation of indentured laborers from India, China and Madeira. The highly stratified slave and post-abolition society mirrored a pyramid structure with Whites (usually British expatriates) at the top, free coloreds[2] in the middle, and the vast majority of dark-complexioned Blacks at the lowest rung (Wesley, 1932).

Within this hierarchical context, the Anglophone Caribbean linguistic situation evolved. The language contact of former slaves and indentured laborers from various ethnic and linguistic groups coupled with English-speaking slave masters engendered the development of a complex spectrum of language varieties ranging from a Creole (the mass vernacular) to varieties of Creole English and standardized Caribbean English. Typically, language use is highly correlated with socioeconomic class and education. Creole speakers are usually at the lower strata of the society, and the more English-proficient, educated middle and upper classes are above them. This sociolinguistic stratification is most visibly manifested in, and reproduced through, the education system.

Prior to gaining independence from Great Britain in the 1960s and 1970s, most Anglophone Caribbean countries followed a British model of education. Gordon (1963) notes that one of the two landmark resolutions in the history of the British West Indies passed by the British House of Commons in 1833 was the provision for the introduction of universal elementary education. (The other was the act to emancipate slaves.) The British colonial system was highly stratified in terms of educational opportunity. Only a small percentage of the population – mostly the children of British expatriates, and a handful of the local upper middle class – was afforded the opportunity to attend secondary school, and an even smaller percentage could aspire to tertiary education. This system was institutionalized by having differentially-resourced schools along with assessment mechanisms based mostly on high stakes tests at the primary and secondary levels, in which proficiency in standard English, among other factors, would be a prerequisite for passing. Performance on these tests was also used as the principal benchmark for determining entrance to, and exit from, various schools. Moreover, the rigidly-stratified colonies ensured that the Creole-speaking majority remained at the bottom of the social order by denying them access to high-quality education, and by extension, opportunities for access to literacy and use of standard English (Gordon, 1963).

Jamaican Education and Language Policy

Colonial language education policy

The education system in Jamaica, prior to its independence in 1962, was part of this British colonial structure. One area in which the structure was palpably manifested was in the language education policy during the colonial period. English was not only the sole medium of instruction in schools; it also served an ideological role in terms of the power and political capital that accrued to those who had access to and proficiency in it. Skutnabb-Kangas captures this phenomenon in the term *linguicism*, defined as:

> ideologies and structures which are used to legitimate, effectuate and reproduce an unequal division of power and resources (both material and non-material) between groups which are defined on the basis of language (on the basis of their mother tongues). (Skutnabb-Kangas, 1988: 13)

The Creole-speaking majority became the worst victims of linguicism. McCourtie (1998: 110) asserts that 'social, political and linguistic stratification acted as determinants of the type of education for the Creole-speaking population', so that, in effect, education not only became a form of social control but perpetuated a view of schooling that guaranteed success to the lighter-skinned, English-proficient expatriates and free-coloreds, and underachievement or failure for everyone else (Keith, 1978).

Not surprisingly, as early as the 1890s, Sterry (1895) recognized the chronic underachievement of large numbers of students from the Creole-speaking underclass, lamenting the fact that students leave elementary school no more proficient in standard English than those who had not been schooled at all. But the response to this problem was an eradicationist approach. Colonial educators erroneously conceived Creole as corrupt or broken English, and embarked on a pedagogy of correction (of all so-called mistakes made by Creole speakers) with the eventual hope of eradication of Creole features (McCourtie, 1998). Needless to say, it was a mistaken policy and practice. This state of affairs can be blamed in large part on what DeGraff (2005, Chapter 7 this volume) calls a 'dangerous myth' created by linguists – that Creoles are 'exceptional' or 'abnormal' languages 'viewed as handicaps for the intellectual development of their speakers' (DeGraff, 2005: 579). This persistent myth has created a vicious cycle for Creole speakers that has allowed the institutionalized devaluation of Creole languages and their speakers in school, denying them access to the curriculum in their mother tongue, thereby setting Creole speakers on a path for academic underachievement or failure, which is then attributed to their language, among other factors.

Education reform

It wasn't until 1966, with the popularization of a Ministry document entitled *A New Deal for Education in Independent Jamaica* (MOEYC, 1966) that serious consideration was given to reforming the education system with the explicit purpose of making it more accessible for the masses and redressing the social inequalities that the system of secondary education had formerly promoted. Recognizing the widespread academic underachievement of large sections of the population, the Jamaican government committed to a large-scale reform of its education system under the direction of its Ministry of Education, Youth and Culture (MOEYC). The first stage in the reform effort came in the early 1970s with the introduction of universally free secondary and college education and a campaign to eliminate illiteracy. Not only were more primary and secondary schools built, but there was also a proliferation of various types and levels of secondary and tertiary institutions – traditional academic, as well as technical, trade and vocational schools (US Library of Congress, Country Studies, n.d.).

A major aspect of reform was in the area of assessment. This is critical in that, as noted earlier, most curricula and instruction in Jamaica and elsewhere in the Anglophone Caribbean have been examination driven. At the primary level, the Common Entrance Examination, a national, locally-authored and administered standardized test, traditionally given in the sixth grade to determine entrance into hierarchically-ranked secondary schools, was phased out in Jamaica in 1998 and replaced by a curriculum-based National Assessment Program (Jamaica Information Service, n.d.).

At the secondary level, Jamaican schools switched from the British-authored and controlled General Certification of Education (GCE) exams to the Caribbean Examinations Council (CXC)-authored exams as the principal credential for showing completion of traditional secondary schools and for entrance to tertiary institutions. This was part of a broader movement organized under the Reform of Secondary Education (ROSE) Program, launched in 1993. However, in a comprehensive study of Jamaican secondary education, Dwyer *et al.* (2003) found that the current system in terms of curriculum and examinations is still set up to better serve the higher-achieving students – students who would have, in any case, attended traditional academic secondary schools and fared well. Their study showed that, while middle- and lower-achieving students are now entering and remaining in secondary school in larger numbers, they have little to show in terms of knowledge gained, as evidenced by poor test performance. Examination performance continues to be the primary criterion used to document learning, and many of these students are tracked into schools and/or classes that do not prepare them adequately for high-stakes exams like the CXC. The critical issue of tracking is therefore taken up in the following section.

Streaming (Tracking)

Despite the educational reform efforts underway in Jamaica discussed above, the underlying structure of the education system as traditionally set up is still in place. As noted by Carlson and Quello (2002: 1) in their social assessment of Jamaican education, 'The educational structure is highly stratified and remains so in spite of policy interventions in the 1990s to reduce stratification'. Nowhere is this more evident than in the time-honored tradition of streaming (hereafter called 'tracking'). Evans (2001) offers an insightful analysis of the practice of tracking in Jamaican schools. She defines tracking as 'a method of organizing teaching whereby students are categorized according to their academic ability and placed in different classes at the same grade level or in different groups within a class' (Evans, 2001: 90). Evans asserts that the practice of tracking in Jamaican schools is deeply engrained and internalized by students, parents and teachers. Many teachers, for example, strongly believe that tracking makes their job easier since they only have students of similar ability levels in various groups. Students and parents, for their part, believe that if a student is placed in a high track, it automatically means the student is more intelligent, and conversely, if placed in a low track the student is a 'dunce'.

One of the most noteworthy findings of Evans's research in primary and all-age schools is that there is a perceptible relationship between tracking and socioeconomic class such that students placed in low tracks are typically children of unskilled laborers and children in high tracks are children of professionals. Carlson and Quello's findings echo the correlation between tracking and socioeconomic background. They characterize tracking as 'destructive' and 'the major problem holding back student achievement' (Carlson & Quello, 2002: 5).

In practice, tracking is done by placing students in A, B or C classes corresponding to high, middle and low tracks respectively, or in mixed ability classes by grouping the high, middle and low achievers separately for classroom instruction. Once students are tracked, Evans (2001: 92) contends, 'they are treated and taught differentially'. She further suggests that 'streaming influences the teacher's expectations and hence, the evaluations which they make of the students' (Evans, 2001: 92). The track becomes not only an academic unit but also a social one, which labels students' identities in a very public way. Thus, the student in the A class is seen not only as being in a high-achieving class, but is deemed a high-achieving person, and conversely, the student in the C class becomes a low achiever, slow learner or 'dunce' – labels that are often internalized by the students themselves, and that influence how they are assessed by teachers and how they assess themselves and each other. The tracking and resulting labeling extend to the school itself, which has pernicious long-term effects on students' self image and the image of their schools. Evans notes that, while it is theoretically possible to move from a lower to a higher track, many students, in fact, end up spending their entire school career in a low track.

How is language reflected in tracking? We know that languages and language varieties do not cause poor performance, but language is used as an *index* of a speaker's social class and academic ability, and this becomes a vicious cycle in terms of eventual chances for academic success. The following excerpts from Yusuf-Khalil's research in two all-age schools and one primary school in Jamaica (cited in Evans, 2001: 99) illustrate the differential language use of sixth grade students in different tracks (A and C):

(1) C-track students discussing other students:

Student 1: 6A children dem in brighter class.

Researcher: How do you know?

Student 2: Teacher dem talk an wi hear. Teacher dem sey we inna dunce class.

(2) A-track students evaluating themselves:
Student 1: We're in the brightest class.
Student 2: I would cry if I was sent to 6C – I would feel shame.
Student 3: I wouldn't want to go to school.

(3) C-track students' description of their evaluation by teachers:
Student 1: Dem sey wi don't know 'A' from bull foot.
Researcher: How does that make you feel?
Group: We feel bad.
Student 2: She tell wi sey wi a cruff.[3]
Student 3: She say wi no learning anything we guan end up planting ganja; bun coal, tun dreadlocks!
Student 4: When she talk the children laugh at yu and mek you feel shame.
Student 5: See unu,[4] that's why you don't learn, because you won't listen.

These excerpts reflect the spectrum of language use in Jamaica from the basilect (Creole) to the mesolect (Creole English) to the acrolect (standard English). Not so coincidentally, the C-track students' speech (excerpt 1) show more Creole features (e.g. 'children dem', 'teacher dem', 'an wi hear') while the language of the A-track students (excerpt 2) is more standardized. The last line in excerpt 3 shows the student capturing the teacher's language, which is a mixture of Creole (e.g. 'see unu') and standard English.

The students' language is an identity marker not only for their track but also for how they are perceived and evaluated by fellow students and school authorities. Thus the A-track students are marked for success and the C-track students for underachievement. This academic and social sorting of students in Jamaica is the beginning of the construction of the parallel narratives of success and failure, which continue when students migrate to North America. McCourtie (1998) suggests that this practice is not deliberate, although I believe its pervasiveness certainly gives that impression. She writes, 'the systemic failure of Creole speakers resulted from a complex interplay of historical, political and pedagogical forces rather than from an explicit attempt to prevent pupils' acquisition of English and thwart their success' (McCourtie, 1998: 121).

Current Language Education Policy in Jamaica

McCourtie's work is enlightening in that it brings into sharp focus the politics of Creole language education in Jamaica in the span of a century (1890s to 1990s), and the recognition that there has been a marked shift in language policy and attitude in Jamaica since the colonial era, even if fraught with tensions. Credit for this shift can be given in part to the research and advocacy of many Creole linguists, sociolinguists and educators, whose work over the last 50 years has raised public awareness of the history, structure and validity of Creole languages and of the unique language situation in former plantation colonies in the Caribbean (Alleyne, 1980; Bryan, 2004; Carrington, 1992; Christie, 2003; Craig, 1983, 2006; Devonish, 1986; Pollard, 1998; Rickford, 1987; Roberts, 1988; Schnepel, Chapter 8, this volume). To be sure, one of the more positive attitude changes that has emanated from the post-independence era has been greater use and acceptance of Creole in the public sphere, in the media, in the performing arts and in literature as an expression of true Jamaican identity.

By the 1970s, the MOEYC officially recognized in its curriculum guidelines that, although English is the official language, Jamaica is a bilingual country, with the vast majority of people speaking Jamaican Creole (JC) as their mother tongue and a small minority speaking Standard Jamaican English (SJE) (MOEYC, n.d.). The objective of language education, according to the policy, was to strive to make Jamaican children more proficient in Standard English. McCourtie (1998: 115) called the recognition of Jamaica's bilingualism 'an important policy watershed' for it laid the groundwork for a real language policy change. The MOEYC came to the understanding that, in order to legitimize this bilingual reality and to redress past practice of de facto language discrimination, a new comprehensive language education policy needed to be written and institutionalized. This was finally accomplished in 2001 with the publication of its *Language Education Policy* (LEP).

In its current LEP, the MOEYC has tried to reverse the colonial policy of stratification by emphasizing access, equity and quality. In its executive summary, the LEP stipulates that the MOEYC:

> has adopted a policy position which recognizes Jamaica as a bilingual country. It retains SJE as the official language and advocates the policy option which promotes oral use of the home language in schools, while facilitating the development of skills in SJE. (MOEYC, 2001: 4)

The policy also seeks to capture the unique language typology in Jamaica, which spans a blurry spectrum of language varieties from Jamaican Creole to Standard Jamaican English in various domains.

How is the LEP actually implemented in the classroom? First, the policy allows teachers to use the children's home language in the early years (kindergarten to Grade 3), while facilitating the development of literacy in English. This might include the teacher's giving directions or explaining a concept or task in Creole. It also allows for 'guidance by linguistically aware teachers who can appreciate the importance of Creole' and 'increased exposure to English, and particularly to idiomatic English, through different types of immersion' (MOEYC, 2001: 24). But Evans (2001: 102) found that in low stream classes 'Creole was often used to show the teacher's contempt for a particular individual', so that, instead of being appreciated, as stated in the LEP, Creole seems to have negative associations in the school context. Furthermore, many teachers, especially in the low-track classes, are not fluent in SJE themselves, and so are not able to provide models of SJE to the students who most need it. Bryan (2004: 89) noted this phenomenon in her work: 'students and teachers might think they are using English when often they are not', attributing their inability to make the distinction to the fact that JC and SJE are lexically related. I would add that the inability to make the distinction is also due to the strong self-ascribed 'English-speaking' identity among teachers and students alike – a legacy of British colonization. So while the LEP calls for 'opportunities to hear and speak the target language in a variety of situations' (MOEYC, 2001: 24), and 'modeling of the target language in the classroom' (MOEYC, 2001: 25), Bryan found that a very different reality obtained in many Jamaican schools. She observes that the school language is not given enough attention in day-to-day classroom interaction:

> In essence, there is still very little sense of the child as a language learner, rather s/he learns *about* language, with a great emphasis on structure in language teaching and covering a prescribed syllabus, to the exclusion of meaningful practice. (Bryan, 2004: 89)

In addition to the challenges of implementation noted by Bryan (2004), the MOEYC also acknowledged three other critical issues in education:

(1) the continued high status of SJE and the low status of Creole (despite the latter's wider use) and the 'inhibitions of many learners who are affected by the ambivalent attitude towards the use of Jamaican Creole in the school and society' (MOEYC, 2001: 5);
(2) the continuing 'unsatisfactory performance of many candidates in English language examinations at all levels' (MOEYC, 2001: 5);
(3) perhaps most important, the persistently low levels of literacy in schools (especially non-traditional ones) and the lack of preparedness of secondary school graduates for higher education or the workforce.

Thus, while the LEP's objective for greater access, equity and quality is to be commended, the underlying structure of the Jamaican education system precludes full realization of this objective, as language and socioeconomic background determine placement into differentially-resourced schools and classes, which in turn influence students' literacy levels, their performance on standardized tests and their ultimate academic prospects beyond secondary school.

What Can Be Done?

In Jamaica

The foregoing discussion raises a number of important issues that relate equally to language, education and social stratification. It is clear that the highly-stratified Jamaican society that exists today as part of the colonial legacy continues to deny equal access to quality education for the poor masses. On a macro-level, socioeconomic and class disparities need to be addressed starting with high-level, targeted government policies and programs. The specifics of the types of programs that would begin to address these disparities are beyond the scope of this chapter. However, in the educational arena, it seems evident that the tracking system needs to be abolished. Several researchers and educators (Allard, 2003; Carlson & Quello, 2002; Dwyer *et al.*, 2003; Evans, 2001) have called for the dismantling of the tracking system, as it sets in motion a rigidly-defined path to success or failure for different students based on circumstances beyond their control – socioeconomic class and language. Educational reform efforts that do not abolish the tracking system are largely cosmetic, and are not likely to yield substantive changes in the long run. Abolishing the tracking system, however, is easier said than done. It would require a societal attitude shift with respect to who is entitled to a good education. And this cannot (should not) depend on one's socioeconomic background. Such an attitude shift is slowly beginning to take hold, but there is still much to be accomplished, as one of the more destructive legacies of colonization is the assumption that rigid social stratification is both normal and desirable.

True educational reform has to demonstrate the political will buttressed by the necessary financial support to provide high quality teachers, a comprehensive curriculum and adequate materials in *every type* of school for *all* students. Within schools, there should be no A, B or C classes. There should simply be classes. Moreover, if the MOEYC's LEP is to be true to its recognition that Jamaica is a bilingual country and that the majority of people speak Creole, then large numbers of Creole speakers should not be marginalized into C schools and/or C classes, where they are not being educated bilingually, and are, in fact, receiving a substandard education. Creole-dominant speakers should be in *all* schools with the same access to a curriculum that recognizes the importance of both Creole and Standard English.

Although many Jamaican students and teachers are aware of the importance of Standard English, many teachers themselves are not proficient in it. This points to the need for a cadre of highly-trained teachers who are competent in standard written and spoken English such that they can provide good models for Creole speakers to help them achieve literacy in standard English. At the same time, teachers may not necessarily be aware of the structure of Creole, even though they speak it. Therefore, they would also need to be sufficiently trained in linguistics to understand the basic history, structure and uses of Creole, its connection to students' identities and the most effective pedagogical approaches for Creole speakers. In this regard, teacher training institutions today have the benefit of being informed by the work of Creole linguists and applied linguists cited above, unlike the days of the colonial language policy. Thus, today's teachers can be provided with well-designed pre- and in-service professional development training to help them implement more effective contrastive, bidialectal and/or bilingual approaches to facilitate the language and literacy development of Creole speakers. Craig's (2006) work, for example, offers linguistically-informed, sound policies and procedures for working with vernacular speakers. Also, Devonish and Carpenter (2007) have reported on a successful bilingual program for JC speakers, which they designed and implemented in Grades 1 to 4 in three Jamaican primary schools.

In the US

This chapter began with my noting the disparity in perception of Anglophone Caribbean students in the US, evidenced in the narratives of 'success' or 'failure' in the literature. Such narratives play out in the classroom. Because Jamaicans have the highest migration rate of Anglophone Caribbean natives to the United States (US Census, 2000), teachers in US schools, especially in urban areas, are likely to encounter Jamaicans in their classrooms. Teachers may find that these students have distinctly different levels of spoken and written English proficiency despite their self-ascribed 'English-speaking' identity for the reasons discussed in this chapter. Furthermore, teachers in schools in metropolitan areas such as New York City with large Caribbean populations are witnessing a rapidly growing number of Creole-dominant speakers, reflecting the current trend in migration. The language use and needs of these students continue to challenge educators to find appropriate and effective strategies to address them.

Many of these students are from lower socioeconomic classes and/or attended low-performing schools in the Caribbean. Often, they continue 'on track' for failure in US schools, as their lack of proficiency in standard written English hinders successful performance in academic subjects, which are heavily dependent on writing. On the other hand, Caribbean students who attended high-performing schools back home usually continue to fare well in US schools, perpetuating the successful immigrant narrative, but at the same time increasing the discrepancy in perception of Caribbean students.

How best to address the linguistic needs of Jamaican and other Anglophone Caribbean students in American schools and colleges has been a highly-contested topic However, as a first step, I believe language awareness training in undergraduate and graduate teacher preparation programs, with particular focus on Creole speakers, such as described earlier for Jamaican teachers, would enhance American teachers' understanding of the history, structure, use of and attitudes towards Creoles. It would also be a more principled basis on which to make placement decisions for Creole-speaking students, and to enact appropriate pedagogical strategies to address their needs. Such training could also be implemented through ongoing in-service professional development.

The second step, how to translate training into effective pedagogical practice, is debatable. Should Creole speakers be placed in mainstream English, bilingual, English as a Second Language (ESL) or English as a Second Dialect (ESD) classes? Several linguists and educators have offered insightful recommendations for teaching Creole speakers in US classrooms (Clachar, 2004; DeKleine, Chapter 10, this volume; Pratt-Johnson, 2006; Winer, 2006). I have argued elsewhere (Nero, 2000, 2001) that traditional ESL classes that serve the needs of second language learners such as Spanish speakers do not effectively address the unique linguistic needs of Jamaican Creole speakers. Because of (1) students' strong self-identification with English, (2) students'receptive knowledge of English, and (3) the inability of some Creole speakers to distinguish between Creole and English, Creole speakers often are not inclined or motivated to participate in ESL classes. Rather, an ESD approach might be more helpful where the students' vernacular is taken into account in the classroom, selectively using contrastive approaches. Clachar's (2004) work on the differences between ESD (Creole) and ESL speakers with regard to the acquisition of tense-aspect in English underscores the need for curriculum to be tailored to the unique needs of Creole speakers.

Still, in New York City, a group of educators successfully lobbied the New York State Education Department in 2001 to provide funding and support for ESL classes for English-based Creole speakers from the Caribbean by arguing that 'Patois' (or Creole) should be recognized as a separate language. While the policy has been official for some six years, its implementation in schools has been uneven at best. A small number of schools in Queens and Brooklyn provide ESD (rather than ESL) classes for newly-arrived Creole speakers who are struggling readers and writers. Other schools provide assistance for this population in resource rooms or in after-school programs. For eaxmple, in one middle school in Queens, a literacy-based 'newcomer class' is offered for this population (Joseph Gates, school principal – personal communication, December 10, 2007).

Siegel (2007: 68) provides other examples of the translation of linguistic training into two types of instructional programs:

(1) *accommodation programs* where the use of students' home language is accepted in classroom interaction, storytelling and creative writing, as well as the study of vernacular literature;
(2) *awareness programs* that include accommodations in addition to two other components: (a) a sociolinguistic component where students learn about different language varieties, dialects and Creoles, and how one variety comes to be privileged and accepted as the standard; and (b) a contrastive component where students contrast the phonological, morphosyntactic and pragmatic features of their vernacular with the standard variety. The Caribbean Academic Program in Evanston, Illinois is an example of such a language awareness program.

Also, the wide range of language and academic ability among Caribbean students could be addressed by a curriculum that includes an equally wide range of language and literature. For example, students should be encouraged to read literature written in both Standard English and in the vernacular, and should be encouraged to write the same. Too often, schools take a narrowly prescriptive approach to reading and writing, giving students the impression that only the standard variety counts for any medium of communication in school, leaving Creole speakers at a decided disadvantage, and unintentionally privileging speakers who are already proficient in the standard variety. If we are to halt the cycle of linguistic tracking, then schools would do well to make language variation an object of study (Adger *et al.*, 2007), and also give all students multiple opportunities to exercise and expand their linguistic repertoire through reading, writing, listening and speaking in many language varieties appropriate to the context.

Between the Caribbean and the US

American and Caribbean educators would do well to familiarize themselves with the education system in each other's countries in order to have some understanding of the various types of educational and linguistic experiences students might have had prior to migrating to the US, and what Caribbean students might expect coming into an American classroom. Such knowledge can be gained through teacher exchange programs, comparative education conferences and even video conferencing as part of professional development.

The recommendations here are by no means a panacea. They are, however, an attempt to address a system that sets up students for success or failure. Caribbean students, like all other students, run the gamut in their academic abilities. Yet, language, tracking and social stratification can unwittingly create differential paths for them that may not reflect their real abilities. A critical re-examination of the current system, including educational structure, language attitudes, teacher-preparation and practice, would begin a more equitable realignment of the social order, view language as an asset for all rather than a liability for some, and allow *all* students a chance to succeed.

Notes

1. The term Anglophone Caribbean (also known as the West Indies) refers here to the following islands and/or countries: Anguilla, Antigua and Barbuda, The Bahamas, Barbados, The British Virgin Islands, Caricou, The Cayman Islands, Dominica, Grenada, Jamaica, Montserrat, St. Kitts-Nevis, St. Lucia, St. Vincent and the Grenadines, Trinidad and Tobago, Turks and Caicos Island, Belize in Central America and Guyana on the South American mainland. All of these islands/countries share a history of British colonization, and English is their official language.
2. Free coloreds were persons of full or partial African descent who were not enslaved. They were often the mixed race offspring of a White slave master and Black female slave (Wesley, 1932).
3. Creole word: *cruff* – a worthless person.
4. Creole word: *unu* – you all (second person plural pronoun).

References

Adger, C.T., Wolfram, W. and Christian, D. (2007) *Dialects in Schools and Communities* (2nd edn). Mahwah, NJ: Erlbaum.

Allard, L. (2003) Access to secondary education in Anglophone Caribbean countries. In T. Bastick and A. Ezenne (eds) *Researching Change in Caribbean Education: Curriculum, Teaching and Administration* (pp. 329–354). Mona: Department of Educational Studies, University of the West Indies.

Alleyne, M. (1980) *Comparative Afro-American*. Ann Arbor, MI: Karoma Publishers.

Bryan, B. (2004) Language and literacy in a Creole-dominant environment: A study of primary schools in Jamaica. *Language, Culture and Curriculum* 17 (2), 87–96.

Carlson, B. and Quello, J. (2002) *Social Assessment* (of Jamaican education). Ministry of Education Youth and Culture. On WWW at http://www.moec.gov.jm/projects/rose/socialassessment.htm. Accessed 24.5.06.

Carrington, L. (1992) Caribbean English. In T. McArthur (ed.) *The Oxford Companion to the English Language* (pp. 191–193). Oxford: Oxford University Press.

Christie, P. (2003) *Language in Jamaica*. Kingston: Arawak Press.

Clachar, A. (2004) The construction of Creole-speaking students' linguistic profile and contradictions in ESL literacy programs. *TESOL Quarterly* 38 (1), 153–165.

Craig, D. (1983) Teaching standard English to nonstandard speakers: Some methodological issues. *Journal of Negro Education* 52 (1), 65–74.

Craig, D. (2006) *From Vernacular to Standard English: Teaching Language and Literacy to Caribbean Students*. Miami, FL: Ian Randle Publishers.

DeGraff, M. (2005) Linguists' most dangerous myth: The fallacy of Creole exceptionalism. *Language in Society* 34 (4), 533–591.

Devonish, H. (1986) *Language and Liberation: Creole Language Politics in the Caribbean*. London: Karia Press.

Devonish, H. and Carpenter, K. (2007) Full bilingual education in a creole situation: The Jamaican bilingual primary education project. *Occasional Paper, No. 35*. St Augustine, Trinidad: Society for Caribbean Linguistics.

Dwyer, C.A., Harris, A. and Anderson, L. (2003) *National and Regional Secondary Level Examinations and the Reform of Secondary Education (ROSE II)*. Prepared for the Ministry of Education, Youth and Culture, Government of Jamaica.

Evans, H. (2001) *Inside Jamaican Schools*. Mona: University of the West Indies Press.

Gordon, S. (1963) *A Century of West Indian Education*. London: Longmans Green.

Jamaica Information Service (n.d.) *Government of Jamaica*. On WWW at http://www.jis.gov.jm/gov_ja/education.asp. Accessed 24.5.06.

Kalmijn, M. (1996) The socioeconomic assimilation of Caribbean American Blacks. *Social Forces* 74, 911–930.

Kao, G. and Tienda, M. (1995) Optimism and achievement: The educational performance of immigrant youth. *Social Science Quarterly* 76 (1), 1–19.

Keith, S. (1978) An historical overview of the state and educational policy in Jamaica. *Latin American Perspectives* 5 (2), 37–52.

Kirkwood, T.F. (2002) Jamaican students of color in the American classroom: Problems and possibilities in education. *Intercultural Education* 13 (3), 305–313.

McCourtie, L. (1998) The politics of Creole language education in Jamaica: 1891–1921 and the 1990s. *Journal of Multilingual and Multicultural Development* 19 (2), 108–127.

MOEYC (1966) *A New Deal for Education in Independent Jamaica*. Kingston: Ministry of Education,Youth and Culture.

MOEYC (2001) *Language Education Policy*. Ministry of Education, Youth and Culture (Jamaica). On WWW at http://www.moec.gov.jm/policies/languagepolicy.pdf. Accessed 23.5.06.

MOEYC (nd) *Curriculum Guidelines for Grades 7–9*. Kingston: Ministry of Education,Youth and Culture.

Model, S. (1991) Caribbean immigrants: A Black success story? *International Migration Review* 24, 248–276.

Nero, S. (2000) The changing faces of English: A Caribbean perspective. *TESOL Quarterly* 34 (3), 483–510.

Nero, S. (2001) *Englishes in Contact: Anglophone Caribbean Students in an Urban College*. Cresskill, NJ: Hampton Press.

Pollard, V. (1998) Code-switching and code mixing: Language in the Jamaican classroom. *Caribbean Journal of Education* 20 (1), 9–21.

Pratt-Johnson, Y. (2006) Teaching Jamaican Creole-speaking students. In S. Nero (ed.) *Dialects, Englishes, Creoles and Education* (pp. 119–136). Mahwah, NJ: Lawrence Erlbaum Associates.

Rickford, J. (1987) *Dimensions of a Creole Continuum*. Stanford, CT: Stanford University Press.

Roberts, P. (1988) *West Indians and Their Language*. Cambridge: Cambridge University Press.

Rong, X.L. and Brown, F (2001) The effects of immigrant generation and ethnicity on educational attainment among young African and Caribbean blacks in the United States. *Harvard Educational Review* 71 (3), 536–565.

Siegel, J. (2007) Creoles and minority dialects in education: An update. *Language and Education* 21 (1), 66–86.

Skutnabb-Kangas, T. (1988) Multilingualism and the education of minority children. In T. Skutnabb-Kangas and J. Cummins (eds) *Minority Education: From Shame to Struggle* (pp. 9–44). Clevedon: Multilingual Matters.

Sontag, D. (1992) Caribbean pupils' English seems barrier, not bridge. *The New York Times*, November 28, pp. A1, A22.

Sterry, C. (1895) *Jamaica Annual Report of the Superintending Inspector of Industrial Schools and of the Board of Education for the Year Ended 31st March, 1984*. Kingston: Jamaica Government Printing Office.

United States Census (2000) Online at www.census.gov. Accessed 8.9.08.

US Library of Congress. Country Studies (n.d.) *Jamaica Education*. On WWW at http://countrystudies.us/caribbean-islands/22.htm. Accessed 24.5.06.

Wesley, C. (1932) The Negro in the West Indies, slavery and freedom. *The Journal of Negro History* 17 (1), 51–66.

West-White, C. (2003) Caribbean student speakers' education and experiences in American schools: A constant struggle with varied results. In T. Bastick and A. Ezenne (eds) *Teaching Caribbean Students: Research on Social Issues in the Caribbean and Abroad* (pp. 251–248). Mona Department of Educational Studies, University of the West Indies.

Winer, L. (2006) Teaching English to Caribbean English-Creole speaking students in the Caribbean and North America. In S. Nero (ed.) *Dialects, Englishes, Creoles and Education* (pp. 105–118). Mahwah, NJ: Erlbaum.

Chapter 10

Sierra Leonean and Liberian Students in ESL Programs in the US: The Role of Creole English

CHRISTA DE KLEINE

With increased globalization, and the concomitant spreading dominance of the English language, varieties of English continue to develop around the world. Similarly, with increased mobility of speakers of these diverse varieties of English, we are now experiencing increasing numbers of speakers of 'other' varieties of English – particularly those labeled 'Outer Circle' varieties (cf. Kachru, 1992) – in classrooms in 'Inner Circle' countries. The first Inner Circle country to witness this trend was the UK, primarily in the 1960s and 1970s, followed by Canada in the 1980s. More recently, the US has seen a rise – in some urban areas, such as New York, Miami and Washington, a very sharp one– in immigrant students from Outer Circle countries, in particular from Anglophone Caribbean and West African countries.

Immigrant students from English-speaking parts of West Africa and the Caribbean face significant challenges in US schools (Crandall, 2003; de Kleine, 2006a, forthcoming-a; Narvaez & Garcia, 1992; Nero, 2001, 2006; Pratt-Johnson, 1993; Sewell, 1997). Some of these challenges are similar to those that many immigrant students experience, such as adjusting to a new culture, functioning in a different educational system, dealing with the economic hardship that living in a new country may bring, coping with family separation issues, and so forth. From a linguistic perspective, though, they face a different task: while most immigrant students have to adjust to a school language that is typologically different from their native language (L1), students from the Anglophone West Africa and the Caribbean – specifically those with an English-lexifier pidgin or creole language background – have to acquire a school language that is in several respects similar to their L1, yet in others very different. This chapter discusses the unique challenges that such a language background brings, focusing on students from Anglophone West Africa who come from Sierra Leone and Liberia and on whom little research has been conducted to date (unlike students from the Anglophone Caribbean, cf. Clachar, 2003, 2004, 2005; Coelho, 1991; de Kleine, forthcoming-a; Edwards, 1979; Nero, 2001; Pratt-Johnson, 1993). It is argued here that while English-lexifier creole language varieties are not (necessarily) exceptional as a group (cf. DeGraff, Chapter 7 this volume), the differences between Creole English (CE) varieties and their lexifier, English, are unique when compared to the differences between other closely-related language varieties. The nature of these differences, it is argued here, contributes significantly to the challenges that CE speakers experience in Standard English (SE) classrooms.

West African Students in US Classrooms

This chapter reports on a study conducted in a large suburban school district on the East Coast (henceforth 'the school district'), which was part of a larger research project that examined the language and literacy development of secondary school students from Anglophone West Africa who were enrolled in ESL classes (see also de Kleine, 2006a, forthcoming b). The research project was originally motivated by a concern in the school district that students from English-speaking West African countries, whose numbers had increased rapidly since the mid-1990s, were struggling linguistically and, consequently, academically. This was most clearly observed among students from Sierra Leone and Liberia and, to a somewhat lesser extent, Ghana. The research discussed here focuses on the role that Sierra Leonean and Liberian students' native CE varieties – Krio and Vernacular Liberian English respectively – play in the students' challenges in US schools.

Despite the fact that, unlike most other immigrant students, the Sierra Leonean and Liberian immigrant students in the school district had typically received education in their home countries in English, intake data on the reading and writing skills of these students indicated that the academic challenges they experienced were nonetheless (at least partly) related to their English language skills. More than 80% of the students tested in the Limited English Proficient (LEP) range, typically resulting in placement in ESL classes – a situation similar to that of many immigrant students from the Anglophone Caribbean (cf. Nero, 2006; Pratt-Johnson, 2006; Winer, 2006).

Several factors are likely to have contributed to the high percentage of Sierra Leonean and Liberian students lacking sufficient language skills to perform at age-appropriate grade levels. I have discussed these in more detail elsewhere (de Kleine, 2006a); they include students' prior education, psychological trauma and – the main factor cited by teachers – interrupted education. Nonetheless, data from the school district show that of the students involved in our research project 'only' a third of all Liberian students and two-thirds of all Sierra Leonean students were reported to have had interrupted education.

While fully acknowledging the potential effects of prior literacy instruction and interrupted education for at least a number of the students, existing research among CE-speaking students from other parts of the world indicates that another factor merits further investigation in the case of Liberian and Sierra Leonean students' linguistic challenges. That factor is their unique English language backgrounds, which typically include a variety of creolized English.

A large body of research spanning over 40 years has shown consistently that students who speak a variety of CE as their home language are at a serious linguistic disadvantage in classrooms that require SE, and that this linguistic disadvantage exerts a considerable influence on literacy development and overall academic performance. In particular, the structural differences between students' home language (CE) and the SE required in the classroom often mean that students find it difficult to express themselves in a language that follows the rules of SE, with significant L1 transfer effects from students' CE varieties. Moreover, teachers' misinterpretation of the role of CE in students' SE development often further exacerbates the challenge for these students, exerting a negative impact on both instruction and assessment. These effects have been observed in a number of different countries (and thus presumably in different cultural contexts, school systems, etc.), including Trinidad (Winer, 1989), Jamaica (Craig, 1966, 1967, 1997, 1999, 2001), the UK (Edwards, 1979), Canada (Coelho, 1991) and the US (Clachar, 2003, 2004, 2005; de Kleine, 2006a, forthcoming-a; Nero, 2001; Pratt-Johnson, 1993, 2006); and at elementary (de Kleine, forthcoming-a), secondary (Clachar, 2004; de Kleine, 2006a) and post secondary (Clachar, 2003, 2005; Nero, 2001) levels. There can thus be little doubt that the language background that CE-speaking students share often forms an important obstacle to academic achievement in settings that require SE.

The Language Background of Sierra Leonean and Liberian Students

Sierra Leone and Liberia are both highly multilingual countries, with 24 languages reported for Sierra Leone and 30 for Liberia (Gordon, 2005). Most of these are indigenous languages, although English remains the official language in both countries. For historical reasons related to colonization and slave resettlement, both in Liberia and Sierra Leone (as in other parts of Anglophone West Africa), pidginized and creolized varieties of English have developed – varieties that share many linguistic features with each other, and also with the CE varieties that developed in the Caribbean. Indeed, the high degree of similarity has led Holm (1989: 415) to label these as varieties of one and the same language, Atlantic Creole English. In Sierra Leone, the CE variety that developed is referred to as Krio, which is widely used across the country as a lingua franca, and as a first language primarily by speakers in Freetown, the capital (Holm, 1989: 412). In Liberia, the situation is more complex, with several (expanded) pidgin and creole varieties being used (for detailed information, see Singler, 1997). However, the variety that is by far the most prevalent – indeed, spoken by almost all Liberians (Singler, 2004) – is Vernacular Liberian English (VLE).

In the current study, information collected on the home language background of the students (assumed to be representative of at least the Sierra Leonean and Liberian students in the school district) revealed that most students had extensive exposure to varieties of CE, with a significant majority employing it as their home language, i.e. as (one of) their first language(s) (for more detailed information, see de Kleine, forthcoming b).

Writing Skills among Sierra Leonean and Liberian ESL Students

To analyze L1 transfer effects of students' CE backgrounds on students' written SE language development, a corpus of 463 writing samples was collected from 41 Sierra Leonean students (346 samples) and 15 Liberian students (117 samples); students were enrolled in ESL classes ranging from lower to advanced level. Essays covered a variety of topics, with an average length of approximately 275 words.

Detailed analysis revealed a number of clear tendencies in the data. First, the samples showed weaknesses with in a number of areas, as could be expected with any group of students, native or non-native speakers, who are developing academic writing skills. For example, many samples contained spelling and punctuation errors, and a fair number displayed organizational and coherence weaknesses. Again as expected, the writing skills of students in lower level ESL classes were generally less developed than those of students in intermediate and, particularly, in advanced ESL classes. Overall, students also struggled to negotiate the use of appropriate academic registers – an issue that greatly challenged all students (see Schleppegrell, 2004). But an interesting additional tendency emerged: while lower-level students' writings displayed weaknesses in most if not all areas, the weaknesses of intermediate and, particularly, advanced ESL level students were heavily concentrated in the area of grammar. In other words, while students' writing skills did indeed improve (probably at least partly as a result of ESL instruction, though further research is necessary to establish that), *their grammatical accuracy improved relatively much less*. In fact, it was not uncommon to find essays at the advanced ESL level that had a well-developed topic, excellent organization and a rich, appropriate vocabulary for an academic essay, but which contained grammatical errors usually associated with lower-level ESL students, such as lack of past tense marking (cf. Bardovi-Harlig, 2000).

Before an analysis of grammatical error patterns is presented, however, a discussion of the significance of grammatical accuracy and how it is determined is in order. In recent years, various linguists have de-emphasized the role of grammatical accuracy in the literacy development of 'World English' speaking-students. For instance, Canagarajah (2006: 593) writes ... 'rather than focusing on correctness, we should perceive "error" as the learner's active negotiation and exploration of choices and possibilities.' From this perspective, deviations from SE are not viewed as 'errors' but as relatively conscious choices to not abide by the grammar of SE. However, this presumes that the student has a reasonable amount of bidialectal/ bilingual competency. One cannot 'negotiate and explore choices and possibilities' when the range of choices and possibilities is not available to the speaker (or writer), and thus this presumes an awareness of the inventory of features and their underlying meanings in the different varieties. As this chapter will show, that is not always the case for speakers of different varieties of English. The goal of this chapter, then, is to contribute to the information needed to enable speakers of different varieties of (non-standard) English to negotiate and explore the choices and possibilities that crucially include those typically viewed as falling within the realm of SE.

'Error' in this chapter is defined as a deviation from the rules of Standard American English (SAE), as for instance laid down in publications on SAE grammar (e.g. Celce-Murcia & Larsen-Freeman, 1999). This does not imply that this variety of English is superior to other varieties, standardized or non-standardized, but simply that this is the standard used in education in the US and, for better or worse, the standard used to judge students' academic progress.

Detailed analysis of grammatical error patterns in the writings revealed that a small set of error types was particularly prevalent. After identifying all grammatical errors in the corpus, we categorized the errors that occurred at least three times in an individual student's writings, which resulted in a total of 88 types of error. The number of students that had produced a certain error type was then tabulated. This analysis revealed a sharp distinction between errors made by a high percentage of students and those errors made by a relatively low percentage of students. Of all the errors recorded, a small set was produced by at least 75% of all students; by contrast, all other error types were produced by less than 60% of the students, with more than half of all error types (46) produced by less than 25% of all students. The most prevalent error types, i.e. those produced by 75% of all students or more, are shown in Table 10.1.

Several explanations can be invoked to account for these error types. Obviously, particular grammatical structures are more frequently used in English than others (e.g. plural noun phrases are encountered more often than, say, hypothetical clauses), and this in turn will affect the frequency of error types, with increased opportunity for error in the more commonly encountered constructions. Another factor that may influence error frequencies is related to the complexity of certain grammatical forms or patterns in English, with the more complex ones presumably being harder to acquire and thus more prone to errors. A good example in this category is preposition use in English: mastering the SE use of prepositions, in particular those with non-spatial reference, is notoriously difficult for most learners of SE (Celce-Murcia & Larsen-Freeman, 1999: 401). As Table 10.1 shows, CE-speaking students are no exception in this regard (with their native dialects being of little help since there are significant differences in preposition use in CE and SE).

Table 10.1 Prevalent grammatical errors in the writings of Sierra Leonean and Liberian ESL students

Category	*Error (incl. % of students)*	*Example*
Verb phrase	Lack of past tense marking (100%)	*He was 10 years old when his grand father* ***die.***
	Lack of subject-verb agreement (94.6%)	*She* ***live*** *in England.*
	Copula[1] absence (82.1%)	*That Ø how big the land in Sierra Leone is.*
	Modal verb use: *will* for *would* (75%)	*If I was sarina I* ***will*** *always be respectful to my mom and dad.*
Noun phrase	Lack of plural marking (98.2%)	*A lot of* ***student.***
	Zero article (82.1%)	*he was not as old as Ø grandfather could be.*
Prepositional phrase	Preposition omitted (32.1%)	*I want to go [to] a party.*
	Different preposition (87.5%)	*I don't believe* ***on*** *[in] Juju.*

But while grammatical complexity and frequency may have an impact on error types and their frequencies, the error patterns identified here suggest that similar grammatical patterns found in CE – both in VLE and Krio – also play an important role.[2] Analyzed as a group, all errors in Table 10.1 (perhaps with the exception of preposition errors) can be traced to CE. That is, there are corresponding patterns in CE that can explain why it was predominantly these errors that Sierra Leonean and Liberian students made. In addition, several error types do not merely resemble patterns in CE, they also occur in grammatical environments unique to CE, providing further important support for L1 transfer. I will illustrate this with two examples of noun phrase (NP) errors; the reader is referred to de Kleine (forthcoming b) for a more elaborate discussion including all error types identified in Table 10.1.

Nominal plural marking tendencies in the writings illustrate CE effects quite clearly. While in SE nouns are typically inflected for plural, in Krio and VLE, and indeed in most CE varieties, the NP is not obligatorily marked for plural. In fact, the tendency for NPs to be unmarked for number is quite commonly observed in these varieties, especially when the context clarifies the plural reference of the noun, when other elements in the NP indicate plurality (such as a quantifier) or when number is simply not relevant (Singler, 1981; cf. Yillah & Corcoran, 2007). In cases where the NP is marked for plural, a form derived from 'them' is usually used as a free morpheme, which follows the head of the NP, e.g. 'the boy them' (Singler, 1981: 74; Yillah & Corcoran, 2007: 190). For a student whose L1 is VLE or Krio, this means that he or she not only has to learn that the *-s* suffix is used to mark plural in SE but, importantly, also that the underlying system – what governs the use of a plural marker in SE – differs considerably from the system in their L1. Table 10.1 shows that SE plural marking is an area of challenge for CE-speaking students: 98.2% of all students produced this error (and many of them produced it frequently). The data furthermore suggest that the main challenge for students lies with the SE distribution of the inflection. In their writings a clear tendency is observed for NPs to lack inflection when a quantifier indicates plural or when the overall context does so, i.e. when the conditions apply that result in a lack of overt marking in CE, as in 'a lot of student'. In other words, when the students produce errors in SE, these appear fairly consistently in grammatical environments where the form would have been fully acceptable in CE.

The lack of article usage where SE requires it is another example of an NP error that appears frequently in the data (produced by 82.1% of the students); this error primarily affects NPs that require an indefinite article in SE. It concerns a grammatical form, which, while also present in SE, is nonetheless governed by different underlying rules in CE, as a result of its different underlying grammatical function. Unlike in SE, in CE, indefinite article usage is determined by whether a NP has specific or non-specific reference, with specific nouns taking an indefinite article (usually a form derived from 'one' instead of 'a') but nouns with non-specific (generic) reference taking a zero article (Holm 2000: 214). This is the pattern that both VLE and Krio follow:

Krio: When ø snake done bite you ...
(SE: 'When a snake has bitten you', Jones 1971: 85)
VLE: She went to take ø bath (Singler, 1981: 75)

Here, too, the writing samples reflect CE patterning: when NPs appear without an article where SE would have required one, this typically occurs with NPs that would have used an indefinite article in SE. Furthermore, the NPs that contain such errors often have non-specific reference, suggesting that students are confusing the underlying rule systems of CE and SE, as illustrated in the example in Table 10.1, 'he was not as old as ø grandfather could be'.

The NP error types discussed here are traced to CE not only because CE possesses corresponding grammatical structures, but also because CE displays distributional patterns that are frequently mirrored in the student writings. Elsewhere (de Kleine, forthcoming-b) I present additional analyses for verb phrase (VP) error types involving past tense marking and copula absence, arguing that these, too, are patterns for which distributional patterns resemble CE patterns and thus indicate L1 transfer effects. Such evidence is important in light of the fact that many error types prevalent among CE-speakers resemble developmental errors commonly produced among ESL learners, i.e. they are features that are normal manifestations of the second language learning process (Lightbown & Spada, 2006: 81). An examination of distributional patterns unique to CE thus helps us to distinguish developmental errors from L1 transfer errors since developmental errors do not appear predominantly in the same grammatical environments as the errors of CE-speakers, i.e. environments that reflect CE influence.

But such evidence is not available for all predominant error types. Consider for instance lack of subject–verb agreement, manifested in the data on third person singular forms of both regular and irregular verbs. With 94.6% of students producing this error repeatedly, this is a very common error among Sierra Leonean and Liberian students. Since Krio and VLE do not use verbal inflection to mark subject–verb agreement, it seems quite plausible that this error type is also rooted in CE grammar. On the other hand, lack of subject-verb agreement is also a common developmental error among ESL learners (Celce-Murcia & Larsen-Freeman, 1999: 58). As such, additional evidence is needed to establish that, in the case of the language production of Sierra Leonean and Liberian students, it is an error that is the result of CE influence rather than a reflection of a 'normal' developmental step in the L2 acquisition process. Such evidence cannot be found in different distributional patterns for this feature, as CE does not mark for subject–verb agreement at all. However, a comparative quantitative analysis of error frequencies in the writings of advanced-level (Sierra Leonean) Creole English-speaking students and other ESL students has revealed that the former's written language contains twice to four times as many errors of the types discussed here (for details, see de Kleine, forthcoming- b). This provides important additional evidence indicating that these errors, too, are not part of the normal developmental L2 acquisition process for CE speakers as they are for ESL students, and are rooted elsewhere.

Explaining the Effect of Creole English on Students' SE Language Development

While research has established convincingly that the L1 plays an important role in second language acquisition (Gass & Selinker, 1992; Kellerman, 1995; Odlin & Jarvis, 2004; Ringbom, 1987), the acquisition of a closely-related language variety is arguably a different process, one that intuitively seems less challenging. Nonetheless, research findings from a variety of countries (Cheshire *et al.*, 1989) suggest that acquiring a closely-related language variety (usually the standard) as an L2 can be quite challenging (Siegel, 2007).

Several explanations have been proposed to account for the challenges related to the acquisition of a closely-related language variety or dialect. Following Siegel (2003), I will refer to this process as 'second dialect acquisition', in other words I will interpret this process as including the acquisition of a lexifier language by speakers of a creolized language variety. The distinction between 'dialect' and 'language' is problematic, even more so in Creole contexts, and is primarily politically-based rather than linguistically-based (Nero, 2006). Indeed, there is a lack of agreement among linguists as to whether CE varieties should be labeled dialects or not. What is crucial in the current discussion, however, is that – whether we label Krio and VLE separate languages or dialects of English – these language varieties display a large overlap with English, albeit primarily in the lexicon, and as such are closely-related language varieties, and this has implications for acquisition.

Specifically, the great number of similarities between the L1 and L2 in cases of closely-related varieties may result in a learner's failure to notice the differences (Siegel, 2003), particularly when these are relatively minor. Schmidt (1993) has argued that the L2 learner needs to possess a conscious awareness of the structural features that set the target language variety apart in order to acquire these distinguishing features successfully, as captured in his 'noticing hypothesis'. For L2 learners of closely-related varieties, this means that unnoticed minimal differences that distinguish the L2 variety are unlikely to be included in the interlanguage of the learner, even when the learner has ample exposure to the target language variety. When, furthermore, differences between two language varieties do not affect meaning, and thus do not cause cross-linguistic comprehension difficulties, the incentive for the learner to pay attention to details distinguishing the two varieties is reduced and is thus likely to affect the second dialect acquisition process even more.

For instance, in the data of our study we observed that the *-s* inflection marking subject–verb agreement was omitted at a disproportionate rate among CE speakers. This inflection has limited phonetic salience and as such can be labeled a minimal difference between SE and CE; moreover, it does not result in a difference in meaning and thereby fails to impact cross-linguistic comprehension. Difficulties acquiring other inflectional forms including plural *-s* and (regular) past tense *-ed* are no doubt also, at least partly, explained by a lack of phonetic salience and their failure to affect comprehension to a significant extent (given that context often clarifies meaning when inflections are absent). Thus, it is highly plausible that these erroneous attempts at SE production by native CE-speaking students are reflective of a failure to notice phonetically minimal as well as inconsequential differences, which as a result have not been incorporated systematically into students' interlanguages.

However, this does not provide a complete explanation. Following Stewart (1987, 1990), I argue that speakers of Krio and VLE (and indeed, many other CE varieties) who are learning SE face important additional challenges. Stewart (1987) believes that the level of difficulty in second dialect acquisition depends to a great extent on the nature of the differences between the L1 and L2 varieties involved. He posits a difference between what he labels 'traditionally related' dialects, such as regional dialects of English spoken in England, and other closely-related varieties (also referred to as 'dialects' by Stewart) with a formation history that has included large groups of L2 learners, such as African American Vernacular English in the US and CE varieties worldwide. As a result of massive L2 learning and language contact effects, the latter type of language variety has undergone restructuring that distinguishes it more than other dialects from the original 'lexifier' language (in this case English), specifically in the grammatical domain. In other words, while 'traditionally related' dialects are characterized primarily by differences in pronunciation and lexicon, dialects (i.e. closely-related varieties) that have been shaped by large numbers of L2 users display primarily grammatical differences, particularly when the original native language(s) of past speakers was typologically distant from the L2 (Stewart, 1987: 288). Many varieties that have traditionally been labeled pidgin and creole languages are good examples of the latter type of language variety, but are not limited to these – as I argue later in this chapter, using the example of Surinamese Dutch, a variety of Dutch whose grammar has been affected considerably by language contact (de Kleine, 2007).

Crucially, however, because closely-related language varieties that have undergone significant language contact-induced restructuring[3] possess (like all dialects) largely overlapping vocabularies with their lexifier variety, they may contain similar (or even identical) forms that nevertheless carry different underlying grammatical *functions* and/or have a *distribution* governed by a different underlying rule system. In such cases, there is on the surface limited (or no) evidence to suggest to the L2 learner that there is even a difference between the L1 and L2: the true identity of the grammatical differences is (partly) masked. It is not hard to see why acquisition of such grammatical forms and their functions of the target language variety can easily fail, making full acquisition a difficult task (cf. Spears, 1982; Stewart, 1987).

A similar masking effect can explain the level of difficulty that Krio- and VLE- speaking students displayed in the data with, for instance, SE article usage. As discussed, indefinite and zero article usage in Krio and VLE, unlike in SE, is governed by rules that depend on whether the noun (singular or plural) has specific or non-specific reference. But this different rule system governing article use is from the learner's CE perspective, partially masked since, in singular NPs with specific reference, both SE and CE varieties take an indefinite article, though for different reasons. In CE it is to mark the NP for 'specific' (a meaning not grammaticalized in SE) while in SE the use of the indefinite article is determined by definiteness (a meaning not grammaticalized in CE) and (singular) number. In other words, the underlying rule systems governing article use are quite different, with each variety grammaticalizing different meanings, but on the surface (potentially) producing sentences in which article usage appears identical. CE speakers learning SE might thus miss this important distinction between CE and SE; part of the evidence suggests, at least from the perspective of their CE framework, that there is no difference. In addition, importantly, the underlying grammatical function that is distinguished in SE is altogether absent in the student's native language variety, no doubt further enhancing the challenge.

Another example of a SE grammatical function that is partially masked from a CE perspective is that of absolute tense marking. Like most CE varieties, Krio – and possibly also VLE, although this is less clear – (see de Kleine, forthcoming-b, for details) employs a system of relative tense marking. This results in a partial overlap between SE and Krio since both employ finite verbs without inflection; however, in SE these typically carry present tense but in Krio they can carry present or past tense. (Of course, past forms in SE are usually not masked from a CE perspective, presuming that learners indeed perceive the inflection of regular verbs.) The underlying rule system governing tense marking is radically different though, resulting in a different distribution of marked versus unmarked VPs. This cross-linguistic asymmetry then prevents students from using a one-to-one matching strategy of mapping newly-acquired SE forms onto a grammatical tense marking system already known to them, i.e. that of CE. Indeed, this leaves CE-speaking students the challenging task of sorting out a grammatical function largely unknown to them using evidence that is likely to be ambiguous.

A final example of an error type that is likely the result of overlapping grammatical systems is that of copula absence, though it distinguishes itself from previously discussed areas of grammatical difficulty involving masking in that (from the perspective of CE) it does not concern a (partially) camouflaged function. In Krio and VLE, overt copula use is limited to fewer environments, but does nonetheless occur in certain environments in which it is also used in SE (Singler, 1981; Yillah & Corcoran, 2007). This leaves the L2 learner with the task of sorting out – indeed, of noticing in the first place – the additional environments in SE that require copula use when their native variety does not require it. Again, there is no symmetric match of grammatical form use in the different varieties. Plural marking also falls into this category. While there is no difference in terms of grammatical function (i.e. indicating 'more than one') between SE and Krio/VLE, the underlying rule system that governs the use of overt plural marking on NPs (i.e. when marking is required) is quite different in CE varieties, but, again, overlaps significantly on the surface with SE.

In sum, the nature of the linguistic differences can account for the difficulty learners of Krio and VLE experience in acquiring SE. The areas of difficulty for CE speakers are largely congruent with those areas of the grammatical systems of CE and SE that display different underlying grammatical functions or distributions (or both). The obvious explanation that suggests itself then is failure on the part of the learners to fully discern the grammatical discrepancies between language varieties, but further research analyzing learners' perceptions is needed to confirm this.

'Unique' Challenges of Creole English Speakers in ESL Programs: Another Case of Creole Exceptionalism?

An important focus of this volume is linguistic exceptionalism and its damaging effect on education. Specifically, DeGraff (2005, Chapter 7 this volume) has argued against 'creole exceptionalism'. He insists that the classification of 'creole' languages as a unique language type (i.e. different from all other languages) is flawed and that claiming such uniqueness can be harmful in educational settings. While it lies outside the scope of this chapter to address the debate surrounding the validity of creole languages as a separate class (cf. Holm, 1988), it should be emphasized that the claim here is not that CE-speakers are disproportionately challenged because they are speakers of 'creole' languages acquiring 'non-creole' languages. In fact, my claims are quite unrelated to this purported classification. Rather, my claims in this chapter concern language varieties which under the influence of heavy language contact (involving typologically distinct languages) have developed grammatical properties that are very different from those found in the languages that have supplied most of their lexicons (and at least part of their grammars). L2 acquisition involving closely-related varieties with different (underlying) grammatical properties, so I claim, can be deceptively challenging because of the linguistic ambiguity (for the L2 learner at least) on the surface.

A case in point illustrating that the cross-linguistic 'asymmetry' in focus in this chapter does not necessarily involve 'creole' language varieties concerns the variety of Dutch spoken in Suriname in South America (de Kleine, 2007). Surinamese Dutch (SD), as a result of centuries-long language contact with Sranan, the lingua franca of Suriname, has developed a set of grammatical characteristics that is unique among Dutch dialects. Its unique features consist mostly of grammatical forms that are also identified in European Dutch (ED) but which carry very different functions in SD (often with different distributions) – indeed, functions not isolated in any other ED dialect. As I have described in detail elsewhere (de Kleine, 2007), this has produced masking effects similar to those discussed earlier. Thus, although neither SD nor ED is a 'creole' language,[4] a similar cross-linguistic asymmetry described for SE and Krio/VLE exists between ED and SD. So far the evidence suggests that the development of the asymmetry as discussed here is the result of contact-induced grammatical restructuring in the formation history of at least one of the language varieties involved, but further research is necessary to confirm this. What is clear, however, is that asymmetry among closely-related language varieties does not necessarily involve those varieties that have been labeled 'creole'.

Implications for Education: The Language Awareness Approach

There has been a fair amount of discussion of what accommodations, if any, are best for CE-speaking students in educational settings using SE, and several linguists have taken a clear stance against placement in ESL programs (cf. Nero, 2006; Sewell *et al.*, 2003; Winer, 2006), currently the most common choice for US school districts. Reasons have included students' already-existing receptive and (albeit to a lesser extent) productive English skills (Nero, 2006), the poor fit of the ESL curriculum (Crandall, 2003; Sewell, 1997) and CE speakers' self-identity as native speakers of English, which undermines their motivation for ESL instruction, sometimes to the point of sheer resentment (Winer, 2006). However, rather than asking what kind of program might be best for speakers of CE, it is in my view more productive to focus instead on what knowledge these students need to acquire, and who is best positioned in the schools to help them develop this knowledge.

It seems obvious that if failure to perceive differences between two language varieties lies at the root of students' second dialect acquisition challenges – either because the differences are phonetically minimal, or because they are (partially) masked – then language education for such students should focus on helping them become more cognizant of the exact areas of difference between the closely-related language varieties involved, specifically where it concerns differences that are hard to discern, and where considerable exposure may thus be insufficient. Fischer (1992), working with Caribbean students at a high school in Illinois, has demonstrated that a language awareness approach can be very successful with CE-speaking students. An important goal of such an approach is for students to develop explicit knowledge (and appreciation) of their native language background that will allow for a detailed comparison with SE in order to build true bilingual competency. Crucially, though, a language awareness approach does not merely teach about differences between CE and SE. Rather, it provides a framework for understanding the properties of different language varieties (in general), and the reasons why people use different varieties, with special emphasis on the validity, complexity and equality of all human language varieties.

While knowledge of language and language variation is useful for all students (Adger *et al.*, 2002), for students who speak a stigmatized language variety, as CE speakers do, this is arguably even more important. As a result of the stigma attached to their native language variety (including within their own original speech communities), students with a CE background typically hold a deeply-ingrained deficit view of their native English variety, which they often view as a simple, agrammatical form of language. Dispelling the 'Broken English' myth is an absolute prerequisite for working with such students: one cannot expect students to build on their existing knowledge of English (CE) when they misunderstand or reject the validity of this knowledge. It is not until that foundation has been laid that students can begin to explore and appreciate the properties of their native CE, and contrast these to the properties of SE.

Including the student's native language background in this process – indeed, using the student's native language variety as a point of departure – is essential not just for psychological reasons, but also for pedagogical reasons. Failure to take into account a student's L1 variety is likely to result in a corrective approach (particularly regarding grammar), and such an approach has been shown to be highly ineffective when the L2 is a closely-related language variety (cf. Fogel & Ehri, 2000; Taylor, 1991). It is not hard to see why such an approach is often ineffective. Consider for instance a Krio learner of SE who consistently fails to mark verbs for past as a result of employing an underlying system of relative tense marking, as required in Krio (rather than absolute tense marking, as found in SE). When a teacher corrects, i.e. focuses only on those uninflected verb forms that require inflection in SE but fails to focus on those forms that the student did mark for tense (but for the wrong reasons), in other words when the teacher fails to explain the system as a whole, it is unlikely that the student will be able to apply SE tense marking rules consistently in the future. In fact, the result of a corrective approach is often excessive hypercorrection, indicating that the student is aware of his or her tendency to produce errors in certain areas but unable to discern the correct conditions under which a rule applies. Furthermore, a corrective approach can be ineffective, and indeed, damaging, when the student–teacher miscommunication that often results leads to flat-out rejection of SE by the student. In such cases, language instruction backfires and can leave students seriously demotivated.

The second question to be addressed concerns who is best positioned to help students develop language awareness and, ultimately, bridge the gap to SE. Clearly, this can be done only by teachers who have the professional preparation to understand issues of linguistic diversity, in particular as these relate to variation involving closely-related language varieties. In reality, for good reasons, ESL teachers are more likely than 'mainstream' (i.e. general education) teachers to have received extensive professional training in linguistic diversity issues – structural properties of (related) language varieties, identity and choice of language variety, language and power issues, etc. Indeed, National Council for Accreditation of Teacher Education (NCATE) standards recently published by the Teachers of English to Speakers of Other Languages (TESOL) association include an explicit requirement for ESL teacher candidates to be able to 'demonstrate understanding of the nature and value of World Englishes and dialect variation, and build on the language that ESOL students bring in order to extend their linguistic repertoire' (TESOL, 2003: 22). While ideally all teachers should possess such in-depth knowledge, the reality is that this knowledge is often not (sufficiently) present among mainstream teachers in the US (cf. Adger *et al.*, 2002). Furthermore, with the 'escalating demands that the educational system places on teachers' (Adger *et al.*, 2002: 1), demands that are, no doubt, exacerbated today by requirements and pressures resulting from the *No Child Left Behind* Act, it may not be reasonable to expect in the near future that the majority of mainstream teachers will be equipped with the necessary knowledge and skills to help speakers of CE effectively with their SE language development. Until more mainstream teachers have developed knowledge necessary to help CE-speaking students effectively, I argue that the additional language support that these students urgently need is best provided by ESL teachers. This can be done in special classes for CE speakers, as advocated by Fisher (1992) and Winer (2006), among others. However, in most school districts (with the exception of New York City and Miami, which have unusually large percentages of CE speakers), this is not a feasible option. Even in the large, affluent suburban school district where we conducted our research, which enrolled over 400 students from Anglophone countries who qualified for additional language support (representing approximately 5% of the ESL population), logistics prevented separate classes. In light of this reality, I believe that placement in ESL classes constitutes an excellent alternative. Crucial to ensuring success, however, is the modification of the ESL curriculum to accommodate the unique needs of speakers of restructured dialects of English. In this way, students get the additional linguistic support that they need from professionals who have the basic training needed to understand the relatively unique and often complex challenges of CE-speaking students. At the same time the students benefit from the additional support that ESL classes provide to sharpen their overall literacy skills – skills that foreign-born students, who may have had different or interrupted education at home, often still require as well. (For details on approaches and strategies for CE speakers in ESL classes, see de Kleine, 2006b.)

Conclusion

This chapter has argued that L1 transfer from CE plays a significant role in the SE writing skills development of Liberian and Sierra Leonean immigrant students. While overall literacy skills obviously include much more than the ability to manipulate SE according to its grammatical rules, this ability is nonetheless an important part of literacy development in a US setting and, for the speakers involved in our research, a disproportionately challenging one. This chapter has laid out areas of L1 influence that are particularly relevant for students from Liberia and Sierra Leone (and given the similarities across CE varieties, presumably for other CE-speaking students as well) and has argued for modified instruction to help students overcome these linguistic challenges.

The main issue at stake is students' full access to SE, and our central role as educators in helping them gain this access so as to be able to develop full SE proficiency. As argued in this chapter, mere exposure to SE is not going to provide them with the tools to fully acquire the standard. This does not imply that the objective is for students to replace their English varieties with SE (i.e. develop SE at the expense of their original varieties of English). In fact, even in the SE-dominant classroom, inclusion of CE varieties is a necessity, both as a way to analyze the properties of these varieties and to learn more about contexts in which non-SE is more appropriate, thus validating students' language backgrounds. This knowledge, understanding and appreciation form the essential foundation for students to develop genuine bilingual competency, enabling them to use each language variety as appropriate. As Canagarajah (2006: 593) has put it, 'Rather than simply *joining* a speech community, students should learn to *shuttle* between communities in contextually relevant ways' [emphases in original].

In order for students to be able to 'shuttle' to and from SE, they need to have full access to SE – one cannot shuttle between two points when one of the points is out of reach. This calls for a focus on grammar for students who otherwise will not be able to develop full competency in SE. In recent years, the benefits and promotion of a single 'canonical' standard in education has been questioned and critiqued (cf. Canagarajah, 2006; New London Group, 1996), and with it, there has been a movement away from focusing on grammatical 'accuracy' (i.e. from a SE perspective). From an intellectual point of view, such a position is certainly defendable; however, the US reality in education remains one that dictates one (fairly) uniform standard. As Nero (2006: 505) has highlighted, teachers are, like society at large, notoriously intolerant of grammatical deviations from the SE norm and view the ability to manipulate the grammar of SE according to the norms agreed upon by society as a benchmark of academic ability, level of education and general potential. Failure to abide by the rules of SE thus has serious negative consequences, both in education and society at large, ironically resulting in precisely the barrier to success that progressive educators who have advocated increased linguistic tolerance and inclusion have tried to avoid. Therefore, if we genuinely want to ensure that language does not form a barrier to social advancement, then we have a duty to enable all students to access the dominant language code of society at large, i.e. the standard. For CE-speaking students, so I have argued in this chapter, access to the standard must be provided through language education that includes an explicit focus on the properties of SE and the way these relate to the properties of their own English varieties. If we fail to provide such education, students will be unable to 'shuttle' between their native English varieties and the one that serves as a gateway to full participation in the society in which they now live.

Notes

1. A copula is a linking verb like 'be' or 'seem' that identifies the predicate with the subject of the sentence.
2. The possibility should always be considered that foreign-born students from Anglophone countries may be producing language that follows the rules of their local SE varieties. (Although the grammars of Sierra Leonean and Liberian SE largely overlap with Inner Circle SE – the American variant for Liberian English, and the British for Sierra Leone – there are nonetheless areas of difference, cf. Ahulu, 1994, 1995, 1998; Bamgbose, 1998; Ngovo, 1998.) This, as the discussion of error types in this chapter shows, is not the case for the students under consideration here. Grammatical patterns as they appear in the data are simply too inconsistent, and more importantly, in all but one case (*will* for *would*) have not been attested for West African varieties of SE.
3. Of course, all dialects – indeed, all language varieties – undergo grammatical restructuring over time. Here reference is made to language varieties which have experienced more rapid and thus more profound grammatical restructuring as a result of language contact.
4. It so happens that Sranan is an English-lexifier creole language, but this is entirely irrelevant to the argument here as there never was any 'creolization' (as defined for instance in Thomason & Kaufman, 1988) in Dutch in Suriname, and thus SD, much as it is very distinct from ED, is definitely not 'Creole' Dutch.

References

Adger, C.A., Snow, C. and Christian, D. (2002) *What Teachers Need to Know about Language*. McHenry, IL: Delta Systems and the Center for Applied Linguistics.

Ahulu, S. (1994) Styles of Standard English. *English Today* 40, 10–17.

Ahulu, S. (1995) Variation in the use of complex verbs in international English. *English Today* 42, 28–34.

Abulu, S. (1998) Grammatical variation in international English. *English Today* 56, 19–25.

Bamgbose, A. (1998) Torn between norms: Innovations in World Englishes. *World Englishes* 17, 1–14.

Bardovi-Harlig, K. (2000) *Tense and Aspect in Second Language Acquisition: Form, Meaning and Use*. Malden, MA: Blackwell.

Canagarajah, A.S. (2006) The place of World Englishes in composition: Pluralization continued. *College Composition and Communication* 57 (4), 586–619.

Celce-Murcia, M. and Larsen-Freeman, D. (1999) *The Grammar Book: An ESL/EFL Teacher's Course* (2nd edn). Boston, MA: Heinle and Heinle.

Cheshire, J., Edwards, V., Münsterman, H. and Weltens, B. (1989) *Dialect and Education*. Clevedon: Multilingual Matters.

Clachar, A. (2003) Paratactic conjunctions in creole speakers' and ESL learners' academic writing. *World Englishes* 22 (3), 271–289.

Clachar, A. (2004) The construction of Creole-speaking students' linguistic profile and contradictions in ESL literacy programs. *TESOL Quarterly* 38 (1), 153–165.

Clachar, A. (2005) Creole-English speakers' treatment of tense-aspect morphology in English interlanguage written discourse. *Language Learning* 55 (2), 275–334.

Coelho, E. (1991) *Caribbean Students in Canadian Schools: Book* 2. Markham, ON: Pippin.

Craig, D.R. (1966) Teaching English to Jamaican Creole speakers: A model of a multi-dialect situation. *Language Learning* 16 (1 & 2), 49–61.

Craig, D.R. (1967) Some early indications of learning a second dialect. *Language Learning* 17 (3 & 4), 133–140.

Craig, D.R. (1997) The English of West Indian university students. In E. Schneider (ed.) *Englishes around the World* (Vol. 2; pp. 11–24). Philadelphia: John Benjamins.

Craig, D.R. (1999) *Teaching Language and Literacy: Policies and Procedures for Vernacular Situations*. Georgetown: Education and Development Services Inc.

Craig, D.R. (2001) Language education revisited in the Commonwealth Caribbean. In P. Christie (ed.) *Due Respect. Papers on English and English-related Creoles in the Caribbean in Honour of Professor Robert Le Page* (pp. 61–78). Barbados, Jamaica, Trinidad & Tobago: University of the West Indies Press.

Crandall, J.A. (2003) They DO speak English: World Englishes in US schools. *ERIC/CLL News Bulletin* 26 (3), Summer/Fall.

DeGraff, M. (2005) Linguists' most dangerous myth: The fallacy of Creole Exceptionalism. *Language in Society* 34 (4), 533–591.

de Kleine, C. (2006a) West African World English speakers in US classrooms: The role of West African Pidgin English. In S. Nero (ed.) *Dialects, Englishes, Creoles and Education* (pp. 205–232). Mahwah, NJ: Lawrence Erlbaum.

de Kleine, C. (2006b) Towards a better understanding of the linguistic challenges of World English-speaking students in ESOL classrooms: A teacher manual. Unpublished manuscript.

de Kleine, C. (2007) *A Morphosyntactic Analysis of Surinamese Dutch*. Munich: Lincom Europa.

de Kleine, C. (forthcoming-a) The acquisition of Standard American English by speakers of Creole English: Interference in the writings of K–12 students in the Baltimore City Public Schools System. In A.K. Spears (ed.) *Black Language in the US and Caribbean: Education, History, Styles and Structure*. Lanham, MD: Lexington Books.

de Kleine, C. (forthcoming-b) Grammatical transfer from Creole English in the writings of Sierra Leonean students in ESL classes.

Edwards, V. (1979) *The West Indian Language Issue in British Schools: Challenges and Responses*. London: Routledge and Kegan Paul.

Fischer, K. (1992) Educating speakers of Caribbean English Creole in the United States. In J. Siegel (ed.) *Pidgins, Creoles and Nonstandard Dialects in Education. Occasional Papers Applied Linguistics Association of Australia 12* (pp. 99–123). Clayton: Monash University ePress.

Fogel, H. and Ehri, L. (2000) Teaching elementary students who speak Black English Vernacular to write in Standard English: Effects of dialect transformation practice. *Contemporary Educational Psychology* 25, 121–235.

Gass, S. and Selinker, L. (eds) (1992) *Language Transfer in Language Learning* (rev. edn). Philadelphia, PA: John Benjamins.

Gordon Jr, R.G. (ed.) (2005) *Ethnologue: Languages of the World*, (15th edn). Dallas, TX: SIL International. Online at http://www.ethnologue.com/. Accessed 10.1.08.

Holm, J.A. (1988) *Pidgins and Creoles* (Vol. 1): *Theory and Structure*. Cambridge: Cambridge University Press.

Holm, J.A. (1989) *Pidgins and Creoles* (Vol. 2): *Reference Survey*. Cambridge: Cambridge University Press.

Holm, J.A. (2000) *An Introduction to Pidgins and Creoles*. Cambridge: Cambridge University Press.

Jones, E. (1971) Krio: An English-based language of Sierra Leone. In J. Spencer (ed.) *The English Language in West Africa* (pp. 66–94). London: Longman.

Kachru, B.B. (1992) Teaching World Englishes. In B.B. Kachru (ed.) *The Other Tongue* (pp. 355–365). Urbana, IL: University of Illinois Press.

Kellerman, E. (1995) Cross-linguistic influence: Transfer to nowhere? *Annual Review of Applied Linguistics* 15, 125–150.

Lightbown, P. and Spada, N. (2006) *How Languages are Learned* (3rd edn). Oxford: Oxford University Press.

Narvaez, D.H. and Garcia, M.L. (1992) Meeting the needs of newly-arrived West Indian students in New York public schools. New York: National Origin Unit, Equity Assistance Center, Baruch College, CUNY. (ERIC Document Reproduction Service Center No. ED359307.)

Nero, S. (2001) *Englishes in Contact: Anglophone Caribbean Students in an Urban College*. Cresskill, NJ: Hampton Press.

Nero, S. (2006a) Language, identity and education of Caribbean English speakers. *World Englishes* 25 (3/4), 501–511.

New London Group (1996) A pedagogy of multiliteracies: Designing social futures. *Harvard Educational Review* 66 (1), 60–92.

Ngovo, B. (1998) English in Liberia. *English Today* 54, 46–50.

Odlin, T. and Jarvis, S. (2004) Same source, different outcomes: A study of Swedish influence on the acquisition of English in Finland. *The International Journal of Multilingualism* 1 (2), 123–140.

Pratt-Johnson, Y. (1993) Curriculum for Jamaican Creole-speaking students in New York City. *World Englishes* 12, 257–264.

Pratt-Johnson, Y. (2006) Teaching Jamaican Creole-speaking students. In S. Nero (ed.) *Dialects, Englishes, Creoles and Education* (pp. 119–136). Mahwah, NJ: Erlbaum.

Ringbom, H. (1987) *The Role of the First Language in Foreign Language Learning*. Clevedon: Multilingual Matters.

Schleppegrell, M.J. (2004) *The Language of Schooling: A Functional Linguistics Perspective*. Mahwah, NJ: Erlbaum.

Schmidt, R. (1993) Awareness and second language acquisition. *Annual Review of Applied Linguistics* 13, 206–226.

Sewell, D. (1997) World English speakers in ESL classes: Not a perfect match. *TESOL Matters* 7 (June/July), 1/22.

Sewell, D., Rodriguez-McCleary, B. and Staehr, D. (2003) Working with World English-speakers from the Outer Circle. *WATESOL News* 34 (1–2),10.

Siegel, J. (2003) Social context. In C.J. Doughty and M.H. Long (eds) *The Handbook of Second Language Acquisition* (pp. 178–223). Malden, MA: Blackwell.

Siegel, J. (2007) Creole and minority dialects in education: An update. *Language and Education* 21 (1), 66–86.

Singler, J.V. (1981) *An Introduction to Liberian English*. East Lansing: Peace Corps/ Michigan State University, African Studies Center.

Singler, J.V. (1997) The configuration of Liberia's Englishes. *World Englishes* 16, 205–231.

Singler, J.V. (2004) Positioning Vernacular Liberian English relative to other West African Pidgin Englishes. Paper presented at the 24th West African Languages Congress, University of Ibadan, Nigeria.

Spears, A.K. (1982) The Black English semi-auxiliary *come*. *Language* 58 (4), 850–872.

Stewart, W.A. (1987) Coping or groping? Psycholinguistic problems in the acquisition of receptive and productive competence across dialects. In P. Homel, M. Palij and D. Aaronson (eds) *Childhood Bilingualism: Aspects of Linguistic, Cognitive and Social Development* (pp. 281–298). Hillsdale, NJ: Lawrence Erlbaum.

Stewart, W.A. (1990) From xenolect to mimolect to pseudocomprehension: Structural mimicry and its functional consequences in decreolization. In E. Bendix (ed.) *The Uses of Linguistics* (pp. 33–47). New York: New York Academy of Sciences.

Taylor, H.U. (1991) *Standard English, Black English and Bidialectalism: A Controversy*. New York: Peter Lang.

TESOL (2003) *TESOL/NCATE Program Standards: Standards for the Accreditation of Initial Programs in P-12 ESL Teacher Education*. Alexandria, VA: TESOL.

Thomason, S.G. and Kaufman, T. (1988) *Language Contact, Creolization and Genetic Linguistics*. Berkeley: University of California Press.

Winer, L. (1989) Variation and transfer in English Creole-standard English language learning. In M. Eisenstein (ed.) *The Dynamic Interlanguage. Empirical Studies in Second Language Variation* (pp. 155–173). New York: Plenum.

Winer, L. (2006) Teaching English to Caribbean Creole English-speaking students in the Caribbean and North America. In S. Nero (ed.) *Dialects, Englishes, Creoles and Education* (pp.105–118). Mahwah, NJ: Erlbaum.

Yillah, S.M. and Corcoran, C. (2007) Krio (Creole English). In J. Holm and P. Patrick (eds) *Comparative Creole Syntax. Westminster Creolistics Series 7*. London: Battlebridge.

Chapter 11

Continued Marginalization: The Social Cost of Exceptionalism for African Refugee Learners of English

DORIS S. WARRINER

In response to war, famine and religious persecution in Somalia, the Sudan, the Congo, Rwanda and other sub-Saharan African contexts, a large number of African immigrants and refugees have come to the US in search of political or religious freedom, economic security and a chance at a 'better life'. This dramatic increase in the number of African immigrant students enrolled in adult ESL programs and public schools presents challenges to educators striving to incorporate and build on these students' linguistic, cultural and social resources while also helping them learn English, act in ways that are socioculturally 'appropriate' in the US, and succeed academically. Added to these challenges are the unique stresses that refugees face as a result of the trauma of living through war or persecution.

In this chapter, I examine how widely-circulating discourses about English (e.g. as a language of power and prestige, commerce and globalization) shape English language learners' beliefs about the value of English language learning, the deficiencies of languages other than English and the 'problems' with their own 'accented English'. The analysis demonstrates the specific, situated ways that 'exceptionalist assumptions' (DeGraff, 2005) influence the beliefs and practices of learners themselves while challenging policy-makers, teachers and learners to not only recognize those beliefs but also confront them in their daily practice.

After describing the discursive and ideological context of adult instruction in the US, I provide background information on the research context and include biographical sketches of three Sudanese women refugees. I then examine the various ways in which the women take up, reject or reconstitute discursive and ideological influences. After analyzing how such ideologies of language support practices of exclusion and marginalization, I address the implications of these findings for educational research, applied linguistics, the development of social and educational policy and engaged advocacy.

The Discursive and Ideological Context

With a view of the English language classroom as a 'site of cultural politics', Pennycook has argued that the growing dominance of English on the global scene is bolstered not only by the increased use and teaching of the English language but also by increased *talk about* the value of learning English:

> the teaching practices themselves represent particular visions of the world and thus make the English language classroom a site of cultural politics, a place where different versions of how the world is and should be are struggled over. (Pennycook, 1994/1996: 146)

Pennycook (1998, 2000) draws attention to the static cultural representations of the 'other' in much of the theory and practice behind ESL (English as a Second Language)/TESOL (Teaching English to Speakers of Other Languages) instruction. He urges English language teachers and researchers to examine how such discourses influence the ways that teachers, learners and the general public talk about the value of English and the importance of learning English as a second language.

Despite assumptions about positive effects of English proficiency, a close examination of the experiences of individual immigrants reveals that proficiency in English does not often result in the academic achievement, economic stability or social mobility promised by these discourses. The presence of an accent, for example, becomes an additional marker of difference (or object of attack) (Lippi-Green, 1997; Wiley & Lukes, 1996). Given this social-political-historical-cultural context, it is critical to examine closely what learners say about why they are studying English if we are to understand the hegemonic nature of the ideologies at work.

With history, politics and discursive influences in constant tension, *standard* English language proficiency has come to index both membership in a specific community of practice and also claims to particular rights and resources that accompany this membership. Even when this 'community' is largely imagined (Anderson, 1991; Kanno & Norton, 2003), this 'standard' English language proficiency serves as a powerful indicator of what constitutes insider status, access to goods and resources (symbolic and material) and legitimacy. This complicated relationship between how languages are used, the discourses that support or devalue different ways of using language, and the ideological control that is achieved as a result of such processes is also taken up in recent work by Makoni and Pennycook (2006) which explores the culturally specific ways that 'languages' are defined, described, viewed and valued. They claim that 'the concept of language, and indeed the "metadiscursive regimes" used to describe languages are firmly located in Western linguistic and cultural suppositions' (Makoni & Pennycook, 2006: 147). They also recommend that we 'understand the interrelationships among metadiscursive regimes, language inventions, colonial history, language effects, alternative ways of understanding language, and strategies of disinvention and reconstitution' (Makoni & Pennycook, 2006: 138). Or, as Makoni and Trudell have written about the construct of diversity in language planning:

> it is ... important to understand the discursive source of these beliefs [about the nature of linguistic diversity], the perspectives to which each discourse is hospitable, and how the different discourses complement or contradict each other. (Makoni &Trudell, 2006: 14)

Elsewhere, I have described the prevalence of certain dominant, sometimes hegemonic, discourses about English and English language learning – and illustrated how the women's lived experiences represent a challenge to those discursive forces and ideological influences (Warriner, 2003, 2007). Here, I highlight the women's discourses in order to understand, not only the specifics of their language-learning experiences, but also the situated ways that they each responded to, took up and reframed these various discursive and ideological constructs. With a view of ESL instruction as a site of cultural politics and ideological control, this work demonstrates that *standard* English language proficiency has become the goal not only of institutional actors but also of the learners themselves – in ways that result in their continued marginalization from the communities of practice they wish to join.

Research Context

The data examined here come from a larger ethnographic study (Warriner, 2003) in which I examined the experiences of seven women refugees (from Bosnia, Iran and the Sudan), who were enrolled in an adult ESL program located in the heart of a mid-sized city in the western US. The adult ESL program at Valley Instruction and Training Center[1] is locally and nationally recognized for its unique educational programs. Among the services that the program provides are: ESL and high school completion courses, GED prep class, in-house technical and vocational instruction, access to educational and workplace technology, onsite childcare, assistance securing employment through a school-to-work program and an on-site Department of Workforce Services (DWS) representative, partnerships with business and community-based agencies, scholarships, subsidized transportation, driver's education courses, citizenship courses and health and medical screening. There are 10 levels of ESL instruction in the program, ranging from pre-literate (for students unable to read or write in their native language) to advanced (someone who has obtained a high score on the standardized reading test in English that is administered to all incoming students during orientation), and there are two programs, a daytime program offered five days per week and one in the evening, three nights per week.

Data sources for the larger study included field notes collected while conducting extensive participant observation in school and home contexts; document collection from the adult ESL program; audio-recorded interviews with women refugee learners, their teachers and the ESL coordinator; and informal conversations with students and their teachers. As a former teacher and orientation coordinator in the program, when I began data collection in 2001 I had an 'insider's' understanding of the policies and practices of the program as well as the challenges faced by the teachers and administrators.

The grant applications and other institutional documents show that the primary purpose of this ESL program is 'to move newly arriving and public assistance refugees toward self-sufficiency and self-reliance, in as short a time as possible.' Many of the refugee students are referred or brought to the day program by a number of sources, including two resettlement agencies (International Rescue Committee and Catholic Community Services), the local (state-run) Refugee Employment and Community Center and friends or relatives. Through conversations with the ESL coordinator, I learned that one of the greatest challenges of his position was finding a balance between focusing on the day-to-day administrative tasks (such as ordering books, enrolling new students or 'putting out fires') and taking a step back to reflect on what long-term changes might be made with regard to curriculum and instruction. He stated that an important goal of the program was to help students access resources in the community: 'It isn't so much grammatical fluency or proficiency as it would be being able to get a job at an entry level perhaps and then quickly improving that to a higher paying job.' With regard to this, one change that the ESL coordinator said he would like to make was to increase opportunities for students to get more involved in the community and use English in more 'authentic situations'. He questioned the value of structured classroom learning in relation to real-life, hands-on experiences and suggested that combining classroom learning with real-life ('work') experiences might be an ideal way to foster second language learning. Given this institutional context, I introduce the stories told by three refugee women who were students in the program.

Ayak, Mary and Moría

Ayak, who is from the Sudan, was 27 years old, married and the mother of two young children when I met her in the winter of 2001. Before arriving in the US in 1998, Ayak, her husband and her children lived in Egypt for 10 months. As soon as they arrived in the US, Ayak and her husband began studying ESL in the Center. Ayak started in Level P, a level designated for those who cannot read or write in their own language, while her husband started at a slightly higher level. During one of our interviews, Ayak told me that it had been very difficult to live in the US at first because she knew no one and because she spoke no English. She indicated her initial ambivalence about leaving Egypt to come to the US, stating that she had often asked her husband why they had come at all. But her husband reassured her that she would make friends when she learned some English.

Later, Ayak was enrolled in Level 4 and considered a 'high-intermediate' student in the program. Because the program is so heavily structured, Level 4 students have little choice regarding what classes they will take, and Ayak consequently had ESL classes from 8:30 to 3:00 every day. Her husband, also a student in this adult ESL program, was in a Level 6 class – in part because of his greater initial proficiency in English and in part because he had not taken any time off while enrolled in the program as Ayak did when she had her second child. During an interview with Ayak in April 2001, I learned that she had recently taken a job at a fast-food restaurant in the airport and that she was happy to have this job; nevertheless, she already wanted to find 'a better job'. At that time, Ayak also shared the plans her family had made to get her mother to the US from Egypt, and the problems with paperwork associated with that pursuit. Ayak hoped her mother would be able to live with them and take care of their children so Ayak could work and go to school more easily. As Ayak said, 'when she [my mother] come here, I don't look for babysitter. She stays with my children.'

Mary, who is also from the Sudan, came to the US with three children on February 23, 2000. Mary was a single mother because her husband was killed in the war in Sudan. Although the refugee resettlement agency had found her a three-bedroom home and furnished it, it took some time for Mary and her children to get settled and comfortable. While describing to me her first week living in the US, Mary said her food ran out after three days, and she couldn't figure out how or where to get more. She also talked about not having heat in her house and not having enough 'language' to solve the problems she encountered. Finally, after seven days in her unheated apartment and after four days with no food, Mary decided to walk down the road in search of help. A woman she met ended up taking her to a local discount grocery store and helping her with the grocery shopping. To her relief and surprise, the plastic card given to her by the refugee resettlement agency 'worked', and Mary was able to buy food.

Mary began studying ESL on March 23, 2000, one month after her arrival in the US and one year before I began interviewing her for this study. When I met Mary in the spring of 2001, she was enrolled in Level 6, the highest level in the adult ESL program. She was taking classes such as pronunciation, English grammar, algebra, information processing, math/science and computers. She told me she wanted to go to college and get a good job. She said she had been an accountant and bookkeeper in Sudan and wanted a similar job in the US. In these conversations, Mary emphasized that although she wanted 'to work and study as much as possible,' she was concerned about who would take care of her children when she had to work, especially during the summer when they were not in school. When I interviewed Mary for this study, her oldest son was 11, her second son was nine, and her daughter was seven years old. They all attended the same school and, because there is only one ESL class at the school, they were enrolled in the same ESL class. During each of our interviews, Mary was very concerned about finding someone to help her children with their reading and writing homework because she wanted them to do well in school.

Moría and her husband are from the Sudan and have two children. When we met (winter 2001), Moría was 38; she had a four-year-old daughter and a 14-month-old son. At that time, she was in Level 5, and taking classes such as TOEFL prep, advisory, advanced grammar, four information processing classes, childcare and English (a high school completion class). Moría was quite proficient in English, and she told me that the classes she was taking were not difficult, but that she had enrolled in the program because it had childcare facilities on the premises and because it was 'better than to stay at home.' She told me that she was grateful for the opportunity to practice her English, because even though she had studied it for a long time, she never had a chance to use it.

In the Sudan, Moría received a degree in accounting from the university and then worked as an accountant for five years before moving to Cairo, Egypt. In Cairo, she worked as a housekeeper for a year and a half while waiting for paperwork to be processed so that she and her family could resettle in the US. By the time I met Moría, her husband had a full-time job working as a machine operator for a computer manufacturing company. Because of her husband's income, the family did not qualify for assistance from the Department of Workforce Services or for Medicaid. Moría planned to continue studying English and to take all the required exams until the end of the program's fifth session before looking for a job. When we discussed what kind of work she might like to have, she said she might be able to be a cashier, a salesperson or an employee of the local post office. When I asked her what she would do about childcare once she started working, Moría said she and her husband were 'going to exchange' shifts, with her husband working at night and Moría working during the day so that one of them would always be with their children. Moría wanted to go to the community college to study accounting so that she could pursue the same kind of work she had in Sudan. However, when her husband's hours at the computer company were later reduced to part-time, Moría decided that she needed to work rather than take classes at the college.

For Moría, the most difficult aspect of living in a new context was raising her children alone. At the same time, she said that, comparatively, things weren't that bad and that one great benefit of living in the US would be that her children would learn and speak English: 'Here I'm alone, no one is help me, everything, they need me. No relatives. But not too difficult. Children are learning English, they like it.'

Taking Up, Rejecting, Re-constituting the Discursive and Ideological

Ayak, Mary and Moría all frequently stated how important they thought it was to learn English. Ayak, for instance, connected English language learning with both personal and professional goals. Initially, when I first asked her why she came to this school, she said, 'I come, I want to learn English, I get, I looking for better job.' Later, when I asked her about her future, she stressed the importance of studying English to reach her professional goals:

> Maybe in the future, when I take the diploma at [this school], I want to go to college ... when I finish college, maybe I can learn more. I looking for the better job. Now the [restaurant] is very far away for me ... I like daycare, the program for daycare ... Maybe I finish, I take training for daycare ... Maybe when I finish college, I take training, maybe I open daycare ... maybe I open daycare in my own house, cheaper than another daycare.

In this excerpt, there is evidence of a connection in Ayak's mind between studying English, obtaining a diploma and finding a better job or getting training in an area that interests her (childcare). Ayak has clearly given this a lot of thought, and serious career goals motivate her current efforts to learn English. Ayak appears motivated to study English in order to pursue long-term professional goals.

Other excerpts show her belief that studying English will help her make friends, especially with other immigrants and refugees. When I asked her to tell me about her arrival in the US, she said:

> I didn't know anybody, I didn't speak English, no TV, no chair ... I say to my husband, 'why I come here?' I had many friends in Egypt, auntie and uncle, sometimes they come visit me in my house, sometime I go with them, but here nobody. My husband say, 'you have to wait, when you learn English, you speak, you have a lot of friends. You stay here, you know everything. It's not "you come today you know everything today." Need time.' I tell him, 'I try.' Now it's okay. I make a lot of friend from Mexico, from Bosnia (laugh), and Sudanese, and the American people.

Ayak's observations reflect ideologies of language that connect English language learning with job opportunities, continued education at the community college level, personal growth and fulfillment through friendships.

Mary, too, explicitly connected English language proficiency with employment opportunities as well as a better life. For instance, in response to my question 'do you like studying English?' Mary said:

> I want to know English. I want to study English because I want to go to the college. Yeah, to train in accounting, because I take many years, so I forgot, so I want to go to the college, that maybe help me in the future.

Later, Mary connected English language proficiency with the ability to help her children do better in school. Repeatedly, after identifying her own limited English ability – or more accurately, her non-standard pronunciation of English words – as one of the factors contributing to her children's difficulties doing their reading and writing homework, she expressed shame about her non-standard English:

> Yeah, my problem now is my English is not good. So when I do homework with them, and I pronounce the word, they say, 'it's different from the pronunciation of the teacher' [...] so it's difficult for me to help them.

In this very short excerpt, there are at least two kinds of ideologies of language and language learning at work. First, there is evidence of Mary's belief in the importance of improving both her own English language proficiency and her children's. Also, we see that, in part because of the value and importance she attaches to English, Mary has internalized ideologies that devalue her developing English and nonstandard pronunciation. Rather than focus on what she *can* do (speak multiple languages and thereby participate in multiple communities of practice) and what resources she *has*, Mary is overwhelmed by what she has come to view as deficiencies. In these ways, Mary's comments demonstrate an acceptance and internalization of dominant discourses about the importance of English (to her children's academic success and to her own) as well as the value and prestige associated with 'standard' English.

Ironically, even though Mary has completed all the requirements of her ESL program and 'graduated' with a high school completion certificate, she feels unable to help her children with their homework, ill-equipped to advocate for them in school and unsure of her ability to find a job that would allow her to be home with her children. In these ways, Mary's own continued exclusion threatens to influence whether and how her children become excluded from the practices of schooling that would grant them entry into local communities of practice. Her comments thus reflect ideologies about languages other than English (and the developing English of language learners) and the discourses widely circulating that rely on, promote and further constitute those ideologies.

Language ideologies were also evident in the comments the Sudanese women made about the need for their children to learn English or the ways that English language proficiency might be intimately connected to their children's future academic and personal successes. Moría, for example, was very pleased that her three-year old daughter was learning English while in daycare:

> My daughter is good ... she knows a, b, c, d. She knows the color and she knows 1, 2, up to 13. She can say weekday, Monday, Tuesday ... It's good. I like it. She cannot speak our dialect very well but she can speak English very good.

Indeed, Moría values English even more than she values the maintenance of her children's first language, Madi, a dialect spoken in Sudan. The fact that it is not considered problematic for English to replace her daughter's first language reflects the high status associated with speaking English in Moría's eyes. Ayak also commented on the importance of English language learning for her children. With respect to her oldest son, in particular, she saw a connection between going to school, learning English and getting a good job

> When the people they don't go to school, I don't like. Yeah. Now, I tell my son, when you have five years, you go to school, you study English, maybe you can be doctor. Yeah I tell my son like that, you be doctor, I like you be doctor ... He say, yeah, I be doctor.

Ayak's comments demonstrate her belief that learning English is a large part of the educational equation that will allow her child to become a doctor here in the US. These same comments also reflect a lack of understanding of the historically and discursively influenced barriers that so-called 'non-standard' speakers of English often face, in spite of their growing English language proficiency and academic achievement. In the case of African immigrants and refugees, the linguistic insecurity that accompanies speaking English with an accent (Lippi-Green, 1997; Rampton, 2006) is only exacerbated by the growing realization that their identities are differently racialized in the US context.

Collectively, the interview excerpts examined here demonstrate how individual learners of English take up, internalize and reconstitute larger discursive influences that have historically positioned them in deficit ways (e.g. as individuals without linguistic or cultural resources who need to be 'fixed' in order to succeed academically, socially, or economically). The three women's views demonstrate the powerful influence of such widely circulating discourses (e.g. those that equate English language proficiency with improving one's circumstances, obtaining a 'good' job, pursuing advanced education or training and achieving success in the future). They have each positioned themselves (and their children) as individuals who need to learn English in order to survive and prosper in this context. In the women's talk, then, we see in action metalinguistic regimes (Makoni & Pennycook, 2006; DeGraff, 2005) that value English language learning above all else.

Contradiction and Contestation: Ideologies of Language as Practices of Exclusion

In work that has greatly influenced the study of language ideology as a field of inquiry, Susan Gal (1998: 319) describes language ideologies 'as verbalized, thematized discussion and as the implicit understandings and unspoken assumptions embedded and reproduced in the structure of institutions and their everyday practices.' Woolard (1998: 3) describes language ideologies as 'representations, whether explicit or implicit, that construe the intersection of language and human beings in a social world.' Ideologies of language are both spoken and implied, explicit and tacit, within our conceptual grasp and beyond it – and all simultaneously. They are also multi-sited, reproduced within and outside of institutional contexts and sustained, challenged and even transformed at the level of discourse as well as at the level of social practice. That is, language ideologies achieve their power and effect in large part because they are simultaneously dispersed (or shared) *and* revealed in the actions and talk of local actors situated in specific contexts.

With an acute awareness of the identities indexed by accented English, Ayak, Mary and Moría often found themselves in a precarious position with regard to how to 'locate' themselves on the ideological landscape of US debates over the role of English language proficiency in attaining membership and belonging. However, because their individual efforts to learn English (in order to access symbolic, material and cultural 'goods') are not considered complete nor sufficient, they are relegated to second-language learning status (and the exceptionalist beliefs attached to this) in spite of their increased proficiency in English, and their improved knowledge of how things 'work' in this context. Such contradictions raise questions for practitioners and policy makers alike about the influence of widely-circulating discourses of immigration and difference as well as the costs associated with replacing first languages with English, replacing accented English with 'standard' English, and replacing learners' daily practices with the practices of the communities they wish to join.

With limited resources and time, the adult ESL program that Ayak, Mary and Moría attended aimed to fulfill the short-term needs of the large numbers of refugee and non-refugee students that continually entered the program in search of the English language knowledge and skills they were told would give them access to the world of work. However, in spite of its noble goals, the program, albeit unwittingly, supported and enacted ideologies of language and language learning that devalue new immigrants and the languages they speak and ultimately confined the students of this program to 'dead-end' jobs with little potential for advancement or social mobility.

Exceptionalist ideologies, beliefs and practices often influence speakers to devalue not only their own cultural understandings and community resources (including their home languages), but also their own developing English. Comments made by the three women demonstrate that their ideologies of language and language learning are influenced by a complicated set of paradigms and practices, including English-as-panacea rhetoric and anti-inclusive discourses; they also serve to further bolster arguments made in favor of those practices in adult ESL instruction. In such ways, the hegemonic power of language ideologies (particularly exceptionalist ones) is both far-reaching and consequential. We see how the women both internalize the ideologies of language that devalue their own accented English *and* perpetuate those ideologies by passing on those expectations to their children – even when their first-hand experiences demonstrate that English language learning in and of itself is not enough. While linguists correctly argue that all languages are created equal (e.g. DeGraff, Chapter 7, this volume), they are not equal in the eyes of most speakers of those languages, and especially in the eyes of already-disenfranchised immigrants trying to 'make it' in the politically-ideologically influenced terrain of ESL instruction. As any language learner will tell us, certain languages (such as English) and certain varieties (standard) are afforded greater prestige and value in social, cultural, educational and employment contexts; this makes them a powerful currency to have.

Implications, Remaining Challenges and Conclusions

Ricento argues that the most important question facing educational researchers interested in the connections between language use, language policies and language ideologies is:

> Why do individuals opt to use (or cease to use) particular languages and varieties for specified functions in different domains, and how do those choices influence – and how are they influenced by – institutional language policy decision-making (local to national to supranational)? (Ricento, 2000: 23)

The examination of individual actors' ideologies of language and language learning through a critical lens affords many productive and illuminating insights about why individuals choose to use (or not to use) a particular language, as well as how their choices are shaped by policies and paradigms that reach far beyond the individual or the institution. As such, the comments of Ayak, Mary and Moría indicate the power of widespread negative views toward speakers of non-dominant languages and the languages they speak (whether it be their mother tongue or their accented English), as well as how those views are often internalized by speakers themselves.

The analysis provided here raises a number of important questions. For instance, in order to create spaces that promote different kinds of ideologies (e.g. of multilingualism, diversity or community rather than ideologies of monolingualism, assimilation or individualism), what kinds of institutional support mechanisms, educational policies and pedagogical/assessment practices would need to be in place? And, in what ways do ideologies of language like those described here create a sort of manufactured consent that serves to perpetuate inequities and injustices, even while masking them – making them appear fair and meritocratic when they are not? Further, in what ways are ideologies of language not primarily about language at all?

One important implication of this work is the need for critical language awareness among teachers and learners alike, whereby hegemonic discourses that contribute to the continued economic and social marginalization of learners are identified and challenged. A challenge associated with this work will be to find ways to increase language and dialect awareness among ESL teachers and their students as well as among the government officials and agency representatives who create policies that motivate or justify particular practices. Another related challenge will be finding ways to represent and engage with the many contradictory views that learners themselves hold about the different languages they speak, especially given how resilient and robust those views are. One promising direction for teacher education would be to focus on students' funds of knowledge (Gonzalez *et al.*, 2005) or *cultural repertoires of practice* (Lee, 2007) as resources for raising our collective critical consciousness while creating a space for valuing difference.

Both educational researchers and teacher educators might also benefit from turning to recent work that asserts the impossibility of disentangling the 'color line' from the 'language line' (Hopson, 2003) in the study of those factors that contribute to the continued marginalization of certain racialized (immigrant and non-immigrant) groups living in the US context. Calling this 'the challenge of the 21st century', Hopson (2003: 229) argues that 'language is central to the reproduction of racialized identities at school and in our larger society for the American of African descent.' For African immigrants learning English as a second language, Hopson argues that the language line intersects with the color line in similar kinds of ways. He observes that:

> to these learners, the dominant language and variety exists as a double-edged sword. This is the key to vertical mobility and symbol of American identity, but not the key to socioeconomic equality and equity on which it often is portrayed. (Hopson, 2003: 241)

By illuminating how macro-level discourses might influence local policies, pedagogical practices and learners' individual subject positions, this analysis extends the insights of existing research on the language-learning experiences of refugees in two key ways. First, it increases our understanding of the views and priorities of the learners in adult ESL classroom contexts. Second, it raises timely questions about the paradigms and practices that continue to dominate adult ESL instruction in spite of the growing interest in the intersections between immigration, language learning, race, ethnicity, nationalism and class in the fields of applied linguistics and educational anthropology (see e.g. Alim, 2005; Ibrahim, 1999; Kubota & Lin, 2006). Linguists and anthropologists have an important role to play in increasing our understanding of the educational, social and economic costs associated with exceptionalist assumptions and then using this knowledge to improve policies and practices accordingly. As part of this agenda, scholars in linguistics, anthropology and education might play a central role in increasing language awareness among learners, teachers and policy-makers such that linguistic diversity would be valued (Makoni & Trudell, Chapter 2, this volume) and exceptionalist assumptions (DeGraff, Chapter 7; Wolfram, Chapter 14) would be forcibly challenged.

Acknowledgements

My work continues to be inspired by the important work of my mentor, Nancy Hornberger, and I thank her for her wise counsel and careful guidance. I also appreciate the unwavering support of Bryan Brayboy, professionally and personally. I wish to thank Jo Anne Kleifgen for her patience as well as her insightful comments on multiple versions of this chapter. Most of all, I appreciate the courage, wisdom and compassion that Ayak, Mary and Moría continue to demonstrate and embody, even in the face of continued hardship and, sadly, continued marginalization.

Note

1. The names of the program and all participants are pseudonyms.

References

Alim, H.S. (2005) Critical Language Awareness in the United States: Revisiting issues and revising pedagogies in a resegregated society. *Educational Researcher* 34 (7), 24–31.

Anderson, B. (1991) *Imagined Communities: Reflections on the Origins and the Spread of Nationalism* (rev. edn). London: Verso.

DeGraff, M. (2005) Linguists' most dangerous myth: The fallacy of Creole Exceptionalism. *Language in Society* 34, 533–591.

Gal, S. (1998) Multiplicity and contention among language ideologies: A commentary. In B. Schieffelin, K. Woolard and P. Kroskrity (eds) *Language Ideologies: Practice and Theory* (pp. 317–331). New York: Oxford University Press.

Gonzalez, N., Moll, L. and Amanti, C. (eds) (2005) *Funds of Knowledge: Theorizing Practices in Households, Schools and Communities*. Mahwah, NJ: Erlbaum.

Hopson, R. (2003) The problem of the language line: Cultural and social reproduction of hegemonic structures for learners of African descent in the USA. *Race, Ethnicity and Education* 6 (3), 227–245.

Ibrahim, A. (1999) Becoming black: Rap and hip-hop, race, gender, identity and the politics of ESL learning. *TESOL Quarterly* 33 (3), 349–369.

Kanno, Y. and Norton, B. (2003) Imagined communities and educational possibilities: Introduction. *Journal of Language, Identity and Education* 2 (4), 241–249.

Kubota, R. and Lin, A. (2006) Race and TESOL: Introduction to concepts and theories. *TESOL Quarterly* 40 (3), 471–493.

Lee, C. (2007) *Culture, Literacy and Learning: Taking Bloom in the Midst of the Whirlwind*. New York: Teachers College Press.

Lippi-Green, R. (1997) *English with an Accent: Language, Ideology and Discrimination in the United States.* New York: Routledge.

Makoni, S. and Pennycook, A. (eds) (2006) *Disinventing and Reconstituting Languages.* Clevedon: Multilingual Matters.

Makoni, S. and Trudell, B. (2006) Complementary and conflicting discourses of linguistic diversity: Implications for language planning. *Per Linguam* 22 (2), 14–28.

Pennycook, A. (1994/1996) *The Cultural Politics of English as an International Language.* New York: Longman.

Pennycook, A. (1998) *English and the Discourses of Colonialism.* New York: Routledge.

Pennycook, A. (2000) English, politics and ideology: From colonial celebration to postcolonial performativity. In T. Ricento (ed.) *Ideology, Politics and Language Policies: Focus on English* (pp. 107–120). Philadelphia, PA: John Benjamins.

Rampton, B. (2006) *Language in Late Modernity: Interaction in an Urban School.* New York: Cambridge University Press.

Ricento, T. (2000) *Ideologies, Politics and Language Policies: Focus on English.* Philadelphia, PA: John Benjamins.

Warriner, D.S. (2003) 'Here without English you are dead': Language ideologies and the experiences of women refugees in an adult ESL program. PhD dissertation, University of Pennsylvania.

Warriner, D.S. (2007) Language learning and the politics of belonging: Sudanese women refugees *becoming* and *being* 'American'. *Anthropology and Education Quarterly* 38 (4), 343–361.

Wiley, T.G. and Lukes, M. (1996) English-only and standard English ideologies in the US. *TESOL Quarterly* 30 (3), 511–535.

Woolard, K. (1998) Language ideology as a field of Inquiry. In B. Schieffelin, K. Woolard and P. Kroskrity (eds) *Language Ideologies: Practice and Theory* (pp. 3–47). New York: Oxford University Press.

Chapter 12

Linguistic Profiling, Education and the Law within and beyond the African Diaspora

JOHN BAUGH

For almost as long as the study of language has been around, linguists have offered various explanations for the apparent privileging of certain languages or dialects over others. During the early formulations of linguistic science, Sapir (1921: 219) proposed a relationship between language and race, concluding, 'When it comes to linguistic form, Plato walks with the Macedonia swineherd, Confucius with the headhunting savage of Assam'. Without making any explicit racial attribution, Bloomfield (1933: 48) noted that in the United States, 'The most striking line of cleavage in our speech is one of social class. ... Less fortunate children become speakers of "bad" or "vulgar" or, as the linguist prefers to call it, non-standard English.'

The 'social class' differences in speech that Bloomfield described have been well known for centuries, as evidenced by scribes who documented differences between elite 'classical' Latin and the so-called 'vulgar' Latin spoken by the uneducated masses. Conquests, wars and colonialism throughout history have had direct and indirect linguistic consequences that, regrettably, have distorted folk notions about language, race and poverty. Within the US, Haugen's (1972) emphasis on the 'ecology of language' focused primarily on bilingualism, calling special attention to the plight of voluntary immigrants to America who endured discrimination as a result of trying to master English as a second language. Meanwhile, in England, Bernstein (1971, 1975) focused on social class differences in speech embodied in 'elaborated codes' among the well educated upper classes versus 'restricted codes' as employed by working and lower class speakers. Weinreich (1953) provided a broader survey of languages in contact and asserted that intelligibility is the basis upon which linguistic science should classify distinctive languages and dialects. Although Weinreich does not emphasize the linguistic plight of American slave descendants per se, his magnificent treatise on *Languages in Contact* is directly relevant to the linguistic dislocation suffered by African captives who survived the Atlantic passage and were sold into slavery. The international foundations of the Ebonics debate grow directly from the multilingual and multinational contacts that resulted from the African slave trade, which far exceed the linguistic circumstances experienced by any other (voluntary) immigrant group in the United States (Alim & Baugh, 2007; Baugh, 2000; Rickford & Rickford, 2000; Smitherman, 2000a; Williams, 1975).

Whereas voluntary immigrants to America typically arrived in poverty, speaking languages other than English, they brought their native languages and cultures with them (Wolfram & Schilling-Estes, 1998, 2006). Ethnic enclaves where languages other than English flourished have always been common throughout the development and expansion of the United States, and new immigrants still maintain this tradition today (Valdés, 1996; Zentella, 1997). By striking contrast, enslaved Africans did not come to America of their own free will, and their linguistic circumstances have been devalued and greatly misunderstood throughout American history (Baugh, 1999; Mufwene, 2001; Poplack & Tagliamonte, 2001; Rickford, 1999; Wolfram & Thomas, 2002).

Various studies of diversity in African American English offer tremendous insights with regard to questions of racial justice, as do studies of American linguistic diversity (Finegan & Rickford, 2004; Ferguson *et al.*, 1981; Lippi-Green, 1997; Wolfram & Schilling-Estes, 1998). Sociolinguists in other parts of the world, including England (Trudgill, 1990; Bernstein, 1971), Ireland (Milroy, 1987), Australia (Horvath, 1985), Brazil (Bortoni-Ricardo, 1985), South Africa (Alexander, 2000; Ball, 2006; McCormick, 2002; Mesthrie, 2002) and throughout the European Union (Fairclough, 1995; Reisigl & Wodak, 2000) confirm that the social stratification of linguistic diversity in most advanced industrial societies frequently coincides with parallel racial stratification (Kontra *et al.*, 1999; Skutnabb-Kangas *et al.*, 1994).

The Devaluation of Black Speech in Global Perspective

Many people of African descent in France, South Africa and the US (among other countries) share similar linguistic stereotypes in supposing that Blacks who speak the dominant language poorly must also lack intelligence (Baugh, 2005, 2006; Mandela, 1994; Steele, 1990). Moreover, in South Africa and the US, prevailing linguistic stereotypes about 'Black speech' are often detrimental to their native speakers, particularly in the wake of bygone legal statutes intended to maintain racial segregation. From a diachronic perspective, Mesthrie (1995) and Mufwene (2001) stress different historical orientations for the linguistic heritage of slaves who were transported to North and South America. Mesthrie *et al.*'s (2000) 'slave triangle' emphasizes the fact that Africans who were transported to North and South America did so as European captives. Mufwene's views do not contradict Mesthrie's observations, but emphasize European influences with greater primacy in ways that are supported by Poplack and Tagliamonte (2001).

Regardless of historical linguistic controversies regarding the birth and evolution of African American English, ensuing devaluation of the language and culture of enslaved Africans has been a barrier to racial equality since the inception of slavery, to say little of the combined detrimental impact of statutes intended to deny slaves (or their posterity) full access to literacy or fair treatment under the law. Such explicit anti-Black laws propped up historical myths intended to perpetuate racial segregation.

The passage of antislavery laws in the US and Brazil did little to assuage anti-Black sentiment among racist bigots who felt superior to slaves and/or their descendants. Anti-Black sentiments in South Africa differ, in part, because of differences in racial classification and the fact that White supremacy in Africa occurs where Blacks remain a majority (Mandela, 1994; McCormick, 2002; Mesthrie, 2002). Unlike patterns of overwhelming White immigration to the US from Europe, White immigration to South Africa has been comparatively slight, resulting in a sustained Black, indigenous majority. To be sure, Whites became the dominant (and oppressive) group, bolstered by their notorious legacy of apartheid, but so too were parts of the US once governed by Jim Crow laws and horrific racially-targeted terrorism that was explicitly intended to oppress all Black people (Franklin & Moss, 2000; Wright, 1985). During these historical periods of legally-sanctioned racial discrimination, neither the American South nor South Africa was considered a desirable destination for voluntary Black migration from other parts of the world. Owing to major legal changes, and to the strength of their respective economies, Black immigration to the US and South Africa has greatly increased. Ironically, this influx of Black immigrants has complicated efforts to advance racial reconciliation, since not all Black residents in the US or South Africa share the same personal or historical circumstances, or the same ancestral connection to slavery (Alim, 2003; Baugh, 2006).

Evidence of Linguistic Profiling in Black and Brown Communities

As part of a larger effort in sociolinguistic research to advance racial justice, we have conducted several studies in collaboration with various local fair housing agencies, most of which are affiliated with the National

Fair Housing Alliance.[1] In our case, we have expanded upon previous studies by Purnell *et al.* (1999) and Massey and Lundy (2001) by developing a multidialectal version of Lambert's (1972) matched guise experiments. African American vernacular English (AAVE), Chicano English (ChE), and Standard American English (SAE) were employed in controlled experiments using the telephone to request appointments to visit vacant apartments for rent. In independent studies, Purnell *et al.* (1999) and Massey and Lundy (2001) demonstrated that speakers of nonstandard English were less likely to be granted appointments to view apartments than speakers using Standard English.

Since then, the issue of 'sounding Black' (or 'sounding Latino/a', or 'sounding Gay') during telephone conversations has been the object of scholarly inquiry among various anthropologists, educators, legal scholars, linguists and sociologists (Alim, 2005; Baugh, 2003, 2005; Massey & Lundy, 2001; Smalls, 2004). Unlike racial discrimination derived from visual cues during face-to-face interaction, linguistic profiling frequently reveals prejudice based on the sound of someone's voice. Within the US, many people who have lived most of their lives in one region of the country may develop and maintain negative linguistic stereotypes about speakers from other regions (MacNeil & Cran, 2005).

A clear pattern emerged from experimentally-controlled phone calls in which prospective renters called to inquire about apartment vacancies, always using the phrase 'Hello, I'm calling about the apartment you have advertised in the paper,' albeit in three distinctive renditions, associated with (1) Standard American English (SAE, frequently described as 'White speech'), (2) African American vernacular English (AAVE) and (3) Chicano English (ChE).

Figure 12.1 contains the residential distribution of five communities within the San Francisco Bay Area based on race. There is a clear pattern reflecting a vast majority of Whites in the most affluent communities, and the greatest number of non-Whites in lower income neighborhoods.

Figure 12.2 illustrates the results of successful appointment requests that were granted in response to phone calls that, again, experimentally manipulated different American English dialects uttering the same request (Purnell *et al.*, 1999). The ensuing pattern of acceptances and rejections, illustrated in Figure 12.2 reflects clear trends of much greater rejection of minority dialects, which – for experimental purposes – were always introduced prior to calls made in Standard English.[2]

These findings suggest that many non-Whites are being denied equal access to housing, especially in more affluent areas. Discrimination that results from linguistic profiling is often undetected by those who fall prey

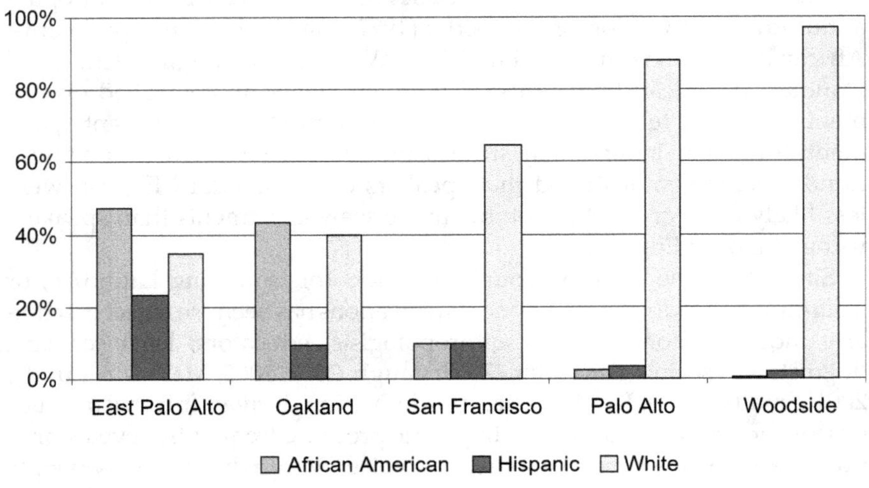

Figure 12.1 Residential distribution by racial classification

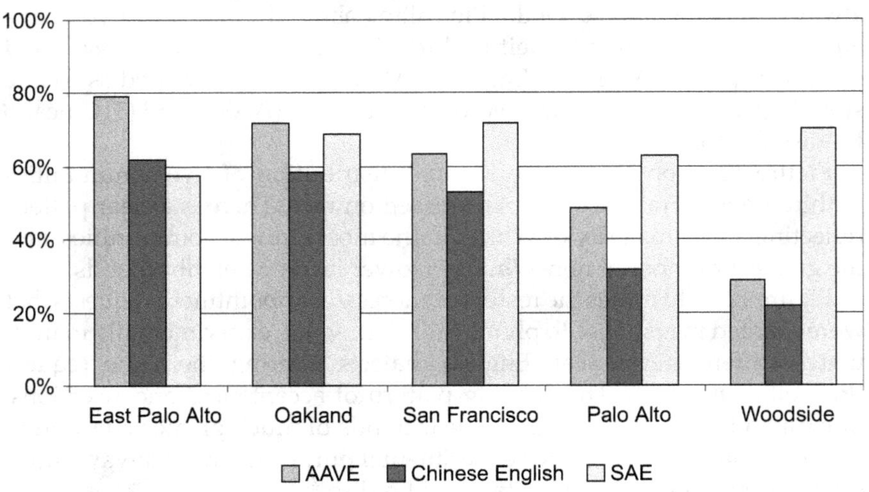

Figure 12.2 Experimental evaluations of confirmed appointments in San Francisco Bay area

to its exclusionary tactics. Our research has the benefit of statistical comparison (Purnell *et al.*, 1999) confirmed in other independent research (Massey & Lundy, 2001). However, from the standpoint of the individual who has been denied an apartment or loan, there is rarely any basis for comparing how others who speak differently were treated by the same service providers. Indeed, it is for this reason that we have found it so important to conduct this research (Alim, 2005; Baugh, 2000; Smalls, 2004).

Research shows that unequal access to housing has consequences for educational opportunities. Nelson (2006) conducted an innovative economic analysis in collaboration with private lending institutions that explored lending bias against qualified African American homebuyers who paid substantially higher interest rates than White homebuyers of comparable socioeconomic status. Since public education funds are allocated based on residential tax bases, any financial or linguistic restriction to housing could easily result in restricted access to better public schools.

Clearly, the quest for justice and racial reconciliation demands the kind of political inquiry that surrounds policies intended to overcome past discrimination, such as affirmative action (Gibson, 2004; Sniderman & Piazza, 2002). But, because many of these political discussions fail to consider linguistic facts, their ultimate utility for social or legal resolutions may be limited. For example, South Africa now has 11 official languages, whereas under apartheid only English and Afrikaans shared official sanction. However, despite their new status as official languages, South Africa's indigenous Black languages have yet to attain equal status with either English or Afrikaans.

We are faced with the apparent contradiction between Sapir's (1921) edict of universal linguistic equality among human languages and the political reality that those who lack fluency in the language(s) of officially sanctioned power also frequently lack the capacity to take advantage of employment, housing or educational opportunities afforded to linguistic elites (Fishman *et al.*, 1996).

Linguistic Profiling and the Law

Smalls (2004) and Wiehl (2002) have surveyed legal cases where voice identification proved to be central. Their findings confirm cases where linguistic research has direct relevance to the advancement of racial justice. Wiehl (2002) concentrated on the *Clifford v. Kentucky* (1999) criminal wiretap case, in which a police officer – who had never seen the alleged drug dealer in person – claimed to be able to identify an African American defendant based solely on the sound of his voice. The court concluded that the officer, having served in the police for over a decade, could credibly distinguish between 'Black' and 'White' speakers based exclusively on hearing their voices. Wiehl (2002) brings up many essential concerns, including the fact that voice identification of this kind, merely suggesting that a speaker belongs to a particular race, does not meet the legal gold standard of individual voice identification.

Whereas Wiehl (2002) devotes primary attention to a single case and its legal and linguistic consequences, Smalls (2004) provides a broader legal survey of criminal and civil cases in which voice identification, particularly identification of African American voices, proved an essential aspect of each case. Based on her survey, Smalls devotes considerable attention to the definition of an 'expert witness' in voice identification cases. She concludes that individuals who are most familiar with the languages or dialects that are central to a given case are more likely to accurately identify someone whose linguistic background is similar to their own. Thus, in a case in which the witness lacks familiarity with the language or dialect of the defendant, the potential for unreliable testimony may increase.

We are currently engaged in new studies that explore the creation of auditory line-ups, where witnesses in critical voice identification cases (both criminal and civil) can be tested to increase the reliability of their voice identification. Stated in other terms, in much the same manner that eye-witness testimony is frequently challenged by asking witnesses to identify suspects from a comparison of photos or a human line-up, our studies of linguistic profiling confirm the need to establish legal comparative standards for 'earwitness testimony'. At present, courts in the US and elsewhere do not have clear standards regarding the ways in which witnesses may be tested to establish the credibility and veracity of their voice-identification abilities.

Language law varies greatly throughout the world, frequently reflecting provincial norms where those with the greatest political power usually determine which languages, and which dialects within those languages, are the most influential and used to maintain government, commerce, education and the law. Our studies confirm that the Biblical attestations of Shibboleths, once delivered face-to-face with potentially fatal consequences, still thrive and may be enhanced with the global proliferation of telephones and cell phones.

Linguistic Leadership: Future Challenges for Educational Leaders and Policy Makers

Drawing upon Goffman's (1959) sociological formulation of 'teams' and 'players', we recognize that many social problems like linguistic profiling demand linguistic leadership among administrators of schools that serve linguistically diverse constituents. Most advanced industrialized societies reflect a social stratification of linguistic diversity, and human linguistic capital is locally reflected by language and cultural norms that vary from one community to the next. Thus, the speaker who is comfortable and at ease in one or more languages will be less effective, from a communicative point of view, working with speech communities where s/he has insufficient linguistic or communicative competence.

When viewed in terms of the social stratification of language, we typically find three subdivisions within any given speech community:

(1) native speakers of the dominant language(s);
(2) native speakers of non-standard dialects of the dominant language(s);
(3) those for whom the dominant language(s) is/are not native.

Figure 12.3 is inspired by Hymes' (1964, 1974) formulation of the ethnography of communication, and his universal observation that human communication must take place between *senders* and *receivers* who alternate roles during discourse. Although this figure can be applied to any complex organization, in this instance, we consider the communicative demands of educational institutions, where individuals within the school must not only communicate among themselves, but also with the students and their respective sociolinguistic communities.

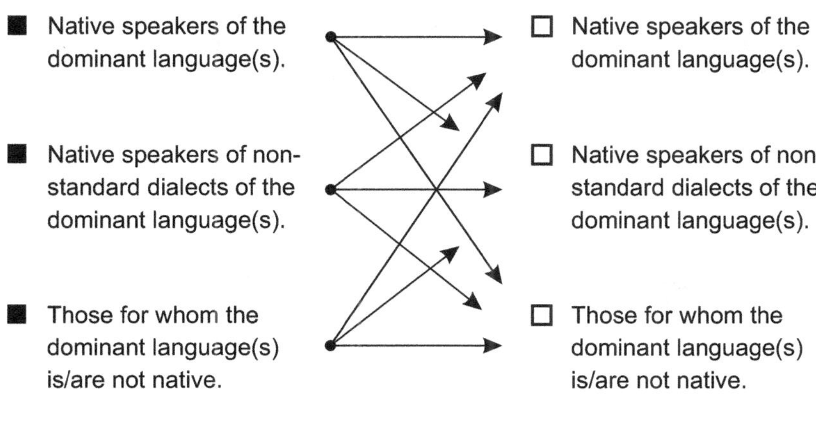

Figure 12.3 The communication demands within complex organizations

Figure 12.3 is provided for illustrative purposes and is not intended to be comprehensive. For example, it fails to capture important distinctions between public and private conversations, to say nothing of highly confidential conversations, or remarks that may have been inadvertently overheard. However, Figure 12.3 does illustrate the potential flow of discourse within an educational organization and those it serves. Rather than describe every possible connection illustrated in Figure 12.3, it is best to recognize that linguistic leadership in educational settings will accrue to those who can effectively manage communication among members within their own organization, as well as those they seek to serve, including those students and their families whose backgrounds may in fact be quite different from those of the school.

It is my contention that many linguists have, in some instances unwittingly, offered substantial evidence that is vital to the advancement of racial justice and equal educational opportunity. This is due in large measure to misconceptions about language, race, intelligence and misplaced linguistic elitism. In some instances, such as the 1979 Black English trial in Ann Arbor, Michigan, well-intended educators were simply unaware of the linguistic bias and demands that they placed upon their young African American students (Labov, 1982a; Smitherman, 1981). In other instances, linguistic prejudice can be overt, even if it is benign. Many people are simply unaware of their personal linguistic preferences, or how potentially hurtful their well-intended comments can be (Steele, 1990).

Challenges Confronting Students from Non-Dominant Linguistic Backgrounds at Home and Abroad

Many scholars have written about how best to address the language education needs of African American students with explicit contemporary relevance (Adger *et al.*, 1999; Baugh, 2000, 2005; Perry & Delpit, 1998; Rickford & Rickford, 2000; Smitherman, 2000a). For example, the emergence of global Hip Hop studies has opened new research venues among anthropologists, linguists and educators regarding effective and appropriate ways to educate urban youth (Alim, 2003; Ball & Lardner, 2005; Darling-Hammond & Baratz-Snowden, 2005; Foster, 1997; Ladson-Billings, 1994; Lee, 1993; Morgan, 2002; Perry & Delpit, 1998; Smitherman, 2000b; Spady *et al.*, 1999; Yasin, Chapter 15, this volume).

Ball's (2006) comparison of the education and literacy development of Black students in the US and South Africa affirms important differences in educational opportunities available to students from low-income backgrounds, who lack fluency in academic modes of discourse (Baugh, 2004;

Heath, 1983). Fluency in academic discourse, whether in Cape Town, Paris or St Louis, will enhance students' prospects for higher education and eventual access to higher-paying employment. Educational researchers have attempted to find ways to improve teacher effectiveness and literacy (Ball, 2006; Ball & Lardner, 2005; Foster, 1997; Hollins *et al.*, 1993; Ladson-Billings, 1994; Lee, 1993) and to ensure that every student, anywhere, has the right to learn (Darling-Hammond *et al.*, 2002).

Cultural barriers and competing linguistic loyalties account, in part, for the fact that many African American students have not fared well educationally, including upper-middle class Blacks who attend affluent public schools where they represent a small minority of the school's population. Ogbu (2003) and Ogbu and Fordham (1986) attribute much of the low academic performance of African Americans to a desire on the part of Black students to avoid 'acting White'. In addition, Steele's (1992) observations regarding stereotype threat may also account for some of this lower academic performance among Black students. However, elsewhere (Baugh, 1999, 2006) I posit that some of this low achievement may be the result of low teacher expectations and the lack of political will to provide incentives and investment to create educational opportunities that have the capacity to advance the well-being of all students, but particularly students for whom Standard American English is not native (Lippi-Green, 1997). Such students would include those for whom English is not native, but also those who are native English speakers but for whom Standard English is not native (Baugh, 1998; LeMoine, 2007).

Alim (2003, 2005) has taught high school students from non-dominant groups, who are keenly aware of the competing linguistic demands in their lives. Whereas Ogbu's (1999) ethnographic studies of Black language usage in urban schools introduced such concepts as 'correct English' and 'proper English', in contrast to 'slang' (i.e. AAVE?), many of the African American consultants I have interviewed spoke infrequently of 'proper English', while making clear distinctions between 'talking Black' versus 'talking White' or 'acting White'. Clearly, from the point of view of linguistic science, all of this terminology is imprecise and therefore problematic, but these (somewhat misleading) linguistic labels underlie many of the myths about race and language that perpetuate misunderstanding in the US and other nations that reflect social stratification with racial relevance. Corresponding historical hardships, or inherited advantages, exceed the plight and perils of the African Diaspora and find relevance in the universal quest for human rights and justice that exist throughout the world. Nevertheless, because of the historical exploitation of Africa, educational prospects for students of African descent throughout the world are neither adequate nor globally competitive. The educational challenges facing students throughout the African Diaspora are enormous and extremely complex, but new and old technologies may combine in innovative ways to provide alternative educational supplements to students who remain eager to learn, and who are willing to work hard and compete, if only they are provided with the necessary instructional tools and environmental support to nurture their academic development (see www.thinkquest.com).[3]

Enhanced educational professionalism will be vital to closing these educational gaps in Africa, America[4] and France, including no-nonsense evaluations of educational malpractice wherever it occurs (Baugh, 1999; Bridges, 1992). Educational researchers and countless dedicated teachers have performed, and will continue to perform, marvelous educational achievements with less fortunate students, but we must do all we can to expand these successful efforts rather than let them wane. Linguists have demonstrated great educational leadership regarding support for students from non-dominant linguistic backgrounds, frequently exposing legal discrepancies with profound relevance to the advancement of racial justice (Adger *et al.*, 1999; Baratz & Shuy, 1969; Fasold, 1972; Gutierrez, 2002; Hakuta, 1986; Labov, 1972; McCormick, 2002; Mesthrie, 2002; Wolfram, 1979, 1991; Zentella, 1997).

Conclusion

> [An] eloquent English-speaker said, 'How can we seniors be overthrown by a backward fellow from the countryside like Mandela, a fellow who cannot even speak English properly!' Nelson Mandela (1994: 45)

Many people who do not consider themselves to be 'eloquent' – be they 'from the countryside' or from the urban ghettos of the poor – may share Mandela's experience of linguistic castigation. This may be particularly true for Black people living in English (or French) speech communities where they are frequently criticized because of 'improper' language usage. Ironically, it was this very issue, including the 'difference versus deficit' debate described by Wolfram (2007) that first attracted me to linguistic science in the form of Labov's (1969a, 1969b) seminal papers titled 'The Logic of Nonstandard English' and 'Contraction, Deletion and Inherent Variability of the English Copula.' Labov's analyses of African American vernacular English stood in direct empirical contrast to the racially-charged genetic hypothesis of White intellectual superiority espoused by Jensen (1969). It is to Labov's pioneering sociolinguistic efforts, and that of many other skilled and dedicated linguists who have devoted their research to the advancement of education, human rights and justice, that I seek to pay tribute here.

The linguistic and social strife that have been the object of Fishman's (1971, 1972) long-standing cultivation of The Sociology of Language are quite evident throughout the African Diaspora, particularly in Black communities where African languages have been displaced by European languages (as a result of colonization and the African slave trade). My myopic attention to the plight of Black speakers throughout the African Diaspora is partially a reflection of administrative responsibilities as director of a program in African and African American Studies. Our mission, to advance distinguished scholarship of and by people of African descent in all fields of intellectual inquiry, is embodied in our studies of linguistic profiling in Black communities throughout the world (Alim, 2005; Baugh, 2003; Smalls, 2004). The historical devaluation of Black speech and corresponding policy implications in medicine, education, business, public policy and the law are pertinent throughout the African Diaspora.

In closing tribute to my mentors, the universal scientific implications embodied in the writings of Labov (1972, 1982b, 1994), Hymes (1964, 1974, 1995, 2004) and Goffman (1959, 1971, 1981) do much more than establish a strong empirical research tradition of language usage in speech communities throughout the world. They also embody an ethos of human equality among all people, and therein lie the direct and indirect relevance to the global quest for racial justice within and beyond the African Diaspora. As with the US Civil Rights movement and the South African struggle to overcome apartheid, lessons learned in Black communities devoted to the advancement of justice and equality have been beneficial to others, including many who have been marginalized and excluded from fair and equal access to quality education, housing, wealth, health care, justice and effective political engagement.

Acknowledgements

The research on linguistic profiling described herein has been supported by generous grants from the Ford Foundation to explore the relationship between linguistic discrimination and potential racial bias in fair housing, education, employment and the law. I am extremely grateful to Natalie Schilling-Estes, Charla Larrimore Baugh, H. Samy Alim, Dawn Smalls, Ashlyn Nelson, Cerena Sweetland-Gil, Aaron Welborn and Jo Anne Kleifgen for their original ideas, support, encouragement and insightful critiques of early formulations of this paper. I have benefited greatly from their independent research contributions in anthropology, economics, education, ethnography, linguistics and the law. Some of the policy implications of their research are outlined in this paper, although I alone am responsible for any limitations.

Notes

1. The National Fair Housing Alliance is a non-profit organization devoted to providing equal and open access to affordable housing for those who might otherwise be denied legal access to fair housing, fair lending and available access to insurance. Their website is at www.nationalfairhousing.org (accessed 14.8.08).
2. The procedure that was employed was one where initial phone calls were randomly made in either AAVE or ChE, based on the toss of a coin. A series of three phone calls would then be made to the same landlord, separated by a period of no less than 45 minutes. The second call would be made in whichever non-dominant dialect had not been selected by the coin toss. Standard English was routinely used during the final phone call in the series of three phone calls to insure that we could more closely scrutinize situations where prospective landlords would reject one or both of the first two requests for an appointment, only to grant an ensuing request to a speaker of Standard English (i.e. someone who might be perceived as 'White' during a telephone conversation).
3. ThinkQuest inspires students to think, connect, create and share. Students work in teams to build innovative and educational websites to share with the world. Along the way, they learn research, writing, teamwork and technology skills, and compete for exciting prizes. Online at www.thinkquest.com (accessed 14.8.08).
4. Throughout this chapter I have tried to make a distinction between 'America' – that is, including both North American and South America – and the 'US'. I regret any inconsistency in advance, owing to my prior habit of using 'America' and the 'US' as synonyms.

References

Adger, C., Christian D. and Taylor O. (eds) (1999) *Making the Connection: Language and Academic Achievement among African American Students: Proceedings of a Conference of the Coalition on Language Diversity in Education.* McHenry, IL: Delta Systems Co.

Alexander, N. (2000) *English Unassailable but Unattainable: The Dilemma of Language Policy in South African Education.* Rondebosch: Project for the Study of Alternative Education in South Africa (PRAESA).

Alim, H.S. (2003) *You Know my Steez: An Ethnographic and Sociolinguistic Study of Styleshifting in a Black American Speech Community.* Durham, NC: Duke University Press.

Alim, H.S. (2005) Critical language awareness in the United States: Revisiting issues and revising pedagogies in a resegregated society. *Educational Researcher* 34 (7), 24–31.

Alim, H.S. and Baugh, J. (eds) (2007) *Talking Black Talk: Language, Education and Social Change.* New York: Teachers College Press.

Ball, A.F. (2006) *Multicultural Strategies for Education and Social Change: Carriers of the Torch in the United States and South Africa.* New York: Teachers College Press.

Ball, A.F. and Lardner, T. (2005) *African American Literacies Unleashed: Vernacular English and the Composition Classroom.* Carbondale, IL: Southern Illinois University Press.

Baratz, J.C. and Shuy, R.W. (eds) (1969) *Teaching Black Children to Read.* Arlington, VA: Center for Applied Linguistics.

Baugh, J. (1998) Linguistics, education and the law: Educational reform for African-American language minority students. In S. Mufwene, J. Rickford, G. Bailey and J. Baugh (eds) *African-American English: Structure, History and Use* (pp. 282–301). London: Routledge.

Baugh, J. (1999) *Out of the Mouths of Slaves: African American Language and Educational Malpractice.* Austin, TX: University of Texas Press.

Baugh, J. (2000) *Beyond Ebonics. Linguistic Pride and Racial Prejudice.* New York: Oxford University Press.

Baugh, J. (2003) Linguistic profiling. In S. Makoni, G. Smitherman, A.F. Ball and A.K. Spears (eds) *Black Linguistics: Language, Society and Politics in Africa and the Americas* (pp. 155–168). London: Routledge.

Baugh, J. (2004) Standard English and Academic English (dialect) learners in the African diaspora. In A. Curzan and A. Beckford (eds) *Journal of English Linguistics* 33 (1), 1–13.

Baugh, J. (2005) Conveniently Black: Self-delusion and the racial exploitation of African America. *Du Bois Review* 2 (1), 1–14.

Baugh, J. (2006) It ain't about race: Some lingering (linguistic) consequences of the African slave trade and their relevance to your personal historical hardship index. *Du Bois Review* 3 (1), 145–159.

Bernstein, B. (1971) *Class, Codes and Control.* London: Routledge and Kegan Paul.

Bernstein, B. (1975) *Class and Pedagogies, Visible and Invisible.* Paris: Organization for Economic Cooperation and Development.

Bloomfield, L. (1933) *Language.* New York: Holt, Rinehart and Winston.

Bortoni-Ricardo, S.M. (1985) *The Urbanization of Rural Dialect Speakers: A Sociolinguistic Study in Brazil.* New York: Cambridge University Press.

Bridges, E.M. (1992) *The Incompetent Teacher: Managerial Responses.* Washington, DC: Falmer Press.

Clifford v. Kentucky,7 SW 3d 371 (Ky. 1999).

Darling-Hammond, L., French J. and Garcia-Lopez, S.P. (eds) (2002) *Learning to Teach for Social Justice.* New York: Teachers College Press.

Darling-Hammond, L. and Baratz-Snowden J. (eds) (2005) *A Good Teacher in Every Classroom: Preparing the Highly Qualified Teachers Our Children Deserve.* San Francisco: Jossey-Bass.

Fairclough, N. (1995) *Critical Discourse Analysis: Papers in the Critical Study of Language.* New York: Longman.

Fasold, R.W. (1972) *Tense Marking in Black English: A Linguistic and Social Analysis.* Arlington, VA: Center for Applied Linguistics.

Ferguson, C.A., Brice Heath, S.B. and Hwang D. (eds) (1981) *Language in the USA.* New York: Cambridge University Press.

Finegan, E. and Rickford, J. (eds) (2004) *Language in the USA: Themes for the Twenty-first Century.* New York: Cambridge University Press.

Fishman, J.A. (ed.) (1971) *Advances in the Sociology of Language.* The Hague: Mouton.

Fishman, J.A. (1972) *The Sociology of Language: An Interdisciplinary Social Science Approach to Language in Society.* Rowley, MA: Newbury House.

Fishman, J.A., Conrad, A.W. and Rubal-Lopez A. (eds) (1996) *Post-Imperial English: Status Change in Former British and American Colonies, 1940–1990.* New York: Mouton de Gruyter.

Foster, M. (1997) *Black Teachers on Teaching*. New York: New Press.
Franklin, J.H. and Moss, A.A. (2000) *From Slavery to Freedom: A History of African Americans* (8th edn). New York: A.A. Knopf.
Gibson, J.L. (2004) *Overcoming Apartheid: Can Truth Reconcile a Divided Nation?* New York: Russell Sage Foundation.
Goffman, E. (1959) *The Presentation of Self in Everyday Life*. New York: Anchor.
Goffman, E. (1971) *Relations in Public: Microstudies of the Public Order*. New York: Harper & Row.
Goffman, E. (1981) *Forms of Talk*. Philadelphia: University of Pennsylvania Press.
Gutierrez, K. (2002) Studying cultural practices in urban learning communities. *Human Development* 45 (4), 312–321.
Hakuta, K. (1986) *Mirror of Language: The Debate on Bilingualism*. New York: Basic Books.
Haugen, E. (1972) *The Ecology of Language*. Stanford, CT: Stanford University Press.
Heath, S.B. (1983) *Ways with Words: Language, Life and Work in Communities and Classrooms*. Cambridge: Cambridge University Press.
Hollins, E.R., King, J.E. and Hayman, W.C. (eds) (1993) *Teaching Diverse Populations: Formulating a Knowledge Base*. Albany, NY: State University of New York Press.
Horvath, B.M. (1985) *Variation in Australian English: The Sociolects of Sydney*. New York: Cambridge University Press.
Hymes, D. (ed.) (1964) *Language in Culture and Society: A Reader in Linguistics and Anthropology*. New York: Harper & Row.
Hymes, D. (1974) *Foundations in Sociolinguistics: An Ethnographic Approach*. Philadelphia, PA: University of Pennsylvania Press.
Hymes, D. (1995) *Ethnography, Linguistics, Narrative Inequality: Toward an Understanding of Voice*. Washington, DC: Taylor & Francis.
Hymes, D. (2004) *'In Vain I Tried to Tell You': Essays in Native American Ethnopoetics*. Lincoln, NE: University of Nebraska Press.
Jensen, A. (1969) How much can we boost IQ? *Harvard Educational Review* 39 (1), 1–123.
Kontra, M., Skutnabb-Kangas, T. and Várady, T. (1999) *Language, a Right and a Resource: Approaching Linguistic Human Rights*. New York: Central European University Press.
Labov, W. (1969a) The logic of nonstandard English. In J.E. Alatis (ed.) *Georgetown Monographs on Language and Linguistics* 22, 1–31.
Labov, W. (1969b) Contraction, deletion and inherent variability of the English copula. *Language* 45, 715–62.
Labov, W. (1972) *Language in the Inner City: Studies in the Black English Vernacular*. Philadelphia: University of Pennsylvania Press.
Labov, W. (1982a) Objectivity and commitment in linguistic science: The case of the Black English trial in Ann Arbor. *Language in Society* 11, 165–202.
Labov, W. (1982b) *Speech Actions and Reactions in Personal Narrative*. Georgetown: Georgetown University Press.
Labov, W. (1994) *Principles of Linguistic Change: Internal Factors*. Oxford: Blackwell.
Ladson-Billings, G. (1994) *The Dreamkeepers: Successful Teachers of African American Children*. San Francisco, CA: Jossey-Bass.
Lambert, W.E. (1972) *Language, Psychology and Culture*. Stanford, CT: Stanford University Press.

Lee, C.D. (1993) *Signifying as a Scaffold for Literary Interpretation: The Pedagogical Implications of an African American Discourse Genre.* Urbana, IL: National Council of Teachers of English.

LeMoine, N. (2007) Developing academic English for Standard English language learners. In H.S. Alim and J. Baugh (eds) *Talking Black Talk: Language, Education and Social Change.* New York: Teachers College Press.

Lippi-Green, R. (1997) *English with an Accent: Language, Ideology and Discrimination in the United States.* New York: Routledge.

MacNeil, R. and Cran, W. (2005) *Do you Speak American?* A companion to the PBS television series. New York: Nan A. Talese/Doubleday.

Mandela, N. (1994) *Long Walk to Freedom: The Autobiography of Nelson Mandela.* Boston: Little, Brown.

Massey, D.S. and Lundy, G. (2001) Use of Black English and racial discrimination in urban housing markets: New methods and findings. *Urban Affairs Review* 36 (4), 452–469.

McCormick, K. (2002) *Language in Cape Town's District Six.* New York: Oxford University Press.

Mesthrie, R. (ed.) (1995) *Language and Social History: Studies in South African Sociolinguistics.* Cape Town: David Philip.

Mesthrie, R. (ed.) (2002) *Language in South Africa.* New York: Cambridge University Press.

Mesthrie, R., Swann J., Deumert, A. and Leap, W.L. (2000) *Introducing Sociolinguistics.* Philadelphia: John Benjamins.

Milroy, L. (1987) *Language and Social Networks* (2nd edn). New York: Blackwell.

Morgan, M. (2002) *Language, Discourse and Power in African American Culture.* New York: Cambridge University Press.

Mufwene, S.S. (2001) *The Ecology of Language Evolution.* New York: Cambridge University Press.

Nelson, A.A. (2006) Better credit, better schools: Credit quality, race and discrete-choice residential sorting. PhD dissertation, Stanford University.

Ogbu, J. (1999) Beyond language: Ebonics, proper English and identity in a Black-American speech community. *American Educational Research Journal* 36 (2), 147–184.

Ogbu, J. (2003) *Black American Students in an Affluent Suburb: A Study of Academic Disengagement.* Mahwah, NJ: Erlbaum.

Ogbu, J. and Fordham, S. (1986) Black students' school success: Coping with the burden of 'Acting White'. *The Urban Review* 18 (3), 176–206.

Perry, T. and Delpit, L. (eds) (1998) *The Real Ebonics Debate: Power, Language and the Education of African-American Children.* Boston: Beacon Press.

Poplack, S. and Tagliamonte, S. (2001) *African American English in the Diaspora.* Malden, MA: Blackwell.

Purnell, T., Idsardi, W. and Baugh, J. (1999) Perceptual and phonetic experiments on American English dialect identification. *Journal of Language and Social Psychology* 18, 10–30.

Reisigl, M. and Wodak, R. (eds) (2000) *The Semiotics of Racism: Approaches in Critical Discourse Analysis.* Vienna: Passagen Verlag.

Rickford, J.R. (1999) *African American Vernacular English: Features, Evolution, Educational Implications.* Malden, MA: Blackwell.

Rickford, J.R. and Rickford, R.J. (2000) *Spoken Soul: The Story of Black English.* New York: John Wiley and Sons.

Sapir, E. (1921) *Language: An Introduction to the Study of Speech*. New York: Harcourt, Brace.

Skutnabb-Kangas, T., Phillipson, R. and Rannut, M. (eds) (1994) *Linguistic Human Rights: Overcoming Linguistic Discrimination*. New York: M. de Gruyter.

Smalls, D. (2004) Linguistic profiling and the law. *Stanford Law and Policy Review* 15, 579–604.

Smitherman, G. (ed.) (1981) *Black English and the Education of Black Children and Youth: Proceedings of the National Invitational Symposium on the King Decision*. Detroit, IL: Center for Black Studies, Wayne State University.

Smitherman, G. (2000a) *Talkin That Talk: Language, Culture and Education in African America*. New York: Routledge.

Smitherman, G. (2000b) *Black Talk: Words and Phrases from the Hood to the Amen Corner* (rev. edn). Boston, MA: Houghton Mifflin.

Sniderman, P.M. and Piazza, T. (2002) *Black Pride and Black Prejudice*. Princeton, MA: Princeton University Press.

Spady, J.G., Lee, C.G. and Alim, H.S. (1999) *Street Conscious Rap*. Philadelphia, PA: Black History Museum, Umum/Loh Publications.

Steele, C. (1992) Race and the schooling of Black Americans. *The Atlantic Monthly* 271, 68–78.

Steele, S. (1990) *The Content of our Character: A New Vision of Race in America*. New York: St Martin's Press.

Trudgill, P. (1990) *The Dialects of England*. Cambridge, MA: Blackwell.

Valdés, G. (1996) *Con Respeto: Bridging the Distances Between Culturally Diverse Families and Schools: An Ethnographic Portrait*. New York: Teachers College Press.

Weinreich, U. (1953) *Languages in Contact*. Paris: Mouton.

Wiehl, L. (2002) 'Sounding Black' in the courtroom: Court sanctioned racial stereotyping. *Harvard Blackletter Law Journal* 18, 185–210.

Williams, R.L. (1975) *Ebonics: The True Language of Black Folks*. St Louis, MO: Robert L. Williams and Associates.

Wolfram, W. (1979) *The Linguist in Speech Pathology*. Arlington, VA: Center for Applied Linguistics.

Wolfram, W. (1991) *Dialects and American English*. Englewood Cliffs, NJ: Prentice Hall.

Wolfram, W. (2007) Sociolinguistic folklore in the study of African American English. *Language and Linguistics Compass* 1 (4), 292–313

Wolfram, W. and Schilling-Estes, N. (1998) *American English: Dialects and Variation*. Malden, MA: Blackwell.

Wolfram, W. and Schilling-Estes, N. (2006) *American English: Dialects and Variation* (2nd edn). Malden, MA: Blackwell.

Wolfram, W. and Thomas, E. (2002) *The Development of African American English*. Malden, MA: Blackwell.

Wright, G.C. (1985) *Life Behind a Veil: Blacks in Louisville, Kentucky, 1865–1930*. Baton Rouge, LA: Louisiana State University Press.

Zentella, A.C. (1997) *Growing Up Bilingual: Puerto Rican Children in New York*. Malden, MA: Blackwell.

Chapter 13

On Shallow Grammar: African American English and the Critique of Exceptionalism

ARTHUR K. SPEARS

Shallow grammar refers to any one or the set of written grammatical descriptions as well as the set of approaches to grammatical study shackled by received theoretical questions, methodologies and inventories of human language grammatical features, all of which contribute to the overlooking of important grammatical features in the languages under study. African American English (AAE) studies offer prime examples of shallow grammar, in terms of research processes and resulting grammatical descriptions. As often noted, the AAE vernacular (AAVE, see below) is the most studied variety of English, outside the standard; yet, no grammar thus far produced even lays out the basic features – formatives and their interactions – of the verbal auxiliary system. Perhaps as many as a third of the auxiliaries in this system have either never been discussed in the literature or have been discussed in only a handful of writings (see Appendix to this chapter). Nevertheless, unbridled theorizing on the history and nature of AAE forges ahead on the thinnest tissue of grammatical understanding. The phenomenon of shallow grammar also renders patently clear the premature and intellectually irresponsible nature of much theorizing on creoles and other contact languages. (In this chapter, I use *creole*, lower case, in reference to the group of languages called creoles. The term refers to a type of language, extensionally defined. When using DeGraff's (2005) term *Creole exceptionalism*, I will capitalize *Creole*, as he does.) The notion of Creole exceptionalism is, among other things, an artifact of shallow grammar.

DeGraff defines *Creole exceptionalism* as 'a set of beliefs, widespread among both linguists and nonlinguists, that Creole languages form an exceptional class on phylogenetic and/or typological grounds' (DeGraff, 2005: 533; see also DeGraff, Chapter 7, this volume). DeGraff speaks of exceptionalism in relation to creole languages and focuses on Haitian

Creole. Exceptionalism is also relevant in the study of AAE; I will return to this relevance shortly. As an AAE researcher and a creolist, I observe that the bottom line regarding Creole exceptionalism with respect to typology is that any creolist can define creoles typologically, as does McWhorter (e.g. 2001, and see the references in DeGraff, 2005) in a number of writings, if s/he manipulates membership in the group of languages called creoles. Membership manipulation makes typologically exceptionalist claims about creoles circular and therefore falsifiable. Phylogenetic exceptionalist claims, such as Bickerton's (1981) Bioprogram Hypothesis and others' revisions of it, have already been disproved (see the discussion in DeGraff, 2005 and Chapter 7). These hypotheses state essentially that creole genesis partially recapitulates phylogeny, the birth of language as a human trait. Views of creole language genesis qua recapitulating phylogeny gave rise to the term *new languages* in respect to creoles.

From a sociohistorical perspective, Creole exceptionalism must be seen as an exercise, whether conscious or unconscious – it matters not, in the maintenance of white supremacist racism, a regime of truth, in the Foucaultian sense, whose logic requires:

(1) the continued debasement of Haiti (whose culture and Creole are discussed at length in DeGraff, 2005) in retaliation for the Haitian Revolution's epistemological 'crime' against white supremacist racism, and
(2) the continual intervention in and destabilization of sub-Saharan ('black') Africa, among other developing regions, whose material resources are indispensable for world industry. These resources are largely controlled by global capitalists in service to the world color order. It is of interest that all of the major recent (post-World War II) hypotheses on Creole exceptionalism were produced in the US, the world headquarters of white supremacist racism (Spears, 1999).

Some Background on AAE's Relation to Creoles

African American English (AAE) is not currently considered a creole by creolists or noncreolists who specialize in AAE study. It has, however, been labeled a *semi-creole,* or labeled by the equivalent and later term *partially restructured language* (Holm, 1992, 2004). Compare this with the term *restructured language* in reference to creoles. The use of either *semi-creole* or *partially restructured language* implies that AAE shares grammatical features with Atlantic creole languages, but not enough of them to be considered a full-fledged language of the creole type. This view can be taken as implying that creole languages either constitute a separate typological class or merely that there is a group of grammatical features that are commonly found in creoles. My view is the latter.

Some earlier views considered AAE to be a decreolized language variety, or post-creole – an erstwhile creole that had undergone gradual linguistic changes over time, becoming close enough in grammar to the ensemble of other American English varieties to be classified as a variety of English, albeit one with some few grammatical remnants of its creole past (Dillard, 1972; Stewart, 1967, 1968). (See Spears, forthcoming, for a fuller discussion of hypotheses on AAE genesis and evolution.)

I have recently demonstrated that AAE has many more creole-associated grammatical features (creolisms) than previously thought and have explained why it does not have the high profile, conspicuous grammatical features typically used as diagnostics, such as, for example, the pronominal and verbal systems typical of creoles (Spears, forthcoming). As noted above, the term *creole language* has no air-tight linguistic or sociohistorical definition, *pace* McWhorter (2001). However, given that there is a set of grammatical features considered as typical of Caribbean creole languages, not all of which have been recorded for every single language traditionally called a creole, I advance the neocreolist claim that most varieties of AAE (leaving aside focal creolisms), can reasonably be termed creoles on the basis of *nonfocal* creole-associated grammatical features (Spears, forthcoming), which have hardly or not at all been discussed in the literature. Focal creolisms, creole grammatical features frequently discussed in the literature, are largely absent from AAE today because of historical assimilationist pressures in the US and the much stronger history in the US of black formal education, relative to the Caribbean. In sum, we might label AAE a *creole-related* language.

Varieties of AAE

Before going further, it must be noted that two main varieties of AAE can be distinguished with reference to the notion of standardness: the nonstandard one, which, following recent literature, I will refer to as African American Vernacular English (AAVE), and African American Standard English (AASE) (Spears, 1988, 2007b, forthcoming). Although standards are commonly considered as attaching to regional groups among others, they are not usually associated with specific ethnic or racial groups, such as African Americans. The term AASE implies that in the case of African Americans there is an ethnic standard variety that satisfies the conditions for standardness and also has distinctive grammatical traits associated with this ethnic group's variety.

The conditions for standard status are basically negative: a standard variety does not have certain grammatical features that are considered non-standard, such as multiple negatives, use of *ain't* and double modals, as in:

(1) We might could do that.
'Maybe we could do that.'

Note, though, that there is not a universally recognized set of features that make up the list of non-standard features. One learns a variety of the standard by growing up interacting with its speakers or through education. Distinctively African American (or *black*) grammatical features (DBGFs) occurring in AASE are not discussed in pedagogical and prescriptive grammars. Also, they are not recognized in the normal case by AAE speakers or other dialect speakers as being distinctively African American. These features have gone unclassified with respect to standardness by those who might want to label them as non-standard because they are distinctively African American and because of the low prestige often attached to any kind of speech labeled 'African American' or 'black.' Were these features better known, we might well see efforts to classify them as non-standard, i.e. to make them 'exceptional', simply because they are distinctive to AAE.

Creole and AAE Exceptionalism

I emphasize the observation that racist ideology is the buttress of shallow grammar (Alim & Baugh, 2007; Makoni *et al.*, 2003; Smitherman, 2000: especially Part 4; Spears, 1999), which in turn lends support to Creole and AAE exceptionalism. Exceptionalism begins with the racist ideological framework that produces an expected outcome – shallow grammar – which then confirms what were erroneous assumptions to begin with. The process is circular.

No parallel ideas of AAE grammatical exceptionalism are current among AAE scholars, practically all of whose research has focused on AAVE. However, its nonlinguistic implications, especially, 'that Creole languages are a "handicap" for their speakers, which has undermined the role that Creoles should play in the education and socioeconomic development of monolingual Creolophones' (DeGraff, 2005: 533), often apply (*mutatis mutandis*) to AAVE in the minds of lay people – and shockingly, some linguists. (Many PhD programs in linguistics do not require students to take any sociolinguistics courses, where they would learn, minimally, about the rule-governedness and communicative adequacy of stigmatized language varieties such as AAVE. As recently as the late 1980s, the National Science Foundation (NSF) grant proposal evaluators erroneously asserted that a proposal to fund a study of African American children's acquisition of AAVE was unfundable because the children were not acquiring a full-fledged language; thus, the study, they thought, would be of questionable usefulness for acquisition research.)

Note that it is AAVE that is labeled as a handicap (few lay persons or linguists are aware of AASE). It, in comparison to the standard, is erroneously assumed to be grammarless, illogical, and communicatively deficient. (As observed above, American standard English is actually a group of standard varieties, classified on regional, ethnic and other bases.)

One way of encapsulating one strand of the Creole exceptionalist view of creole grammar is 'Creole languages have the world's simplest grammars' (McWhorter, 2001). Note in this connection that it is one thing to state that a group of languages *appear, on the basis of our current state of knowledge,* to have the world's simplest grammars. It is another to make an unqualified assertion that they do. Regardless of the difficulties in defining what grammatical simplicity actually means in talking about the entire grammars of individual languages (Faraclas, 2006), taking into account solely the *dual* prosodic systems of a number of Caribbean area creole languages, one must conclude that we have significant research left to do before making claims about simplicity. Research over the last decade has demonstrated that several creole languages make use of *two* prosodic systems (stress and tone) to make lexical contrasts (Saramaccan, Ndjuka, Guyanese, Papiamentu, Jamaican – all discussed in Gooden, 2003), Crucian and Bajan (Barbadian), while their lexifier languages make use of stress alone. (See Faraclas, 2006 and Good, 2006 together for remarks on all of these languages.) In terms of prosody, then, these creoles are more complex than their lexifiers, because, unlike their lexifiers, they have both stress and tone. Stress refers to how prominent syllables are. For example, *produce* (fruit and vegetables) has stress on the first syllable. *Produce* (to bring into existence) has stress on the second syllable. Tone is the use of pitch to distinguish meaning in a precise way (as linguists would say, to signal semantic rather than solely pragmatic distinctions). Pitch ranges from high to low (think of musical notes). Pitch is called tone when precise meaning differences (semantic differences) are signaled by pitch. For example, tone differences in a syllable of a verb in many West African languages change the tense of the verb (e.g. present, past, etc.).

Dual prosodic systems have been detailed since McWhorter's (2001) claims. We can be certain that other areas of grammar will be revealed to be more complex, given that shallow grammars are the norm in creole grammatical studies. This is to be expected since so much of the attention of creolists has focused on sociohistorical questions, and the in-depth study of creole grammars is quite recent and constitutes a relatively small subfield of linguistics, with few practitioners.

Shallow Grammar and AAE

There are several contributing factors to AAE shallow grammar. First, only a small group of grammatical features is studied in depth, primarily in a variationist framework, for example, copula absence and invariant habitual *be*. Copula absence refers to sentences in AAVE that do not have a form of the copula *be*, especially the singular, whose absence distinguishes AAVE from other American dialects, standard and vernacular. Copula absence is exemplified in example (2):

(2) (a) John Ø crazy. (AAVE)
 (b) John's (John is) crazy. (AASE, other American dialects; parentheses here and in other examples contain variants)

Invariant habitual *be* is an auxiliary verb form occurring in AAVE (but not AASE) that is never conjugated; it signals habitual aspect – the occurrence of an event or state over a significantly long period of time (length depending on the social context). Note the following examples and their glosses:

(3) (a) She always be throwing my stuff away. (AAVE)
 'She always throws HABITUAL (is always throwing HABITUAL) my stuff away.'
 (b) He be over at Grandpa house. (AAVE)
 'He is (HABITUAL) over at Grandpa's house.'

In reality, there are a number of distinctively black (i.e. African American) grammatical features (DBGFs) that have seldom been discussed in the literature, though this situation is being corrected (Spears, 1998, 2000, 2001a, 2001b, 2004, 2006a, 2006b, 2007a, 2007b, forthcoming).

Second, few studies approach AAE grammar systemically, whether the whole system of grammar or subsystems, such as the auxiliary system we focus on here, but note Labov's (1998) and Green's (2002) efforts to address this problem.

Third, there has been little attention to communicative practices (Morgan, 2002; Smitherman, 1977; and several publications of Spears are the major exceptions in this regard.) I have pointed out (Spears, 2007a, and below) that a number of grammatical features distinguishing AAE grammar are closely connected with distinctive African American communicative practices. Thus, if due attention is not paid to those practices, there is a strong likelihood that these grammatical features will be overlooked. (Disapproval markers are prominent in this regard, as we shall see below.)

Fourth, in terms of methodology, there is very little collecting and analyzing of speaker-initiated discourses, produced by speakers as they carry out real, everyday, socially-situated tasks requiring speech, i.e. *naturally occurring speech*, ethnographically observed but with a focus on grammatical analysis. Studies have generally focused on researcher-prompted speech outside the context of speakers' normal daily lives, for example, sociolinguistic interviews, researcher prompted narratives and repetition tests.

By *ethnographically observed* speech, I refer to speech recorded or noted in its context of natural occurrence, by participant observation. The kind of *participant observation* I stress refers to researchers' studying the speech of communities of which they are members, as they go about their social business as members of the community. (Participant observers may also, of course, be nonmembers of the community.) Participant-member observation normally assumes native speaker ability in the language of interest, and native speakerhood can provide not only grammatical intuitions but also make possible participant observation and recollection – not just recordings – of socially-situated, naturally-occurring speech. The point here is that all work on AAE involving participant observation, except that of Spears, has been related to the study of communicative practices alone without accounting for grammatical analysis. More important, however, is that naturally-occurring speech, no matter how obtained, is key for observing grammar in its 'natural habitat.'

This leads to the fifth factor, which is that AAE grammar is rarely studied within the context of communicative practices and culture generally, that is, holistically; but, it should be if we are to to avoid the shallow grammar trap. Stated differently, linguists should always keep in mind *ethnogrammar* (my term, cf. *ethnosyntax* (Enfield, 2002; Wierzbicka, 1979)), the interconnections between the cultural knowledge, attitudes and practices of speakers, and the grammatical (including phonology) resources they employ in speech. Ethnogrammar stresses the interconstitutivity of culture and grammar, for example, cultural emphases and speech styles affecting the evolution of grammar (assuming that culture drives grammar more than vice-versa). It also stresses the ways in which grammatical items (constructions and function morphemes) encode cultural values and meta-discursive styles, for example, 'grammatical devices in Russian expressing "emotionality," "non-rationality," "non-agentivity" and "moral passion" (Wierzbicka, 1992)' (quoted in Enfield, 2002: 3).

Ethnographically observed speech is critically important since, as will be explained below:

(1) the incommensurate part of AAE grammar is mostly in evidence in naturally-occurring speech;
(2) the social situatedness of such speech is better for detecting camouflaged forms;
(3) camouflaged forms are much more likely to occur in such speech.

Additionally, forms involved in camouflage and grammatical incommensurability typically relate to important AAE meta-discursive styles, notably directness (Spears, 2001b).

Close attention to naturally-occurring speech, through participant observation, has a snowball effect in bringing new grammatical features to the linguist's attention. A tacit understanding of this fifth factor is no doubt at work in the continual calls for producing more native speaker linguists, not only of AAE but also of the languages of other disadvantaged groups.

Obstacles to Understanding AAE Grammar

To move beyond problems with approaches to studying AAE and how they are implicated in the production of shallow grammar, two principal obstacles to understanding AAE grammar can be singled out: grammatical camouflage and grammatical incommensurability.

Grammatical camouflage refers to the phenomenon whereby AAE function morphemes and other grammatical features are misinterpreted as phonologically similar or identical items occurring in non-AAE dialects. *Grammatical incommensurability* refers to aspects of the grammar of a language x (e.g. AAE) that have no counterparts in language y (e.g. non-African American dialects). An example of grammatical camouflage is a feature occurring in AAVE and AASE called stressed BIN, as in example (4). BIN[1] is uttered with pronounced stress (and high pitch in my dialect) and refers to events that began to occur long ago and still continue. Note that the AASE sentence includes the auxiliary (*-s* < *has*), while the AAVE sentence does not. Stated differently, the AASE sentence segmentally conforms to other standard American English dialects, while the AAVE sentence does not. (*Segmental* refers to vowel and consonant quality, without taking into consideration prosody, i.e. intonation, pitch, tempo, rhythm, stress, etc. In transcriptions of speech, segmentals are written on the line, while suprasegmentals, prosodic indicators, are written above consonant and vowel symbols. *Segment* is the cover term for consonants, vowels – and, of course, glides.)

(4) (a) He's BIN gone. (AASE)
    (b) He BIN gone. (AAVE)
    'He has been gone for a long time and is still gone.'

Segmental conformity is contrasted with suprasegmental, or prosodic, conformity. Prosody includes stress. The AASE sentence, then, segmentally conforms but does not suprasegmentally conform to its counterpart sentence in non-African American standard dialects. The AAVE sentence conforms neither segmentally, having no auxiliary, nor suprasegmentally. Segmental conformity is one of a few wide-ranging processes that produce grammatical camouflage, the grammatical result of historical assimilationist pressures on African Americans, pressures that constrain AASE grammar.

Stressed BIN, like other distinctively African American grammatical features, is highly camouflaged (Spears 1982, 1990). If features are camouflaged, they are not normally recognized by the uninitiated as AAE grammatical features; they are mistakenly assumed to be equivalent to phonemically similar or identical features of non-African American varieties – ones having different meanings and sometimes different grammatical functions. Thus, BIN in AAE, a marker of remote perfect tense, is camouflaged with respect to other American dialects and is mistaken for the past participle of be that occurs in all English dialects. The existence of camouflaged forms such as BIN results from

(1) general societal pressures on African Americans to assimilate, pressures that are the by-product of the subordinate position of African Americans in American society;
(2) the continuing high level of racial segregation, which was lessened but not eliminated in the wake of the Civil Rights Movement of the 1950s through the 1970s.

Some speakers who typically use AASE also use AAVE features, whereas some never do, except self-consciously for some metacommunicative purpose. Thus, the two forms of AAE exist separately, though some speakers deploy both varieties.

One of the main factors leading to shallow grammar is the insufficient attention that linguists often pay to the incommensurability of grammars: languages and dialects have significant numbers of grammatical features that have no analogs in related languages and dialects. As Dell Hymes, the eminent anthropological linguist, once put it, most of language begins where universals leave off (Hymes, 1974). The neglect of incommensurability stems significantly from widespread Chomskyan universals-oriented approaches to the grammars of languages. Linguists often take to the study of language a set of investigative predispositions based on:

(1) received theories and the questions they privilege;
(2) received methodologies;
(3) received inventories of human language grammatical features.

All of these contribute to the linguists overlooking of important grammatical features in the languages they study. Consequently, they fail to find what they have not been open to discovering. Perhaps the scholars most susceptible to the factors leading to shallow grammar are those who study non-standard (vernacular) dialects of European languages and the creoles in whose genesis those European languages played a part.

Disapproval markers (DMs), which express varying degrees of negative evaluation, mostly disapproval and indignation, offer an excellent illustration of both grammatical camouflage and grammatical incommensurability. The semi-auxiliary *come* is one in a group of four; the others are *gone, gone-come* and be *done* (the last in one of its three uses) (Spears, 1990, 2006b). The DM *come* expresses strong disapproval or indignation. Consider:

(5) (a) He come (came) walking in the door.

(Remember that parentheses indicate another variant.) The *come* in this AAE sentence might be the familiar motion verb or the *come* of strong disapproval or indignation, unique to AAE. Segmentally (i.e. without taking prosody into account), there is no way to tell which item *come* is. In other sentences, however, the *come* can only be the disapproval marker (DM) *come* because the familiar motion verb cannot occur in the same context, for example:

(5) (b) She come (DM) being all friendly with me, after she been talking about me behind my back.
'She had the nerve to be (act) all friendly with me ...'

(For simplicity's sake, I will not consider further variation involving the form *come*.) Note that *come*, the motion verb, cannot immediately precede a form of *be*, thus, the ungrammaticality of **He came being all friendly to my door ... , They came being well-dressed to my door ...* . Note also, that *come* the motion verb cannot precede itself: **He come coming up to me.* However, we do get:

(5) (c) He come (DM) coming (MOTION VERB) up to me with all that fool talk ...
'He had the nerve to come up to me ...'

Note also that in some dialects of AAVE, the DM *come* is followed by a bare verb, as in these examples:

(6) (a) She come (DM) come up to me with all that fool talk ... .
'She had the nerve to come up to me with all that fool talk ... .'
(b) He come (DM) tell me I ain't got no sense.
'He had the nerve to tell me I ain't got no sense.'

Thus, in the case of the DM *come*, there are three degrees, so to speak, of camouflage. The first, involves sentences of the type in (7), the second involves sentences of the type in (8) and the third involves sentences of the type (9), which has the standard Simple Past verb form of the homophonous motion verb:

(7) *come* (DM) V (bare verb);
(8) *come* (DM) V+ing;
(9) *came* (DM) V+ing.

In an instance of the first degree, example (7), the DM *come* can indeed be misinterpreted as the familiar motion verb of non-African American dialects; however, there is never segmental conformity with non-African American standards. With the second degree, there can be segmental conformity with non-African American non-standard (but not standard) dialects, as in example (5a), if the *come* is used, which is homophonous with the non-standard Simple Past verb form of the motion verb *come*. The third degree of camouflage is present when the pattern in (9) occurs, with *came*, which is homophonous with the standard Simple Past verb form of the motion verb.[2]

Thus, the semi-auxiliary DM *come* (Spears 1982, 1990) is camouflaged in a number of grammatical contexts. It is easy to overlook it if one is not looking for it. Moreover, *come*, other DMs, other function words distinctive to AAE and other distinctive grammatical features are quite unlike anything found in other dialects of English; it is in this sense that they are part of the incommensurable grammar of AAE. Grammatical incommensurability, it must be remembered, is an objective linguistic fact, but it takes on importance as a phenomenon owing to researchers' motives, predispositions, theoretical orientations and ideological baggage, all of which make them insensitive or less sensitive to the incommensurate part of AAE grammar.

Conclusion

The foregoing discussions contain several implications for linguists and educators. Focusing on the former, I should note that most linguists do not deal with variation – inherent variation, present in the speech of all groups and in the speech of all individual speakers. Variation is principally the province of sociolinguists, anthropological linguists and dialectologists. (These specialties have significant overlapping concerns, but their theories and methodologies are not fully equivalent.)

Above I have emphasized the existence of two major dialect clusters of AAE: AAVE and AASE. Observe, however, that within each of these two clusters there is much diversity. Some AAE speakers use regularly only one or two distinctively black grammatical features (DBGFs). Some speakers' AAE is such only on the basis of prosodic features – intonation, volume, tempo, rhythm, etc. – or the use of distinctive AAE vocabulary.

All sociolinguists know that there are no two speakers of a dialect who speak it exactly the same way. Each individual has her/his own personal *idiolect*, the term sociolinguists use. It must be stressed that this general sociolinguistic principle concerning idiolects applies to AAE speakers too. Each AAE speaker has his/her own idiolect of AAE. We do not want to overstress the diversity within AAE, but we do not want to understress it either. So, for example, teachers must not assume that they will find all or most of the grammatical features commonly discussed in the AAE literature among their AAE-speaking students. Teachers should be aware of all the features of AAVE that they may encounter, but focus on those they actually do encounter and use them to guide their teaching.

Educators must also keep in mind the importance of linguistic training for teachers – all teachers – because all deal to some extent with language arts. A great shortcoming of language arts teacher education especially is that they do not require future teachers to have a grounding in core linguistics (grammar, including the study of sounds/pronunciation) and sociolinguistics (the influence of society and culture on language).

To turn to all linguists as a group, I must emphasize that where there is unawareness of or a diminished sensitivity to grammatical camouflage and grammatical incommensurability, these linguists are more likely to produce shallow grammars and advance unsupportable claims based on them. (Note that all linguists are trained to carry out research on grammatical description and theory.) With such claims may come beliefs and claims that the languages of some oppressed peoples (e.g. creole speakers and AAE speakers) are simpler than the languages of their oppressors.

All linguists must be required to master the fundamentals of language in society and culture so that they will never embarrass the discipline by making uninformed statements about the grammatical adequacy or deficient simplicity of languages and dialects spoken by disenfranchised peoples.

Claims of greater grammatical simplicity do not logically imply inferiority. Nevertheless, taken within the context of white supremacist ideology as it dehumanizes exploited peoples of color and their languages, these claims become for all practical purposes supports for the debasement and exploitation of the speakers of these languages. Shallow grammar, then, seen in this light, becomes not simply a linguistic problem but a political one as well.

Notes

1. BIN is often written with capital letters in the literature to distinguish it from the past participle *been*.
2. Observe that for most AASE and AAVE speakers, the DM is uninflectable. A tiny minority of AASE speakers treat the DM as inflecting like the motion verb for tense: *Every time I see them, they come* (DM) PRESENT TENSE *badmouthing me* vs. *He came* (DM) PAST TENSE *telling me I was crazy.*

Appendix: Some AAVE Auxiliaries

These auxiliaries express primarily tense, mood and aspect. All three are complex concepts; however, a basic explanation of terms is included in the chart (Table 13.1) overleaf. The disapproval markers all have different meanings, which are too complex to differentiate here.

Table 13.1 Some AAVE auxiliaries

<table>
<tr><th>Auxiliary</th><th>Name</th><th>Meaning</th><th>Occurrence in Creoles</th><th>Occurrence in other American English dialects</th></tr>
<tr><td>be</td><td>invariant habitual be</td><td>habitual aspect – expresses a situation in effect, either repeated or continuing, over a significantly long period of time, as determined by social context</td><td>no</td><td>no</td></tr>
<tr><td colspan="5">• She think she be knowin the answer. She thinks she always knows the answer.
• They be watching TV when I get home. They are normally watching TV when I get home.
• He be at Fred house. He's normally/ always/etc. at Fred's house.</td></tr>
<tr><td>BIN [usually written thus]</td><td>stressed BIN</td><td>remote perfect – expresses a situation that either began a long time ago and continues to the present or occurred a king time ago and has present relevance</td><td>no</td><td>no</td></tr>
<tr><td colspan="5">• She BIN married. She has been married a long time and still is.
• I BIN know him. I've known him a long time.
• I BIN knowin him (= preceding example). I've known him a long time.
• I BIN working on this paper. I've been working on this paper a long time.</td></tr>
<tr><td>been [used by a small percentage of AAVE speakers]</td><td>unstressed been</td><td>anterior marker – similar to a past tense marker, but it marks past or past before the past (pluperfect) situations</td><td>yes</td><td>no</td></tr>
<tr><td colspan="5">• But everybody thought she been had that house for years. But everybody thought that she had had that house for years.
• Somebody been broke the window. Somebody broke the window.
• I been know your name (Fasold, 1981: 173). I knew your name (before/already).
• Larry been gone when I come (Mufwene, 1994: 19). Larry had gone when I came.
• I been sleeping when you come (Mufwene, 1994: 19). I was sleeping when you came.</td></tr>
</table>

Table 13.1 – *continued*

Auxiliary	*Name*	*Meaning*	*Occurrence in Creoles*	*Occurrence in other American English dialects*
done	perfect *done*, auxiliary *done*	perfect tense – expresses a situation that began in the past and has present relevance, e.g. the situation still exists: *He done lock the door* (the door is still locked); tends to express intensity and/or disapproval	yes (however, its semantic range is different in subtle ways)	yes (its semantic range is most likely subtly different)
• I done forgot my hat. *I've forgotten my hat.* • He done told your game. *He sure exposed you.*				
STAY [written thus]	stressed *stay*	frequentative, iterative aspect – expresses a situation that occurs repeatedly and frequently	no	no
• She STAY at Grandma house. *She is frequently at Grandma's house.* • He STAY flossin. *He is always well dressed.*				
gone (also *go*)	disapproval marker *gone*, past *gone*	disapproval (mood) marker – expresses the speaker's negative evaluation of a situation expressed by the sentence in which it occurs	yes	no
• Now why he go act like that. *Now why did he act like that.* • And he gone raise the damn window. *And he had the nerve to raise the damn window.*				
come	*come* of indignation (or strong disapproval)	disapproval (mood) marker	yes	no

Table 13.1 – *continued*

Auxiliary	*Name*	*Meaning*	*Occurrence in Creoles*	*Occurrence in other American English dialects*
• He come coming in my house acting a damn fool. *He had the nerve to come in my house, acting like a damn fool.* • She come being all nice (like we were friends or something). *She had the nerve to be/act all nice ...*				
gone-come [the combination of the two is not a simple combination of the meanings of each]	*gone-come*	disapproval (mood) marker [treated as one bimorphemic word]	yes	no
• He gone-come telling me had to change my whole transmission [probably lying]. *He had the nerve to tell me had to change my whole transmission.* • Jane said he gone-come asking her if I could steal one for him [I can't believe he had the nerve]. *Jane said he had the nerve to ask her ...*				
be done (Baugh, 1983)*	disapproval *be done* [to be distinguished from the other two *be done*s]	disapproval (mood) marker, also expresses a rapid reaction of the clause subject to the disapproved situation	no	no
• You do that again, I be done whip your little behind. *If you do that again, I will whip your behind so fast (you won't know what happened).* • If the police shoot anybody again, we be done had a riot up in here. *If the police shoot anybody again, we'll have a riot around here so fast.*				

*Some tense properties of *be done* were first observed in print by Baugh (1983); the modal semantic properties were reported by Spears (1985).

Sources: Baugh (1983); Spears (1980, 1982, 1985, 1990, 2000, 2006a, forthcoming), unless otherwise indicated.

References

Alim, H.S. and Baugh, J. (eds) (2007) *Talkin Black Talk: Language, Education and Social Change.* New York: Teachers College Press.

Baugh, J. (1983) *Black Street Speech.* Austin, TX: University of Texas Press.

Bickerton, D. (1981) *The Roots of Language.* Ann Arbor, MI: Karoma Press.

DeGraff, M. (2005) Linguists' most dangerous myth: The fallacy of Creole Exceptionalism. *Language in Society* 34, 533–591.

Dillard, J.L. (1972) *Black English: Its History and Usage in the United States.* New York: Random House.

Enfield, N.J. (2002) Ethnosyntax: Introduction. In N.J. Enfield (ed.) *Ethnosyntax: Explorations in Grammar and Culture* (pp. 3–30). Oxford: Oxford University Press.

Faraclas, N. (2006) Suprasegmentals and the myth of the simplicity continuum from 'pidgin', to 'creole', to 'natural' languages. Paper presented at the Sixth Creolistics Workshop, Giessen, Germany.

Fasold, R.W. (1981) The relation between black and white speech in the South. *American Speech* 56, 163–89.

Good, J. (2006) The phonetics of tone in Saramaccan. In A. Deumert and S. Durrlemann (eds) *Structure and Variation in Language Contact* (pp. 9–28). Amsterdam: John Benjamins.

Gooden, S.A. (2003) The phonology and phonetics of Jamaican creole reduplication. PhD dissertation, The Ohio State University.

Green, L.J. (2002) *African American English: A Linguistic Introduction.* New York: Cambridge University Press.

Holm, J. (1992) A theoretical model for semi-creolization. Paper presented at the meeting of the Society for Caribbean Linguistics. Barbados.

Holm, J. (2004) *Languages in Contact: The Partial Restructuring of Vernaculars.* New York: Cambridge University Press.

Hymes, D. (1974) *Foundations in Sociolinguistics: An Ethnographic Approach.* Philadelphia, PA: University of Pennsylvania Press.

Labov, W. (1998) Co-existent systems in African-American vernacular English. In S.S. Mufwene, J.R. Rickford, G. Bailey and J. Baugh (eds) *African-American English: Structure, History and Use* (pp. 110–153). New York: Routledge.

Makoni, S., Smitherman, G., Ball, A.F. and Spears, A.K. (eds) (2003) *Black Linguistics.* London: Routledge.

McWhorter, J. (2001) The world's simplest grammars are Creole grammars. *Linguistic Typology* 5 (2), 125–156.

Morgan, M. (2002) *Language, Discourse and Power in African American Culture.* Cambridge: Cambridge University Press.

Mufwene, S.S. (1994) On decreolization: The case of Gullah. In M. Morgan (ed.) *Language and the Social Construction of Identity in Creole Situations* (pp. 63–99). Los Angeles: UCLA Center for Afro-American Studies.

Smitherman, G. (1977) *Talkin and Testifyin.* Detroit: Wayne State University Press.

Smitherman, G. (2000) *Talkin That Talk.* London: Routledge.

Spears, A.K. (1980) The other *come* in Black English. *Working Papers in Socio-Linguistics* 77 (pp. 1–15). Austin, TX: Southwest Education Development Laboratory and National Institute of Education.

Spears, A.K. (1982) The Black English semi-auxiliary *come. Language* 58, 850–872.

Spears, A. K. (1985) Review of *Black Street Speech*, by John Baugh. *Language in Society* 14, 101–108.
Spears, A.K. (1988) Black American English. In J.B. Cole (ed.) *Anthropology for the Nineties* (pp. 96–113). New York: The Free Press. [Reprinted in J.M. Wallace III (ed.) (1990) *Language, Culture and Society: Readings in Linguistic Anthropology* (pp. 87–100). Dubuque, IA: Kendall/Hunt Publishing Co.]
Spears, A.K. (1990) The grammaticalization of disapproval in Black American English. In R. Rieber (ed.) *CUNYForum: Papers in Linguistics* 15 (1 & 2), (pp. 30–44). New York: Linguistics Department, The Graduate School, CUNY.
Spears, A.K. (1998) African-American language use: Ideology and so-called obscenity. In S.S. Mufwene, J.R. Rickford, G. Bailey and J. Baugh (eds) *African American English: Structure, History and Usage* (pp. 226–250). New York: Routledge.
Spears, A.K. (1999) *Race and Ideology: Language, Symbolism and Popular Culture.* Detroit, MI: Wayne State University Press.
Spears, A.K. (2000) Stressed *stay*: A new African-American English aspect marker. Paper presented at the meeting of the American Dialect Society, Chicago.
Spears, A.K. (2001a) Serial verb-like constructions in African-American English. Paper presented at the meeting of the Society for Pidgin and Creole Linguistics. Washington, DC.
Spears, A.K. (2001b) Directness in the use of African-American English. In S.L. Lanehart (ed.) *Sociocultural and Historical Contexts of African-American English* (pp. 239–259). Philadelphia, PA: John Benjamins.
Spears, A.K. (2004) Los Sustantivos sin determinantes en el palenquero y en el inglés afroestadounidense. In M. Fernández, M. Fernádez-Ferreiro and N. Vázquez Veiga (eds) *Los Criollos de Base Ibérica: ACBLPE [Asociación de Criollos de Base Léxica Portuguesa y Española] 2003* (pp. 227–235). Frankfurt am Main: Verveurt Verlag.
Spears, A.K. (2006a) African American English: Pitch and the question of tone. Paper presented at the Society for Pidgin and Creole Linguistics, Winter Meeting. Albuquerque, NM.
Spears, A.K. (2006b) Disapproval markers: A creolism. Paper presented at the Society for Caribbean Linguistics, Roseau, Dominica.
Spears, A.K. (2007a) African American communicative practices: Performativity, semantic license and augmentation. In H.S. Alim and J. Baugh (eds) *Talkin Black Talk* (pp. 100–111). New York: Teachers College Press.
Spears, A.K. (2007b) Bare nouns in African American English. In M. Baptista and J. Guéron (eds) *Noun Phrases in Creole Languages* (pp. 421–434). Philadelphia, PA: John Benjamins.
Spears, A.K. (forthcoming) Pidgins/creoles and African American English. In J.V. Singler and S. Kouwenberg (eds) *The Handbook of Pidgins and Creoles.* Malden, MA: Blackwell.
Stewart, W.A. (1967) Sociolinguistic factors in the history of American Negro dialects. *The Florida FL Reporter* 5 (2), 11, 22, 24, 26.
Stewart, W.A. (1968) Continuity and change in American Negro dialects. *The Florida FL Reporter* 62, 14–16, 18, 304.
Wierzbicka, A. (1979) Ethno-syntax and the philosophy of grammar. *Studies in Language* 3 (3), 313–83.
Wierzbicka, A. (1992) *Semantics, Culture and Cognition.* New York: Oxford University Press.

Chapter 14

African American English and the Public Interest

WALT WOLFRAM

No sociocultural variety of English is more recognized by the public than African American English (AAE), or *Ebonics*, as commonly referred to in the public sector. Furthermore, AAE has figured prominently in several controversies played out in the media over the past half century, including the deficit-difference debate of the 1960s (e.g. Baratz, 1968; Labov, 1972), the Ann Arbor Decision of the late 1970s (Center for Applied Linguistics, 1979; Farr-Whiteman, 1980), the Oakland Ebonics controversy of the 1990s (Baugh, 2000; Rickford, 1999) and linguistic profiling of the 2000s (Baugh, 2003). Everyone seems to have been exposed to AAE from one source or another, and most people have a strong opinion about it. Unfortunately, in most cases, the public understanding derives from the principle of linguistic subordination (Lippi-Green, 1997), whereby the language of socially-subordinate groups is interpreted as linguistically inadequate and deficient by comparison with the language of their socially dominant counterparts. Even among stigmatized varieties of English, AAE is treated as a case of vernacular exceptionalism in a way that parallels DeGraff's depiction of Creole Exceptionalism (DeGraff, 2003, 2004, 2005). Its origin, its historical development and its current trajectory of change are still interpreted as an anomaly among dialects, though it is hardly extraordinary in terms of the general principles of language contact, substrate influence and language variation that have affected its development over time and place.

Meanwhile, AAE has been subjected to more linguistic and sociolinguistic scrutiny than any other variety of English, indicating a professional intrigue that matches the public curiosity. Schneider (1996: 3) reports that AAE has more than five times as many publications devoted to it than any other variety of American English from the mid-1960s through the mid-1990s, and more than twice as many as all other ethnic varieties of English combined. In some respects then, both popular culture and the academy of scholars appear to treat AAE as an exceptional variety, even though sociolinguists would no doubt deny such treatment (Wolfram,

2007). In this regard, the sociolinguistic interpretation of AAE is again not unlike the exceptional status assigned to creoles by professional linguists (DeGraff, 2004).

Though the general public and professional sociolinguists share an interest in AAE, their ideological perspectives are often in great conflict. Sociolinguistic axioms about the nature of language variation stand in stark opposition to folk theories of language differences, resulting in an ongoing controversy over the linguistic integrity and utility of AAE. Since the inception of sociolinguistics more than half a century ago, scholars have disputed popular myths and resolutely attempted to counter the dominant 'deficit model' and the 'correctionist approach' that treat AAE as little more than an unsystematic, unworthy approximation of standard English that should be eradicated.

Despite the significance of language in all spheres of public life and at least 12 years of compulsory public-school education in English and/or language arts, there is still no tradition of English language studies that includes the examination of language diversity as a regular part of this education. The need for informed knowledge about language variation and the dissemination of essential knowledge to the public thus remains an imposing challenge for sociolinguistics. Sociolinguistics is a very small, largely invisible professional field that can be overwhelmed by popular perception and dominant opinion. Accordingly, the public impact of sociolinguistics is severely limited if it does not effectively use a range of media to communicate its message. Though this may seem like an insurmountable hurdle for sociolinguistics, Deborah Tannen's popular books (1990, 1995, 2006) and media presence on topics related to language and social interaction have taught us that it is not an unachievable or even unrealistic ideal to disseminate information about language through the media.

The State of AAE

Research on AAE continues to be a major focus of the sociolinguistic enterprise, with continuing scrutiny and re-examination of some of the now-canonized axioms that emerged from the early tradition of study. The pioneering descriptive studies of AAE in the 1960s focused primarily on the vernacular language of African Americans in large, non-Southern urban areas such as New York City (e.g. Labov *et al.*, 1968; Labov, 1972), Detroit (Wolfram, 1969), Los Angeles (Legum *et al.*, 1971) and Washington, DC (Fasold, 1972). These descriptions set a precedent for decades, and they also established an accompanying interpretive paradigm. The initial focus on urban, vernacular AAE was not accidental, since there was a hypothesized link between it and significant social and educational problems that plagued these urban areas. To some extent, this focus set the stage for the sociolinguistic preoccupation with vernacular structures and basilectal versions of AAE, leading to a kind sociolinguistic nostalgia for the authentic vernacular speaker (Bucholtz, 2003). Though these studies made an essential and significant contribution in terms of their original goals, they also led to a reified set of axioms about AAE and its speakers that has not always been validated by the data.

Recent studies have included a much more diverse, representative set of regional and social demographics for AAE, particularly in the rural South (e.g. Bailey, 2001; Carpenter, 2004, 2005; Childs, 2005; Childs & Mallinson, 2004; Cukor-Avilla, 2001; Mallinson, 2006; Mallinson & Wolfram, 2002; Wolfram, 2003; Wolfram & Thomas, 2002) where it was originally rooted and nurtured. Furthermore, descriptive studies are now complemented by perceptual studies and experimental conditions that offer insight into the interaction of regional, ethnic and social variables in the delimitation of AAE (e.g. Fridland *et al.*, 2004; Graff *et al.*, 1986; Thomas, 2002; Thomas & Reaser, 2004). Finally, there is an expanding body of ethnographic evidence about AAE, including observations by community participants themselves about the distribution of AAE over time and place (Childs & Mallinson, 2006; Mallinson, 2006; Morgan, 2002). Our research over the past decade on small, long-term Southern rural communities in the Southeastern US has led us to challenge several widely-accepted conclusions about language variation and change in AAE (Wolfram, 2007). These include the *supraregional assumption*, the *language change assumption* and the *social stratification assumption*.

The supraregional assumption

One of the conclusions that emerged from the first wave of AAE descriptive studies was the observation that the primary structural features setting apart the vernacular speech of African Americans from their European American cohorts were shared by African American communities regardless of regional context, this is the *supraregional assumption*. Thus, descriptions of morphosyntactic traits such as invariant *be* with a 'habitual' denotation (e.g. *They always be playing*), the absence of copula and auxiliary *be* (e.g. *She nice; she playing ball*), verbal *-s* (e.g. *She play ball*), possessive *-s* (e.g. *The man hat*) and plural *-s* absence (e.g. *Three dog*) were well-documented in the speech of African Americans in urban areas such as New York City (Labov *et al.*, 1968; Labov, 1972), Detroit (Wolfram, 1969), Los Angeles (Legum *et al.*, 1971) and Washington, DC (Fasold, 1972), as were phonological features such as syllable-coda prevocalic consonant cluster reduction (e.g. *wes' area*), labialization of non-initial interdental fricatives (e.g. *baf* for *bath*) and postvocalic *r*-lessness (e.g. *fea'* for *fear*). The apparent common core of AAE structures in quite disparate urban settings seemed quite unlike the regional configuration of dialects for the European American population, leading to the assumption that vernacular AAE revealed a kind of uniformity immune to regionality. This assumption further contributes to the social construction of AAE as an exceptional variety among the vernacular dialects of English.

Though some structural linguistic traits of AAE certainly show trans-regional distribution, the examination of African American communities in Appalachia (Childs & Mallinson, 2004; Childs, 2005; Mallinson, 2006; Mallinson & Wolfram, 2002), the Coastal Plain (D'Andrea, 2005; Rowe, 2005) and the Outer Banks region of North Carolina (Carpenter 2004, 2005; Wolfram & Thomas, 2002) reveals significant regional distribution, both in terms of the accommodation to cohort European American regional varieties and in terms of structures that are part of the structural core of AAE (Charity, 2007). In addition to our objective studies of regional AAE, we have recently conducted a series of perceptual experiments to tease out the intersection of ethnicity and regionality in dialect identification (Childs & Mallinson, 2006; Thomas & Reaser, 2004; Torbert, 2004; Wolfram & Thomas, 2002). Listeners consistently misjudge the ethnic identity of African Americans from Appalachia and the Outer Banks (Childs & Mallinson, 2006; Wolfram & Thomas, 2002), showing that regionality may trump ethnicity in listener perception of African Americans in some settings. The evidence from speaker identification experiments, along with the cross-generational linguistic analysis of dialect features, supports the contention that both the earlier varieties of English spoken by African Americans and the contemporary varieties of AAE may indeed be quite regionalized.

The language change assumption

The *language change assumption* refers to the fact that the past and present trajectory of change in AAE has often been reduced to a unilateral path of convergence or divergence. To some extent, the language change myth is related to the supraregional myth. If one assumes a uniform structure for AAE regardless of regional context, it is a relatively small step to the assumption that AAE has exhibited a unilateral path of change, since both interpretations appear to be fueled by an underlying homogeneity assumption. The study of different communities in the rural Southeast US, however, reveals a number of different trajectories of change with respect both to core AAE structures and to regional accommodation. The empirical evidence reveals at least three different trajectories of change for AAE, one that supports the divergence hypothesis (Wolfram & Thomas, 2002), one that supports the convergence hypothesis (Mallinson & Wolfram, 2002) and one that shows a curvilinear trajectory that includes periods of both convergence and divergence over time and place (Carpenter, 2005; Childs & Mallinson, 2004).

A number of historical, demographic and social factors need to be considered in explaining different trajectories of change. Factors include the regional setting, the size of the community, macro and micro socio-historical events, patterns of contact with adjacent European American communities and with external African American communities, intra-community social divisions and cultural values and ideologies. For example, the Appalachian African American community in Beech Bottom (Mallinson & Wolfram, 2002) is a very small, receding community that has been quite removed from other African American communities geographically and socially over the past half-century. Perhaps more importantly, residents show a value orientation that aligns with the surrounding European American culture (Mallinson, 2004). In this context, convergence seems quite understandable, and speakers are losing remnants of AAE as they fully accommodate the Appalachian English features of the European American dialect community.

In contrast, Hyde County, located on the coast of North Carolina, is a long-term African American community of more than 2000 people that was once highly insulated from outside influences. At present, the younger community members indicate increasing social contact with external African American communities, and many youth reveal a kind of exocentric (i.e. community-external) value orientation that accommodates urban cultural norms (Wolfram & Thomas, 2002). In this context, once-entrenched regional dialect features of the Outer Banks dialect from almost three centuries of co-existence between African American and European American are rapidly receding and linguistic features associated with urban AAE are intensifying.

The cases of Texana in Appalachia (Childs & Mallinson, 2004) and Roanoke Island on the Outer Banks (Carpenter, 2005), which show curvilinear paths of change, are somewhat more complicated by internal social divisions, particularly with respect to external values and norms. Thus, some middle-aged and younger speakers show shifts that correlate with endocentric (i.e. community-internal) and exocentric value orientations, sometimes co-existing within the same community. Both of these communities are relatively small but have differential patterns of external contact that provide choices between traditional rural and encroaching urban value orientations. Dialect change in different communities, both with reference to traditional regional linguistic traits and with reference to traits associated with AAE, shows that the unilateral change assumption simply cannot be applied to variation in AAE.

The social stratification assumption

The *social stratification assumption* refers to the belief that there is an isomorphic correlation between socio-economic status and the use of acrolectal and basilectal[1] AAE. As Weldon observes (2004), there is a prevailing assumption among sociolinguists that AAE is not spoken by middle class African Americans so that there is a fairly straightforward social dichotomy in the social stratification of vernacular AAE. Though there has been considerable discussion of an idealized distinction between standard and vernacular AAE (e.g. Spears, 1999; Weldon, 2004), the social stratification assumption has largely flown under the radar of sociolinguistic critique. There has been surprisingly little empirical study of the social diversification of AAE use within the African American community while there has been an inordinate preoccupation with its canonized set of vernacular linguistic structures.

Our recent study (Kendall & Wolfram, 2006) of social divisions within the African American community moves away from traditional kinds of objective socio-economic status measures used to rank subjects, and focuses instead on a more broadly defined linguistic marketplace related to a system of social sanctions and censorships (Bourdieu, 1991). To examine the social distribution of language from this perspective, we examined the speech of recognized, local African American community leaders and compared their public speech at town meetings and in radio interviews with their speech during sociolinguistic interviews and in other settings. We also compared their speech with the norms for their age and gender cohorts from the community. We contrasted, for example, the use of vernacular structures by the Mayor of Princeville (Eastern NC), the oldest town established by blacks in the United States, and that of a County Commissioner from Roanoke Island, a long-standing small African American Outer Banks community in North Carolina surrounded by a European American population. The leaders from the two communities show contrasting uses of vernacular AAE in public presentations, from the predominant use of vernacular forms by the Mayor of Princeville to the primary use of Standard English forms by the Roanoke Island Commissioner. Furthermore, the speech of local community leaders does not necessarily conform to age and gender norms, but it departs in divergent ways. In Princeville, the female Mayor is among the most vernacular speakers while in Roanoke Island, the female Commissioner is among the least vernacular speakers, though she still shows fossilized vestiges of vernacular forms. Part of this difference may be related to their local leadership roles and to their principal service constituencies. In Princeville, the Mayor's primary service community is centered on the local citizens of a predominantly black municipality that obviously sanctions local vernacular speech. The historical values of Princeville are largely endocentric, and most of the public speaking still occurs within the local, largely autonomous community setting. In fact, it might be hypothesized that vernacularity helps establish solidarity with local community members in Princeville.

By contrast, the constituency of the Roanoke Island Commissioner is largely external to the black community – and has been for decades now given her role as a pioneering leader in a dominant white social order. The Commissioner could not, in fact, win any elected office without a significant white vote; in Princeville, there is no white vote to speak of. The differential contexts, community structures and public constituencies thus correlate with the use of vernacular forms by respective community leaders rather than with traditional socio-economic indices such as education or residency. Both the Mayor and Commissioner have college degrees and post-baccalaureate education, and live in comparable types of residencies within the community, yet their use of vernacular forms in public and private differs dramatically.

The cases of leaders in small rural Southern African American communities reveals that a host of community, contextual, social and personal factors have to be taken into account in understanding the use of vernacular AAE forms and in explaining the public and non-public speech of community leaders in the rural African American South – and probably everywhere for that matter. The relative autonomy of the community, the primary public service constituency, the different social affiliations and divisions within the community, personal background and history and the socialized demands in public presentation all seem to be factors in understanding the use of local vernacular and mainstream standard variants by these speakers. If nothing else, imagined dichotomies between middle-class and working-class speech and between standard and vernacular AAE speech must be abandoned, along with unilateral explanations and simplistic assumptions about the social stratification of AAE within the community.

Studies of a more representative sample of regional contexts and different kinds of communities suggest that AAE is considerably more diverse than often assumed or presented, and that sociolinguists have sometimes overlooked this diversity in time and place. Convenient but unjustified sociolinguistic conclusions do not serve sociolinguists in the study of AAE any better than a misinformed understanding and folk theories of AAE serve the public at large. And these conclusions may ironically serve to exceptionalize the treatment of AAE among sociolinguists, despite their ideological and descriptive differences with popular culture over the nature of the linguistic system. Notwithstanding the great contributions sociolinguists have made to the professional and public understanding of AAE, some current assumptions, constructs and explanations need to be examined more critically with reference to the canon of AAE description.

Public Education and AAE

Very few linguists and classroom teachers have been engaged in systematic formal and informal public education programs related to language diversity, despite the fact that a number of national and state educational agencies affirm the importance of such educational practice. The standards of the National Council of Teachers of English (NCTE) specify that students are to 'develop an understanding of and respect for diversity in language use, patterns and dialects across cultures, ethnic groups, geographic regions and social roles.' The NCTE/NCATE (National Council for Accreditation of Teacher Education) standards for training programs include norms for the preparation of secondary teachers specifically related to language diversity (2003). For example, one of the target goals (3.1.4) states that teachers and students should:

> show extensive knowledge of how and why language varies and changes in different regions, across different cultural groups and across different time periods and incorporate that knowledge into instruction and assessment that acknowledge and show respect for language. (NCTE/NCATE, 2003)

Another target goal (4.4) states that teachers should:

> Create opportunities for students to analyze how social context affects language and to monitor their own language use and behavior in terms of demonstrating respect for individual differences of ethnicity, race, language, culture, gender and ability. (NCTE/NCATE, 2003)

Despite these admirable NCTE/NCATE ideals, explicit training in dialect diversity and systematic educational curricula reflecting these ideals are virtually non-existent in formal public education programs.

Unfortunately, the correction model continues to dominate the public interpretation of language differences, and most public discussions of language differences are still consumed by the discussion of the right and wrong way to use the English language. The persistent use of labels such as 'correct', 'proper', 'right' and 'grammatical' when speaking of the standard variety and 'incorrect', 'improper', 'wrong' and 'ungrammatical' for vernacular forms and varieties is hardly accidental. It directly reflects the underlying belief that non-mainstream varieties of English are simply unworthy deviations from the standard variety. Indeed, the most persistent sociolinguistic challenge in all venues of public education continues to be the widespread application of the principle of linguistic subordination (Lippi-Green, 1997).

An Approach to Public Education

The public impact of sociolinguistics is severely limited if it does not effectively utilize a range of media for public education about language diversity. There are dimensions of language variation that hold broad-based, inherent intrigue for general audiences, and we need to start by connecting language diversity with this public curiosity. Apart from the sporadic language controversies that afford linguists their proverbial 15 minutes of media exposure for a 'teachable moment,' programs targeting language diversity are conspicuously absent from informal public education. In the past two decades, only two TV documentaries related to language diversity have aired on national television, *American Tongues* in 1986 (Alvarez & Kolker, 1986) and *Do You Speak American*? in 2005 (McNeil, 2005). Both of these have informative, useful vignettes on AAE, but this is hardly a representative media representation of language diversity. The notion that media presentations about language should be entertaining may seem somewhat superficial to those focused more on the transmission of knowledge than entertainment quotient, but the use of the media does indeed compete with other types of entertainment, notwithstanding the dedication of some viewers to educational TV stations. One of the reasons that the now-dated documentary *American Tongues* (Alvarez & Kolker, 1986) has been effective for two decades is its high entertainment value. The use of striking dialogue and humor also serve as a non-confrontational method for opening up candid discussions about language attitudes.

Recent documentaries on language diversity that we produced for public TV in North Carolina and beyond (Hutcheson, 2001, 2004, 2005, 2006; Rowe & Grimes, 2006) have shown that it is quite possible to pique the public's interest in language differences if the subject is framed in an appropriate, natural cultural setting. For example, the airing of *Voices of North Carolina* (Hutcheson, 2005) had a rating of 2.3 per 1000 viewing homes, significantly higher than the regular programming in the time slot. Perhaps just as importantly, the viewing audience did not turn the program off; the audience at the beginning and end of the program was stable. While a viewer rating of 2.3 may pale by comparison with the rating of a popular major network program, it does demonstrate that presentations about dialect diversity can compete at least within the restricted audience of potential viewers who watch public television. In fact, the public television station, the state affiliate of PBS, was so impressed by the viewer response to the program that it offered a DVD of *Voices of North Carolina* as an incentive give-away item in its annual fundraising campaign. To my knowledge, this is the only language documentary ever used in this way.

The themes that frame our public presentations of language diversity are typically related to cultural legacy and historical heritage. When language diversity is associated with historical and cultural traditions such as settlement history, social developments and other cultural traditions, a meaningful context for broader cultural and social issues is established for the presentation of language differences. The framing of language diversity in a historical, regional and cultural context is one of the reasons that our dialect awareness curriculum targets the eighth grade social studies program (Reaser & Wolfram, 2007a, 2007b; Reaser, 2006), the grade level when students study state history. The rationale for the choice is straightforward: an important component of the state's historical and cultural development is reflected in language diversity that ranges from the endangered or lost Native American languages to the development of distinct regional and sociocultural varieties of English. Accordingly, our program naturally fits in with the state's mandated course of study for eighth grade social studies that includes curricular themes of 'culture and diversity', 'historic perspectives' and 'geographical relationships' (North Carolina Public Schools Standard Course of Study, 2004). In this context, the goals of the dialect awareness curriculum neatly dovetail with social studies competency goals such as

- Describe the roles and contributions of diverse groups, such as American Indians, African Americans, European immigrants, landed gentry, tradesmen and small farmers to everyday life in colonial North Carolina (Competency Goal 1.07) or
- Assess the importance of regional diversity on the development of economic, social and political institutions in North Carolina. (Competency Goal 8.04)

Though the general public may neither understand nor value the seemingly myopic obsession of linguists with technical structural detail, it can appreciate and identify with the symbolic role that language plays in its representation of historical, regional and cultural development.

One of the attributes of our public outreach programs and formal educational curricula is the focus on the positive dimensions of language diversity rather than on the controversy sometimes associated with language differences. Despite deep-seated ideological differences between sociolinguistic axioms and public interpretations of language differences, we have taken the position that positively-framed presentations of language differences hold a greater likelihood of being received by the public than the direct confrontation of unassailable ideologies. Once a few fundamental sociolinguistic premises about language diversity are established inductively, the discussion of more sensitive social issues related to the conflict between folk theories and sociolinguistic premises may become more meaningful. Furthermore, deductive linguistic proclamations about the legitimacy of language diversity tend only to result in the balkanization of entrenched sociopolitical positions rather than open an honest discussion of language differences. The most effective and permanent education always takes place when learners discover truths for themselves. Inductive, incremental education that begins with a positive, non-threatening perspective on language diversity provides a much more effective opportunity for an authentic discussion of linguistic diversity than the direct opposition to entrenched positions. In the final analysis, we are admittedly ideological brokers but we also want our audiences to come to understand the truth about language diversity for themselves.

Although our informal and formal education programs invariably include a section or vignette on AAE, they do not focus exclusively on this variety of English. Instead, AAE is treated simply as one of the significant sociocultural varieties of English that complements other sociocultural and regional varieties. For example, the documentary *Voices of North Carolina* includes entire segments on two Native American varieties, the Cherokee language and Lumbee English, Spanish and several regional varieties to complement the vignette on AAE. There has sometimes been so much focus on AAE in education to the exclusion of other legitimate varieties that it runs the risk of being interpreted as a special condition of being black in American society, leading to a kind of linguistic and social exceptionalism (DeGraff, 2005). Our presentation of AAE along with other varieties of English is a deliberate attempt to counter the popular belief that this variety is distinct from other varieties of English in terms of its linguistic status. It is important neither to exaggerate nor minimize the status of AAE as a genuine variety of English representing the natural development of sociolinguistic diversity within the English language.

Dialect Awareness Curricula

Much of our educational direction over the past decade has focused on an ambitious program to develop formal curricular materials on language diversity in the public schools (NCSU, n.d.). We have experimented with curricular programs in a number of communities throughout North Carolina and we have taught a program annually in one of the public schools for more than a decade so that an entire generation of students has now been instructed in this dialect awareness curriculum. Unfortunately, formal education about dialect variation is still a relatively novel – and in some cases, controversial – idea. Our pilot program targets the middle-school curriculum in social studies that connects with language arts (Reaser & Wolfram, 2007a, 2007b; Reaser, 2006), but similar units might be designed for other levels of K-12 as well. The rationale for the curriculum has humanistic, scientific and social science goals, and the curriculum engages students on a number of participatory levels. In the process, students learn about dialects as a kind of scientific inquiry as well as a type of humanities and social science study. The examination of dialect differences offers great potential for students to probe the linguistic manifestations of a broad base of behavioral differences, including sociological, psychological, geographical and historical.

Illustrative Curricular Activities

In our present curriculum (Reaser & Wolfram, 2007a, 2007b), exercises focus on AAE along with other regional and social varieties of English. In fact, we deliberately introduce the notion of dialect patterning in other dialects of English in order to show how AAE is no different from other varieties in terms of the general principles of language patterning. These activities are supported by a full set of audiovisual vignettes that are used with the program. In one of the early exercises in the curriculum, we directly ask students to confront the issue of language prejudice by having them view the one-minute ad on linguistic profiling and housing discrimination prepared by National Fair Housing Alliance for the US Department of Housing and Urban Development and Leadership Conference on Civil Rights Education (Ad Council, 2003). The activity from the student workbook (Reaser & Wolfram, 2007b: 2) is presented as described in Figure 14.1.

This reflective activity has a humanistic goal, while other activities have complementary objectives in terms of social science and linguistic science. For example, the exercise on linguistic patterning in AAE (Figure 14.2) demonstrates how the examination of language diversity fulfills a scientific objective (Wolfram, 2007b: 36-37). Prior to the exercise, students are intro-

Video Exercise: Examining Language Prejudice

During phone conversations, it is often possible to tell a number of things about a person based on the characteristics of their voice. You will see a 1-minute commercial produced by the US Department of Housing and Urban Development (HUD). The purpose of this commercial is to raise awareness of how discrimination can occur over the phone. As you watch the video, think of answers to the following:

(1) How common do you think it is for people to be discriminated against on the phone?
(2) How strong are people's prejudices about language?
(3) Why do you think people have such strong prejudices about language?

Figure 14.1 Video exercise, language prejudice

duced to the notion of inner linguistic knowledge and the technical term 'linguistic intuition' as it is used in linguistics. The goals are to have students inductively recognize that dialects are systematically patterned, and not simply haphazard and random deviations from Standard English. Furthermore, the exercise demonstrates that the linguistic notion of grammaticality is different from that of social acceptability. No sociolinguistic axiom is more critical to the study of AAE than the systematic patterning of its grammatical and phonological forms. Before presenting this exercise to students, however, we get students to do a number of exercises with other varieties of English so that they understand that AAE is no different from other social and regional varieties in its rule-governed behavior.

In another exercise (Figure 14.3), students are introduced to the notion of regional and stylistic variation within AAE, another fundamental sociolinguistic axiom. This activity relies on a nine-minute video vignette that illustrates these types of variation and includes commentary about the personal and social factors that come into play in accommodating different norms of language use within and outside of the home community (Reaser & Wolfram, 2007b: 37).

Another exercise (Reaser & Wolfram, 2007b: 39) examines language change in AAE (Figure 14.4). For the segment on AAE, students listen to different speakers representing different generations from an isolated rural area in coastal North Carolina (Wolfram & Thomas, 2002) and consider how AAE has changed over time. Students listen to the different segments while they view a transcript of the passage that highlights some of the features illustrating the changing regional and ethnolinguistic configuration of AAE in this region.

Worksheet: Understanding Linguistic Patterns: Uninflected *be* in African American English

We're going to examine a dialect pattern of African American English. It is important to remember that not all African Americans use this pattern. It is most common in the speech of young African American speakers in large cities. In this construction, the unconjugated form of *be* is used where other dialects use *am*, *is*, or *are*. But *be* is used only in certain contexts! Your job will be to decide what contexts can take *be* and what contexts cannot.

Not all English speakers have intuitions about when *be* can and cannot be used. Instead, only speakers familiar with African American English seem to have strong linguistic intuitions with respect to this feature. Before examining the data, you will test to see if you have intuitions about this feature. Read the sentences in **List A** and write a sentence that tells how you would interpret the sentence given. Be sure and mention when you think the event is happening. We will return to these sentences later.

List A:

1. My mom *be* working.
2. He *be* absent.
3. The students *be* talking in class.

Next, examine the data in **List B**. This list contains data from a forced choice test, where speakers were asked to use their linguistic intuitions to determine which sentence sounded better. The data are from 35 fifth graders in Baltimore, Maryland. All these students were speakers of African American English. Notice that the students had a definite preference for one sentence over the other. This indicated that there is a linguistic pattern guiding their choices. Examine the data to determine what determines when an AAE speaker can use *be* and when they cannot.

List B: Number of Baltimore fifth graders who chose each answer:

1. a. 32 *They usually be tired when they come home.*
   b. 3 They be tired right now.
2. a. 31 *When we play basketball, she be on my team.*
   b. 4 The girl in the picture be my sister.
3. a. 4 James be coming to school right now.
   b. 31 *James always be coming to school.*
4. a. 3 My ankle be broken from the fall.
   b. 32 *Sometimes my ears be itching.*

Figure 14.2 Worksheet on linguistic patterns

Write a rule that describes this pattern:

Examine your translations of the sentences in **List A**. Do you have linguistic intuitions about this feature?

Now that you understand when African American English speakers use *be*, use your rule to predict whether or not a speaker of African American English would use the sentences in **List C**. Write **Y** for **Yes** if the sentence follows the dialect pattern, and **N** for **No** if it does not.

List C: Applying the rule

1. The students always *be* talking in class.
2. The students don't *be* talking right now.
3. Sometimes the teacher *be* early for class.
4. At the moment the teacher *be* in the lounge.

Figure 14.2 – *continued*

Video Exercise: African American English

Despite the fact that African American English is rule-governed and patterned like all dialects, it is often viewed negatively by people. In the following video clip, you will see some African Americans from North Carolina who are proud of their dialect but also switch their speech to Standard English when they feel it is necessary. As you watch this video, think about responses to the following questions.

1. Could you hear differences in the speech of individuals in different situations?
2. Could you tell which African Americans lived in cities and which lived in rural areas?
3. Are these African Americans aware of the fact that they change their speech or not?
4. Why do you think that they feel that they must change their speech in different situations?

Figure 14.3 Video exercise: African American English

Though we have had great personal success teaching a pilot program on dialect awareness in one public school for more than a decade, the real test of such a curriculum is its successful adoption by classroom teachers who have no linguistics training. Reaser (2006) recently field-tested a pilot version of the curriculum taught by several classroom teachers who had no

Listening Exercise: Hyde County

You will hear four different generations of speakers who lived all of their lives in mainland Hyde County. All of the speakers are members of the same family, a long-standing African American family of Hyde County. In this region of Eastern North Carolina, European Americans and African Americans have been living in close proximity since the early 1700s. Because the county is 80% marshland, residents have been more isolated here than in many other areas of North Carolina. The first paved roads into the county arrived in the mid-1900s, and dramatically changed life for the younger generations of Hyde County residents. Listen closely to the speakers and follow along with the transcripts on the screen. Think about the following questions as you listen to the passages.

1. How does the oldest speaker sound compared with the younger speaker? What changes do you see across the generations?
2. What differences in speech take place from generation to generation? What do you think is happening to the Outer Banks Brogue over time in this family?
3. Why do you think that some of these changes are taking place?

Now listen to two European American residents of Hyde County: a middle-aged male and a teenager. Do these two speakers sound similar? Compare the speech of the young European American male to the speech of the youngest speaker in the African American samples that you just listened to. Answer the following questions.

1. What differences do you hear between the younger European American males and the youngest African American speaker you just listened to?
2. Were the two European American speakers more or less similar to each other than the older and younger African American Speakers?
3. What does this comparison tell you about the way language is changing in mainland Hyde County for European Americans and for African Americans?
4. Why do you think these differences in language change are taking place?

Figure 14.4 Listening exercise: Language change

background training in linguistics or sociolinguistics. In fact, the teachers had only an hour of preliminary orientation that focused mostly on the use of the DVDs for the program. The formal evaluation of a pilot version of the curriculum (Reaser, 2006) shows promising results. Reaser devised a pre- and post-curricular survey measure that included items related to both language knowledge and language attitudes. The plot of the pre- and post-test change for the 20-item test is given in Figure 14.5.

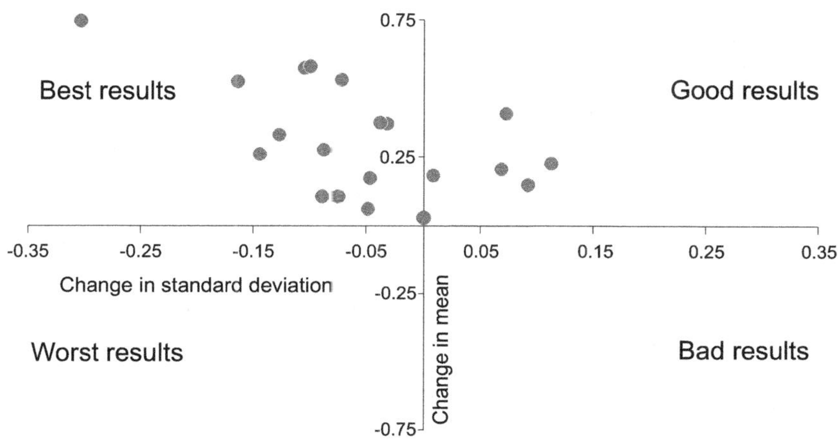

Figure 14.5 Pre-test and post-test change for survey items in dialect awareness curriculum
Source: Reaser (2006: 120)

All the survey items showed change in the direction of increased tolerance and/or knowledge about dialect diversity, and 17 of the 20 items indicated a significant change between pre- and post-curricular surveys. Furthermore, 98% of the 129 students who were involved in the pilot study reported that they learned something surprising about dialects that would change the way that they thought about language, and 88% of the students thought that the information in the curriculum was important for all students to study. With respect to language attitudes, 91% of the students found fault with people who were not aware that dialects show systematic patterning and that dialects have historical and cultural value. In the summative comments about the curriculum, students most frequently mentioned their surprise at the fact that dialects had rules or patterns that governed their use.

Students are not the only ones who profit from the study of dialect diversity. Teachers also found that some of their stereotypes about languages were challenged, and that they became more knowledgeable of and enlightened about language variation in the process of teaching the curriculum. In fact, the classroom teachers who piloted the curriculum were among the most enthusiastic supporters because of the new knowledge they had received in teaching it to their students. The teachers were so enthusiastic that they convinced the rest of their grade-level teachers to adopt the curriculum the following year. Our goal, of course, is to offer the curriculum throughout the state so that every student has the opportunity to learn the truth and consequences about dialect diversity that includes, but is not limited to, AAE.

Conclusion

The preceding presentation reveals that research on AAE has far outdistanced the dissemination of information to the American public. Unfortunately, we are still confronting many of the same issues that we encountered decades ago when sociolinguists challenged folk theories about language diversity. This unrelenting challenge was forcefully underscored when I revisited a school where I had conducted a workshop on language differences 25 years earlier. I forgot that I had conducted the earlier workshop until a participant approached me at the conclusion and reminded me she had attended the earlier workshop. Unfortunately, the questions and the resistance to some of the sociolinguistic axioms by workshop participants indicated that very little had changed in the 25-year interim. Language ideology is among the most entrenched belief systems in society, rivaling religion, morality and nationalism in terms of partisan politics and change does not take place rapidly (Wolfram, 1998). Fundamental change in popular language ideology will take generations to effect, and we must utilize the full range of formal and informal educational media to tell the story of AAE as a natural manifestation of historical development and behavioral differences, as well as the linguistic effects of racism. It requires our most proactive and entrepreneurial endeavors if we ever hope to make a difference; we cannot be limited by past traditions or precedents in public education.

Note

1. The *acrolect* refers to the standard dialect of the language. The *basilect* is a dialect that diverges considerably from the standard.

References

Ad Council (2003) Accents (advertisement). Washington, DC: National Fair Housing Alliance, US Department of Housing and Urban Development and Leadership Conference on Civil Rights Education Fund.

Alvarez, L. and Kolker, A. (1986) *American Tongues*. New York: Center for New American Media.

Bailey, G. (2001) The relationship between African American Vernacular English and white vernaculars in the American South: A sociocultural history and some phonological evidence. In S.J. Lanehart (ed.) *Sociocultural and Historical Contexts of African American English* (pp. 53–92). Philadelphia, PA: John Benjamins.

Baratz, J. (1968) Language in the economically disadvantaged child: A perspective. *ASHA* (April), 143–145.

Baugh, J. (2000) *Beyond Ebonics: Linguistic Pride and Racial Prejudice*. New York: Oxford University Press.

Baugh, J. (2003) Linguistic profiling. In C. Makoni, G. Smitherman, A.F. Ball and A.K. Spears (eds) *Black Linguistics: Language, Society and Politics in Africa and the Americas* (pp. 155–168). New York: Routledge.

Bourdieu, P. (1991) *Language and Symbolic Power*. Cambridge, MA: Harvard University Press.

Bucholtz, M. (2003) Sociolinguistic nostalgia and the authentication of identity. *Journal of Sociolinguistics* 7, 398–416.

Carpenter, J. (2004) The lost community of the Outer Banks: African American speech on Roanoke Island. MA thesis, North Carolina State University.

Carpenter, J. (2005) The invisible community of the lost colony: African American English on Roanoke Island. *American Speech* 80, 227–255.

Center for Applied Linguistics (1979) *Ann Arbor Decision, The Memorandum, Opinion and Order & The Educational Plan*. Washington, DC: Center for Applied Linguistics.

Charity, A.H. (2007) Regional differences in low SES African American children's speech in the school setting. *Language Variation and Change* 19, 281–294.

Childs, R.L. (2005) Investigating the local construction of identity: Sociophonetic variation in Smoky Mountain African American speech. PhD dissertation, University of Georgia.

Childs, R.L. and Mallinson, C. (2004) African American English in Appalachia: Dialect accommodation and substrate influence. *English World-Wide* 25, 27–50.

Childs, R.L. and Mallinson, C. (2006) The significance of lexical items in the construction of ethnolinguistic identity: A case study of adolescent spoken and online language. *American Speech* 81, 3–30.

Cukor-Avilla, P. (2001) Co-existing grammars: The relationship between the evolution of African American and Southern White Vernacular English in the South: A sociocultural history and some phonological evidence. In S.J. Lanehart (ed.) *Sociocultural and Historical Contexts of African American English* (pp. 93–128). Philadelphia, PA: John Benjamins.

D'Andrea, K.D. (2005) African American English in Princeville, NC: Looking at dialect change through the feature of *r*-lessness. Paper presented at American Dialect Society Annual Meeting, Oakland, CA.

DeGraff, M. (2003) Against Creole Exceptionalism. *Language* 79, 391–410.

DeGraff, M. (2004) Against Creole Exceptionalism (redux). *Language* 80, 834–839.

DeGraff, M. (2005) Linguists' most dangerous myth: The fallacy of Creole Exceptionalism. *Language in Society* 34, 533–591.

Farr-Whiteman, M. (ed.) (1980) *Reactions to Ann Arbor: Vernacular Black English and Education*. Washington, DC: Center for Applied Linguistics.

Fasold, R.W. (1972) *Tense Marking in Black English: A Linguistic and Social Analysis*. Arlington, VA: Center for Applied Linguistics.

Fridland, V., Bartlett, K. and Kreuz, R. (2004) Do you hear what I hear? Experimental measurement of the perceptual salience of acoustically manipulated vowel variants by Southern speakers in Memphis, TN. *Language Variation and Change* 16, 1–16.

Graff, D., Labov, W. and Harris, W.A. (1986) Testing listeners' reactions to phonological markers of ethnic identity: A new method for sociolinguistic research. In D. Sankoff (ed.) *Diversity and Diachrony* (pp. 45–58). Philadelphia, PA: John Benjamins.

Hutcheson, N. (producer) (2001) *Indian by Birth: The Lumbee Dialect*. Raleigh, NC: North Carolina Language and Life Project.

Hutcheson, N. (producer) (2004) *Mountain Talk*. Raleigh, NC: North Carolina Language and Life Project.

Hutcheson, N. (producer) (2005) *Voices of North Carolina*. Raleigh, NC: North Carolina Language and Life Project.

Hutcheson, N. (producer) (2006) *The Queen Family: Appalachian Tradition and Back Porch Music*. Raleigh, NC: North Carolina Language and Life Project.

Kendall, T. and Wolfram, W. (2006) Local and external standards in the use of African American English. Paper presented at the American Dialect Society Annual Meeting, Albuquerque, NM, January 7.

Labov, W. (1972) *Language in the Inner City: Studies in the Black English Vernacular.* Philadelphia, PA: University of Pennsylvania Press.

Labov, W., Cohen, P., Robins, C. and Lewis, J. (1968) *A Study of the Non-Standard English of Negro and Puerto Rican Speakers in New York City.* Washington, DC: United States Office of Education Final Report, Research Project 3288.

Legum, S.E., Pfaff, C., Tinnie, G. and Nichols, M. (1971) *The Speech of Young Black Children in Los Angeles*. Inglewood, CA: Southwest Regional Laboratory.

Lippi-Green, R. (1997) *English with an Accent: Language, Ideology and Discrimination in the United States*. New York: Routledge.

McNeil, R. (producer) (2005) *Do you Speak American*? New York: MacNeil/Lehrer Productions.

Mallinson, C. (2004) The construction of ethnolinguistic groups: A sociolinguistic case study. In M. Bender (ed.) *Linguistic Diversity in the South: Changing Codes, Practices and Ideology* (pp. 66–79). Athens, GA: University of Georgia Press.

Mallinson, C. (2006) The dynamic construction of race, class and gender through linguistic practice among women in a Black Appalachian community. PhD dissertation, North Carolina State University.

Mallinson, C. and Wolfram, W. (2002) Dialect accommodation in a bi-ethnic mountain enclave community: More evidence on the development of African American Vernacular English. *Language in Society* 31, 743–775.

Morgan, M. (2002) *Language, Discourse and Power in African American Culture*. New York: Cambridge University Press.

North Carolina Public Schools Standard Course of Study. Eighth grade Social Studies (2004) Online at www.ncpublicschools.org/curriculum/socialstudies/scos/2003-04/050eighthgrade. Accessed 21/8/08.

NCSU (n.d.) *Voices of North Carolina*. Dialect awareness curriculum. Online at http://ncsu.edu/linguistics/research_dialecteducation.php. Accessed 21.8.08.

NCTE/NCATE (2003) *NCTE/NCATE Program Standards: Program for the Initial Preparation of Teachers in Secondary English Language Arts*. Urbana, IL: National Council of Teachers of English.

Reaser, J.L. (2006) The effect of dialect awareness on adolescent knowledge and attitudes. PhD dissertation, Duke University.

Reaser, J.L. and Wolfram, W. (2007a) *Voices of North Carolina: Language and Life from the Atlantic to the Appalachians. Instructor's Manual*. Raleigh, NC: North Carolina Language and Life Project.

Reaser, J.L. and Wolfram, W. (2007b) *Voices of North Carolina: Language and Life from the Atlantic to the Appalachians. Student Workbook.* Raleigh: North Carolina Language and Life Project.

Rickford, J.R. (1999) *African American English: Features, Evolution and Educational Implications*. Malden, MA: Blackwell.

Rowe, R.D. (2005) The development of African American English in the oldest Black town in America: -S absence in Princeville, North Carolina. MA thesis, North Carolina State University.

Rowe, R.D. and Grimes, A. (producers) (2006) *This Side of the River: Self-determination and Survival in Princeville, NC*. Raleigh, NC: North Carolina Language and Life Project.

Schneider, E.W. (ed.) (1996) *Focus on the USA*. Philadelphia, PA: John Benjamins.

Spears, A.K. (1999) Race and ideology: An introduction. In A.K. Spears (ed.) *Race and Ideology: Language, Symbolism and Popular Culture* (pp. 11–58). Detroit, MI: Wayne State University Press.

Tannen, D. (1990) *You Just Don't Understand: Women and Men in Conversation*. New York: Ballantine.

Tannen, D. (1995) *Talking from 9 to 5: Women and Men at Work.* New York: Quill.

Tannen, D. (2006) *You're Wearing That? Understanding Mothers and Daughters in Conversation*. New York: Random House.

Thomas, E.R. (2002) Sociophonetic applications of speech perception experiments. *American Speech* 77, 115–147.

Thomas, E.R. and Reaser, J.L. (2004) Delimiting perceptual cues for the ethnic labeling of African American and European American voices. *Journal of Sociolinguistics* 8, 54–87.

Torbert, B. (2004) Southern vowels and the social construction of salience. PhD dissertation, Duke University.

Weldon, T. (2004) African American English in the middle classes: Exploring the other end of the continuum. Paper presented at NWAV33. Ann Arbor, MI: University of Michigan.

Wolfram, W. (1969) *A Sociolinguistic Description of Detroit Negro Speech*. Washington, DC: Center for Applied Linguistics.

Wolfram, W. (1998) Language ideology and dialect: Understanding the Ebonics controversy. *Journal of English Linguistics* 26, 108–121.

Wolfram, W. (2003) Reexamining the development of African American English: Evidence from isolated communities. *Language* 79, 282–316.

Wolfram, W. (2007) Sociolinguistic folklore in the study of AAE. *Linguistic and Language Compass* 2, 292–313.

Wolfram, W. and Thomas, E.R. (2002) *The Development of African American English*. Malden, MA: Blackwell.

Chapter 15

Rockin' the Classroom: Using Hip Hop as an Educational Tool

JON A. YASIN

Schools have become more diverse because of the growing number of people from various backgrounds including 'people whose native language is not English or not the so-called Standard English. ...[As a result], slowly but surely, previously nonacademic discourses are blending with traditional academic discourses to form the new "mixed" forms' (Bizzell, 2002: 2). Many students bring languages, dialects, registers and other nonacademic elements to the classroom and instructors would benefit from greater understanding of these 'funds of knowledge' (Moll, 1992; Moll & Greenberg, 1990). This tolerance towards what Bizzell identifies as alternative discourses can compel instructors to develop sensitivity to and awareness of language and other symbolic expressions. Language sensitivity and awareness are vital factors in education because 'students actively construct their ways of knowing as they strive to be effective by restoring coherence to the worlds of their personal experiences' (Cobb, 2005: 39). Therefore, certain students may be calling upon non-academic language and symbolic expressions – aspects of their personal experiences – to assist them in constructing knowledge. One such alternative discourse in which many students participate is that of Hip Hop culture, now an international culture. This culture can be appropriately identified as a Discourse, which Gee defines as:

> a socially accepted association among ways of using language, other symbolic expressions, and 'artifacts', of thinking, feeling, believing, valuing and acting that can be used to identify oneself as a member of a socially meaningful group or 'social network' or to signal (that one is playing) a socially meaningful 'role.' (Gee, 1996: 131)

In this chapter, I describe how Hip Hop emerged in the South Bronx section of New York City during the early 1970s in the African American, African Caribbean, Latino and African diasporic communities as a popular recreational activity for local youths. Various elements – deejayin', emceein'/rappin', b[reak] boyin' and b[reak] girlin' (breakdancing), taggin' (graffiti art) and, eventually, knowledge (studying in all disciplines) – quickly evolved into a common culture, which came to be known as Hip Hop. Hip Hop is:

> full of expressions, signs and symbols through which individuals and groups seek creatively to establish their presence, identity and meaning ... [by] expressing or attempting to express something about their actual or potential *cultural significance*. This is the realm of living common culture ...'common' in being shared, having things 'in common.'(Willis, 1990: 1–2)

A source of empowerment for African American and Latino youths early on, Hip Hop culture is now having a similar influence on youths internationally. Once appropriated by mainstream society and institutions in the United States, the Discourse of Hip Hop culture moved quickly into institutions such as business, health and politics. I argue that, because many youth use Hip Hop for everyday, informal learning, more educators should explore this culture as an instructional tool in formal educational institutions.

The Origins of Hip Hop

Considered teachers in the Hip Hop community today, Clive Campbell, known as Deejay Kool Herc, the Father of Hip Hop, and his sister Cindy, the Mother of Hip Hop, migrated with their family from Jamaica in 1967 to the United States. The Campbell family's arrival in the Bronx coincided with two powerful movements: the non-violent Civil Rights Movement, organized in 1955 to confront the social injustices perpetrated against African Americans by racist segments of United States society, and the newly organized activities of the militant Black Power Movement. Because of the success of these movements. the young Clive found various positive changes in the country (such as the re-definition of self), governmental laws changing (such as the passage of the Civil Rights Act of 1964 and the Voting Rights Act of 1965) and the founding of the first Black Studies Program in the country at San Francisco State University as a direct result of the four month student strike organized by the Black Student Union and other student organizations. Clive also found resistance to change by other segments of society. For example, J. Edgar Hoover, Director of the Federal Bureau of Investigation, organized the Counterintelligence Program, COINTELPRO to thwart these movements for social justice. The program 'targeted civil rights movement leaders and black power advocates alike under a "Black Hate Group" caption [and] targeted all of black America under a series of community surveillance programs' (O'Reilly, 1989: 261).

Amidst these movements and counter-movements, Clive saw the emergence of graffiti art, such as the 'tags' of the 'writer' Taki 183 and others, which spread from Philadelphia's neighborhoods of color to New York City. Writers or taggers are graffiti artists who primarily create three types of graffiti art, including tags, which are like signatures; 'throw-ups,' which are bubble letters often colored in; and 'pieces', which are whole scenes. (Figure 15.1 is a 'throw-up' combined with a 'tag'.) Taki's signature was most prevalent throughout New York City because he was a bike messenger from the Washington Heights section of Manhattan, who 'habitually wrote his alias ... throughout his messenger route. ... The idea of signaturing caught on like wildfire' (Miller, 2002: 6), catching Kool Herc, also. Kool Herc recalls being mesmerized by graffiti, which, by 1970, led him to develop his moniker, 'Clyde as Kool' and later 'Kool as Herc' (Herc is an abbreviation for Hercules, because of his large size). This fascination was short-lived however, for one day another crew gained entrance to the building where Herc's family lived and put his tag on the wall. Going downstairs, Herc's father saw the tag and, according to Herc (2006), 'beat my ass 'cause he didn't play that. ... My father is from the West Indies.' Mr Campbell's actions persuaded his son, Herc, to turn his attention to music.

With his attention diverted away from taggin', Kool Herc concentrated on deejayin', an activity in which he sometimes had been engaged using his

Figure 15.1 Graffiti art by tagger, Mauricio Rodriquez

father's sophisticated equipment and recordings of various types of music. Herc developed a two-turntable system, with large amplified speakers, similar to the systems utilized in the neighborhood dance halls in his native Jamaica, which provided music for those in attendance.[1] Because he was gaining a reputation for his deejay skills, in 1973 Kool Herc's sister, Cindy, convinced him to provide the music for a back-to-school dance that she would organize to celebrate the conclusion of her summer program with the Neighborhood Youth Corps. That party's success is considered the birth of Hip Hop. Herc played Soul and Funk music, mixing and blending the music playing on the two turntables. The dance was so successful that Cindy and Herc continued to sponsor parties throughout the year. The following summer, 1974, Kool Herc organized a free block party, taking along members of his 'clique' and Herculoids (his two-turntable-amplified-speaker system) to the street. His 'clique' had always included the emcee Coke La Rock, who, over the music, recited little rhymes and gave shout-outs to their friends and followers through the microphones from the stage. Moreover, Herc introduced Kevin and Keith, the b boy twins, who performed powerful dance moves specific to the records he played. Most notable is the fact that Herc's block parties were overwhelmingly successful because Kool Herc was instrumental in curbing violence by *telling* the people in attendance that *there would be no fights.*

This directive marked the beginning of Hip Hop's first major achievement. Gang leaders, realizing that there would be no fights at Kool Herc's parties and feeling other community pressures, called a truce, which is still in effect more than 30 years later. Afrika Bambaataa, leader of the Black Spades, one of the major gangs, was instrumental in mediating the truce among the leaders of the gangs in the Bronx and organizing those gangs into the social activist organization, the Universal Zulu Nation, now an international association that continues to organize programs and projects. Many of these former gang members, who attended Kool Herc's parties, were studying his techniques, so they were, in essence, his students. They attended Deejay Kool Herc's parties, more interested in honing their skills to battle others with one or more of the elements of Hip Hop culture – as b boys and b girls, as emcees, as deejays – than in battling each other physically. Bambaataa, the second pioneering deejay, known as the Godfather of Hip Hop, honored annually on the anniversary of the Universal Zulu Nation, which culminates with the Sunday conference, the Meeting of the Minds, is now responsible for having guided a plethora of youths around the world to productive lives because of his roles in the neighborhood gang peace process and in Hip Hop culture – another major achievement.

Grandmaster Flash, the third most widely-known pioneer of Hip Hop culture, also studied Kool Herc at his parties and brought his knowledge of electroncs and the technology of the day to deejayin'. Flash is known for introducing many techniques to the mixing of recordings on two turntables, which enhanced musical rhythms by creating a variety of cacophonous sounds unique to Hip Hop music. According to Kool Herc, a major contribution to the culture was Grandmaster Flash's emcees, who brought 'the flow' to the oral recitation over the music. Flash's emcees were the first to *communicate spoken messages in time to the music's beat*, which is alternately referred to as rappin', spittin', flowin', emceein' or rhymin'. In preparation for a battle of skills with another crew, they began to pronounce each syllable of their rhyme in time to the music meter or the beat (Yasin, 1997: 102). Previously, Herc's emcee, Coke La Rock and emcees from other crews had recited poetry and little rhymes and given shout-outs to friends over the microphone. Communicating spoken messages over music is an African oral tradition that is at least 2000 years old, and has continued in the music of the African diaspora, since the arrival of Africans as involuntary immigrants in the Americas during the period of slavery (Yasin, 2001: 201). Grandmaster Flash's mike controllers/emcees added another dimension to the tradition, so that 'by 1977, djs that weren't already rapping ... were looking to line up rap crews as raw as Flash's' (Chang, 2005: 113–114). Thus, a third major achievement of Hip Hop was that its pioneers provided an outlet for many disenfranchised youths to tell their stories through their own voices as Hip Hop emcees, with the assistance of their crew members.

With their homeboys acting as security, these crews of deejays, emcees, b boys and b girls honed their skills in order to entertain the Hip Hop youths at their parties and at their performance battles with other crews to determine which crew had the better skills. The other element of Hip Hop, taggin', became an element of this culture because taggers/writers were enlisted to make posters of various types that would advertise these parties and battles. The party entrance fees for the battles between crews provided the prizes awarded to the winning crew for its outstanding performance of deejayin', emceein', and b boyin' and b girlin' skills. The music from many of these parties and battles was taped and sold out of the trunks of cars, on the streets and at other parties and battles.

According to the Public Enemy emcee Chuck D (2003), Hip Hop was a million-dollar business controlled by the youths producing and participating in the culture before the outside world knew about it. Chuck D, growing up in the town of Roosevelt on Long Island, said that, because they were not able to attend all of the Hip Hop parties and battles in New York City, they engaged the taxi drivers to bring them new audiotapes of the music at the battles, which they then duplicated and sold for five dollars apiece. The profits were controlled by those youths for several years until 1979, when Hip Hop's first two commercial recordings were released. The first commercial recording, 'King Tut' by Brooklyn's Fatback Band, was moderately successful; later that year, 'Rapper's Delight', recorded by the Sugar Hill Gang, introduced rhyming and Hip Hop music and its culture to the global community.

Commercialization of its music drastically changed the dynamics of Hip Hop culture, its participants' control of their creativity, and its relationship to the outside, mainstream society, for the music industry began to profit from production and sales of recordings. However, by this time, those youths of the boroughs of New York City and environs, both performers and spectators, had empowered themselves with a plethora of skills. In addition to honing these Hip Hop performance skills, they learned other skills such as organizing public events and identifying suitable sites, negotiating contracts with deejays and their crews, advertising the events, overseeing the events themselves, exercising all aspects of production and selling of audio cassette tapes of the events, and eventually talking with the media. These informal learning practices constitute the fourth major achievement of Hip Hop. Such skills empowered the pioneers of Hip Hop culture in curbing gang violence, providing guidance and direction for many youths, and giving voices to disenfranchised youths. As this culture has evolved over the decades, the pioneers of Hip Hop have worked hard to empower and to teach this culture to the Hip Hop generation – those children and youths succeeding them.

The Hip Hop Generation

An integral feature of the evolving Hip Hop culture has been the development of a Discourse, which participants have utilized to teach the culture to the succeeding generation. Examples include using language, with clipped words such as 'dis' for 'disrespect', invented words such as 'bling' for that which is opulent, words with extended meanings such as 'ice' for diamonds, and using symbolic expressions, such as the performance elements of Hip Hop and signs, such as holding up the two end fingers while holding down the thumb and two middle fingers to represent the Universal Zulu Nation. The Discourse of Hip Hop is a secondary Discourse for the pioneers of Hip Hop, who, as youths, created this culture past the early socialization process.

> Secondary Discourses are those to which people are apprenticed as part of their socializations within various local, state and national groups and institutions outside early home and peer-group socialization – for example,

> churches, gangs, schools, offices. They constitute the recognizability and meaningfulness of our 'public' (more formal) acts. (Gee, 1996: 137)

However, the pioneers in Hip Hop culture strongly influenced and participated in the socialization and development of their younger siblings, children in their neighborhoods, and those born during the early days of Hip Hop, whom Bakari Kitwana calls the Hip Hop generation:

> those African Americans born between 1965 and 1984 who came of age in the eighties and nineties and who share a specific set of values and attitudes. At the core are our thoughts about family, relationships, child rearing, career, racial identity, race relations and politics. Collectively, these views make up a complex worldview that has not been concretely defined. (Kitwana, 2002: 4)

For this generation of young people, those who were children or born during the flowering of the culture, Hip Hop is a primary Discourse. Gee explains primary Discourses as:

> those to which people are apprenticed early in life during their primary socialization as members of particular families within their sociocultural settings. Primary Discourses consititute our first social identity, and something of a base within which we acquire or resist later Discourses. They form our initial taken-for-granted understandings of *who* we are and *who* people 'like us' are, as well as what sorts of things we ('people like us') do, value and believe when we are not 'in public'. (Gee, 1996: 137)

As an illustration, rhyming is a feature of the primary Discourse of Hip Hop. Emcee Joaquin, a so-called 'basic writing student' and member of the Hip Hop generation, writes rhymes to cope with and negotiate certain social issues. According to Joaquin 'The Big Money Game' (reproduced below with the author's permission), communicates to us that 'life is not a game and we are all accountable for our actions'.

The Big Money Blues

> Let me buckle up my seatbelt and take a trip through yer mind
> And see what you're thinking cause me I'm thinking all the time
> About my friends I use to kick it with after school
> I knew this guy named Craig and yo! He thought he was cool
> He use to stand up on the corner
> Slanging the rocks Dodgein the cops
> When they patrolling the block
> Until one day my friend Craig got caught
> I guess he didn't know he was sellin coke to a cop

And now my friend Craig is 19 years old
Doing 5 months man Ain't that cold
5 months passed away now he's fresh out of jail
And he was thinking to himself
I'm a go back to the block and sell
He jumps out of the car steps into the house
Grabs his stash and ready to bounce
Walks through the hood says 'waas up' to his folks
Chills for a minute Ready to smoke
20 minutes passed now he's ready to ball
He bounced with his friend walked straight through the hall
Then all of a sudden something went wrong
Craig seen these new cats sellin' dope to everyone
Craig got mad Walked right over
Pushed the other cat exchanging words and so so
Then the other cat I think his name is David
Ohh, well he punched him in the face and kicked his head to the pavement
It was a very very bloody scene
Craig got up and destroying everything
He cocked his pistol back and started bustin' shots
David got hit He was pleading for his life
Hours passed and David died
That's just the way I gotta end it-bye
Pe@ce much Love!!! (Emcee Joaquin)

Because Hip Hop is a part of their primary identity, members of the Hip Hop generation, in reality, employ the Discourse of Hip Hop to negotiate a variety of life experiences. Davey discusses how African American soldiers at war in Iraq make use of Hip Hop Discourse to vent their frustrations. '[S]ervice members turn to rap to express, and perhaps relieve, fear, aggression, resentment and exhaustion ... a common part of life during nearly two years of war in Iraq' (Davey, 2005: 2: 1).

Because of the Hip Hop generation's influence, traditional institutions, such as the church, are now taking a Hip Hop 'flava' in their discourse. For example, although now extended to other cities, for several years, the Hip Hop church, organized by Emcee Kurtis Blow, has convened for service each Thursday evening at the Greater Hood African Methodist Episcopal Zion Church in Central Harlem, New York. The service is replete with praise for the Creator, prayer, public announcements that include awards for excellent performances in school, and other features of a traditional service – all in an informal atmosphere.

Politics is another institution, which the Hip Hop generation has chosen to approach in its own way. Authors, attorneys, politicians and other professionals and scholars of the Hip Hop generation organized the 2004 National Hip Hop Political Convention in Newark, New Jersey. The 2004 election and other political, intergenerational, economic, health and social issues dominated the agenda of the official delegates, who came from various states and from around the world. Furthermore, officials have organized Hip Hop Summits regularly across the US, with the assistance of the Hip Hop mogul, Russell Simmons, in order to promote voter registration among the Hip Hop generation. 'Hip Hop summits have encouraged tens of thousands of young adults across the country to register to vote since 2001' (Anderson, 2005: 3).

The Appropriation of Hip Hop

Just as the Hip Hop generation is adapting Hip Hop culture to traditional institutions, such institutions are adopting features of Hip Hop culture for their purposes, as well. Various aspects of Hip Hop culture have been appropriated by mainstream society, such as its distinctive manner of dressing by the fashion industry and its musical performances by advertisers. Perhaps the feature that is most pervasive in mainstream society is Hip Hop culture's Discourse. For at least five years now, at regular intervals as part of the channel's identification, CNN, the Cable News Network, has used their phrase 'Headline News' with Hip Hop's 'twenty-four seven' written below it, meaning 'all the time'. Interestingly, in addition to utilizing a b boy and b girl for its Cobalt automobile television commercial, on visiting certain Chevrolet automobile showrooms one sees the complete phrase written in numerical form, '24/7/365' above the phrase 'WE'LL BE THERE'. Writing numbers in Arabic numeral form within words, phrases and sentences is a custom of participants in Hip Hop, particularly emcees and writers. (Note the use of numbers in 'The Big Money Game' above.) Words, phrases and terms from the Discourse of Hip Hop are quickly becoming entries in the *Oxford English Dictionary (OED).* To date, for instance, words like 'bling', 'ice', 'boo' (girlfriend or boyfriend) and 'thugged out' (tough looking) have been entered into the *OED*. Jesse Sheidlower, the principal editor of the *OED* states 'for most of the last century African American vernacular has been the driving force in American language' (in Siemaszko, 2004: 6).

In addition, Hip Hop Discourse is used by the disenfranchised people of various countries around the world to engage in struggles against social injustice. The African American Hip Hop generation has supported the struggles of the international Hip Hop community and identifies in particular with the social injustices suffered by members of the African diaspora around the world. Hip Hop culture provides these youths with voices to utilize its elements with their local deejays infusing their traditional music into the pronounced beats they play, with their local emcees rhyming about their plight in their native languages, and with their local b boys and b girls infusing their traditional dances into their power moves on the dance floor. For example, Mari Alba Nieves, Toni Blackman and others have stated that Hip Hop emcees are the only people able to discuss the Cuban government critically in public (Nieves, 2001). Thus, as Rose states, 'Hip [H]op is a cultural form that attempts to negotiate the experiences of marginalization, brutally truncated opportunity and oppression within the cultural imperatives of African-American and Caribbean history, identity and community' (Rose, 1994: 21). For these youths in what is now an international Hip Hop community, skin color, race, ethnicity, gender and religion are irrelevant. What count are the skills one has, and this becomes clear when one attends concerts, battles and other competitions, meetings of such organizations as the International Rock Steady Crew and the Universal Zulu Nation, and conferences such as the National Hip Hop Convention. This loosely organized, yet intensely loyal international community's practice of the common culture, Hip Hop, provides an example of the benefits of inclusion, which should be instructive for mainstream global society.

Hip Hop: From Informal Learning to the Classroom

As we have seen, the Hip Hop culture has made an impact both nationally and internationally and at both individual and institutional levels. Perhaps most edifying are the ways in which young people are learning informally through Hip Hop culture and becoming inspired by the same culture to go on to further study, as the following stories exemplify.

- *Hip Hop motivates youths to study.* David Bland, a young African American graduate of Bowling Green University, stated that, as a teenager, he was listening to a recording by Emcee Chuck D and the Public Enemy, who asked, 'And what are you doing, Black man?' At that moment, David said that he knew that he had to go to college. Other students tell similar stories about how Hip Hop has inspired them to turn to further study.
- *Hip Hop's elements are used as study strategies.* Wade Colwell, a soccer star-athlete, received a scholarship to attend Stanford University. He was placed in a calculus class for which he did not have the prerequisite courses. Not having performed well on the examinations and

assignments, Wade approached another student about studying with him for the final examination. During their study session, they wrote a rhyme that included all of the calculus equations and formulas, recorded the rhyme and sent a copy to the professor. The professor responded with a personal telephone call to Wade, stating that, in spite of his earlier poor classroom performances, if he allowed her to use the taped rhyme to help other students and if he would take the final examination, that he would indeed pass the course. Today, Wade is a certified teacher in Tucson, Arizona and co-owns Funkamentals, a company that develops educational materials using Hip Hop culture.

- *Hip Hop Discourse supports students' writing.* In completing academic assignments, writers use experiences from Hip Hop culture as supporting details and evidence for the main idea, for example. In an essay discussing racial profiling written for a freshman expository writing class, Greg Annesse, who today is a graduate of the University of Delaware, wrote that 'the frustration of being pulled over because of skin color has been portrayed in movies and songs such as the movie *Boyz N The Hood* and the song "F**k tha Police", by the rap group NWA.' Because of its dominant status as youth culture, contemporary students draw upon Hip Hop's elements as primary sources of reference for their writing. Other students use the discourse of the classroom to develop their vocabulary skills for rhymes that they compose in bound composition books; they, especially emcees, ask for definitions of words used by the instructor to build their vocabularies for their rhymes.

By using these learning strategies, youths are drawing upon their primary Discourse, which includes Hip Hop as part of their early socialization, in order to learn the secondary Discourse of the educational institution, which is *not* part of peer group and early home socialization. Given the presence of Hip Hop culture in classrooms, instructors could draw on these Discourses in order to establish rapport with our young students, communicate that they and their culture are respected, assist them in understanding the relationship between the classroom and the outside world, foster an interest in the content of the subject being studied and assist in their learning of that content. There are various ways in which Hip Hop can be employed in classroom activities. Instructors can collaborate with students who participate in Hip Hop culture by co-facilitating presentations and discussions where appropriate. For example, once English and writing instructors identify students in class who are involved in the culture, they can ask those students who are emcees to discuss the writing process as they understand it. Although they write rhymes in bars with a hook (the refrain), emcees utilize the writing process, the same process that instructors introduce to students for college composition. In 2005, a young emcee studying at Bergen Community College presented to his cohorts in an introductory course on expository writing the following steps in the process he uses to write Hip Hop rhymes:

Step 1 Get an idea (for a song).
Step 2 Think of supporting ideas and personal experiences.
Step 3 Put ideas in 'story telling' or chronological order.
Step 4 Go back, make sure the story makes sense and everything rhymes.

These steps are similar to those presented by author John Langan (2005, 2006) in his series of books, *English Skills* and *College Writing Skills*. In this situation, it was the instructor's role to guide the student-writer in adapting his choice of words, once designed for oral performance, to the academic writing format, keeping in mind the eventual readers of his work.

Based on their own experiences in protecting their lyrics, emcees can also lead lively discussions on academic plagiarism. These students do not want other emcees to 'bite their lyrics'; that is, they do not want other emcees to claim and to use their rhymes. To prevent this from occurring, emcees do one of several things. Some complete a rhyme, memorize it, then destroy it, leaving no copy. This technique has led to the loss of many brilliant rhymes. For example, Tank and members of his crew wrote an excellent rhyme, a tribute to leaders of Africa and the African diaspora, which they presented at the Ethnography in Education Conference at the University of Pennsylvania. However, not wanting other emcees to 'bite their lyrics', after memorizing the rhyme and performing it several times, they destroyed the written copy. Later, they forgot the rhyme. To prevent such losses, some emcees, upon completion of a rhyme in their composition books, will not show it to anyone. To control 'biting of lyrics', other emcees write in a script legible only to them. Often, these emcees are *taggers* or writers, as well. Such is the case with tagger, Hassan Salaam; Figure 15.2 is an example from his rhyme, 'Masterpieces'. The unique script was used as a camouflage to prevent others from 'biting the lyrics'. In addition to the script in this sample, there are revisions and rewriting for clarity, essential to any writing process.

The classroom instructor can also discuss documentation and research in the context of Hip Hop culture. Students, active in producing the elements of the culture, are familiar with research and its purposes and bring much to these discussions. Emcees wish to be accurate when

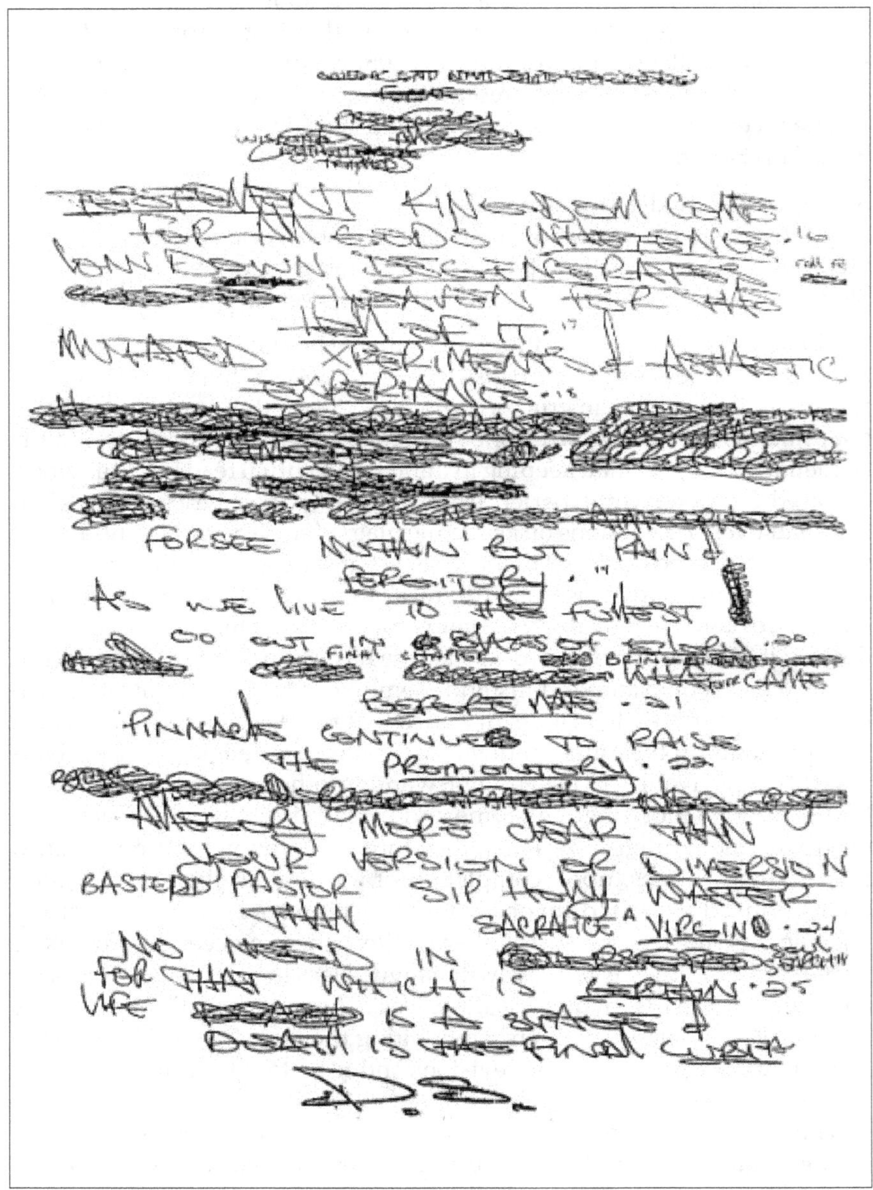

KINGDOM COME
MUTATED XPERIMENTS & AESTHETIC EXPERIANCE
FORSEE NUTHIN' BUT PAIN & PERGITORY
AS WE LIVE TO THE FULLEST
PINNACLE CONTINUES TO RAISE THE PROMONTORY
MORE CLEAR THAN YOUR VERSION OF DIVERSION
BASTERD PASTOR SIP HOLY WATER THAN SACRAFICE A VIRGIN
NO NEED IN
FOR THAT WHICH IS CERTAIN
LIFE IS A STAGE & DEATH IS THE FINAL CURTAIN
D.B.

Figure 15.2 A page from the rhyme 'Masterpieces' by Emcee Hassan Salaam

rhyming about certain topics, as one of Hip Hop's symbolic expressions is 'to keep it real'! During an interview with the author, Tank stated:

> Research! Well ... it's like taking a little piece here, a little piece there and combine it all to make a brand new project. And with your mind and the way you use your style and to put a certain important message across ... is a very unique project. (Yasin, 1997: 147)

Regarding the production of written assignments, on occasion, emcees have stated that they, as students, have nothing to write about. Instructors can suggest that they re-write one of their rhymes in essay form. As an illustration, 'Big Money Blues', the rhyme presented above, was rewritten in paragraph form by Emcee Joaquin. Below (reproduced with the author's permission) is the first draft of an unedited paragraph, in which Joaquin uses the literacy of his primary Discourse to learn a secondary Discourse, that of the educational institution.

> The Big Money Blues is a rap about this guy named Craig. Craig is a drug dealer and a thug, like many, many people I know that have been through the thing that Craig has been through. About his experiences on the streets, one time he sold drugs to a cop and got busted. When he got out five months later, he went back to the block expecting to take up where he left off before he went to jail. When Craig got back to his old spot, this dude David had already taken his place. Craig was furious and attempted to reclaim his turf. Then things, got really, really ugly. David got shot and killed. Life is not a game and we are accountable for what we do to ourselves and others, because when you are hurting others, you are hurting yourself too. And many of us don't know that this is true. (Emcee Joaquin)

Since Joaquin's draft already demonstrates understanding of organizing information, formatting and using specific details; it becomes an excellent tool to assist him in understanding the difference between informal and formal English, the use of conjunctions, the clarification and explanation of details, the use of certain sentence structures and various types of punctuation. To clarify such issues with students, Gary Berke of Bergen Community College has written rhymes with the assistance of his students about rules of grammar and sentence construction (Berke, 2007). Kelli Weiss, a doctoral student at Howard University, uses the hook (refrain) and the verses of bars in Hip Hop lyrics such as 'Aliens' by Outkast, to teach the relationship between the thesis or controlling idea in the academic essay and the supporting paragraphs (Weiss, 2005). With Lyric Shuffle, linguist

John Baugh presents a variety of educational activities using music in the classroom (Baugh, 1999: 31–40).

Some instructors draw on Hip Hop culture in teaching other subject areas. Constance Chapman at Clark Atlanta University uses commercial rhymes and those of emcees who are students to teach figurative language in fiction and in poetry. Alan Singer, professor of history at Hofstra University, uses 'rap in his efforts to engage the students. Though he admits he is an awful rapper, he dons a T-shirt and cap (appropriately askew) and presses on anyway' (Eltman, 2006: 2). Dawn Fisher-Banks now teaches courses in Anthropology with an emphasis on Hip Hop at San Francisco State University. NASA sponsors a program that includes Hip Hop dancing and 'live performers, outrageous stunts and music videos to teach students about Newton's laws of motion' (Shapiro, 2005: 28).

Courses on Hip Hop are being offered, especially in diverse institutions of higher education, such as Syracuse University, Howard University, Essex County College in New Jersey and Rutgers University. Students, primarily of the Hip Hop generation, continuously have organized conferences on Hip Hop, since as early as 1991 at Howard University. And the Hip Hop Archives, initially housed at the W.E.B. Dubois Institute of African American Research and recently relocated to Stanford University, has hosted a Hip Hop Roundtable at each of these institutions. Such courses and conferences provide guidance and direction for the Hip Hop generation by more concretely defining its very complex world view. Ultimately, these venues assist educators and other professionals in making maximum use of this culture to continue exploiting its potential to empower the Hip Hop generation.

Conclusion

Our students 'bring a rich, oral tradition, knowledge and linguistic skills into the classroom. ... [T]hey are far from *tabula rasa* zombies. ... [They] have a wealth of "lived experience" that we can capitalize on' (Smitherman, 2001: 159). For a majority of students of the 21st century, much of this lived experience, similar to Moll's funds of knowledge, is embedded in elements of Hip Hop culture, now a global youth culture. Often overlooked by many educators who are not part of the Hip Hop generation, and denigrated by others, Hip Hop culture is an integral part of the socialization process of many youth born after 1965; that is, for them, it is a primary Discourse. A plethora of our students, who participate in Hip Hop culture, have drawn on its cultural elements to develop empowerment strategies, survival strategies, informal learning practices, and so forth. Furthermore, the creativity they invest in Hip Hop has strongly influenced various mainstream institutions – economic, political, religious and entrepreneurial. Thus, what is keeping educators from using Hip Hop culture as a powerful tool in the contemporary classroom? Elements and creative aspects of the culture, including its contemporary speech forms, provide ample opportunities for teachers and students to collaborate in the teaching–learning process. Educators' acknowledgement of the value of Hip Hop can help them to build a positive rapport with students. Because of its penetration into mainstream society and spread to the African diaspora throughout the world and even to Africa itself, Hip Hop assists students in understanding the relationship between the classroom and the outside world or, to borrow Freire's terms, in reading the word in relation to the world (Freire & Macedo, 1987; see also Richardson, 2006: 55). Furthermore, the diverse global Hip Hop community can be a powerful tool to teach tolerance, awareness and acceptance of others. Our sensitivity to and application of this youth culture to classroom practices allows us to reach some of those students, whom many too often 'write off' as unreachable. Peace!

Note

1. This tradition of playing music for the neighborhood had been seen in the region of M'Backe in Senegal, West Africa, where music was played for the surrounding area for about one hour before the theater opened each evening.

References

Anderson, A.S. (2005) NJ Hip-Hop Summit on a campaign for voters. *The Bergen Record*. October 1, p. A 3.

Baugh, J. (1999) *Out of the Mouths of Slaves*. Austin, TX: University of Texas.

Berke, G. (2007) Using Hip Hop to teach grammar. Paper presented at the Annual Conference on College Composition and Communication: The National Council of Teachers of English, New York, March 21–24.

Bizzell, P. (2002) The intellectual work of 'mixed' forms of academic discourses. In C. Schroeder, H. Fox and P. Bizzell (eds) *Alternative Discourses and the Academy* (pp. 1–10). Portsmouth, NH: Boynton/Cook.

Chang, J. (2005) *Can't Stop Won't Stop: A History of the Hip-Hop Generation*. New York: St. Martin's.

Chuck D (2003) Personal communication. November 9.

Cobb, P. (2005) Where is the mind? A coordination of sociocultural and cognitive constructivist perspectives. In C.T. Fosnet (ed.) *Constructivism: Theory, Perspectives and Practice* (2nd edn; pp. 39–57). New York: Teachers College, Columbia University.

Davey, M. (2005) Fighting words. *The New York Times*. February 20, p. 2:1.

Eltman, F. (2006) Slave lesson hits home for L.I. students. *New York Daily News*. March 20, p. CN: 2.

Freire, P. and Macedo, D. (1987) *Literacy: Reading the Word and the World*. Westport, CT: Bergin & Garvey.

Gee, J.P. (1996) *Social Linguisitics and Literacies* (2nd edn). London: Falmer.

Kitwana, B. (2002) *The Hip Hop Generation: Young Blacks and the Crisis in African American Culture*. New York: Basic Books.

Kool Herc (2006) Personal communication. February 15.

Langan, J. (2005) *College Writing Skills* (6th edn). New York: McGraw-Hill.

Langan, J. (2006) *English Skills* (8th edn). New York: McGraw-Hill.

Miller, I. (2002) *Aerosol Kingdom: Subway Painters of New York City*. Jackson, MS: University Press of Mississippi.

Moll, L.C. (1992) Bilingual classroom studies and community analysis: Some recent trends. *Educational Researcher* 21 (2), 20–24.

Moll, L.C. and Greenberg, J. (1990) Creating zones of possibilities: Combining social contexts for instruction. In L.C. Moll (ed.) *Vygotsky and Education* (pp. 319–348). Cambridge: Cambridge University Press.

Nieves, M. (2001) Presentation at the Conference on Hip Hop in Cuba. New School for Social Research, New York, NY.

O'Reilly, K. (1989) *Racial Matters: The FBI Files on Black America, 1960–1972*. New York: The Free Press.

Richardson, E. (2006) *Hiphop Literacies*. London: Routledge.

Rose, T. (1994) *Black Noise: Rap Music and Black Culture in Contemporary America*. Hanover, NH: Wesleyan University Press.

Shapiro, R. (2005) Newton's laws big laughs for school troupe. *New York Daily News*. September 23, p. 28.

Siemaszko, C. (2004) Crack ho' gains Oxford admissions. *New York Daily News*. December 16, p. 6.

Smitherman, G. (2001) *talking that talk: Language Culture and Education in African America*. London: Routledge.

Weiss, K. (2005) Conference of the College Language Association: Using Hip Hop to Teach Expository Writing. New Orleans, Louisiana.

Willis, P. (1990) *Common Culture: Symbolic Work at Play in the Everyday Cultures of the Young*. Boulder: Westview Press.

Yasin, J.A. (1997) In yo face! Rappin' beats comin' at you: How language is mapped onto musical beats in rap music. Unpublished doctoral dissertation, Teachers College, Columbia University.

Yasin, J.A. (2001) Rap in the African-American music tradition. In A.K. Spears (ed.) *Race and Ideology: Language, Symbolism and Popular Culture* (pp. 197–223). Detroit, MI: Wayne State University.

Index

For Product Safety Concerns and Information please contact our EU Authorised Representative:

Easy Access System Europe

Mustamäe tee 50

10621 Tallinn

Estonia

gpsr.requests@easproject.com

www.ingramcontent.com/pod-product-compliance
Lightning Source LLC
Chambersburg PA
CBHW060148280326
41932CB00012B/1680

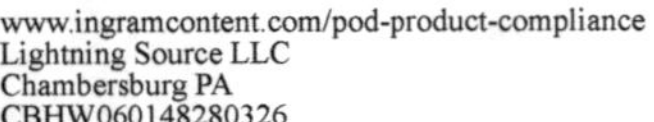